CASES IN
MARKETING
MANAGEMENT

CASES IN MARKETING MANAGEMENT

Luiz Moutinho
University of Wales

 ADDISON-WESLEY PUBLISHING COMPANY

Wokingham, England · Reading, Massachusetts · Menlo Park, California
New York · Don Mills, Ontario · Amsterdam · Bonn
Sydney · Singapore · Tokyo · Madrid · San Juan

Many of the designations used by manufacturers and sellers to distinguish their products are claimed as trademarks. Addison-Wesley has made every attempt to supply trademark information about manufacturers and their products mentioned in this book.

Typeset by Colset Private Limited, Singapore
Cover designed by Crayon Design of Henley-on-Thames
and printed by The Riverside Printing Co. (Reading) Ltd.
Text design by Lesley Stewart.
Printed in Great Britain by Redwood Books, Trowbridge, Wiltshire

First printed 1989. Reprinted 1990, 1992 and 1993.

British Library Cataloguing in Publication Data

Moutinho, Luiz
    Cases in marketing management.
    1. Marketing. Case studies
    I. Title
    658.8′00722

    ISBN 0–201–17570–3
    ISBN 0–201–41632–8 Instructor's manual

Library of Congress Cataloging in Publication Data

Moutinho, Luiz.
        Cases in marketing management/Luiz Moutinho.
            p.   cm.
        Accompanied by instructor's manual.
        Bibliography: p.
        Includes Index.
        ISBN 0–201–17570–3 ISBN 0–201–41632–8
    (instructor's manual)
        1. Marketing—Management—Case studies.   I. Title.
    HF5415, 13.M69   1989
    658.8—dc20   89–14894
                                                                    CIP

To my mother

Preface

This textbook contains twenty-eight cases about marketing management. *Cases in Marketing Management* is designed for use in both undergraduate and graduate marketing management courses. This book of case studies gives many examples of marketing practice, each case concentrating on a particular aspect of marketing management. The cases can be used in the following teaching/learning situations: (1) assignment work; (2) discussion work in class; (3) examination purposes; and (4) role-play exercises. Some instructors may wish to adapt cases so as to make them more suitable for their purposes. Because all cases are recent and are built around existing companies or organizations, you will have the opportunity to analyse actual situations that have occurred recently. Most of the facts and figures presented in the cases are authentic; in some instances, names, locations or other information have been disguised. The types of decisions required and the process for making these decisions are unchanged, however, from what they were in the original situation.

All of the cases in this book are actual business cases and the student is provided with all the information that the managers involved had at their disposal.

In planning this text I have carefully assessed the existing marketing management casebooks and evaluated the needs of the student and instructor. This exercise helped me enormously in writing the text, in selecting cases and in developing a relevant framework for the study of the cases. It is my belief that the most effective and useful casebook must have certain qualities and characteristics. These qualities and characteristics are:

(1) Cases should be related to well-known companies or organizations.
(2) Cases should be as current as possible.
(3) Cases should be of varying length and complexity.
(4) Cases should concern a variety of industries and businesses.
(5) A framework should be provided for studying the cases.

Cases in Marketing Management contains five different parts in its structural format (see Exhibit A).

Exhibit A   *Book structure.*

Part 1 includes six cases in *marketing policy and strategy* dealing with the policy-making process in marketing and the design of marketing strategies.

Part 2 deals with the critical areas of *buyer behaviour analysis, development of a marketing information system and segmentation planning.* This part introduces five comprehensive case studies.

Part 3 presents a diversity of cases related to *managing the marketing mix.* It includes two cases in new product development, two cases in pricing policy, two cases in advertising management, one case in distribution management, one case relating physical distribution issues with the evaluation of a marketing information system, three other cases presenting the many interactions among the marketing mix variables, as well as one case on demarketing. These cases dealing with different decision-making aspects of *marketing management* focus on the stages of analysis, planning, implementation and control in marketing.

Part 4 introduces three interesting cases in *international marketing.* These case studies focus on foreign market entry, transfer of technology issues and the development of international markets.

Part 5 includes two *non-profit marketing* cases. These are challenging and thought-provoking cases, one dealing with the marketing process as applied to a national orchestra and the other with the development of a marketing approach tailored to a football league.

This text has a good blend of short and long cases. However, the text probably has more longer cases than most marketing casebooks. I feel these longer cases are desirable so that students will have sufficient material with which to analyse carefully the companies and organizations involved.

Approximately half of the cases included in the book concern companies and organizations the students know something about and will be interested in studying: British Aerospace, Avis, Massey-Ferguson, Passcard, Scottish Football League, Scottish National Orchestra, among others.

Some other cases deal with smaller companies, but involve situations that students should find interesting and relevant. All the cases deal with real-life, ongoing organizations, and will, I hope, involve students in the realism of the situations. The companies and organizations focused in this casebook are drawn from a wide variety of industries, including retailing, financial services, high technology, hospitality and tourism, manufacturing, electronics, pottery, coatings, packaging, aviation/aerospace, publishing, sports, entertainment, hunting equipment, transportation, car repairing, rent-a-car, agricultural machinery, surgical equipment, alcoholic beverages, heavy and mechanical engineering. A structural framework, managerial in nature, ties the material together, provides section headings for the cases, and gives students a taxonomy for understanding the decision-making process in marketing management.

The cases included in the book are somewhat skewed towards the utilization of Scottish companies as the focal point for case development due to the professional location of the editor and most of the contributors. Nevertheless, one of the paramount objectives for the conception and selection of the cases was the level of their national projectability and representativeness.

This book is the result of all the contributors' efforts. I wish to express my gratitude to these individuals for their labour with the cases and their kindness in granting us permission to use them: David A. Buchanan; Douglas T. Brownlie; Matthew J.T. Caminer; Peter Coyne; Martin Davidson; Anthony W. Dnes; Paul S.A. Ettinger; Gordon Foxall; Brian Johnston; Rob W. Lawson; Tom Lloyd; Howard Lyons; James McCalman; Arthur Meidan; Stanley J. Paliwoda; Sharon Paterson; Gerard J. Shepherd; N. Craig Smith; Leonard Sym; and David Martin Taylor. Allison King, Commissioning Editor, offered invaluable assistance at all stages of manuscript development.

This book only became a manageable project with the outstanding cooperation of all these individuals. Please accept this statement of gratitude.

I also wish to express thanks to those executives who provided important data and material about their companies and organizations and, as a result, facilitated our efforts to capture the essence of a marketing situation at a particular time. And, because we were able to test these cases in both undergraduate and graduate classes, we would like to thank our students for their feedback.

I hope that you will find this book a useful new teaching resource and I wish you well in using this casebook. I hope you find it informative, challenging and thought provoking.

Luiz Moutinho
Glasgow, November 1988

Contents

Preface   vii

Introduction to Case Analysis   1

Part 1   Marketing Policy and Strategy   13

Case 1	**E & R Products**		
	Strategic Marketing		19
Case 2	**Dawson & Company Limited**		
	Strategic Marketing		24
Case 3	**Scottish Foam Limited**		
	Strategic Marketing		35
Case 4	**Bovill & Boyd Limited**		
	Strategic Marketing		53
Case 5	**George Hobson Limited**		
	Marketing Policy and Strategy		58
Case 6	**Passcard**		
	Strategic Marketing		69

Part 2   Buyer Behaviour, Marketing Information System and Segmentation   73

Case 7	**Clydesdale Products**		
	Organizational Buying Behaviour		79
Case 8	**Southern Precision Engineering**		
	Organizational Buying Behaviour/Personal Selling		104
Case 9	**Weighill Hotel, Glasgow**		
	Marketing Information Systems		118
Case 10	**Deckgard**		
	Marketing Orientation/Marketing Information Systems		130

Case 11   Independent Bookshop Limited
Segmentation and Targeting   135

Part 3   Managing the Marketing Mix   153

Case 12   British Aerospace Warton
New Product Development   158

Case 13   INFORAK
New Product Development   168

Case 14   MIT Tractors
Pricing Policy   187

Case 15   POK Electronic Systems
Pricing Policy   190

Case 16   Kilroy Products
Advertising Management   196

Case 17   The Langport Building Society
Advertising Management   201

Case 18   AVIS Rent-a-Car Limited
Distribution Management   207

Case 19   Scottish Express International
Physical Distribution/Marketing Information
Systems   216

Case 20   Bartels paperbacks
Marketing Mix Strategies   225

Case 21   Strathspey Ski Centre
Marketing Mix Strategies   232

Case 22   Auto-Main
Marketing Mix Strategies   246

Case 23   The Anglo-Saxon Artist Limited
Marketing Mix Strategies   255

Part 4   International Marketing   257

**Case 24   Massey-Ferguson–Agromet-Motoimport
[Poland]**
International Marketing   262

Case 25   Flexible Technology Limited
International Marketing   284

Case 26   Europack
International Marketing   295

Part 5   **Non-Profit Marketing**   303

           Case 27   **The Scottish National Orchestra**
                          Non-Profit Marketing   308

           Case 28   **The Scottish Football League**
                          Non-Profit Marketing   320

Case Index   329

Introduction to Case Analysis

A case enables you to bridge the gap between academia and the 'real business world'. Another benefit from case analysis is the further development of necessary marketing management skills. Case analysis requires you to examine a critical point in the life of a business. You are put in the position of the decision maker. In a real business situation, the key decision will have to be made logically, objectively and in a timely manner. In a case analysis, you will have to apply your analytical skills to identify and solve whatever problems appear in the case. Studying cases will help you to develop the experience to make these decisions.

An additional benefit should occur as you become involved in the operation of the interesting and different kinds of organizations presented in this book. Cases range from small retail stores to financial institutions, from a national orchestra and football league to some of the world's largest corporations; they will expose you to many different situations requiring many different types of decisions. You will become familiar with different organizational structures, different philosophies of business, and alternative techniques of marketing products, all of which should broaden your knowledge of business and marketing in particular.

The whole process involved in preparing a case analysis will benefit you in other ways. You will develop your communication skills as you write and present your final report. The cases will give you an opportunity to use your initiative, decide on a course of action and follow it through. If your work in groups, you will develop your ability to work with other people – a crucial skill in todays's business world.

All the relevant information necessary to make critical decisions is there. You will learn by doing.

Format for Case Analysis

Analysing a business situation needs a formalized plan of action. In a marketing case analysis the goal of the process is the pursuit of knowledge. The case analyst tries to understand all elements in a particular business situation so that he or she can recommend action to improve that situation. The entire process must be systematic. In a marketing case analysis, there should be a systematic set of principles and procedures followed in examining a particular situation and making appropriate recommendations.

There are many ways for students to approach the analysis of business cases. Each instructor has his or her own ideas on the number and nature of the steps that are involved. A logical format should be used for analysing any business situation. The following four-step procedure is a practical way to begin:

(1) Define the problem.
(2) Formulate the alternatives.
(3) Analyse the alternatives.
(4) Recommend a solution.

The case method becomes an effective teaching device when students are encouraged to analyse the data presented and to formulate their own set of recommendations.

Case Overview

Suppose for a moment that you are a marketing consultant who has just been asked to analyse an organization and advise it on its marketing strategy. Where would you begin? First, you would acquaint yourself with the entire organization, including its products, processes, situation and any other relevant general factors. You would try to get a broad picture in your mind of the whole organization. With this overview, you would then be able to deal with specific elements of the situation.

Your first objective should be to get an overall feel for the case, an overview of what is going on. Do this by skimming over the case quickly, perusing its highlights. Try to anwer these general types of questions: What kind of organization is it? What are some of the general factors at work in the case? What kinds of problems is the organization having?

After you have this overview of the case, go over it again, reading it carefully, underlining or identifying key statements in the case. During this in-depth reading of the case, you should not only try to understand the case situation but also identify, at least on a preliminary basis, some of the problem areas. These problems will be formally delineated later. In writing up the first section of your case analysis, present a brief overview of the situation; this will set the stage for your analysis.

Situation Analysis

After having understood the case and identified the key problem areas, you should break the case down into parts so you can evaluate critically all aspects of the organization. Look closely at all details of the case, then try to pull this information together into a more manageable form. The situation analysis stage involves analysing four general areas: the organization, the customer, the competition and the environment. Although these four areas of study are important, the most extensive analysis will be of the internal operation of the organization. Here is an outline to help you organize your situation analysis:

Company Analysis

(1) **Financial situation**

(a) Balance sheet/income statement analysis
You should analyse the financial statements both vertically and horizontally. *Vertical analysis* involves the calculation of meaningful figures from the financial statements of one year. For the balance sheet, each item may be expressed as a percentage of total assets. For the income statement, each item may be expressed as a percentage of sales. These figures can then be compared with industry figures, competitors, or other divisions of the same company.

    Horizontal analysis consists of comparing items on the financial statements, or calculations derived from the vertical analysis, with the same items in other time periods. A comparison of key items over a five-year period can be especially enlightening. For example, you might analyse sales trends over the past five years, calculating the percentage change from one year to the next. You might do the same for other key items such as cost of goods sold or net income. Not only can these figures be compared between years, but they may also be compared with industry trends, those of competitors, or other divisions of the same company.

(b) Ratio analysis
To obtain an accurate measure of a firm's financial position, it is best to calculate several financial ratios. Some of the more frequently used financial ratios are shown in Exhibit I.1. These ratios might be calculated for two or more years to uncover any significant trend in the company's financial performance.

(c) Other quantitative analyses
Depending on the information provided in the case, you may be able to carry out other quantitative analyses. For example, *break-even analysis* is a helpful technique for analysing the relationship among fixed costs, variable costs and revenue. *Marketing profitability analysis* examines the profitability of various segments of the company or of various market segments served by the company.

Exhibit I.1   Selected Financial Ratios

Ratio	How calculated	What it measures
(1) *Liquidity Ratios*		
(a) Current ratio	$\dfrac{\text{Current assets}}{\text{Current liabilities}}$	Measures the ability of the firm to meet short-term debt. The rule-of-thumb for this ratio is 2.
(b) Quick (acid test) ratio	$\dfrac{\text{Current assets} - \text{Inventory}}{\text{Current liabilities}}$	A more accurate measure of a firm's ability to pay off immediately its short-term debt.
(c) Inventory to working capital	$\dfrac{\text{Inventory}}{\text{Current assets} - \text{Current liabilities}}$	Measures the extent to which the firm's working capital is tied up in inventory.
(2) *Profitability Ratios*		
(a) Return on net worth (return on equity)	$\dfrac{\text{Profit after taxes}}{\text{Net worth}}$	Measures the rate of return on stockholders' equity.
(b) Return on assets (return on investment)	$\dfrac{\text{Profit after taxes}}{\text{Total assets}}$	Measures the return on total investment in the firm.
(c) Net profit margin (return on sales)	$\dfrac{\text{Profit after taxes}}{\text{Sales}}$	Indicates return on sales.
(3) *Leverage Ratios*		
(a) Debt to assets ratio	$\dfrac{\text{Total liabilities}}{\text{Total assets}}$	Measures the extent to which borrowed funds have been used to finance the operation of the business.
(b) Debt to equity ratio	$\dfrac{\text{Total liabilities}}{\text{Stockholders' equity}}$	Provides a comparison of the equity of the owners with the funds provided by the creditors.
(4) *Activity Ratios*		
(a) Inventory turnover	$\dfrac{\text{Sales}}{\text{Inventory}}$	Measures the number of times the average inventory is turned over in the year.
(b) Fixed assets turnover	$\dfrac{\text{Sales}}{\text{Fixed assets}}$	Measures the sales productivity and utilization of plant and equipment.
(c) Total assets turnover	$\dfrac{\text{Sales}}{\text{Total assets}}$	Measures the sales productivity and utilization of all the firm's assets.

You should evaluate carefully all of the quantitative information you are given in a case and ask yourself, 'What can I do with this data to make it more meaningful?'

(d) Overall financial assessment

After you have scrutinized all of the financial information in the case, you should be able to make some general statements regarding the financial position of the firm. For example, you may have determined from your ratio analysis that the firm is in a precarious position relative to its liquidity. You should draw attention to this, since it limits what the company is able to do in the short run and, thus, what you are able to recommend. It is imperative that you state concisely the firm's financial position since it directly impacts on future marketing strategy.

(2) Organization structure

Examine all aspects of the organization structure: the various components, the formal lines of authority and responsibility, the communication flow, as well as the management style and capabilities.

(3) Marketing system

Evaluate critically all elements of the marketing system: product(s); marketing channel(s); physical distribution; pricing strategy; and promotion strategy.

(4) Other aspects

Examine other relevant aspects of the company: corporate philosophy; mission or purpose; attitudes in the company; key individuals, etc.

Customer (Market) Analysis

Since the customer should be the focal point of the business, take a careful look at the market for the company's products: Who are the customers? Why do they buy the product? When or how frequently do they buy? Has the organization segmented the market properly and clearly defined its target market? Ask yourself questions like these to get some feel for the type of people who are likely customers for the company. You can then evaluate whether the company is reaching this market. Also carefully analyse what changes are taking place in the market and how the market of the future will be different from today's.

Competitive Analysis

It is important to understand the competitive structure of the industry. Where does the company stand relative to the competition? Is the company a leader, a follower, or a 'nicher' (that is, after a special market segment)? What are the organization's strengths and weaknesses relative to the competition? What changes are occurring in the industry?

Environmental Analysis

In addition to the company, customers and competition, evaluate the external environment. Are there any changes taking place, or expected to take place, in the political, legal, technological, or economic environment that may affect the organization? Look for environmental *threats* as well as environmental *opportunities*; realize, however, that what at first may appear to be a threat may actually be a great opportunity for the firm.

The student must add to the facts by making reasonable assumptions regarding many aspects of the situation. Business decision making is rarely based on perfect information. What is required in these situations is the making of reasonable assumptions and learning to make decisions under uncertainty. The ability to make decisions based on well-reasoned assumptions is a skill that must be developed for a manager to be truly effective.

You should always ensure that a logical analysis is given.

Problem Identification

Now that you understand the case and have critically evaluated all of its key elements, you are ready to formalize the problems existing in the organization. Not only is this normally the most difficult part of the case analysis, it is also the most crucial. Since the remainder of the case analysis evolves around solving the problems defined at this stage, it is important to consider the problem areas very carefully.

A good way to start is to define all of the problem areas you see in the case. Then go over each of these, and try to sort out the symptoms of problems from the actual problems themselves. You may have to search to find the problem behind the symptoms. A company may be having problems with increasing inventory costs, declining profitability and declining customer services quality. After examining all aspects of the situation, you may conclude that the company's major problem is poor product management, particularly the lack of a formal product elimination strategy. As you carry out this process, you may find that there is more than one problem in the case. In this situation you need to prioritize the problems into major and minor. Focus your case analysis around what you define as the one major problem. On occasion, you may identify two major problems. If so, treat them separately: solve one completely, then solve the other. In most situations, try to pick out the one problem that is more immediate than any other and focus your analysis on it. However, you should not disregard the minor problems; deal with them fully at the end of the case analysis.

In writing up this section of your case analysis, define concisely the major problem (or, occasionally, problems). Also list the appropriate symptoms. Following this statement of the major problem, list all of the minor problems, along with the corresponding symptoms.

Problem definition is also a matter of delineating a suitable framework within which to deal with what may be posed in the case as an immediate question. The problem scope should not be unrealistically and unmanageably broad. Good problem definition names the immediate problems and defines them in a way that calls for action-oriented answers.

Statement and Evaluation of Alternatives

Now that you have identified the major problem, you are ready to solve it. Develop as many possible solutions as you can, and then screen out those ideas that are illogical until you have a set of realistic alternatives. You can then examine the advantages and disadvantages of these remaining alternatives to reach a solution.

The initial process of alternative generation is similar to idea generation in the creative process. The objective is to generate as many alternative courses of action as possible. The next step involves mentally making a pass over each of these to eliminate any that are not feasible. This process should leave you with some realistic alternatives to be assessed more critically.

In writing up your case analysis, list these realistic alternatives, making sure that each relates to the major problem you defined. Each alternative should be a potential solution to the major problem in the case; the alternatives should be completely different ways of solving the problem, independent of one another and mutually exclusive. Then, list the specific advantages and disadvantages of carrying out each alternative. You may even wish to construct a 'T-account' for each alternative, listing the pros on one side and the cons on the other. If you stated more than one major problem, you should follow this same procedure for each. In a poor analysis there is no explicit discussion of the pros and cons of each alternative. Problem and opportunity statments serve as the basis of your pro (opportunities) and con (problems) discussion. Different ones relate to specific alternatives.

Recommended Solution and Justification

After following this logical approach to identifying potential solutions to the major problem and evaluating the alternatives, you should be in a position to recommend a course of action. In this section of your case analysis, state the alternative you selected and explain why. In cases where you defined more than one major problem and set of realistic alternatives, select and justify an alternative for each problem. Remember that, ideally, no more than one alternative should be selected. If you could select more than one, it is probably because (1) the alternatives in that set were not really independent and mutually exclusive, or (2) your major problem statement is too general and should be more specific. Recommend the solution you think is most suitable, offering reasons for your decision. In your recommendations and implementation, beware of constraints on the organization. Some important constraints include strength of competition, company resources, production capacity, budgets, and philosophies and capabilities of top management. You must reach a clear decision. Part of the skill of decision making is to be forced to reach a decision under ambiguous circumstances and then be prepared to defend this decision. In reaching a decision, a good analysis reaches a decision that is logically consistent with the situation analysis that was done. This is the ultimate test of an analysis.

Implementation

You may feel that after you have recommended a solution the case analysis is finished. However, in many respects the important decisions have yet to be made. All you have accomplished so far is to decide on a specific course of action for the future. Now you must answer such questions as:

- How will it be accomplished?
- When will it be accomplished (short term, long term)?
- Who will do it?
- Where will it be done?
- How much will it cost?
- How much is the projected revenue?
- How much is the projected contribution?

A good proportion of your written analysis will be devoted to your plans for implementation. In addition, you may have a technical appendix at the end of your paper in which you specify each part of your plan, along with the corresponding cost and revenue projections. In your recommendations for the organization, also consider how these plans will impact on the minor problems you identified earlier in the case analysis. Address each of these minor problems and make appropriate recommendations for their solution as well.

The final paragraph should attempt to tie a bow around your analysis. Briefly summarize how your recommendations will solve the major and minor problems faced by the organization. Suggest what the organization should do in the future and how it will be better off because of it.

Writing the Report

Students who prepare written reports do a better job of analysing business problems. Writing a good report takes a certain skill.

When instructors read reports, they check to see whether students fully understand the situation and whether their interpretations of the facts are reasonable. They also like to see papers that are objective, balanced, consistent and decisive. Perhaps the most common error made by students in writing case reports is to repeat the facts that have been provided. Instead of analysing the data in light of the alternatives, students frequently repeat statements that appear in the cases, with no clear objective in mind. Another deficiency often observed in writing reports is a lack of organization. The end result is a paper that has no beginning and no end, and often consists of one long paragraph. To avoid this problem, some instructors require that reports be presented in outline form. The condensed nature of such reports sometimes makes them hard to follow, and the more readable narrative approach is preferred.

One system of organization that has proved effective divides the report into three sections. The sections are designated and arranged in the following order:

- Problem statement
- Analysis containing subheadings
- Recommendations

The problem statement should be brief. The analysis section makes up the bulk of the report and should include a number of subheadings. The first subheading might be a statement of the possible alternatives. Other subheadings might include evaluations of the data or discussions of the influence of the data on the various alternatives. Some of the topics that might be considered in the analysis section are the following:

(1) Customer demand
(2) Competitive structure and reactions
(3) Product characteristics
(4) Price analysis
(5) Advertising and promotional efforts
(6) Distribution channels
(7) Effects on organization sales, costs and profits

The recommendations section should be relatively short and concise.

There is no optimum length for a written case analysis. It depends on the amount of data provided, the preference of the instructor and the number of cases turned in by the student during the course. The report should be long enough to cover adequately the subject but not so long as to bore the instructor and the class. It is fairly obvious that written reports must be neat, legible and free of grammatical and spelling errors. Instructors expect certain minimum standards of performance in written expression. Their standards for written work are reflections of what the business community expects from college graduates.

Final Suggestions

How do you know when you have done a good analysis? As you develop your analyses of the cases, keep the following points in mind:

(1)   *Place yourself in the role of a marketing consultant or a particular decision maker in the organization, and address your comments to the appropriate company executive.*

(2)   *As with any report sent to an executive, you should keep it as concise as possible*   Do not rehash all the information contained in the case. Stick with a critical evaluation of the facts.

(3)   *Remember to operate within the time frame of the case*   Do not spend your time trying to find out what the organization actually did and then recommend that as your solution. This destroys the whole purpose of the case analysis. And just because the organization did something does not mean it was right. A solution you come up with may be better than what the organization actually did.

(4)   *Do not use the expression 'I need more information'*   The information provided for you in each case is sufficient for making a decision. Marketing managers would always like to have more data, but cost and time limitations prevent this. Assume you have all the possible information and make a decision based on it.

(5)   *Be complete*   It is imperative that the case analysis be complete. Each area of the situation analysis must be discussed, problems and opportunities must be identified, alternatives must be presented and evaluated using the situation analysis and the relevant financial analysis, and a decision must be made. Each area above must be covered in good depth and with insight.

(6)   *Avoid rehashing case facts*   A good analysis uses facts that are relevant to the situation at hand to make summary points of analysis. A poor analysis just restates or rehashes these facts without making relevant summary comments.

(7)   *Make reasonable assumptions*   Every case is incomplete in terms of some piece of information that you would like to have. Incomplete information is an accurate reflection of the real world. All marketing decisions are made on the basis of incomplete information. A good case analysis must make realistic assumptions to fill in the gaps of information in the case. It is better to make your assumptions explicit and incorporate them in your analysis than to use them implicitly or not make them at all. If we make explicit assumptions we can later come back and see if our assumptions were correct or not.

(8)   *Do not confuse symptoms with problems*   For example, one might list one problem as decreasing sales volume. This would not be correct. This is a symptom. The real problem is identified by answering the question:

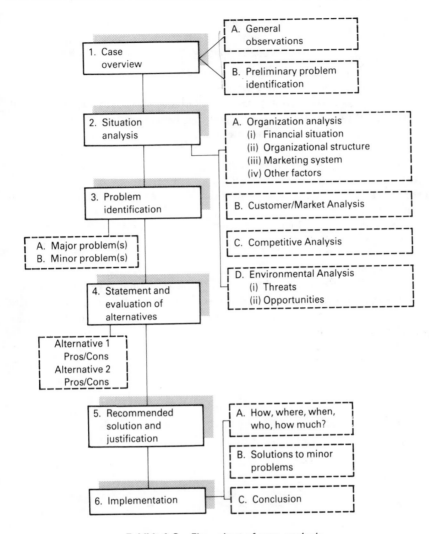

Exhibit 1.2   *Flow chart of case analysis.*

Why are sales down? For example, sales volume may be low due to inadequate salesforce training. But this may not yet be the root problem. You still need to ask: Why is sales training inadequate? It may be due to poor sales management policies. What you do is keep asking 'why' until you are satisfied that you have identified the root problem.

(9)   *Do not confuse opportunities with taking action*   One can recognize a market opportunity but not take any action related to it. A company may decide not to compete in this market due to lack of resources or skills or the existence of strong competition. Decisions involve the complex trading-off of many problems and opportunities.

(10)   *Recognize alternatives*   A good analysis explicitly recognizes and discusses alternative action plans. You must do your situation analysis and recognize alternatives before evaluating them and reaching a decision.

(11)   *Make effective use of financial and other quantitative information*   Financial data (break-even points and so on) and information derived from other quantitative analyses can add a great deal to a good case analysis. Totally ignoring these aspects or handling them improperly results in a poor case analysis.

The cases give you the opportunity to relate the theoretical content of your marketing course to the business world, and will be helpful in developing your marketing skills. You will find that your case study technique will improve with practice.

Remember to take a logical approach to identifying and solving problems. Exhibit I. 2, a flow chart of the recommended case analysis process, will aid your efforts.

Perhaps the greatest pedagogical benefit of the case method is that it generates a high degree of involvement in the learning process. Much of the challenge and satisfaction of case teaching comes from the interaction between students and instructors. The author hopes that you enjoy tackling these case studies and find the approach to be a stimulating learning experience.

PART 1

Marketing Policy and Strategy

Case 1 **E & R Products**   19
Strategic Marketing
Case 2 **Dawson & Company Limited**   24
Strategic Marketing
Case 3 **Scottish Foam Limited**   35
Strategic Marketing
Case 4 **Bovill & Boyd Limited**   53
Strategic Marketing
Case 5 **George Hobson Limited**   58
Marketing Policy and Strategy
Case 6 **Passcard**   69
Strategic Marketing

Strategic planning deals with the relationship of the organization to its environment and thus relates to all areas of a business. Among all the areas of a business, however, marketing is most susceptible to outside influences. Thus, marketing concerns become pivotal in strategic planning. The strategic perspective of the marketing side of business assumes significance in defining a company's purpose. Business definition and the strategic plan, which are usually completed at the same time, must precede the marketing plan. Marketing should be the central function in developing a plan because any significant action ultimately responds to a market need and is affected by competition in the marketplace. This applies to the obvious, such as new products or distribution, and the not so obvious, such as mechanization, cost reduction, fundamental R & D programmes, or new financial control systems.

One of the major strategic planning activities of marketing involves the development of strategies and policies designed to capture preferred positions in the market. This will necessarily involve attempts to gain a competitive advantage over firms pursuing similar positioning strategies.

The experience of companies well versed in strategic planning indicates that failure on the marketing front can block the way to the goals established by strategic planning. Strategic marketing decisions usually have far-reaching implications. Strategic marketing is a commitment, not an act.

A variety of factors point to an increasingly important role for strategic marketing in future years. Firstly, the battle for market share is intensifying in many industries as a result of delining growth rates. Faced with insignificant growth, companies have no choice but to grasp for new weapons to increase their share, and strategic marketing could provide extra leverage in share battles. Secondly, deregulation in many industries is mandating a move to strategic marketing. Emphasis on strategic marketing is no longer a matter of choice if companies are to perform well. Thirdly, many packaged-goods companies are acquiring companies in non-marketing-oriented industries and are attempting to gain market share through strategic marketing. Fourthly, competition from overseas companies is intensifying. More and more countries around the world are developing the capacity to compete aggressively in world markets. To cope with worldwide competition, renewed emphasis on marketing strategy achieves significance. In the strategic marketing approach, market segments are formed to identify the groups(s) that would provide the company with a sustainable economic advantage over competition. A strategic sector is one in which you can obtain a competitive advantage and exploit it. Strategic sectors are the key to strategy because each sector's frame of reference is competition.

In strategic marketing, objectives are systematically defined at different levels after a thorough examination of necessary inputs. Resources are allocated to maximize overall corporate performance. Strategic marketing requires a manager to forego short-term performance in the interest of long-term results. Strategic marketing is inductive and intuitive. Strategic marketing starts from the premise that different businesses have varying roles for the company. The practice of strategic marketing seeks first to examine each product/market before determining its appropriate role. Further, different products/markets are synergistically related to maximize total marketing effort.

Strategic marketing concentrates on the market to serve, the competition to be tackled, and the timing of market entry/exit and related moves. Marketing management deals with developing a marketing mix to serve the designated market.

An ineffective strategic plan is based on past experience, instead of on market research geared to the future needs of the target market.

Competitive marketing strategy is taking offensive or defensive action in order to strengthen a company's position in relation to the competitive forces – positioning the company so that its capabilities provide the best defence against the existing array of competitive forces, influencing the balance of forces through strategic moves that improve the company's relative position or anticipating shifts in the factors underlying the forces and responding so as to exploit change by choosing a strategy appropriate to the new competitive balance before rivals recognize it.

Marketing strategy is dependent on each company's size and position in its industry. Large firms can practise certain strategies not affordable by small firms. Being large, however, is not enough, and, as there are some winning strategies for large firms, there are also some losing strategies for large firms. Small firms can often find strategies to achieve as good or better a rate of return as large firms. Marketing strategies are also dependent on whether the company is a market leader, challenger, follower, or nicher.

After the company's marketing executives have assessed the opportunities existing for the firm's products, they are in a position to establish goals and objectives for their various products and to assist top management in developing goals for the company as a whole. Objectives and strategies determine what marketing activities are required. Marketing management can be defined as the analysis, planning, implementation and control of programmes designed to bring about desired exchanges with target markets for the purpose of achieving organizational objectives. The product-market objectives along with competitive strengths, industry dynamics and demand form the basis for determining strategic thrust. Marketing management may be viewed generically as the problem of regulating the level, timing and character of demand for one or more products of an organization.

A recurrent issue in marketing management is determining the consistency of different product-market strategies with the organization's mission and capacity, market capacity and behaviour, environmental forces, and competitive activities.

What distinguishes marketing management are the problems and techniques of the manager as he or she seeks to maintain demand for the company's productive resources. Because marketing management problems are broad in scope, their solution calls for information and insights provided by production and financial management as well as marketing management. The particular responsibility of marketing management, however, is to interpret conditions in the marketplace. Exogenous forces significantly influence the direction and success of a firm's marketing programmes. A sensitivity to problems of data collection in decision making should become a major objective for marketing management. It is this dynamic feature of business management, the constant interpretation of exogenous forces and adjustment of the company's resources, that provides the real challenge to management.

The interface of marketing management with other managerial functions of the organization will always be challenging to the marketing executive. Every effort should be made to appreciate the problems and potentials of these other segments of the business. However, the main concern of the marketing manager is with the effective development and implementation of marketing strategies and programmes that will ensure a demand for the company's products or services.

The marketing process involves establishing an overall product-market strategy to meet organizational objectives and then developing detailed sub-strategies involving each element of the marketing mix. Decisions must be made concerning the nature of the product itself, how it is to be delivered to customers, how it is to be priced and what information should be communicated to potential customers. These decisions must be oriented towards the needs and characteristics of each of the market segments at which the product is targeted. They must also take into account the strategies employed by competitors.

There are three kinds of marketing plans, each representing a different level of activity. The keystone plan sets marketing's overall goals; the functional plans summarize the overall objectives, strategies and tasks of each of marketing's functions; and the detailed plans direct and control the weekly and monthly actions of most marketing functions.

Marketing programmes and controls refer to the strategy and structure issues in marketing. The key factor in determining the method for organizing and controlling the marketing function is the environment in which the marketing function is to be performed. Managerial marketing, rather than a singular effort to build or maintain sales, is a complex game with many scripts.

The *E & R Products* case provides a realistic account of the fortunes of a company that grew to dominance as a result of innovative and entrepreneurial flair. In maturity, however, it witnessed the emasculation of its competitive position as a result of the entry to the market of an aggresive, market-led competitor. The case is designed to reinforced the applicability of basic marketing concepts such as marketing myopia, marketing orientation, marketing audit, market segmentation, diffusion of innovation, and product life cycle as diagnostic aids. It also gives students the opportunity to formulate an offensive marketing strategy.

In the *Dawson & Company Limited* case students should be examining the strategic choices open to a company in corporate and in marketing terms. The case requires the application of financial and market opportunity analyses in order to allow for the generation and evaluation of strategic options. The critical issues involved in the case include the development of a mission statement, Strengths, Weaknesses, Opportunities and Threats (SWOT) analysis, market segmentation plan, selection of corporate and marketing strategies, as well as the utilization of the portfolio analysis concept.

The *Scottish Foam Limited* case examines the marketing approach of a small company to see whether marketing at 'the sharp end' follows the same basic principles as those which apply in large companies. The case is designed to introduce the students into a pragmatic application of strategic marketing in the context of a small business. The case also helps to develop decision-making skills related to the implementation of marketing strategies and to gain experience in the process of critical evaluation of alternative marketing strategies.

The *Bovill & Boyd Limited* case is designed to bring to the attention of students the management buy-out process, particularly in the light of the recent upward trend in buy-outs. The advantages and disadvantages of undertaking this course of action are evaluated in the case. The case calls for the development of a marketing audit and SWOT analysis, market research plan, marketing strategies, channels of communication and marketing organizational structure.

The *George Hobson Limited* case illustrates the need for an integrated management system which relates other aspects of the firm, especially production, to marketing effort. The case examines some of the organizational problems that can be encountered in implementing a marketing function. It is also designed to understand the limitations of the practical marketing developments that can be undertaken in the short run and to develop an understanding of marketing strategies available to a company with rapidly changing markets and powerful competition. Finally, the case is intended to develop an appreciation of channel relationships, the importance of channel strategies and the issue of budget allocation to support marketing activities.

Finally, the *Passcard* case introduces students to the difficulty of forecasting success for a small company with limited resources to be allocated in marketing efforts. The case focuses on strategic decisions, the trade-off between options in the future and the impact on the present customer base. The case is designed to indicate the effect of price on marketing strategy and to show the use of break-even analysis in assessing bulk rate effectiveness. The major marketing aspects discussed in the case include market targeting, pricing structure, methods and policy, organization of the salesforce, corporate image, as well as advertising strategy and budget allocation.

CASE 1
E & R Products
Strategic Marketing

Douglas T. Brownlie
Glasgow Business School, University of Glasgow

Introduction

The E & R Company was established in Manchester in 1908 as a manufacturer of portable sources of low-voltage electric power. Since the 1920s it has been a leading innovator in the field of zinc–carbon cell technology which it has utilized with much success in the development of a range of small batteries for a variety of applications.

E & R has long held a very strong competitive position in the UK battery market, largely as a result of its early and sustained investment in a sound product-technology base and in a system of direct retail distribution. By means of its own fleet of delivery vehicles the company has attained an extensive coverage of retail outlets. In the 1960s, 70% of all battery sales were made through what was then a highly fragmented body of specialist high street retailers (see Exhibit 1.1).

Although the battery has been with us now for almost 60 years, it was not until the 1950s that growth started to take off. During the consumer boom of the 1960s sales of transistor radios and other small electrical appliances grew rapidly. E & R was quick to seize this opportunity and as a result established itself as clear market leader, so that in the early 1970s it was supplying some 60% to 70% of all batteries sold in the United Kingdom (see Exhibit 1.2). Indeed, by 1977, three out of every four zinc–carbon batteries that were bought were E & R products.

Dominance of E & R

The rise to dominance of E & R was engineered by a strong, driving management team. Over the years, it has implemented a policy of responding to most technological innovations in electrical and electronic goods that required battery power.

Exhibit 1.1   *Distribution outlets.*

Outlet type	Retail sales (% by value)	
	1971	1981
Specialty retailers	62	30
(Chemists, Photographic stores)		
Electric appliances stores	17	15
Supermarkets	10	50
Department stores	8	4
Others	3	1

Exhibit 1.2   *Historical sales trends.*

								(Expected)	
Sales	1970	1976	1977	1978	1979	1980	1981	1982	1983
Total sales (M1 units)	280	440	471	492	493	468	504	515	508
Total sales (Value £m)	35	75	88	94	105	131	156	175	172
E & R sales (£m)	23	50	62	63	65	66	68	71	69
E & R net profit (£m)	4.8	7.2	8.6	8.9	8.8	6.6	5.8	4.4	2.1

In this way, the firm has evolved a very wide range of zinc–carbon batteries which is particularly suited to low drainage and intermittent applications, such as transistor radios, torches, toys and shavers. Of the 14 batteries in its current product range the UG2 and EX4 generated some 70% of the company's sales turnover. (Both products are aimed at the bottom end of the market where sales of zinc–carbon batteries are strong.)

By virtue of a large equity stake in a small independent alkaline battery manufacturer, E & R has also been involved, since the 1940s, in the low-volume manufacture of alkaline manganese button-cells, which are designed for specialist high-power applications. But, in the wake of a Monopolies Commission investigation of the battery industry, E & R divested itself of this equity in 1977.

In 1979, the E & R board rejected an approach by a major supermarket chain to supply it with batteries it would market as its own-label product. The board was then of the view that this sort of operation would not be consistent with its policy of evolving and maintaining a long-term competitive advantage based on a strongly branded product range.

In recent years, the company's research and development effort has been exclusively spent in two major areas: firstly, in improving quality control, labour productivity and working practices, and secondly, in examining the problem of leakage from its zinc–carbon batteries and possible ways in which to improve their average life, particularly for applications where continuous use is to be expected. The problem of chemical failure was one that E & R had wrestled with for some years since it not only restricted battery not-in-use life, but also made the product unsuitable for long continuous use applications.

Despite increasing pressure on its margins, it has also spent heavily on above- and below-the-line promotional effort in order to maintain customer loyalty for its branded product range. In 1983, the main thrust of this effort was to be in television advertising, to which some 80% of the £5 million budget was allocated.

Competition

Early in 1977, a major US battery manufacturer laid plans to establish a UK manufacturing subsidiary in Milton Keynes – DLC Products. The parent company specialized in the manufacture of alkaline–manganese batteries, sales of which at the time were accounting for over 65% of the total US battery market.

At the heart of DLC's strategic planning was the assumption that the long-term patterns of battery sales in the United States and United Kingdom were very similar, with the UK market lagging the US by some six or seven years. In the mid-1970s, sales of alkaline–manganese batteries in the United States had suddenly rocketed with the rapid development of the markets for portable high-power cassettes and radios. Although these batteries were much more difficult to manufacture than their zinc–carbon counterpart, they made use of chemical properties that imparted high performance characteristics which made them very well suited to high drainage applications, particularly of the motorized variety such as cassette players, where continuous use is to be expected. DLC's marketing strategy took advantage of what it found to be surprisingly fluid purchase habits and customer attitudes to the product. It rapidly gained market share not only by encouraging existing consumers to switch from zinc–carbon to alkaline–manganese batteries, but also by attracting new customers so that it also generated modest growth in total unit sales by as much as 5% per year.

Since launching its UK product range in 1978, DLC has implemented a strategy of building market share which has increased its sales from around £4 million in 1978 to over £40 million in 1982. The growth in UK sales of alkaline–manganese batteries from £2 million in 1976 to £52 million in 1982 (see Exhibit 1.3) is largely attributed to the marketing activity of DLC.

The early success of DLC's differentiated marketing approach is attributed to its avoidance of direct competition in the traditional strongholds of zinc–carbon battery sales, that is, applications where long continuous use is not needed. Heavy spending on the promotional element of the mix has enabled the company to develop consumer awareness and so stimulate trial purchase. A simple and consistent promotional message has been used which stresses the longer life and higher performance of DLC's batteries in specific applications, especially cassettes and electronic toys.

Exhibit 1.3   *Sales by type of battery.*

Type of battery technology	Retail sales (% by value)	
	1976	1982
Zinc–carbon	95	67
Alkaline–manganese	2	29
Special designs	3	4

In order to foster and promote brand loyalty, DLC was preparing itself to make sustained large promotional expenditures well into the 1980s. It was planning to use television advertisements which compared the performance of its batteries in specific applications with the traditional zinc–carbon batteries that most consumers were already familiar with. It was also planning to introduce point-of-sale material, as well as packaging and product design features that would make it easy for the consumer to associate DLC batteries with specific applications. Negotiations concerning the implementation of the merchandising policy were well under way by 1983 with several large retailers including Tesco, Asda, Sainsbury and Gateway.

Although the price of DLC batteries was almost twice that of their E & R counterparts, the fact that they lasted up to six times as long in continuous use (and have a longer not-in-use life) was considered to be a sufficiently strong selling point to persuade many customers to switch brands as well as trade up. DLC's product range consists of five battery sizes, which it claims has been conceived to serve 90% of current applications (see Exhibit 1.4).

Exhibit 1.4   *Battery sales by applications.*

Battery application	Total 1982 (1976) battery sales (% by value)	
	Zinc–carbon	Alkaline–manganese
Transistor radios	29 (50)	7
Lighting, torches	14 (18)	1
Photographic	4 (4)	4 (1)
Motorized products	5 (8)	12
(cameras, cassette players, clocks)		
Electronic toys/games	9 (6)	3
Shavers/calculators	2 (6)	1
Others	4 (6)	1 (1)

E & R was slowly becoming sensitive to the view that some of DLC's success could be partly attributed to its own defensive response to DLC's aggressive intrusion into the market. An offensive response was felt at the time to have at its core the development of E & R's own alkaline battery. The mood of the firm, however, in 1979 was against new product development since it would have meant heavy investment and a subsequent decline in short-term performance, in addition to the prospect of the end-product cannibalizing sales of zinc–carbon batteries. By early 1981, it was becoming clear that strong measures needed to be taken against DLC, since E & R was finding itself with a large share of a declining market, and no presence in the growth areas. After much heartsearching, the firm moved on two fronts. Firstly, it discarded its universally known brand name in favour of a new one and introduced a severely rationalized brand livery. And, secondly, it initiated efforts to develop its own alkaline battery and to devise a marketing platform that would avoid the 'me too' trap for the envisaged product.

However, by 1983, the declining proportion of battery sales taken by zinc–carbon products and the falling profitability of E & R's sales had not only persisted, but grown to crisis proportions. The findings of the market research study the E & R board had commissioned (see Exhibit 1.5) pointed to some major weaknesses in the company's marketing strategy.

Exhibit 1.5   UK Battery Market: Independent Research Study (1983)

Summary Findings

Brand Awareness:	E & R Products	– 72%
	DLC products	– 46%
Advertising Awareness:	E & R	– 37%
	DLC	– 60%
Market Penetration:	E & R	– 80%
(% retail outlets stocking products)	DLC	– 56%

Consumer confusion over the very wide range of battery sizes and types, and the applications for which they are suited.
   62% of purchases were made by women, up to the age of 35, compared with 48% in 1978.
   Over 67% of consumers held strongly negative attitudes to the generic products' performance – reflecting the view that 'batteries never last long enough'.

Growth areas:

(i)   'Ghetto blasters' market for high-powered portable radios and cassette players where continuous use for periods of up to 2 hours of more is expected.
(ii)   Electronic toys and games.

The end-use pattern for batteries is difficult to predict, but some industry analysts believe that less emphasis will be placed on continuous running applications in the late 1980s.

Perceived benefits:
Mobility; convenience; comfort; image-status enhancement.

Important product attributes:
Power; durability; price; ease of use; suitability for application; weight; ease of identification; and association with application.

Competition
High rates of recognition of DLC products and unprompted recall of positioning statement. Attributable not only to a high exposure rates, but also to simple application information and clear positioning as technically superior and better value for money.

CASE 2
Dawson & Company Limited
Strategic Marketing

Peter Coyne
British Waterways Board

Company History

Because of the particularly good quality of the spring water in Birton, beer has been brewed there since the Middle Ages. Ewan Dawson established his brewery at Birton in 1830 on the site of the spring still sourced by the company today. When the brewery was rebuilt in 1850 ownership passed to the Wallace family. Wallace McNiall died in 1958 and death duty liabilities resulted in the disposal of the majority of the company's managed houses.

The Company's Products

The company produces seven types of beer: 60/-, 70/-, 80/- and porter real ales plus Light, Special and Export keg ales. In addition, the company factors a full range of other beers, wines and spirits. So as to provide a one-stop shop for the licensed on trade, glasses, bar accessories, stationery and catering can be provided together with stocktaking and audit services.

Sales of Dawson's ales have been dropping by about 2% in real terms per annum since the early 1970s. It has been necessary to carry a full range of products in order to maintain the interest of the free trade and even to supply other ales which compete directly with the company's own products. The only way that the company has been able to keep the rate of decline as low as 2% has been to expand the managed house portfolio to its current level of eight pubs and one hotel and to secure sales convenants with freetraders by way of property purchase finance arrangements.

The Commercial Manager recognizes not the consumer but the retailer as his customer. There are many good standard beers on the market and most consumers do not select between retail establishments on the basis of the beer available. As the retailer is interested in trading profitably and securely it is his needs for financial and product supply service that the company is seeking to satisfy. The retailer is prepared to put Dawson's ales on his counter if the package deal with the company is satisfactory. However, often the retailer expresses concern that Dawson's ales are relatively unknown to consumers and may not be recognized as a good standard beer. Consequently he negotiates on the premise that the company must also supply competitors' products. 1986 turnover breaks between products are shown in Exhibit 2.1.

Exhibit 2.1 *Turnover breakdown figures for Dawson's products, 1986.*

Turnover (%)	Product	Turnover (£'000)	Mean gross margin (%)	Gross profit (£'000)
3	Dawson's real ale	215	35	75
12	Dawson's keg ale	862	35	301.5
28	Factored keg lager	2,011	16.5	331
7	Factored keg ales	502	16	80
33	Wines and spirits	2,370	5	118.5
7	Factored bottled beer	503	15	75
5	Factored canned beer	360	3	11
5	Minerals, etc.	360	22	79
100	Brewing and whole-sale	7,183	15	1,071

Production of Beer Products

The technology employed is traditional and uncomplicated. Although the company has the capacity to malt and mill its own barley, this raw material is now bought in as flour from one of a handful of suppliers to the industry on a three-year advance purchase agreement. In order to avoid a stock-out large paper stocks of the paid for flour are held.

The barley is brewed in open vats then boiled and mashed in closed copper vats in a process that lasts about five days. At this time the production may be split between real or keg and both products are then processed within a further five to ten days. Unit production costs are similar for each of the range of beers.

An average production run is currently about 40% of capacity and the most efficient level of capacity utilization is estimated at 80% by the Director of Production.

There are 26 employees, including management, engaged in production, one less than in previous years and it is felt that this number could handle a doubling of output with overtime in the short term. One or two additional men might be necessary in the longer term in such circumstances.

Although the company has no bottling facility it has provisionally negotiated the subcontracting of this to another firm. As a means of utilizing the production slack, the sales potential of bottled Dawson's ales is being tested. The feasibility of launching a new bottled premium beer, aimed at the export market, is also under consideration. The Commercial Manager feels that this could successfully become a status product in North America and parts of Europe.

Consideration is being given to the introduction of large plastic non-returnable ale packs for the off trade.

Over the last 20 years the trend has been away from dark ales and towards lagers. At present the company sells twice as much factored lager as its own beers and the Director of Production has indicated that the existing plant is capable of producing lager along with ale in an integrated batch production system. However, the raw materials are different for lager and beer and the present advance purchase arrangements would mean a three-year lead time in production planning. This effectively means that the company would be committed to a further three years of raw materials cost before the first year's product test had been completed. Raw materials approximate to 23% of sales value.

Culture and Resources

The company is privately owned and there are 11 separate shareholdings. United Kingdom Brewers holds 20% of shares through historical accident, former directors and their families own another 25% or thereabouts, while the majority of shares are held by Wallace & McGrigor (Holdings) Limited, which was established at the time of Wallace McNiall's intestate death and in which the venture capitalists Investors In Industry have a major interest.

The Commercial Manager describes the company as 'small, fiercely independent, Scottish, traditional and conservative – a low profile real ale brewer which has responded to the demand for keg beer'.

There is almost a 'family' culture in the company with many long-serving employees, low staff turnover and a tendency to promote from within. The company directors are mainly full-time, long-serving employees and tasks tend to be managed with fairly loose functional demarcation.

Reporting to the Managing Director are the Production Director, the Company Secretary, the Commercial Manager and the Retail Manager. The Production Director controls 25 production staff including a biologist research assistant, and 20 draymen. Some 19 administrative staff report to the Secretary, and the Commercial Manager is responsible for three salesmen. The Retail Manager controls 122 full-time and part-time staff employed in the managed pubs and hotel.

Training has traditionally meant learning the job and the company has not perceived any need for management or marketing skills training in staff, nor has the company ever required to engage consultants or market researchers. Much of the company's market information is fed from the salesforce as it encounters demand 'at the sharp end'. However, PR consultants have recently been appointed 'to raise the profile of the company'.

Financially, the company does not feel that there is a problem. Full details of accounts are shown in Exhibit 2.2 at the end of this case study. As the Commercial Manager commented '. . .we are extremely sound at the moment, but I wonder where we will be in ten years time'.

Sales Management

The salesmen mainly service existing accounts and there is very little cold calling. Most new business is by referral by existing clients to acquaintances and 50% of these calls are successful.

The three salesmen each have about 12 years of experience on the job. They are all on fixed incomes and there is no formal performance measurement. Sales are generally expressed at retail prices less discount and the salesmen have discretion to negotiate discount according to guidelines. *Ad hoc* sales meetings are held from time to time to exchange information on prices and products. There have been no sales promotions as such but occasionally discounting incentives are made to push one particular product, usually in response to a general trade promotion of a factored product. Generally prices are set at the market rate.

The annual advertising budget is £43,000 (4% of own product sales).

The Market

The Brewers' Society publishes production statistics for the principal brewers in the United Kingdom. From this and from other informal sources the company estimates its market share to be between 1% and 1.5% in Scotland and between 0.015% and 0.10% in the United Kingdom. United Kingdom and Scottish brewers are considered to control almost 85% of the Scottish market between them.

Because the free trade is largely indifferent to which beer it stocks, market share is gained by getting freetraders locked into the product by capital financing arrangements or by competing on trade service provision. But the most secure way to capture market share is to expand the managed estate and that is the main thrust of many of the brewers now. The company is aiming to expand its portfolio by a minimum of one unit each year into higher quality, higher yielding units.

In order to compete on the capital financing of retail units the company has introduced, as a first on the market, a unit linked endowment scheme whereby the retailer is bound only to stock Dawson's ales and other beers may be stocked so long as display, maintenance and availability is not unfavourable to Dawson's. By this means the company plans to expand the tied estate to 50 units from the current 29 in the medium term.

While the company's sales are almost entirely within the free trade recent discussions have been held with major brewers on the subject of bulk brewing real ale on a contract arrangement for distribution as a product item on the major's range. These discussions have been productive, if as yet inconclusive, and there is now a good possibility of increasing production towards capacity over the next few years.

The Future

The Commercial Manager, in considering the company's strategic position, wishes to secure long-term growth and profitability. He asks himself whether this is inevitably attained as a factor or contract brewer or whether the company can grow as a traditional independent branded brewer.

Exhibit 2.2 Company Accounts and Notes

Profit and Loss Account for the Year ended 30th September 1986

	Notes	1986 (£)	1985 (£)
Turnover	2	7,967,940	7,139,711
Cost of sales		6,750,821	5,996,911
Gross profit		1,217,119	1,142,800
Net operating expenses	3	844,770	750,920
Operating profit	4	372,349	391,880
Income from other fixed asset investments		48,168	41,900
Other interest receivable and similar income		20,363	19,022
Interest payable and similar charges		—	(15)
		440,880	452,787
Exceptional item	5	78,008	—
Profit before taxation		518,888	452,787
Tax on profit on ordinary activities	8	239,109	236,749
Profit on ordinary activities after taxation		279,779	216,038
Dividends paid and proposed	9	99,498	77,188
Retained profit for the year		£180,281	£138,850

Statement of Retained Profits

Retained profits at 1st October 1985	1,396,221	1,257,371
Retained profits for the year	180,281	138,850
Retained profits at 30th September 1986	£1,576,502	£1,396,221

Balance Sheet – 30th September 1986

	Notes	1986 (£)	1986 (£)	1985 (£)	1985 (£)
Fixed Assets					
Tangible assets	10		2,935,256		2,914,047
Investments:					
Loans to group companies	11		—		2,000
Other investments other					
than loans	11		3,075		3,075
Other loans	11		900,839		772,181
Current Assets			903,914		777,256
Stocks	12	383,430		433,897	
Debtors	13	1,084,267		1,035,549	
Cash at bank and in hand		286,215		299,215	
		1,753,912		1,768,661	
Creditors – amounts falling due within one year	14	1,104,147		1,111,764	
Net Current Assets			649,765		656,897
Total assets less current liabilities			4,488,935		4,348,200
Less: Non current liabilities					
Creditors – amounts falling due after more than one year	15	199,401		207,019	

Exhibit 2.2 *continued*

	Notes	1986 (£)	(£)	1985 (£)	(£)
Provisions for Liabilities and Charges					
Deferred Taxation	16	62,672		67,166	
			262,073		274,185
			£4,226,862		£4,074,015
Capital and Reserves					
Called up share capital	17		1,410,000		1,410,000
Revaluation reserve	18		1,240,360		1,267,794
Profit and loss account			1,576,502		1,396,221
			£4,226,862		£4,074,015

These accounts were approved by the board on 14 November 1986.

Directors

Notes to the Accounts – 30th September 1986 (continued)

1. **Principal Accounting Policies** (continued)

(d) *Turnover*
Turnover which excludes value added tax represents the value of sales invoiced during the year.

(e) *Taxation*
The charge for taxation is based on the profit for the year as adjusted for disallowable items. Tax deferred or accelerated is accounted for in respect of all material timing differences to the extent that it is probable that a liability or asset will crystallise. Timing differences arise from the inclusion of items of income and expenditure in tax computations in periods different from those in which they are included in the accounts. Provision is made at the rate which is expected to be applied when the liability or asset is expected to crystallise. Where this is not known the latest estimate of the long term tax rate applicable has been adopted. The amount of unprovided deferred tax is calculated at the best estimate of corporation tax rates in the longer term and is analysed into its major components.

2. **Turnover**
The contributions of the various activities of the company to turnover and profit before taxation, are set out below:–

	1986		1985	
Principal activities	*Turnover* (£)	*Profit before Taxation* (£)	*Turnover* (£)	*Profit before Taxation* (£)
The brewing of beers and the wholesaling of beer and spirits	7,183,256	371,934	6,344,201	257,190
Ownership and management of public houses and hotels	784,684	146,954	795,510	195,597
	£7,967,940	£518,888	£7,139,711	£452,787

During the year the company changed its method of categorising turnover between principal activities. Accordingly the 1985 figures have been stated.
The company's entire operation is based in Scotland.

Exhibit 2.2 *continued*

3. Net Operating Expenses

Net operating expenses are made up as follows:–

	1986 (£)	1985 (£)
Distribution costs	157,250	160,489
Administrative expenses	687,520	590,431
	£844,770	£750,920

4. Operating Profit

Operating profit is stated after charging:–

	Notes	1986 £	1985 £
Depreciation	10	190,304	147,905
Directors emoluments:–	6		
As directors		900	1,100
For management		93,811	137,579
		£94,711	£138,679
Auditor's remuneration		£6,900	£8,600
and after crediting:–			
Gain/(loss) on sale of fixed assets		£16,842	£(3,317)
Net revenue from property		£68,311	£59,274

5. Exceptional Item

A repayment of £78,008 was received from the company pension scheme during the year in respect of overfunding.

6. Directors Emoluments

Particulars of the emoluments of the directors of the company, excluding pension contributions, disclosed in accordance with Sections 22–34, Schedule 5 Part V of the Companies Act 1985, are as follows:–

	1986	1985
Emoluments of the Chairman	£8,230	£7,449
Emoluments of the highest paid director	£25,953	£26,238
Number of other directors whose emoluments were within the ranges:–		
£Nil – £5,000	2	1
£ 5,001 – £10,000	1	–
£20,001 – £25,000	1	2

Notes to the Accounts – 30th September 1984 *(continued)*

1. Principal Accounting Policies (continued)

(d) *Turnover*

Turnover which excludes value added tax represents the value of sales invoiced during the year.

(e) *Taxation*

The charge for taxation is based on the profit for the year as adjusted for disallowable items, and for timing differences, to the extent that they are unlikely to result in an actual tax liability in the foreseeable future.

Exhibit 2.2   *continued*

Timing differences arise from the recognition for tax purposes of certain items of income and expenses in a different accounting period from that in which they are recognised in the accounts. The tax effect of other timing differences as reduced by the tax benefit of any accumulated losses is treated as a deferred tax liability.

2. Turnover

The contributions of the various activities of the company to turnover and profit before taxation, are set out below:–

| | 1984 | | 1983 | |
| | | Profit before Taxation | | Profit before Taxation |
Principal activities	Turnover (£)	Taxation (£)	Turnover (£)	Taxation (£)
The brewing of beers and the wholesaling of beer and spirits	5,388,942	231,697	5,321,479	338,808
Ownership and management of public houses and hotels	781,528	168,676	757,962	94,968
	£6,170,470	£400,373	£6,079,441	£433,776

The company's entire operation is based in Scotland.

3. Net Operating Expenses

Net operating expenses are made up as follows:–

	1984 (£)	1983 (£)
Distribution costs	156,727	148,667
Administrative expenses	529,012	510,510
	£685,739	£659,177

Balance Sheet – 30th September 1984

	Notes	1984 (£)	(£)	1983 (£)	(£)
Fixed Assets					
Tangible assets	10		1,849,438		1,918,236
Investments:					
Loans to group companies	11	2,000		2,000	
Other investments other than loans	11	3,075		3,075	
Other loans	11	678,802		581,199	
			683,877		586,274
Current Assets					
Stocks	12	405,857		362,561	
Debtors	13	1,032,926		1,023,377	
Cash at bank and in hand		371,215		174,215	
		1,809,998		1,560,153	
Creditors – amounts falling due within one year	14	1,125,319		925,694	
Net Current Assets			684,679		634,459
Total assets less current liabilities			3,217,994		3,138,969
Less: Non current liabilities					

Exhibit 2.2 *continued*

	Notes	1984 (£)	(£)	1983 (£)	(£)
Creditors – amounts falling due after more than one year	15	200,454		207,645	
Provisions for Liabilities and Charges	16	77,956		135,830	
			278,410		343,475
			£2,939,584		£2,795,494
Capital and Reserves					
Called up share capital	17		1,410,000		1,410,000
Revaluation reserve	18		272,213		272,213
Profit and loss account			1,257,371		1,113,281
			£2,939,584		£2,795,494

These accounts were approved by the board on 15 November 1984.

)
) Directors
)

Notes to the Accounts – 30th September 1982 (continued)

1. Principal Accounting Policies (continued)

(d) *Turnover*
Turnover which excludes value added tax represents the value of sales invoiced during the year.

(e) *Taxation*
The charge for taxation is based on the profit for the year as adjusted for disallowable items, and for timing differences, to the extent that they are unlikely to result in an actual tax liability in the foreseeable future. Timing differences arise from the recognition for tax purposes of certain items of income and expenses in a different accounting period from that in which they are recognised in the accounts. The tax effect of other timing differences as reduced by the tax benefit of any accumulated losses is treated as a deferred tax liability.

2. Turnover
The contributions of the various activities of the company to turnover and profit before taxation, are set out below:–

	1982 Turnover (£)	Profit before Taxation (£)	1981 Turnover (£)	Profit before Taxation (£)
The brewing of beers and the wholesaling of beer and spirits	4,949,262	239,539	4,570,057	236,820
Ownership and management of public houses and hotels	722,617	39,154	723,490	33,577
	£5,671,879	£278,693	£5,293,547	£270,397

The company's entire operation is based in Scotland.

Exhibit 2.2   *continued*

3. Net Operating Expenses

Net operating expenses are made up as follows:–

	1982 (£)	1981 (£)
Distribution costs	136,359	132,311
Administrative expenses	497,079	459,001
	£633,438	£591,312

Balance Sheet – 30th September 1982

Fixed Assets	Notes	1982 (£)	1982 (£)	1981 (£)	1981 (£)
Tangible assets	11		1,971,096		2,012,879
Investments:					
Shares in group companies	12	–		1,850	
Loans to group companies	12	2,000		–	
Other investments other					
than loans	12	3,075		3,075	
Other loans	12	573,394		444,700	
			578,469		449,625
Current Assets					
Stocks	13	343,412		411,654	
Debtors	14	936,869		744,871	
Cash at bank and in hand		55,215		69,900	
		1,335,496		1,226,425	
Creditors – amounts falling due within one year	15	910,870		781,404	
Net Current Assets			424,626		445,021
Total assets less current liabilities			2,974,191		2,907,525
Less: Non current liabilities					
Creditors – amounts falling due after more than one year	16	170,198		166,972	
Provisions for Liabilities and Charges					
Taxation, including deferred taxation	17	125,369		143,178	
			295,567		310,150
			£2,678,624		£2,597,375
Capital and Reserves					
Called up share capital	18		1,410,000		1,410,000
Revaluation reserve	19		273,053		273,053
Other reserves	20		–		4,760
Profit and loss account			995,571		909,562
			£2,678,624		£2,597,375

)
) Directors
)

CASE 3
Scottish Foam Limited
Strategic Marketing

Martin Davidson
Tyne & Weir Development Corporation

Company History

Scottish Foam Limited is a small Scottish company which was formed in 1983 to service the Scottish Electronics Industry. The company is located in a recently built factory in Clydebank Enterprise Zone.

The founding members of the company, now the Managing, Marketing, Sales and Production Directors were until 1983 employed by the Scottish branch of Kay Metzler, an international packaging company.

In the early 1980s Alistair Nicol, a director of Kay Metzler, was aware that the impact on Kay Metzler of rising oil prices and the recession might well lead to the closure of its branch plant in Scotland. Together with colleagues he investigated two ways forward:

- A management buy-out of the foam converting operation of Kay Metzler.
- Going it alone and forming a new company.

Even though foam converting is neither a technically sophisticated nor capital intensive industry, should it be necessary to form a new company, such a company would have to compete in a market which, at that time, was occupied by only two companies, each of which was a subsidiary of a major foam manufacturer.

Kay Metzler would not agree to a management buyout and Mr Nicol and his colleagues decided to form a new company and to trade on their own account.

A business plan had already been prepared and after a number of meetings in England and Scotland Scottish financial support was obtained.

A shelf company was bought in May 1983 and a new company, with three employees, began trading on 1 July 1983.

The company name, Scottish Foam Limited, was seen as an important promotional tool, Scottish Foam being the only wholly Scottish company in that market segment. The name proved difficult to get from the registrar since a company using Scottish or English in its title would normally have to occupy a prominent position in its market – something a newly formed company could hardly be expected to do. Nevertheless, the company's solicitor persevered and Scottish Foam Limited began trading on 1 September 1983. The five shareholders were those who had originally agreed to leave Kay Metzler.

Since 1 September 1983 the company's results have exceeded those predicted in the original business plan:

Year	Target turnover	Actual turnover
1983	£400,000	£600,000
1984	£600,000	£1,100,000
1985	£800,000	£1,000,000 (estimated)

In 1986 the company had a total workforce of 32.

Company Objectives

The main company objectives are long-term survival and growth by the following methods:

- Increasing market share at competitors' expense. This is necessary since the market is only growing at an estimated 5 to 10% per annum.
- Broadening the customer base and thus placing less reliance on one or two major customers such as IBM.
- Replacing other similar products such as rubber with the company's foam products.
- Introducing new forms of specific packaging applications.
- Introducing higher performance foams.
- Introducing new foams and new techniques such as polystyrene moulding.
- Manufacturing consumer products which are new to the company, for example pot scourers, insulation lagging for pipes. Both of these can be sold through the same wholesale outlets.
- Extending the services the company provides to cover film wrapping, inspection, packaging and part assembly.
- Horizonal integration by buying a cardboard box manufacturer so that Scottish Foam can provide the complete packaging service.

Certain of these items may be done by more aggressive selling and better customer service to increase market share, while others are extensions of the company's existing product/service line.

Some, like the purchasing of new foams will follow their being made available by the foam manufacturers but diversifications such as cardboard box making and polystyrene foam moulding will require substantial capital investment by the company.

A clearer picture of the company can be provided by analysing its strengths, weaknesses, opportunities and threats as shown below.

SWOT Analysis

Company Strengths

- A competent, aggressive and well-motivated management with excellent knowledge of the cushion packaging industry.
- Local control in the hands of a few people which allows decisions to be taken quickly.
- Well-established company name.
- Good financial relationships with banks, suppliers and customers.
- Efficient credit control.
- Flexible plant and workforce with low overheads.
- Good return on capital.
- A quick build-up in market share showing good relationships/service to customers.

Company Weaknesses

- Although flexible, the manufacturing process is limited and requires substantial capital investment to develop. This would commit the company to achieving high volume to get a satisfactory return on investment.
- Too much time may be being spent on small one-off products such as pot scourers, etc., thus taking effort away from developing the company's main strategy.
- The company is still too dependant on one or two major customers.
- The foam product is not a stand-alone product. Tenders usually have to be made with a cardboard box supplier.
- Market position is weakened by the lack of a total package (that is, including the carton) and by lack of polystyrene moulding facilities.
- Technical knowledge in the company tends to be restricted to foam conversion.
- Financial resources are limited compared with national competitors.
- Company success is very dependant on high quality personal service which is expensive and may be difficult to sustain over a long period.

Opportunities

- Packaging is a very large market in which the company has undoubted expertise and contacts.
- The need for high quality and personal service in packaging could be extended to other parts of the packaging industry.
- There may be opportunities for the company to use its flexible plant to move into consumer goods.
- The company may well be in a good position to diversify into other areas of packaging.
- There is demand in the packaging industry for an integrated cardboard box/cushion packaging product/service.

Threats

- The market in which Scottish Foam operates has a low cost entry point which is perhaps one of the reasons that Scottish Foam has made such quick penetration.
- There may be a danger of being squeezed out by a big foam manufacturer whose main concern is turnover and who can dump foam on the market. With a material cost of 58% of finished product cost this is a possibility.
- The size of goods being packaged, especially electronics goods, is getting smaller, a system of mark-up on cost will therefore result in reduced turnover and therefore reduced profits.
- Many goods, particularly electronics, are imported. Package buying decisions may increasingly be made in London and abroad.
- Most company headquarters are in London hence buying decisions will be made there.
- The carton manufacturers may get more easily into foam than foam converters into cardboard manufacture due to the low entry cost.

Products and Services

Scottish Foam Limited operates within the UK packaging market – which is extremely wide and varied – from high-volume card and paper packaging to low-volume specialist packaging. Scottish Foam Limited operates at the low volume/specialist end of the market, having segmented its market by identifying customers requiring polyurethane and polyethylene foam cushioning as part of their packaging requirements and by concentrating on Scottish companies.

The company attempts to differentiate itself and its product by promoting itself as the only wholly Scottish company in this particular market segment and by providing quickly, specific designs to each customer's requirements together with fast reliable delivery and a high degree of after-sales service.

In addition to general packaging the company also provides:

- contract seating, furniture and bedding foams;
- leisure and sports products such as caravan and boat bedding, judo mats, etc.;
- industrial foams for insulation, filters and sponges;
- contract packing including shrink wrapping, glass repacking, assembly, inspection, storage and distribution.

At present these services represent only 7% to 10% of turnover.

Scottish Foam Limited does not manufacture the various foams required. These are imported from manufacturers in England. Scottish Foam's expertise is in designing, cutting and forming the raw material into specialist shapes, sometimes in association with other packaging media, such as corrugated cardboard, to suit each client's requirements. In this sense the company is a service industry. The service it sells is the ability to design, cut and reform foam to each customer's requirements.

The flexibility of the material and the company's manufacturing processes give the company a wide product line curtailed only by the specifications inherent on the raw material and its ability to meet the client's requirements.

The average breakdown of finished product costs is as follows:

Labour	12%	
Material	58%	(this includes polyurethane and polyethylene foam and various cardboards)
Distribution	5%	
Margin	25%	(overheads are absorbed in this margin)

The low level of capital employed in the business in machinery and stocks (only two and a half weeks' supply are kept on hand) and the low level of fixed costs compared with the high level of variable costs mean that the company's return on capital employed is potentially very good.

The product is low value/high volume which means that companies tend to serve local markets – the high freight cost and varying order size mediating against wider distribution and hence a wider geographical spread of customers.

The product is also a throw-away part of a large and more expensive item, for example an electronic component. As a filler to packaging the product is normally used in conjunction with another product, for example an outer casing or carton.

Suppliers

There are nine UK suppliers of the raw foam material which the company converts into packaging cushioning. All are located in England and are part of large industrial companies such as ICI and Dow Chemicals. The constituents of foam are the by-products of the oil refining industry. It is estimated that there is presently three to four times overcapacity in foam manufacturing.

Scottish Foam Limited obtains foam from three or four suppliers at present and, although the manufacturing companies are quick to pass on any price increases, there appears to be no price advantage in attempting to play one manufacturer off against another. New types of foam come on the market from time to time but this is very much in the hands of the manufacturers.

Scottish Foam's sources of supply look secure for the foreseeable future.

Because the company's products are generally used along with other packaging products the company has reciprocal trade arrangements with other packaging companies. Where Scottish Foam and a cardboard box manufacturer compete for the same contract, each may have previously agreed to use the other's product if it wins the contract.

Pricing

Scottish Foam Limited is primarily in the industrial buying/selling market and therefore has to provide prices in three main circumstances:

- as a competitive quotation;
- as a repeat order;
- as a small one-off batch.

Where the job is sufficiently large, price is arrived at by a full allocation of costs plus a 10% margin. This can easily be replicated, with adjustment as necessary, for repeat orders. Given that the company's two competitors in the market are divisions of much larger companies with higher fixed costs, this may give Scottish Foam a competitive edge.

Where contracts are small they are priced on a materials plus 40/50% margin.

The cost plus method of pricing is probably quite reasonable in a situation where material and labour costs are fairly well known and where a small number of companies compete on design ability, speed of response, reliability and after-sales service.

Where the company is involved in the consumer market, for example selling pot scourers, price is determined by reference to the current market/quality price – the company first ensuring that it can make the product at a cost that will allow it to be sold at a reasonable profit.

The company intends to computerize its costing system. This will enable it to control cost allocation and pricing more easily.

The Market

The company's generic market is the UK foam conversion market. This it has segmented by product – the cushion packaging market – because of the company's expertise in polyurethane and polyethylene foam, and by location – Central Scotland – because of high transport costs (although the company does a small amount of business in other areas of Scotland and England).

The company has also dabbled in other markets such as shrink wrapping, inspection, storage and delivery.

Market Size/Share and Competitors

The value of the Scottish polyurethane/polyethylene foam conversion market has been estimated at 3 million to 4 million and this is divided among three companies as follows:

Scottish Foam Limited 40%
Kay Metzler Limited 40% (down from 60% over the last three years)
Vitafoam 30%

The market is thought to be growing at about 5% to 10% per annum which means that to increase market share Scottish Foam must take it from one or both of its competitors, Kay Metzler or Vitafoam, both of which are part of much larger foam manufacturing companies.

Given the closed nature of the market and the low component value of the product, companies compete on design, delivery and service rather than on price.

Seasonality

Demand is not truly seasonal. The only fluctuations in demand occur around the summer holiday period.

Customers

The main customers in the market are the major electronic companies – IBM had 40% to 60% of the market in 1984 – Hewlett Packard, Wang, Honeywell, National Semiconductor, Burroughs and their many subcontractors. This can lead to an over-reliance on IBM and, as happened in 1985, when that company's requirements fell dramatically, there can be serious knock-on effects on suppliers such as Scottish Foam.

Product Range

A specific standard product range, other than cushion packaging, is hard to identify – each order requiring individual design and make-up. On the other hand the specific products manufactured run into hundreds and new ones are being continuously created. However, there is a need for one company to offer a complete packaging service which would integrate card/carton manufacturing and the foam/cushioning element.

Geographical Location of Market

Scottish Foam's market is found in Central Scotland where the users of its product are located. Selling is direct to the companies who use the product or to intermediaries such as carton makers. The costs of distribution are high relative to product value and Central Scotland will probably remain the company's main market for some time to come. The personalized service required by customers also suggests a local market.

Marketing Strategy

The company's marketing strategy comprises the following:

- Increasing the cushion packaging market share by broadening the customer base. This would be done by targeting customers with known packaging requirements, for example electronic subcontractors, by expanding the salesforce, by aggressive selling, better design and after-sales service and competitive pricing.
- Increasing the penetration of the packaging market by introducing new but related products such as 'Jiffy Bags', shrink wrapping.
- Increasing the company's wholesale market share of foam-related products such as sponges and foam pipe lagging.
- Long-term entry to complete packaging systems comprising the existing foams, polystyrene moulding and cardboard box manufacture.
- Continuing to provide high quality, personal before-/after-sales service.
- Introducing computerized pricing to ensure competitiveness and protect margins.
- Introducing a wider range of polyurethane and polyethylene foams and their applications to a broader customer base.

Marketing Orientation

Scottish Foam clearly has a marketing orientation rather than a product or selling orientation. This derives in part from the need for close ties with customers to design specific packagings and in part from company policy. Nevertheless, in the move towards the use of existing plant and equipment to manufacture small consumer items such as pot scourers, one senses the need to create turnover by putting machinery to work and then trying to sell the goods produced rather than a response to consumer demand.

Marketing Budget

The marketing budget is set on a yearly basis as follows:

- Agreeing sales estimates
- Deducting
- – material costs
- – labour costs
- – distribution costs
- – overheads
- Arriving at profit

A view is then taken on what the company can afford to spend on marketing.

In reality this is the advertising and promotion budget. Marketing activities such as intelligence gathering, research, product development and agreement on marketing strategy are done by the directors as part of their normal workload. What proportion of their time is spent on these activities is very difficult to estimate.

The marketing budget for 1985 was £10,000 and was spent in four areas:

- Design and reproduction of brochures (copy enclosed)
- Advertising in trade journals, Yellow Pages
- Mail shots
- Seasonal gifts of whisky, calendars, Christmas cards, etc.

The main objectives of this form of advertising are to introduce and reinforce the company name in the minds of existing and possible future customers. The company attempts to evaluate the worth of some of the advertising by asking the customers to identify the sources from which they heard about the company, but one suspects that given the nature and size of the market most new customers would come through personal contacts and recommendation in the trade and the efforts of the three-man sales team.

Marketing Activities

Market Intelligence and Market Research

The size, type and geographical location of the company's present market suggests that trade journals, regular business contacts and the activities of the salesforce are adequate to provide sufficient market intelligence for the company's needs, even if this is collected in an informal manner. Close contacts among managers will ensure that important information is quickly disseminated.

Market research, although once again informal and to some extent unstructured, is close to its customers. The company works closely with potential customers to develop new ideas and applications and these are clearly transferable from customer to customer. The company feels that useful market research would be difficult and therefore costly.

New Product Development

New product development in cushion packaging comes from the close contact with customers outlined above and has so far proved successful. Other products and services appear to be added in a slightly haphazard way on the basis of 'what else can we do to make money' rather than a strategic development of the firm's objectives.

However, the firm does innovate at all levels and this creates an exciting atmosphere of change and development rather than a more bureaucratic and ritualized atmosphere which might exist in larger companies.

Selling

About 95% of the company's products are sold to other manufacturers through a third party on tenders obtained by the company's salesforce. This comprises three people, two of whom are directors (the Sales and Marketing Directors). IBM is dealt with personally by the Managing Director.

Sales targets are set by the salesforce and agreed by the board. They are based on:

- Turnover
- New accounts

The Managing Director has a policy of always seting targets 5%–10% above possible.

Remuneration is by salary – there is no commission.

On joining the company, new salesmen spend four weeks on product training and two weeks on selling training.

Exhibit 3.1 *Financial information (see Appendix 3.1 for accounts).*

	1985	1984
Operating ratios		
Return on capital employed	67%	–
Gross profit margin	42.8%	37%
Trading profit/sales	6.6%	–
New profit/sales	4.5%	–
Trade debts/sales – collection time	64 days	80 days
Stock/sales	4.6%	6.7%
Financial ratios		
Gearing: Debt as percentage of capital employed	47.4%	76%
Liquidity: Current ratio	1.33%	1.6%
Quick ratio	1.05%	0.8%

Taking into account all the elements presented in this marketing audit (Exhibit 3.1), the managers of Scottish Foam Limited are confronted now with a difficult decision-making process with regard to the development of an effective marketing strategy. Should the company adopt a diversification strategy? Should it develop new uses for the existing product? Should it fight for market share?

Should the company introduce new products? Should it extend its product range and launch complementary products? Many strategic marketing routes are now open to the company. The problem lies in finding the total value (by weighting its benefits and drawbacks) of each alternative strategy.

Appendix 3.1   Scottish Foam Limited Financial Statements 31 December 1985

Exhibit 3.2   *Directors' Report*

The Directors submit their report together with the financial statements for the year to 31 December 1985.

Principal Activities
The company is principally engaged in polyurethene foam conversion.

Review of the Business and Future Developments
The profit for the year after taxation amounted to £48,747. The directors do not recommend payment of a dividend and the profit has therefore been retained.

The Directors have continued to develop the business of the company in the light of prevailing trading conditions and the position at 31 December 1985 is reflected in the audited financial statements for the period ended on that date. The present intention is to continue the development of the existing business of the company.

Post Balance Sheet Event
Since 31 December 1985 the company has agreed to become a 75% subsidiary of Beaverco plc, a company registered in England. In addition the company is disposing of its investment in Scottish Foam (Transport) Limited at par.

Directors and their Interests
The interests of the directors in the ordinary share capital of the company are as set out below. All served on the Board throughout the year.

	31 December 1985	31 December 1984
A.M. Nicol	9,200	9,200
J.W. Craig	3,400	3,400
J.W. Shaw	2,000	2,000
Z. Lipka	2,400	2,400

In accordance with the article of association, J.W. Craig retires by rotation and being eligible offers himself for re-election.

Tangible Fixed Assets
Details of movements in tangible fixed assets are shown in note 6 to the financial statements.

Auditors
Grant Thornton (formerly Thornton Baker) offer themselves for re-appointment as auditors in accordance with Section 384(1) of the Companies Act 1985.

By Order of the Board,

M. Milne
Secretary.

27 March 1986

Exhibit 3.3   *Report of the Auditors to the Members of Scottish Foam Limited*

We have audited the financial statements [Exhibits 3.4–3.8] in accordance with approved Auditing Standards.

In our opinion the financial statements, which have been prepared under the historical cost convention, give a true and fair view of the state of the company's affairs at 31 December 1985 and of its results and source and application of funds for the year then ended and comply with the Companies Act 1985.

Grant Thornton
Chartered Accountants,
Glasgow.

27 March 1986

Exhibit 3.4   *Accounting Policies 12 Months to 31 December 1985*

The financial statements have been prepared under the historical cost convention. The principal accounting policies of the company are set out below.

Turnover
Turnover is the total amount receivable by the company in the ordinary course of business for goods supplied, exclusive of V.A.T.

Depreciation
Depreciation is calculated to write down the cost of fixed assets by equal annual instalments over their expected useful lives.

The rates generally applicable are:

Property Improvements	20%
Office Fittings	20%
Plant and Machinery	10%, 20% and 25%
Motor Vehicles	100%

Regional Development Grants
Regional Development Grants are being credited to profit and loss account in equal annual amounts over the expected future life of the fixed assets to which they relate. The deferred income in the balance sheet represents total grants receivable to date, less amounts credited to profit and loss account.

Stock
Stocks and work in progress are stated at the lower of cost and net realisable value. In the case of raw materials cost means purchase price calculated on a first-in, first-out basis. In the case of work in progress and finished goods, cost consists of direct materials, direct labour and attributable production overheads.

Leased Assets
At the moment, payments under both operating and finance leases are charged to the profit and loss account on a straight line basis over the lease term.

Deferred Taxation
Deferred taxation is the taxation attributable to timing differences between profits computed for taxation purposes and profits as stated in the financial statements. Provision is made for deferred taxation, except to the extent that there is a reasonable probability of the tax not falling due for payment in the foreseeable future. Such tax not provided for is disclosed as a contingent liability.

Appendix 3.1 *continued*

Group Accounts

The company does not prepare consolidated financial statements for the group. The activities of its trading subsidiary, Scottish Foam (Transport) Ltd. are dissimilar to that of the holding company and in view of the insignificant amounts involved, it is not considered consolidated accounts would be of value to the members of the company.

Exhibit 3.5 *Profit and Loss Account 12 Months to 31 December 1985*

	Notes	12 months to 31 December 1985		16 months to 31 December 1984	
		(£)	(£)	(£)	(£)
Turnover	1		1,072,883		682,167
Cost of sales			751,538		496,738
Gross profit			321,345		185,429
Distribution & selling costs		73,900		58,794	
Administrative expenses		176,864		135,340	
			250,764		194,134
Operating profit/(loss)	2		70,581		(8,705)
Interest	3		8,238		9,391
Profit/(loss) on ordinary activities before taxation			62,343		(18,096)
Taxation charge	4		13,596		—
Profit/(loss) for period after taxation			48,747		(18,096)
Statement of retained profits:					
Deficit on reserves as 1 January 1985			(18,096)		—
Profit/(loss) for period			48,747		(18,096)
Retained profits at 31 December 1985			30,651		(18,096)

The accounting policies [Exhibit 3.4] and the notes [Exhibit 3.8] form part of these financial statements.

Exhibit 3.6 *Balance Sheet 31 December 1985*

	Notes	31 December 1985		31 December 1984	
		(£)	(£)	(£)	(£)
Fixed Assets					
Tangible fixed assets	6		34,658		37,826
Investment	7		4,000		4,000
Current Assets					
Stock	8	49,652		46,056	
Debtors	9	187,925		151,359	
Cash at bank and in hand		314		198	
		237,891		197,613	
Creditors: amounts falling due within one year	10a	177,859		186,741	
Net Current Assets			60,032		10,872

Appendix 3.1   *continued*

	Notes	31 December 1985 (£)	(£)	31 December 1984 (£)	(£)
Total Assets Less Current Liabilities			98,690		52,698
Creditors: amounts falling due after more than one year	10b		33,465		43,822
			65,225		8,876
Deferred Income					
Regional Development Grants	11		5,756		6,972
Provisions for Liabilities and Charges					
Deferred taxation	12		8,818		—
			50,651		1,904
Capital and Reserves					
Called-up share capital	16		20,000		20,000
Profit and loss account			30,651		(18,096)
			50,651		1,904

27 March 1986   Date of Approval

A M Nicol   Director

J W Craig   Director

The accounting policies [Exhibit 3.4] and the notes [Exhibit 3.8] form part of these financial statements.

Exhibit 3.7   *Statement of Source and Application of Funds 12 Months to 31 December 1985*

	12 months to 31 December 1985 (£)	(£)	16 months to 31 December 1984 (£)	(£)
Source of funds				
Profit/(loss) on ordinary activities before taxation		62,343		(18,096)
Adjustments for items not involving the movement of funds:				
Depreciation	8,341		8,469	
Loss on sale of tangible fixed assets	—		250	
Grant release	(1,216)		(1,216)	
		7,125		7,503
		69,468		(10,593)
Funds from other sources:				
Government grants	—		7,369	
Disposal proceeds of tangible fixed assets	—		400	
Share capital introduced	—		20,000	
Loans received	—		60,000	
				87,769
		69,468		77,176
Application of funds:				
Purchase of tangible fixed assets	5,173		46,945	
Purchase of investment	—		4,000	
Loans repaid	8,357		7,321	
		(13,530)		(58,266)
		55,938		18,910

Appendix 3.1 *continued*

	12 months to 31 December 1985		16 months to 31 December 1984	
	(£)	(£)	(£)	(£)
Working capital:				
Stocks		3,596		46,056
Debtors		36,566		150,539
Creditors		4,536		(165,759)
		44,698		30,836
Movement in net liquid funds:				
Cash and bank balances		11,240		(11,926)
		55,938		18,910

Exhibit 3.8 *Notes to the Financial Statements 12 Months to 31 December 1985*

1. **Turnover**

   Turnover comprises sales invoiced to customers net of value added tax. All turnover was earned within the United Kingdom.

2. **Operating Profit/(Loss)**	12 months to 31 December 1985	16 months to 31 December 1984
The operating profit/(loss) is stated after charging:	(£)	(£)
Leasing charges	16,506	15,422
Depreciation	8,341	8,469
Auditors' remuneration	1,625	1,500
and crediting:		
Grant release	1,216	1,216

	12 months to 31 December 1985	16 months to 31 December 1984
3. **Interest**	(£)	(£)
Bank overdraft interest	1,762	3,542
Interest payable on loans repayable within 5 years	2,572	2,300
Interest payable on loans repayable in more than 5 years	3,904	3,263
Other interest	—	286
	8,238	9,391

4. **Taxation**	1985	1984
The taxation charge based on the results for the period is made up as follows:	(£)	(£)
Corporation tax at 30%	4,073	—
Payment in respect of group relief	705	—
Deferred taxation	8,818	—
	13,596	—

5. **Directors' and Employees' Remuneration**	12 months to 31 December 1985	16 months to 31 December 1984
Staff costs during the period:	(£)	(£)
Wages and salaries	212,748	162,116
Social security costs	19,771	16,205
Pension costs	8,965	1,485
	241,484	179,806

The average number of persons employed during the period was 25. All employees were engaged in polyurethane foam conversion.

Appendix 3.1   *continued*

Staff costs include remuneration in respect of directors, as follows:

	12 months to 31 December 1985 (£)	16 months to 31 December 1984 (£)
Management remuneration (including pension contributions)	68,528	68,490

6. **Tangible Fixed Assets**	Leasehold Property Improvements (£)	Plant and Machinery (£)	Office Fittings (£)	Motor Vehicles (£)	Total (£)
Cost					
At 1 January 1985	3,710	40,760	550	1,275	46,295
Additions	1,892	2,355	926	—	5,173
At 31 December 1985	5,602	43,115	1,476	1,275	51,468
Depreciation					
At 1 January 1985	618	6,466	110	1,275	8,469
Charge for year	1,120	6,925	296	—	8,341
At 31 December 1985	1,738	13,391•	406	1,275	16,810
Net Book Value					
At 31 December 1985	3,864	29,724	1,070	—	34,658
At 31 December 1984	3,092	34,294	440	—	37,826

7. **Investment**
   This represents 80% of the issued share capital of Scottish Foam (Transport) Ltd., a company registered in Scotland. This company did not start to trade until 1 January 1985.

8. **Stocks**	1985 (£)	1984 (£)
Raw materials	37,399	41,278
Work in Progress	814	791
Finished Goods	11,439	3,987
	49,652	46,056

There were no significant differences between the replacement cost and the values disclosed for stock.

9. **Debtors** Amounts falling due within one year:	1985 (£)	1984 (£)
Trade debtors	163,565	145,245
Amount owed by subsidiary	8,000	—
Other debtors	820	820
Prepayments	15,540	5,294
	187,925	151,359

10a **Creditors** – Amounts falling due within one year:	1985 (£)	1984 (£)
Trade creditors	136,096	137,864
Amount owed to subsidiary	1,981	—
Bank overdraft	1,000	12,124
Loans	8,000	6,000

Appendix 3.1 *continued*

	1985 (£)	1984 (£)
Clydebank Enterprise Fund loan	2,857	2,857
Social security and other taxes	8,921	15,616
Sundry creditors and accruals	14,931	12,280
Corporation tax	4,073	—
	177,859	186,741

10b **Creditors** – Amounts falling due after more than one year:	1985 (£)	1984 (£)
Loans	22,751	30,250
Clydebank Enterprise Fund loan	10,714	13,572
	33,465	43,822

The loan from the Clydebank Enterprise Fund bears interest at a rate of 5% per annum and is repayable in 28 quarterly instalments of £714.29 from November 1983, the last instalment being due in August 1990.

The loans represent two loans received under the Department of Industry Small Firms Loan Guarantee Scheme.

The first loan for £15,000 was received in September 1983. Capital repayments of £250 per month commenced in November 1985, the last instalment being due in October 1990.

The second loan for £25,000 was received in March 1984. Capital repayments of £416.66 per month commenced in April 1984, the last instalment being due in March 1989.

These loans bear interest at 3% per annum over the bank's base rate. The company's bankers hold a bond and floating charge and personal guarantees by the directors as security for the bank overdraft and the element of the small firm loans not secured by the Department of Industry.

11. **Deferred Income** Regional Development Grants	1985 (£)	1984 (£)
Grants receivable on tangible fixed asset additions	6,972	8,188
Released to profit and loss account	(1,216)	(1,216)
	5,756	6,972

12. **Deferred Taxation**
The following shows the total potential liability for deferred taxation at 30% in respect of timing differences:

	1985 (£)	1984 (£)
Accelerated capital allowances	8,818	10,400
Trading losses	—	(10,400)
	8,818	—

13. **Future Capital Expenditure**	1985 (£)	1984 (£)
Items authorized but not contracted for	Nil	Nil
Items contracted for but not invoiced	Nil	Nil

Appendix 3.1   *continued*

14. Pension Commitments
Individual contributory pension schemes are in force for the directors and certain senior employees funded on a money purchase basis. There are no other pension commitments.

15. Leasing Commitments
The company has commitments in respect of operating and finance leases as follows:

	1985 (£)	1984 (£)
Payable in next financial year	17,056	13,441
Payable between two and five years	7,556	11,695

16. Called-up Share Capital

	1985 (£)	1984 (£)
Authorized:		
100,000 ordinary shares of £1 each	100,000	100,000
Allotted, called-up and fully paid:		
20,000 ordinary shares of £1 each	20,000	20,000

CASE 4
Bovill & Boyd Limited
Strategic Marketing

Sharon Paterson
Grampian Marketing Services

Case History

In 1860, Thomas Ashton set up in business delivering paraffin and engineering products to local companies. The firm soon expanded to supply wholesale and retail electrical and engineering parts from one large shop in Sheffield. Thomas Ashton Limited grew into a successful medium sized firm in the North-East of England.

When its Chairman died just after the Second World War, the business passed to his brothers, who joined forces to push their nephew out of the family firm. However, Bill Wills was undeterred and promptly went into business himself at the age of 18, specializing in asbestos work and using Ashton labour on a contract basis.

Towards the end of the 1950s a compulsory purchase order was placed on the Thomas Ashton Limited's Sheffield premises, and using shares left to him by his mother, Bill Wills was able to take over the family firm himself, though he kept Ashton's company name.

Bill Wills began building the company up from a base of industrial leather and asbestos products, manufacturing and selling them himself. However, it was mainly during the period 1965–80 that the company grew most rapidly, particularly after Ashton's became the largest distributor for Dowty Seals Limited selling industrial consumables like 'O' rings, bonded seals, etc., to industrial buyers.

In 1973 Ashton's employed Mr John Bovill as the General Manager; by this time the company had offices in five areas: Sheffield (the main office), London, Manchester, Nottingham, and finally in East Kilbride in Scotland. Soon after John Bovill joined the company he became concerned over some of the actions taken by the Joint Managing Director, who with a sales management track record had been appointed in 1974 by Bill Wills himself. The Joint Managing Director was very keen to increase his salesforce in the belief that the more salesmen he had, the more sales he would achieve and the bigger the company's profits would be. By 1979 he had accumulated a salesforce of 27 men in the five areas and true to his belief, sales had increased rapidly. However, so had the costs of those sales. The salesforce eventually represented a very substantial proportion of the company's costs.

At the same time as the Joint Managing Director was expanding his salesforce, he decided simultaneously to concentrate on expanding Ashton's OEM (Original Equipment Manufacturers) sales, selling more highly technical equipment for a higher price, thus, in his opinion, leaving more room to adjust the gross margin on sales to certain customers. However, he did not give enough consideration to the technical expertise of the salesmen he had taken on and customers soon began to complain about the lack of technical advice offered to them, leading to confusion over products and their uses, and to general customer dissatisfaction.

In the meantime Ashton's had installed a centralized computer system in its Sheffield office through which all customer orders and specifications were to be processed. This had led to habitual time delays and more customer dissatisfaction.

With the advent of 1980, the recession took a firm hold over the engineering industry in Britain, and Ashton's found itself in a difficult position as more and of its customers failed. Very heavy costs coupled with a dramatic cut in sales led to the closure over the next 18 months of the London, Manchester and Nottingham branches. The salesforce was cut to eight men and plans were underway to close the Scottish office at East Kilbride. Ashton's 'blanket' sales strategy had failed with disastrous results.

At this point John Bovill, who had risen through the ranks to become the Marketing and Scottish Director, approached Bill Boyd, the Scottish Manager he had appointed the year before, with a business proposition. After great discussion both men approached Thomas Ashton and offered a management buy-out of the Scottish operation.

Ashton's was very enthusiastic; it had a great deal to lose having committed itself to a further four years on the lease of the East Kilbride office, to contract hire of company cars in Scotland, to the staff it would have to make redundant, and finally to the surplus stock held in the stores in East Kilbride.

Negotiations proved to be mutually beneficial. Ashton's was able to withdraw from Scotland with fewer losses than anticipated, and the new company, Bovill & Boyd Limited, was able to take over everything in running order, as well as being able to maintain telephone and telex numbers, and the old company's address.

John Bovill and Bill Boyd had ten weeks (from 21 October 1982 to 1 January 1983) to raise sufficient finance. They succeeded through the Small Loans Guarantee Scheme, and with a start-up loan of £25,000 they were in business. Although Thomas Ashton still manufactured, it mainly sold other manufacturers' products. No manufacturing took place in Scotland. John Bovill and Bill Boyd had in effect bought a distributorship.

What was it that had convinced John Bovill and subsequently Bill Boyd that they could succeed where Thomas Ashton's had failed? The Scottish office, like the other branches, had had to cover not only its own costs but also to pay a proportion of the main office costs. This proportion, particularly after the computer system had been installed, had become a very heavy burden on the branches. John Bovill had identified this upward trend and had considered that without this burden the Scottish office could hold its own.

The two men had decided to go into business on an equal footing. They each invested the same in the company and decided there was no need for a Chairman, only for two Directors. The East Kilbride office had two divisions under Ashton's and the two men decided that this should stay the same. John Bovill was to be the Director in charge of the Engineering Division and Bill Boyd the Director of the Partitioning Division (see Exhibit 4.1).

The Engineering Division supplies mainly small engineering firms with a variety of industrial consumables, most of which (with the exception of precision mouldings) are simple rebuys (see Exhibit 4.2). The Partitioning Division, on the other hand, supplies and assembles, using subcontractors, capital equipment such as office and factory partitioning, and suspended ceilings (see Exhibit 4.3). Where

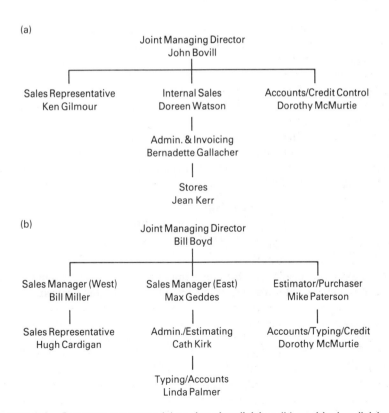

Exhibit 4.1 *Company structure: (a) engineering division; (b) partitioning division.*

Exhibit 4.2   Engineering Division

Product Sheet

Seals:
Imperial and metric 'O' rings in nitrile, vitron, silicone, neoprene and EPDMPTFE back-up rings
Bonded seals
Lock washers
Single and double acting cylinder seals and one piece piston seals
Wiper rings
Rubber and fabric cups
Rotary shaft seals
Forsheda 'V' rings

Rubber Mouldings (precision and non-precision):
A wide range of products in a variety of materials to meet customers' individual requirements
Rubber extrusions to customers' design

Hydraulic & Pneumatic Fittings:
Imperial and metric couplings to BS specifications in brass, mild steel and stainless steel
Hydraulic tubing to appropriate BS or din. specifications. Seamless in mild steel or stainless steel
A wide range of hydraulic valves

Industrial Plastics:
Tufnol range of industrial laminates
Polycarbonate sheet
Tough bar, rod, tube and sheet
Grease guns, grease nipples, and accessories

the engineering side tends to have small but regular customers, the partitioning side of the business tends to have large, one buy-only customers.

Bovill & Boyd Limited is only prepared to distribute good quality products, from a variety of manufacturers and suppliers, some of which Ashton's had used. Bill Boyd said:

'We will only supply the goods that the manufacturers are best at producing, i.e., we will supply their strong products to our customers but we won't supply a weak product if we can get a better one elsewhere. It's like picking the best fruit from a tree and leaving the rest alone.'

John Bovill is also keen that the company should become known for its technical expertise, and after 'teething troubles' when some salesmen left, he made sure that he only took on salesmen who were also time-served engineers. He said:

'I want to build a solid, secure company; not necessarily the biggest of its kind, but one that is regarded as a specialist organisation.'

On the subject of the company's goals and objectives, Mr Bovill went on to add:

Exhibit 4.3 Partitioning Division

Product Sheet

Single Skin Partitioning: A low-cost screening system

Double Skin Partitioning: A modular and versatile demountable partition

Composite Partitioning: An anodized aluminium frame to accommodate a variety of cores with a wide range of finishes. Includes sound and fire systems

Ceiling Systems: Suspended ceilings to suit most applications

Work Stations and Free Standing Screens: Individual, mobile, and acoustic screen system with aesthetic appeal

Raised Storage Areas: An economical way of utilizing existing space

Pallet Racking: A heavy duty adjustable racking system

Slotted Angle Shelving: The simplest of constructional materials for shelving, frameworks, benches, screens, etc.

British Standard Shelving: To BS826: 1955. Includes rolled edge shelving, cupboards, and mobile racking

Containers and Louvred Panels: A comprehensive small part storage system

Personnel Lockers: A complete system with range of sizes, colours, locks, etc.

Square and Round Tube System: An elegant, simple construction system for items to be displayed as well as stored

PVC Strip Curtains: Door curtains from PVC transparent strip to reduce draughts and heat loss

---

'These may have to change over time, but I see that we have three main objectives at the moment. Firstly, to build a company with a solid foundation from which it can expand to benefit all those with the organisation. Secondly, to make the company financially bullet-proof so that I can sleep at night. And thirdly, to ensure that the company can adapt to the changing market environment.'

John Bovill and Bill Boyd had to decide how they were going to instill confidence in their customers and their potential customers, and 'win over' any of those considering going to other distributors after Ashton's had withdrawn; that is, how and what they should communicate.

They had to decide on a marketing strategy that would show the company in its best light, while conveying the range of products it supplied, from two very diverse divisions, dealing in very different products and price ranges, to very different customers.

CASE 5

George Hobson Limited
Marketing Policy and Strategy

Rob W. Lawson
University of Otago, New Zealand

D. Taylor
Huddersfield Polytechnic, UK

Case History

Based in Birmingham, one of the traditional homes of Britain's high quality steel industry, George Hobson had been manufacturing surgical instruments since the early nineteenth century. By the 1980s the company had developed a product range of over 2,000 hand-held, stainless steel instruments including such things as artery forceps, bone cutters and surgical scissors. By and large the company's product range represented the basic instruments commonly used in most surgical procedures. It also produced a small number of specialist instruments for use in particular types of surgery such as orthopaedics and gynaecology, but it had no instruments for many of the most modern and highly specialized branches of surgery such as open-heart, ophthalmics or micro-surgery.

In 1985 the company employed 150 staff. There was a small management team of six supported by an administrative staff of five and the remaining 139 employees were all directly involved in production.

Mr James Treeton, the Managing Director, 52 years of age, had worked at Hobson all his life and 13 years previously had inherited his position as MD together with the majority of the company's shares, from his father.

Alongside Mr Treeton was a long-standing and faithful management team. Mr Beck, the General Manager/Finance Director, 58 years old, had been with the company for 25 years. He was generally regarded as second in command and was proud to say that over the years he had done most jobs in the firm from packing parcels to production chasing. Mr Lambert, the Sales Director, 64 years of age, had spent his lifetime in the surgical instrument trade and had been with Hobson for 12 years. He prided himself on being able to identify all of the company's 2,000 products at a glance and being able to describe in detail their uses in surgical procedures. He had a real love for the products; this he believed was the essential foundation for any approach to successfully selling or marketing surgical instruments. The other members of the management team were all in their mid-thirties. They had each been with the company for about 10 years and consequently were well schooled in the company's philosophies and methods of operating. Although there was no formalized management structure, the *de facto* situation can be summarized as in Exhibit 5.1, with each member of the management team reporting directly, individually and usually informally to the MD.

Mr Treeton was able to take a direct interest in most aspects of the company and was involved in decision making on matters both large and small. His real interest, however, and most of his attention, focused on the 'works' side of the company and in particular on the purchase of new machinery and the development of new or improved production techniques. His main contribution to the firm's sales and promotional activity was his annual visit in February to the company's major export customers in Australia and South Africa.

The small administrative staff comprised a secretary, an export clerk/telephonist, a computer operator, a wages clerk and a sales/order clerk. These people were frequently overworked and it was often necessary for the members of the management to assist in dealing with daily tasks such as sales enquiries, or arranging the logistics of export consignments.

Throughout the 1960s and 1970s Mr Treeton and the management team had regarded the company's main problem to be insufficient production capacity, as there was an almost continuous back-order situation. This had been brought about both by a steady growth in hospitals within the National Health Service and by a fairly buoyant world health market. In the latter, demand was led primarily by massive spending in the Middle East as the oil-rich countries developed their quite lavish health infrastructure.

At Hobson's all effort was devoted to increasing the daily volume of output and this culminated in 1979 with the opening of a factory extension which doubled the size of the plant. The management had understandably been deeply disturbed and very surprised when the year-end sales figures for 1979 recorded a

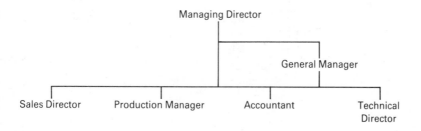

Exhibit 5.1 *Company organizational structure.*

decline in sales volume for the first time in living memory. Rather belatedly, this decline was rationalized in the company as being due to the world economic recession and Thatcherite public spending policy in Britain.

The Market for Surgical Instruments

The market for surgical instruments was split into two broad categories: theatre instruments and ward instruments. Theatre instruments are those used by surgeons when carrying out operations and consequently are required to be of the highest quality and precision. The performance of many of these instruments is critical to the patients' well-being although a number of theatre instruments, such as towel clips and swab holders, are regarded as non-critical.

Ward instruments are those used by nurses on hospital wards for non-critical procedures such as cutting dressings or clamping drip tubes, where there is generally no real requirement for a high quality expensive product. On the other hand, there is a much higher volume of ward instruments used, because of the ratio of wards to theatres in hospitals and because of a high replacement demand due to loss or theft of items such as scissors.

In the past Hobson instruments had been used for both theatre and ward purposes, but by the 1980s the demand was mainly for theatre use. This was due to increasing cost consciousness among hospital buyers and the availability of very cheap, albeit poor quality, imports of instruments suitable for ward use.

The main competition in surgical instrument manufacture came from two areas: Germany and Pakistan.

In Germany instrument production was concentrated almost entirely in the town of Tuttlingen where an estimated 8,000 people were involved in the industry. Production was carried out by a large number of small 'cottage industry' type firms. These frequently employed less than six people and were housed in the basements or outbuildings of the owners' homes to minimize overheads. In addition, there were six large firms, each five times larger than Hobson's. These large companies manufactured a selection of products but primarily acted as marketing outlets through which the cottage producers could sell their goods. In consequence the large firms were able to produce catalogues offering a comprehensive range of surgical instruments, in some cases listing in excess of 20,000 products.

The Germans were the acknowledged market leaders in the supply of top quality instruments and were active in every major country.

The second major concentration of instrument production was found in the town of Sialhot, Pakistan, where an estimated 20,000 people were engaged in the industry. The labour-intensive nature of production, together with a requirement for only low-level technology, made it an ideal candidate for a developing Third World economy. Production had started in Pakistan in the 1950s and although product quality was initially very poor, the industry had grown on the basis of supplying instruments to Third World markets where a low price was of paramount importance. As product quality steadily improved the Pakistanis had stealthily captured a large share of the ward instrument market not only in the United Kingdom, but in most other Western markets including the United States. Furthermore, as quality improved, many Pakistan instruments were being used in the theatre for both non-critical and sometimes critical procedures, a trend which in Britain was encouraged by increasingly tight hospital budgets.

In the late 1970s the large German companies had responded to this competition by establishing their own manufacturing plants in Pakistan and other Far Eastern countries, in order to secure their own supplies of low-cost, high-volume instruments for the ward market. At the same time the small German firms had been forced into producing increasingly intricate and specialized instruments, which although only sold in low volumes did command a high price. It was also widely believed in the trade that the German companies were selling Pakistan instruments as top theatre quality under German brand names which enabled them not only to make substantial profits but also to set their prices just below the equivalent British product.

In light of the lead taken by the Germans, Hobson's had entered into a joint venture with a Pakistan company. In 1983 a factory had been established in Pakistan, equipped with Hobson machinery and run by local management and labour. The company was to produce a small range of theatre-quality instruments using British raw materials, part-worked in Birmingham, finished in Pakistan and quality controlled back in Birmingham. The products were to be sold as a separate brand under the name of Regal. Initially the brand was to be marketed only in the United States at a price one-third below Hobson's Birmingham made products.

Although on a world scale Hobson faced intense competition from Germany and Pakistan, the situation in Britain looked a little more favourable in that competition was diminishing. Traditionally, the domestic market had been served by a significant number of small instrument manufacturers together with seven or eight larger companies of which Hobson was one. By 1984, 90% of the small manufacturers had disappeared together with four out of the eight large firms. In 1985 Darwin, one of the remaining major producers, reduced its workforce by half which left Hobson as the largest remaining UK instrument manufacturer. It was estimated that there were no more than 650 people employed directly in making instruments in Britain, of which 150 were at Hobson's. The industry had no data on the size of the UK market and only the accumulated sales data shown in Exhibit 5.2 was available to Hobson's management. Exhibit 5.3 shows the pattern of orders received in 1985.

The UK Situation

In the domestic market all Hobson's customers were 'trade houses', that is, retailers of a range of medical equipment only part of which was surgical instruments. However, there were a small number of retailers, of which Storth was the largest, for whom surgical instruments comprised the main product line.

Exhibit 5.2 *Annual total order values (£'000s).*

	Storth	Thorsby	Darwin	Massey	UK others	South African Medical Company	Australian hospital supplies	Surgical supplies Canada	USA	Export others	Annual total	Pretax profit (£000)
1976	183	157	36		300					266	942	141
1977	366	463	74		283					454	1,640	262
1978	673	419	45		511					284	1,932	270
1979	489	338	53		370					218	1,468	132
1980	459	423	13	95	242	59	65	33	20	86	1,495	149
1981	449	459	17	130	350	42	86	65	30	134	1,762	158
1982	543	741	92	157	521	53	77	64	29	56	2,333	209
1983	406	589	82	330	591	68	149	51	29	83	2,378	214
1984	701	519	83	135	633	95	170	75	53	149	2,613	182
1985	445	365	227	226	768	143	77	86	598	273	3,208	192

Exhibit 5.3 *Pattern of orders received (1985).*

	Four major domestic customers	UK others	Three major export customers	Export others
Average order value £'s	1,800	200	6,800	1,100
Averge no. of days between orders	7	21	25	30
Average no. of catalogue lines per order	30	8	50	25
Percentage of lines ordered by quantity (See Note 1)				
1– 9 instruments	8	44	5	20
10–99 instruments	62	50	80	70
>100 instruments	30	6	15	10
Minimum acceptable order quantity per line	1	1	1	1

Note 1 Price Discount Structure:

Quantity ordered per line	Discount from basic price
1– 9 instruments	0
10–99 instruments	7½ %
>100 instruments	15 %

None of the large UK customers used Hobson as their exclusive source of intruments and would purchase instruments from Germany, Pakistan or other small UK manufacturers. On a few occasions, Hobson had made direct sales of a few thousand pounds value to small private hospitals, but each time the action had resulted in a direct protest from one or more of the major customers.

Apart from the major clients there was no readily available breakdown of sales to individual customers. In fact, no one within the company had ever taken a comprehensive list of UK customers from the computer. The Sales Director estimated the total customers at between 60 and 100. The small accounts ranged from long-established firms doing a significant amount of business, for example, £50,000 plus per annum, to many small distributors purchasing less than £1,000 per annum. Many smaller customers were not well known to Hobson's as they tended to be regarded as insignificant and something of a nuisance because of their small order values. In fact, pre-1979 such customers were actively discouraged either by being refused products or given very long delivery times, as the company had more than enough orders from its main customers. Traditionally, Hobson had supplied the large trade houses with products branded with the distributor's own label. This policy had been continued as new distributors were added to the customers' list, so that in the United Kingdom no Hobson branded products were sold.

Frequently, new distributors asked Hobson to supply a Hobson branded product. This request was always refused as it was felt that branding would put Hobson into a competitive situation with its major customers.

Contact with UK customers was maintained primarily through telephone conversations when customers placed orders or requested information on product availability. Such conversations almost always elicited the question 'How's business?' – which was the opening to pass on news and gossip about the trade and was the company's main method of collecting information on the market. Contact with the major customers was rather more formalized in that two or three times a year, visits were made to Hobson by senior management from each of the major distributors and there was an ongoing visiting pattern between Hobson and these companies at middle management level.

Overall, Hobson's valued its customer relationships highly and was always willing to produce 'specials' in the form of variations in the design or weight of catalogued instruments in response to the desires or whims of particular surgeons that distributors were trying to please. There were in fact over 2,500 such specials listed on the computer records. Furthermore, the company was proud of its reputation for not overpricing such products, usually adding on only a small percentage to the price of the equivalent standard product despite the sometimes considerable disruption to production.

Overseas Trade

Although the total volume of Hobson's export business was not particularly high, the company had a wide spread of overseas markets in most of which it sold instruments under its own brand name. Hobson had exported for many years, the primary markets being Australia, South Africa and Canada. In each of these countries there was a long-standing, exclusive distributor arrangement with a particular company. Although business with each of these distributors tended to fluctuate from year to year, all three were regarded as good customers and approaches or offers of business from other companies in these countries were always rejected.

In 1980, Hobson's reaction to falling sales revenue was to look to the further development of export markets. The United States was selected as the best possibility because it was the largest and richest medical products market in the world, plus it was English-speaking and relatively easy to access from the United Kingdom. In consequence the Sales Director was commissioned to go and get business in the United States, a task which he undertook by making frequent trips to the United States armed with the names and addresses of American surgical instrument distributors. By 1984, the MD regarded these efforts as a failure, a fact which he clearly conveyed to the Sales Director and the rest of the management team. The Sales Director claimed that he had been successful in securing initial orders with a number of companies but efforts to develop long-term business had been undermined by poor delivery times and problems with product quality.

The MD himself made a number of visits to the United States and in 1984 had been successful in securing a one-year contract worth £455,000 to supply instruments to a US Government department through a distributor in New York. These instruments were of the 'Regal' type being machined in Britain, shipped to Pakistan for intensive finishing and returned to Birmingham for quality control before being finally shipped to the United States. The contract was dogged throughout by late deliveries from Pakistan and poor quality products, which in some cases required large batches of products to be completely reworked in Birmingham. Failure to meet contract deadlines and quality standards finally resulted in the US Government refusing to accept the last £150,000 worth of instruments which were left on Hobson's hands.

A further attempt to penetrate the American market developed out of a chance meeting between James Treeton and Elmer Collins, the owner/manager of Collins Instruments, a small, financially ailing instrument manufacturing company in Boise, Idaho. The meeting eventually led to Hobson buying a half share in Collins Instruments, thus providing sufficient funds to keep the American company afloat and providing Hobson with a distribution base from which to attack the market in western United States. The initial plan was to develop sales in 10 states using 10 manufacturer's representatives served from an inventory of £50,000 worth of instruments held in Boise. The sales target for 1985, the first year of operation, was set at £300,000 and everyone, including the reps, was confident this could be achieved. The main basis of competition was seen as price, therefore, Hobson prices were set at a level which was thought to be roughly 10% lower than local competition. By June 1985, sales had only reached £20,000, Collins Instruments was in deepening financial trouble and Hobson's accountant was sent to Boise to try and avert financial disaster. The reps claimed they had received orders across the whole of Hobson's product range but had been unable to fulfil many orders or secure repeat business because of lack of stock in Idaho and delivery times which were frequently as long as three months on items required from the United Kingdom. In an attempt to increase sales and stave off the financial collapse, the accountant agreed to take on seven more reps covering a further seven states. On his return to England, however, he was unable to persuade Hobson's management to increase stock levels in Idaho; it being argued that until sales picked up the company could not afford to keep more stock in the United States. Furthermore, no one seemed able or confident enough to suggest what additional lines should be placed in the United States if stock were to increase, and the sporadic sales record of the first six months offered no meaningful trends.

The year 1984 had not only witnessed the negotiations to establish a Hobson American base but it had also been the period in which the company embarked on the establishment of Hobson Italy Limited, a wholly owned Italian subsidiary based in Trieste. Again the function of this company was to act as a stockholding and distribution base for Italy. Sales were to be made direct to hospitals and the company engaged three commission-only agents to cover the whole of Italy. The Italian company was set up and run by Mr Treeton's daughter who had recently completed a degree in Italian, which she followed by a year working on the development of promotional materials at Hobson. The idea for the company had come initially from one of the Italian agents who had approached Hobson and convinced the management that there was scope for a range of British surgical instruments in Italy. This was in spite of strong competition from the Germans and an indigenous Italian instrument industry of similar size to that in Britain. By mid-1985, sales in Italy were averaging £6,000 per month against the £30,000 per month needed to cover the costs of running the Trieste office. The problems in Italy were compounded when one agent deserted the company and a second had a heart attack after which he was only able to work two days per week.

In addition to direct efforts in America and Italy, Hobson was also involved in many other export markets. In Exhibit 5.2, the column headed 'Export others' was made up of an ever-changing list of about 20 distributors in various countries each of whom would place sporadic orders with the company. In some territories distributors had asked for and been granted 'exclusivity' but it was surprising that in many instances these companies proved to be the worst performers and often produced no business after an initial flurry of activity. However, the list of export customers was slowly growing longer.

Hobson received a steady flow of enquiries from around the world from companies wishing to distribute British surgical instruments. In most cases, Hobson would agree to supply such companies although enquiries from the Middle East and Black Africa were refused as these were respectively regarded as the markets of Thorsby and Storth, and Hobson had a gentlemen's agreement not to compete in these areas. However, there was never any indication from Thorsby or Storth as to the level of business or market share they achieved in these areas.

The Present Situation

Though Hobson's had continued to produce profits, there had been no real recovery in the company's sales by 1985 and the company's response was to appoint the firm's first marketing manager. The person chosen for the part was a recent MBA graduate, Alistair Telford, whose previous industrial experience was limited to specialized distribution work in a large freight company. The appointment had been made after a series of informal interviews with Treeton who had firmly stated that 'Our company needs marketing, although I'm not sure what marketing is'. Telford was excited by the challenge of introducing marketing into a traditional manufacturing company. Although he acknowledged that he had little industrial experience prior to his MBA he was confident that his studies had given him a firm understanding of marketing concepts with which to approach the job. He had also been impressed by Treeton's forward-looking and fairly adventurous attitude in that the company had recently established three overseas subsidiary companies. In his first week with the company, Telford set about trying to get a feel of both the company and the industry in which he now found himself. The other members of the management team were very welcoming and willing to give him their views on all these matters, but he was initially rather dismayed to find seemingly an almost complete lack of data or structured information on the company's internal performance indicators, its markets or its competition.

The company had a computer which had been operational for three years and he was sure that it would hold a significant level of relevant information once data requirements were specified. The computer had been purchased on the initiative of the company's accountant to carry out fairly basic daily functions such as accounting stock control, monitoring work in progress, etc., and the accountant was the only member of the company who fully understood the system and could write or alter programs. In the early weeks, Telford made several unsuccessful approaches to the accountant with requests for information from the computer or suggestions as to programs that would provide valuable marketing information.

One such request was for a ranked listing showing the percentage profit on each product line. The accountant's reply was that the company did not know the profit margin on each product as production costs per product were not shown. This prompted Telford to ask how prices were set. It transpired that at the time each new product had been added to the product range, a price was set by the MD or Production Manager on the basis of what he thought the job was worth or the product would fetch. These prices were then increased each year by the same percentage as the company's wage settlement.

The situation with the company's promotional activities was, if nothing else, fairly straightforward. The only promotional literature used by the firm was the *Hobson Catalogue* which just contained a full listing of the company's product codes and product descriptions together with pictures of most of the instruments. A new version of the catalogue had been produced two years earlier by a local design and advertising consultancy and it was generally agreed that it was very professional, created a modern image and was very easy to use. Copies of the catalogue were sent to all customers and any potential new distributors who approached Hobson for information about the company or its products.

As Hobson was well known to all its major customers, the feeling in the company was that there was no need to advertise. This was further reinforced by the MD's belief that advertising was an unnecessary overhead that could easily run away with large sums of money with nothing to show in return. Beyond production of 10,000 copies of the new catalogue at a cost of £2 each, the company's main promotional expenditure over the previous three years had been devoted to exhibiting at three international trade shows, two in Germany and one in the United States. These had each cost over £10,000 but no one was really sure what they had achieved, other than bringing in a large number of enquiries from distributors immediately after each show. However, few of these enquiries had resulted in long-term business.

Telford had frequent discussions with Lambert, the Sales Director, regarding Hobson's markets and possible methods to develop new business. One of Lambert's basic beliefs was that the company could not make a bigger impact in the market until it extended its product range. He pointed out that although Hobson listed some 2,000 items in the catalogue, this only represented a small proportion of the total range of surgical instruments used in hospitals. He felt that the only way to attract more interest from distributors was steadily to increase the product range and at the same time make every effort to bring down prices relative to the competition.

Production of the existing range of 2,000 products did not seem to be achieved without some problems. Hobson's main supplier of raw materials was G. T. Blanks Limited, a local company of which Hobson owned 20% of the equity. G. T. preferred to supply a full stamping of 5,000 blanks and had a minimum order requirement for 3,000. Quantities of blanks from 10 upwards were available from Germany but at a much higher unit cost. Telford thought the manufacturing lead times were quite long, frequently two or three months, and many lines seemed to be in a back-order situation despite the fact that the company was holding over £800,000 of finished stocks (Exhibits 5.4 and 5.5). Telephone calls were received every day from customers chasing products. At the same time, there was a steady stream of products returned to the company because of product faults. No proper record of these returns was kept and so it was not possible to put a figure on the number received, although the Production Manager assured Telford it was probably as low as 2% or 3%.

Exhibit 5.4 *Sales/stock levels (1985).*

	Annual sales volume (number of instruments)		
	> 1,000	200–1,000	< 200
Number of products	88	290	1,570
Number of products with raw material stocks	86	261	950
Number of products with WIP	23	116	520
Finished stock relative to average monthly sales levels:			
Zero months' supply	31	44	276
0–2 months' supply	39	128	188
2–12 months' supply	14	95	730
12–60 months' supply	4	23	326
over 60 months' supply	0	0	50

Exhibit 5.5 *Stock values.*

Selling price of goods	(£'000)
Raw materials	711
WIP	754
Finished stock	845

Four weeks after joining the company, Alistair Telford sat quietly at home and mused on the situation he had so far discovered at Hobson's. The company seemed to have very significant problems in every direction and he wondered what he should do in order to start trying to make an effective contribution as the company's new Marketing Manager. He also began to question whether his MBA training had given him an unrealistic expectation of how companies actually performed in the 'real world'. After all, as the General Manager had pointed out, Hobson's had never had a year in which it had failed to make a profit.

CASE 6
Passcard
Strategic Marketing

Leonard A. Sym

Glasgow Business School, University of Glasgow

Introduction

This was the first time in a number of weeks Garry Wilson had reason to sit back and feel contented with his business. He had just heard from his lawyers that a long protracted case had finished in his favour. A financial institution had agreed to buy the name of his product. He now had the opportunity to change his company and product name, to relaunch and perhaps move into another, as yet untapped market segment. He had a lot of different avenues in front of him. Which should he take? How did these possibilities relate to him now and to each other? If he opened one door, how many others, now half open, would close?

Background and Company History

It was only four years ago that Garry had graduated in history and drama from Glasgow University. He now owns and manages the only locally based discount card in Scotland. He founded Passcard 18 months before, after completing a small business start-up programme aimed at graduates. However, the origins predate this course and his university career. Garry is a natural entrepreneur: at the age of 12 he was running a casino in the garage of his parents' house. Before leaving school, he was organizing trips to Blackpool. The idea for Passcard came about accidentally when he was organizing a de-mob night at a Glasgow dancehall. The theme for the evening extended into the 1945s atmosphere and clothes. In his quest to get as many people into de-mob suits, he arranged discounts with the owners of antique clothes shops in the city. The way it worked was that de-mob night ticket holders were given a 10% discount in any of the shops that were advertised on the back of the tickets. This proved to be very successful. There were queues into the streets from these shops on the day before the event. This was to be the style of service he would provide in Passcard. The customer of the card gets a discount from a limited number of outlets and the outlets get free publicity and more custom. He was helping the 'invisible hand' of Adam Smith bringing people together in a win–win situation. The idea would work as long as outlets got more custom and the customer got a bargain or discount.

In the first year of trading, Passcard put 10,000 subscribers on its books. Discounts range from 10 to 50% in any of the 2,000 outlets that subscribe to Passcard. The customers pay £14.50 per year. For this they receive a Passcard which is the size of a credit card and a booklet listing the outlets. The outlets pay £25 for inclusion in the booklet. This is a one-off joining fee and for it they get a captive market. Passcard employs 12 salesmen full time. They are young and able to relate to the market segment Passcard is aimed at, that is, students. Passcard is a leisure-oriented discount card. Many of the outlets are discos, shops, car-hire companies and pubs, and the clients are predominantly students. Students are relatively poor and go for a bargain. Spend £14.50 and save £400 in a year. There are not many better bargains than that!

Cost

The operating cost of Passcard is low. The salesmen work on a commission-only basis and the cost of the card and booklet are low. The cost of the card is £1,000 per 5,000 run or £7,000 per 100,000 run, that is, from 7 pence to 20 pence per card. The booklet has fixed costs of £1,000 and variable costs of £2,500 for a 5,000 run or £10,000 for a 100,000 run, that is, between 10 pence and 50 pence. At the lowest run prices, card and booklet cost 90 pence and salesman's commission @ 25% is £3.63, and this means a contribution of at least £9.97 towards office costs and profit. However, there is a gradation of costs. The relationship is shown in Exhibit 6.1.

Office overheads are £50,000 per year. Break-even is around 5,013 customers at £14.50, providing three lowest quantity runs are made. If, on the other hand,

Exhibit 6.1   *Cost relationships.*

Run size	Card cost	Booklet fixed cost	Booklet variable cost	Total cost	Cost per card
<4,999	£1,000	£1,000	£2,500	£4,500	0.90p
5–9,999	£2,000	£1,000	£3,500	£6,500	0.65p
10–29,990	£3,000	£1,000	£5,000	£9,000	0.30p
30–44,999	£4,500	£1,000	£6,000	£11,500	0.26p
45–49,999	£5,000	£1,000	£6,500	£12,500	0.25p
50–59,999	£5,500	£1,000	£7,000	£13,500	0.23p
60–69,999	£6,000	£1,000	£8,000	£15,000	0.22p
71–89,999	£6,500	£1,000	£9,000	£16,500	0.18p
90–100,000	£7,000	£1,000	£10,000	£18,000	0.18p

one run of 10,000 is made, break-even is then 4,890, due to lower printing costs. Of the 10,000 current cardholders, 5,000 have taken out a subscription at £14.50. This is automatically renewed by banker's order each year.

Competition

Since Passcard was launched, 12 other discount cards have been launched in Scotland. All of these are locally based, and all have been unsuccessful, and are now believed bankrupt. The reason is that a discount service is just very difficult to organize and run. There has to be substantial investment in financial terms, in creating a good network of outlets and getting a good balance between outlets and customers. It is also difficult to market, as customers do not value it according to the benefits that they could receive from it. People are reluctant to spend £14.50 on something that could save them hundreds of pounds.

Passcard has one major competitor on the British market. This competition has 1¼ million members. It is an international organization with a presence in Europe, North America and the Far East. It is based in England but its overall coverage of its markets as compared to Passcard is scant. It started out in the early 1970s and has grown substantially since. It is targeted at a mass market. It is very definitely not up-market. Scotland is covered, but to a far lesser extent than by Passcard. The British discount card sells in bulk orders of 10,000 at very much less than standard subscription, that is at between £1 and £3. Its subscription cost is a similar figure to that of Passcard.

New Markets

The question to be resolved in Garry's mind is two-fold. With the settling of the legal case and the monies he got from it, should he relaunch his discount card with, firstly, another name and, secondly, a different market. If yes, which name and which market. The new name is relatively easy. It will be Passkey. The second question is to be resolved. The market up until now has been the student population at a high subscription rate. Within the last six months or so, Garry has been approached by various organizations requesting him to supply Passkey in bulk at a lost cost. He has had 16 offers to date, eight of which are being looked at closely. What is difficult to gauge is, if he leaves his bread-and-butter market in the university and college campuses around Scotland, how will his new market react and affect his profitability? The new markets and their potential are as follows:

Major stores group This company wishes to give Passkey away to 91,000 account holders. It will arrange extra discounts for all cardholders with ten major high street retailers. The company will pay £2 per card.

Tourist board   A tourist board wants Passkey either to be sold or given away via the tourist board to airline/tour operators. The board is anxious to give away Passkey rather than sell it. If this were the case, it guarantees 100,000 users in the first year. It will pay £0.90 per card.

White-collar union   A white-collar union wishes to use Passkey. It wishes to publicize the card to all its members at a special price. Further, it is willing to produce and pay for all publicity materials, postage, etc. The union dues are £0.62 per week and it has 72,000 members. No price is specified.

Transport group   A public transport group wishes to give Passkey away as a bonus to its monthly season ticket holders. No cards need to be produced as the group will overprint the back of their monthly tickets. The group has 60,000 monthly ticket holders at present. These holders are reasonably stable in so far as turnover is relatively small. The implication is that 60,000 holders will be stable over one year. They will pay £2 per card.

Newspaper   A Scottish national newspaper wants to give the card to its readers who take out a subscription on the paper. The newspaper will provide a large amount of expensive advertising. The circulation of the newspaper is presently 400,000. The paper wants it for nothing.

Factory workers' union   A factory workers' union wishes to purchase the card for its members. The union dues are £52 per year and it has 45,000 members. It will only pay £1 as the union knows the price quoted by Passkey's competitor.

Students' organization   This organization, whose members are Garry's present target market, wishes its own staff to approach their members and sell Passkey at a special rate. This rate is unspecified. The organization has 100,000 members. To sell here would mean the complete loss of the present market.

Fashion chain   A chain of shops wishes to give the card away to purchasing customers. This will involve their shifting 30,000 cards in the first year. They will pay £2.50 per card.

Garry has decided that he could use price differentiation but how radical could it be? If he were going to drop his price per card substantially for bulk orders, could he still sell to individuals at £14.50? His dilemma is: how should he reposition his company marketing strategy? Which bulk orders should he choose and, most importantly, how should he price Passkey given the level of savings that can be made and the price of his competitors?

PART 2

Buyer Behaviour, Marketing Information System and Segmentation

Case   7   Clydesdale Products   79
Organizational Buying Behaviour
Case   8   Southern Precision Engineering   104
Organizational Buying Behaviour/Personal Selling
Case   9   Weighill Hotel, Glasgow   118
Marketing Information Systems
Case 10   Deckgard   130
Marketing Orientation/Marketing Information Systems
Case 11   Independent Bookshop Limited   135
Segmentation and Targeting

Buyer Behaviour

Information on buyer behaviour is generally used to predict or diagnose buyers' actions in markets. Because managers are responsible for the outcome of their decisions, they ought to be sure that buyer behaviour information is relevant to the decision situation.

Consumer behaviour refers to the behaviour of a type of customer in the marketplace – the final consumer. An equally important category of customer is the organizational buyer as represented by the industrial purchaser and by the institutional purchaser.

Organizational buying behaviour represents a larger segment of the economy by sales volume than consumer behaviour.

Organizational buyer behaviour has certain similarities to consumer buying behaviour, but the needs, decision processes and behaviour of organizational buyers are different enough from those of consumer buyers to warrant separate consideration. Recognition of these differences and the consequent differences in marketing strategies have resulted in many studies of organizational buyer behaviour.

The notion of an organizational buyer operating by personal as well as organizational motives, and by subjective attitudes and perceptions as well as economic utility, means that certain components of the model of consumer behaviour may apply equally well to organizational buyer behaviour. The organizational buyer develops attitudes towards vendors on the basis of past experience, the vendor's marketing strategy and the buyer's own predispositions. Clearly, organizational buying cannot be understood by economic analysis alone. Behavioural principles must be applied within a framework of buyer behaviour research. The differences between organizational and consumer buying require a fuller understanding of the process of organizational buying. One important distinction between organizational and consumer buying is that organizational buying requires a decision for selecting both a vendor and a product. Frequently the two are intertwined, but different criteria are used to select vendors (delivery, sales, personnel, reliability) and to select products (price, quality, engineering specifications). The inputs of individual expectations, product and organizational characteristics, environmental influences, and individual versus joint decision making, will lead to a decision regarding a supplier and brand. The criteria used in evaluating alternative suppliers are likely to differ from those used in evaluating product alternatives. An important input into the process of selecting a supplier is the nature and source of information on the suppliers' capabilities and offerings.

Organizational buyer behaviour is generally a process of group decision making, especially in new buy situations. Therefore, an understanding of organizational buyer behaviour requires an understanding of the buying unit within the organization. Central to an understanding of decision making in a buying unit are the different roles of members of the buying group. A logical out-growth of joint purchasing responsibilities is conflict between members of the buying centre. Because of the varying organizational positions and perspectives of members of the buying group, some conflict is inevitable in the buying decision. Such conflict is likely to be resolved if it deals with differences over product or vendor selection, or differences regarding the criteria for evaluation. But when differences focus on personalities or decision styles, conflict may not lead to the attainment of organizational objectives.

Organizational buyer behaviour consists of three distinct aspects. The first aspect is the psychological world of the individuals involved in organizational buying decisions. The second aspect relates to the conditions which precipitate joint decisions among these individuals. The final aspect is the process of joint decision making with the inevitable conflict among the decision makers and its resolution by resorting to a variety of tactics.

The *Clydesdale Products* case introduces many of the critical issues involved in organizational buying behaviour, such as: analysis of the decision-making unit (DMU), sources of conflict within the DMU, product and vendor selection criteria, as well as marketing actions available to suppliers in order to exert a favourable influence on the customer.

The *Southern Precision Engineering* case evolves around the interface relationship between organizational buying behaviour effects and personal selling plans. The case is designed according to a role-playing format, whereby some students would be assigned to either the buying team or the selling team. Instructions would be given to both teams, which would help them develop their game plans in order to reach the most effective level of negotiation and conclusive results.

Marketing Information System

Most progressive companies have a formal system of collecting and reporting market information. The major feature of this arrangement, termed a marketing information system (MKIS), is that the company systematically collects and reports data in such a way that it is of major value in assisting decision making. Marketing information systems extend marketing research from a project-to-project basis to a continuous management information function. Marketing information systems are integrated combinations of information, processing tools and analysis equipment, software, and information specialists that serve the various analysis, planning and control needs of marketing decision makers.

Marketing managers need to monitor market environments continuously and make appropriate adjustments. The marketing information system (MKIS) is designed to provide a continuously updated information base that is readily available as problems occur or when plans need to be made or changed. MKIS is a system which provides a continuous flow of marketing information useful for management decisions.

Organizations face an often bewildering stream of data and information from a number of sources: personal contacts, the salesforce, competitors, business publications, trade associations, government, and marketing research data, as well as the multitude of business transactions such as customers' orders, shipments and records of internal actions.

Trends in the marketing environment are picked up and analysed through four subsystems making up the marketing information system in the internal accounting system, marketing intelligence system, marketing research system and analytical marketing system. An analytical marketing system consists of a statistical bank and a model bank. The statistical bank is a collection of statistical procedures for extracting meaningful information from data. The model bank is a collection of models that will help marketers develop better marketing decisions.

Regardless of the type of marketing information system, its function is to support the marketing decision process. The more advanced the system the more it should add to the efficiency with which decisions are made. A key determinant of the system's contribution to the decision process is the way the system is structured. Although the composition of MKISs varies, certain basic components are present. A decision maker must activate the MKIS in some manner, such as requesting needed information. The result is an 'output' that feeds back to the decision maker. The system comprises three interrelated components: a database (accumulated information); various capabilities for processing information; and system functions (file creation, report generation, etc.).

The marketing decision support system (MDSS) is another sophisticated form of the MKIS. It is a technology that integrates data, software and hardware to provide the marketing executive with information needed for decision making. The MDSS differs from a basic MKIS in that it concentrates on: (1) analysis rather than retrieval; (2) provision of relevant data; (3) use of models to investigate relationships between marketing variables; and (4) interactive computer analysis.

The *Weighill Hotel, Glasgow* case describes applications of computing and information systems. This case study helps the student to identify the main managerial and organizational problems in developing marketing-oriented systems in a service environment, as well as to understand the problems in developing both operational and competitive advantage from information systems. The case clearly demonstrates the marketing opportunities created by applications of management information systems, as well as some critical trade-offs involved in the development of these systems and procedures.

Segmentation

Market selection begins with market segmentation. Market segmentation helps the firm to gear a specific product or service to the likes or requirements of a particular target group. Marketers may compare the benefits against the costs associated with addressing a certain segment of the market. Market segmentation represents a middle way between a strategy of market aggregation, in which all customers are treated similarly, and one of market disaggregation, in which each consumer is treated uniquely. The important thing to keep in mind is that a segmentation scheme is simply a way of grouping like buying units for the purpose of determining what products to offer them and what marketing strategies to formulate to assure success in turning potential demand into sales and profits. Market segmentation plans thus provide the frameworks for formulating strategies.

The choice of a market segment is based on both identifying a significant pocket of demand and assessing the strength of competitive entries in that segment or space.

As markets grow and mature, segmentation changes. Often there is a proliferation of market segments. Total demand becomes increasingly segmented, with product offerings and strategies for each segment being highly tailored to that segment's needs and buying behaviour. In a mature state, consumer goods markets in particular tend to be segmented psychographically, with subtle differences among segments regarding the meaning of the product.

Marketing management needs to find the best basis for showing the segment in which a buyer belongs. Segmentation bases are characteristics on which potential buyers differ and reflect preferences for brand marketing offers. Ideally, a segmentation basis would be a direct measure of response elasticities to entire marketing offers. In practice, segmentation bases are typically characteristic of potential buyers that are, at best, proxy measures of response elasticities.

The requirements for effective segmentation include measurability, accessibility, substantiality and actionability. Market segments must be large, distinct, measurable and reachable. Some of the most important steps involved in a segmentation strategy include the formation of segments, profiling the segments of interest, financially and strategically evaluating the segments and selecting one or more target markets.

Marketing management should be concerned with segmentation policies at each of the levels of aggregation since segmentation is used to: (1) achieve a better competitive position for existing and new products; (2) more effectively position an existing or new product by appealing to a limited market; (3) identify gaps in the market which represent new product opportunities; and (4) identify market potentials and new consumers for the product or service. Segmentation is not a static strategy. It must evolve as consumer needs, tastes, preferences and trends alter and as competitive pressures change.

The *Deckgard* case demonstrates the importance of being close to the customer. Deckgard is a useful case for highlighting the importance of a marketing orientation. It shows that even companies which have been successful by understanding customer requirements may subsequently make mistakes. The effective use of a marketing information system may be considered using this case, as well as the relationship between marketing and R & D, and (by implication) other managerial functions in the company.

The *Independent Bookshop Limited* case study provides an unusual opportunity to look at marketing issues in general, and market segmentation issues in particular. The case is designed to develop decision-making skills in the area of market segmentation and targeting, based on the relevance of factors, such as market demand, competitive structure and cost allocation. The case also demonstrates the importance of developing effective marketing mix strategies as a subsequent stage of the application of a segmentation and targeting approach.

CASE 7
Clydesdale Products
Organizational Buying Behaviour

Douglas T. Brownlie

Glasgow Business School, University of Glasgow

Value and Purpose of Seminars

Since his early days as a buyer's clerk in the steel industry, Ron Naismith had always taken an active interest in the affairs of the Institute of Purchasing and Supply (IPS). Over the years he had grown to recognize the wisdom of his early enthusiasm as he developed and capitalized on an enviable network of contacts in professional buying and selling circles in the United Kingdom and overseas. Indeed, he was known to joke that the only reason he had been headhunted to his recent appointment as purchasing director of a large manufacturer of air compressors was that he was on first name terms with so many senior purchasing and sales executives in the UK engineering industry.

As the immediate past Chairman of the IPS's Education and Training Committee, he had often helped to organize updating seminars for members and other interested parties. He even spoke at several of them.

When the current incumbent first mooted the idea of running a seminar on 'Modelling the Industrial Buying Decision Process', his first thoughts had been those of the mildly disinterested cynic. The source of his reservation was what he interpreted to be a rather arcane and academic subject. Naismith knew from his own experience that members were used to, and seemed to expect a down to earth treatment of practical managerial topics in purchasing. He wondered what value there would be in taking such an apparently academic approach to a topic of relevance to the top management of the purchasing function. The last thing the IPS wanted to do was to sponsor activities that might alienate the membership. But, on the other hand, Naismith thought he was always bemoaning the cinderella status of purchasing as a subject for serious academic enquiry. He could only agree that by bringing academics and practitioners together, the proposed seminar should stimulate opportunities for advancing research and knowledge in the area of purchasing and supply.

Despite his initial ambivalence, Naismith felt the invisible hand of his own self-interest being provoked into action as he perused the advance publicity for the seminar contained in the latest issue of the *IPS Journal*. The seminar was to be led by a Dr Muir of the Glasgow University Business School. He was intrigued to learn that since 1980 she had been building a bank of in-depth case studies of purchasing decision making, and that each case study documented in some detail the factors that led to the decision; the procedures and techniques that enabled it to be taken; and the roles of the people involved during the various stages of the decision process.

Naismith thought Dr Muir's approach to be novel and promising. In the past, he had helped several researchers to conduct large-scale surveys of industrial buying practice. Without exception, however, he had been disappointed, if not entirely surprised, by the sterility and inconclusiveness of their findings. These were usually dismissed by him as mere head counting that contributed little insight to our understanding of the real issues.

In his current position, Naismith often found himself wondering how he could make more effective use of the resources at his disposal. He knew that to do so, he would somehow have to improve the organization of his staff and the use they made of the available purchasing technology. Management development and training of the sort offered by the IPS was helping him to deal with the latter. It was his policy for all purchasing staff to become qualified IPS members. But, the question of organizational design and effectiveness was clearly his to resolve.

Despite his wealth of experience, Naismith could not help feeling inadequately equipped to draw firm conclusions about how to improve effectiveness. Indeed, he often wished there was a theory that could at least point him in the right direction, if not provide the firm solutions he so desired. Of one thing he felt he could be sure, internal pressure to improve his department's effectiveness would continue to mount, not only because of its immediate impact on direct costs and margins, but also because the profit leverage of marketing-based initiatives was declining as volume growth in the compressor market stagnated and price stability was threatened by capacity expansion worldwide.

With these thoughts formulating in his mind, Naismith very quickly found himself engaged in an interesting telephone conversation with Dr Muir. She explained that the particular research she was proposing to build the seminar around was not concerned with routine purchasing decisions, but those associated with capital investment. She believed that the job of the purchaser was made more difficult and less effective in non-routine situations, where the responsibility for the decision was dispersed throughout the firm. Both of these conditions characterized the purchase of capital plant and equipment. Dr Muir summarized the purpose of the seminar as being, firstly, to examine how several firms have organized themselves to take the purchasing decisions associated with their capital investment plans; secondly, to establish criteria by which to judge how successful their endeavours have been; thirdly, to distil from the experiences of those firms the essence of best practice; and fourthly, for participants to reflect on the value of these lessons for the purchasing of capital items in their own firms.

As he rang off, Naismith was glad he had called Dr Muir. She seemed to know what she was talking about. She had also helped clarify his doubts about the purpose of the seminar and its value to him. Indeed, he was beginning to think that the topic of the seminar would be as relevant to executives in sales or marketing as it was to those of us in purchasing. After all, he mused, few could know as well as he did the ground rules for lasting and mutually profitable relationships between buyers and suppliers. And he had to check a sudden wave of smugness on recalling the embarrassing lack of professionalism of some salesmen who had beset him last week, not only unannounced, but ill-informed. He liked to think that he had much more respect for his staff, and for the suppliers and customers with whom they had to work, than to let them loose in the field so ill-equipped and poorly prepared. He wondered what was happening to British sales and marketing management these days. With so much mismanagement, mistrust and misinformation around, would UK industry survive in a deregulating Europe?

Despite the onset of these phlegmatic visions, he was beginning to feel that it would be worth the £180 fee just to discover what specific conclusions Dr Muir would draw from her research about the questions of effectiveness that he predicted would be uppermost in the minds of the audience. She had also promised to send him in advance and free of charge a copy of one of her early case studies which was by now sufficiently disguised to be made public (Appendix 7.1).

Being an optimist, Naismith felt inclined to reserve his place on the seminar, even before he had had the chance to review the case study. After all, he thought, if the worst came to the worst, he could always cancel his place, forfeiting only his £25 deposit.

Appendix 7.1   Dr Muir's Case Study

Industrial Buying Research Group Case Study No. 4,
Working Paper 3
CLYDESDALE PRODUCTS
L. H. C. Muir
University of Glasgow
Department of Management Studies

Abstract

This working paper is the latest of three which document the progress of an in-depth study of purchasing decision making in a large British manufacturing concern. It is the product of a ten-month period of 'action research' in which the author took the role of an observer of the decision-making activity of a group of senior managers and their advisors.

The paper records the sequence of activities which was initiated by the decision, taken at group director level, to expand the production capacity of one of the firm's major manufacturing plants, in anticipation of a cyclical upsurge in the demand for its products. It discusses the composition of the decision-making group whose responsibility it eventually became to recommend a supplier of the capital equipment required to fulfil the compressed air demands of the additional manufacturing capacity. It also considers issues such as the interaction of the members of the group, in terms of the patterns of communication they established while retrieving decision-pertinent information. The roles and relative decision-making influence of group members are also examined.

Summary

In 1982 Clydesdale Products, a large British-owned heavy engineering combine, laid plans to expand the production capacity of one of its major manufacturing plants. A surge in the demand for the products of this plant had been anticipated as a result of the growth in the worldwide exploration and development of offshore oil fields. The small diameter steel pipes it was geared to produce were seen to have applications offshore as riser pipes, drill pipes and small bore flowlines.

The decision to embark on the capital investment programme was clearly seen as having far-reaching implications for most management areas within the plant, especially line functions. Three so-called project groups were formed to conduct exploratory technical studies which would determine what changes needed to be made in those areas most affected by the expansion.

One of the project groups was charged with the responsibility for *determining and implementing* the changes to be made to the factory's compressed-air system: a budget of £60,000 was made available to fund these changes.

It was envisaged that the demand for compressed air would increase by 40% to 7,000 cubic feet per minute (CFM) as a result of the planned expansion of the tube-making forge. Compressed air was used as a power medium throughout the factory because of its versatility and relative safety. In addition to being used to operate pneumatic power tools, it also powered the automated and manually controlled heavy-handling gear which was needed to manipulate heavy goods during various stages of the manufacturing process.

Members of the Compressed Air Project Group included the General Manager of the plant, the Production Manager, the Purchasing Manager, the Area Technical Services Manager, and the Engineering Services Manager – all of whom were senior staff with considerable experience in positions of authority and responsibility, both in a managerial and technical vein. One of the primary conclusions of this group was that it would be necessary to purchase additional compressed air machinery and ancillary equipment (air compressor, air cooler, moisture extractor, noise suppressor and distribution pipework).

After some deliberation and many heated exchanges, the group, in consultation with representatives of other departments, established some tentative requirements which potential suppliers would be expected to satisfy. Several suppliers of compressed-air equipment were soon involved in the process of recommending which machines or 'systems' best met the requirements, or which total package was most attractive. Ultimately, the decision of which supplier to favour was the responsibility of the project group.

Research Setting

The empirical work was undertaken by the author during the period June 1983 to March 1984. It was conducted in one of the major operating units (approximate 1983 turnover £85 million; employees 2,430) of a large UK based heavy engineering combine.

Early in 1982, the group had begun to lay its plans to expand the production capacity of its Clydesdale Products plant. A surge in the demand for Clydesdale's products had been anticipated as a result of the recent return to growth in the worldwide exploration and development of offshore oil fields. The small diameter steel pipes the plant was geared to produce were seen to have applications offshore as riser pipes, drill pipes and small bore flowlines.

The decision to expand production capacity was taken at group director level. It was one of a stream of decisions which flowed from the ambitious growth component of the group's strategic plan for the five years until 1987. This decision having been taken, the director of the Clydesdale plant initiated various exploratory technical studies to determine in detail the changes to be made to the factory in order to meet the new supply requirements.

Company observers thought it to be a very brave and forward-looking decision to take under the circumstances. The market for oil drillpipe and well casing had been very depressed in the wake of the contraction in exploration and development activity which had been precipitated by the US over-reaction to the Iranian revolution of 1979. In subsequent years, several manufacturers and stockholders had gone out of business, but, by 1982, Clydesdale had seen almost three years of a bearish market and felt the bottom of the cycle to be very close. It was then looking ahead to 1987 and beyond when it was confident that there would be an upsurge in offshore exploration and development, and a return to a buoyant market.

The decision to embark on such a capital investment programme was clearly seen as having far-reaching implications for most areas within the organization, especially line functions. Three so-called project groups were formed to direct the exploratory studies in those areas of manufacturing most likely to be influenced by the expansion. This paper documents the activities and behaviour of the group with responsibility for determining the changes to be made to the factory's compressed air system.

The project group consisted of four leading members, or protagonists (in order of seniority): the General Manager (GM); Area Technical Manager (ATM); Production Manager (PM); and Works Engineering Services Manager (WESM) – all were senior managers with experience in positions of authority and responsibility both in a managerial and technical/engineering vein. They were selected by the plant director not only because of their imputed technical and managerial expertise, but also because of their previous experience in directing such projects, and success in finding and implementing solutions to the problems they represent. Of the areas of managerial responsibility of the protagonists, those of the Production Manager and the Works Engineering Services Manager were likely to be most affected by the additional manufacturing capacity. The plant director assigned to the project group the responsibility of fulfilling the primary objective of the exploratory study, which he had established to be:

- To determine the engineering changes to be made to the existing compressed air system in order to meet the increased demand for compressed air which you foresee as a result of the planned expansion of the production capacity of no. 1 manufacturing line.

- To take the necessary decisions to instigate these changes within a proposed budget ceiling of £60,000 (to include the total cost of purchasing, installing and commissioning the necessary air compressors, distribution pipework, control valves, operating cylinders and ancillary equipment). Projected Completion Date: May 1984.

Although the group had been given decision-making authority, ultimate responsibility lay with the plant director who reported to the group board. He also sat on this board. However, in this particular instance the plant director's involvement was limited to sanctioning the decisions taken by the project group and ensuring that budgetary control was maintained. He was to submit progress reports to the group board at monthly intervals.

In addition to the protagonists, the author observed that some 16 other members of the factory staff were, in some small way, involved in the activities of the project group (see Exhibits 7.1 and 7.6). However, only three members were observed to be contributing directly to the work of the project group:

(1) A *Technical Services Engineer* (TSE) who reported directly to the ATM. On two occasions he made presentations of the results of his work to the group as a whole. He was heavily committed (450 man-hours – see Exhibit 7.2) to the preliminary enquiry which provided the information with which to take decisions I and II (see Exhibits 7.1 and 7.3).

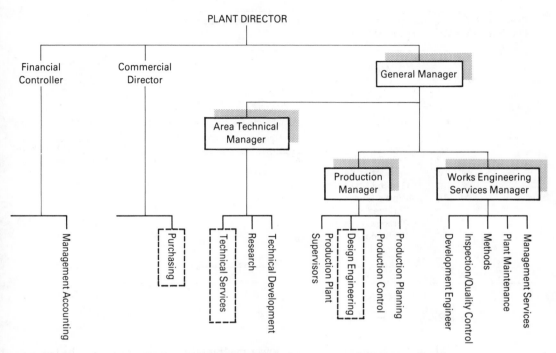

Exhibit 7.1 *Organizational chart showing only those departments which were at least involved on the fringe of the decision-making group's activities. Members of this group are bounded by a rectangle. Departments extensively involved in the exercise are bounded by broken lines.*

(2) A *Design Engineer* (DE) who reported directly to the PM, and on one occasion made a presentation of the results of his work to the group as a whole. He was also heavily committed (320 man-hours – see Exhibit 7.2) to the preliminary stages of the problem-solving exercise.

(3) The *Purchasing Manager†* who established contacts and helped arrange meetings with potential suppliers, where necessary. The tender and specification documents of preferred suppliers were subject to his perusal. His contact with participants in the group was minimal (18 man-hours in all), involving a commitment mainly when the group was assessing the offers of alternative suppliers (15 man-hours).

† Much of the day-to-day work of the purchasing department dealt with the placing and chasing of a large number of low-value orders and repeat orders for raw materials and consumables (straight/modified rebuys) specified elsewhere in the organization. User departments frequently obtained their own quotations for specific pieces of equipment or services where the order value was less than £500. Quotations were then submitted with purchase requests to the purchasing department. Any non-routine order exceeding £500 in value had to be approved by the plant director.

Exhibit 7.2   Commitment (man-hours) of the Participants at Each Stage of the Decision-Making Process

		BUY PHASES	
	MAIN PARTICIPANTS	Identify needs	Establish specifications
		← 24 weeks →	
Code no.	Title	Precipitating decisions (DI + DII)	Product specification
		Approximate time (man-hours)	
2	Area Technical Manager	100	35
3	Production Manager	80	30
1	General Manager	20	5
4	Works Engineering Services Manager	50	10
5	Purchasing Manager	0	2
16	Technical Services Engineer	450	70
11	Design Engineer	320	50
	TOTALS	1,020	202

Preliminary Activity

The use of compressed air as a power medium throughout the factory had grown rapidly over the past decade, mainly because of its versatility and relative safety. In addition to being used to operate pneumatic power tools, it also powered the automated and manually controlled heavy-handling gear which was needed to manipulate heavy goods during the various stages of their manufacturing process. A complex and somewhat haphazard network of piping had been built to distribute compressed air from a centralized compressor house to the location of demand. It was as a direct result of having anticipated the considerable size and complexity of the existing compressed air system (delivering upwards of 5,000 cubic feet per minute of compressed air at 100 psig, through approximately 10 miles of small- and medium-bore pipework) and the consequences of this for the decision-making process, that the plant director decided to establish a project group which included senior managers to plan, what was to the firm in budget terms, a medium-scale capital investment programme.

The first stage of the exercise was to explore the various dimensions of the problem of how best to develop the compressed air system. A preferred approach to finding possible solutions to it could then be decided. Adept problem definition was considered to be critical at this point because the adequacy of any eventual solution would be largely determined by the initial assessment and structuring of the problem.

The firm usually set up project groups to plan and execute capital investments. The composition of the groups varied. Senior managers would form the core of the group and would share the responsibility for *taking* decisions. Their subordinates would support the work of the group in an advisory and often

Exhibit 7.2 *continued*

		BUY PHASES		
Identify	*Evaluate*			
alternatives	*alternatives*	*Select supplier*		
←————————— 7 Weeks —————————→			1 week	
			Commitment	
	Supplier selection		*decision*	*TOTALS*
devoted to each stage of the compressed air system project group				
		30	4	169
		40	4	154
		10	4	39
		5	4	18
		15	1	69
		40	0	560
		0	0	370
		130	17	1,379

influential capacity. But, their involvement was principally in analysis and decision *making.*

On behalf of the project group, the Production Manager and the Area Technical Manager delegated a large part of the work associated with problem definition to two subordinates: respectively, a Design Engineer and a Technical Services Engineer. They then set about collecting and compiling data that would help to take, what the project group had identified as, 'the two important preliminary problem-solving decisions' (DI and DII – see Exhibits 7.3 and 7.4). That is:

- Is the existing compressed air system capable of supplying the additional demand for compressed air?

- If improvements were to be made to the existing compressed air system, could it meet the demands of the new production equipment cost-effectively?

In order to take these decisions the TSE and the DE provided the project group with information which helped to answer several 'lower-order' questions. Exhibit 7.3 illustrates, in the form of two simple decision trees, some of the avenues of enquiry pursued in order to lay the foundations upon which to base the decision-making process. This stage of the exercise took approximately 24 weeks to complete (see Exhibits 7.2 and 7.4). It involved a total commitment of some 1,010 man-hours: 75% of this figure was accounted for by the extensive preliminary work undertaken by the subordinates. The remaining 25% represented a substantial commitment of senior management time. It indicates the

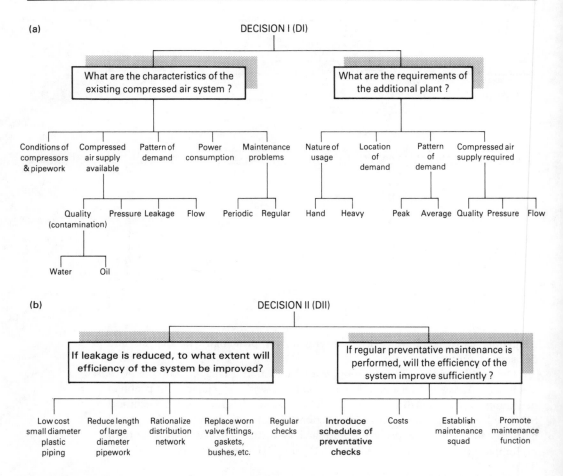

Exhibit 7.3   *Decision trees detailing some of the areas of investigation which provided information on which to base (a): decision I and (b): decision II.*

extent to which the operation of the project group involved senior managers in the requesting and processing of decision-pertinent information; in providing it to the other members of the group; and in meeting suppliers. In this respect the project group can be a counter-productive mechanism if not managed carefully.

The composition of the project group was not seen to vary at any point during the exercise. However, the degree to which participants were involved at different stages of the decision-making process was seen to change (see Exhibit 7.2). Of the total commitment of the main participants, measured in man-hours, 90% was made during the first two phases of the decision process, over a period of about 24 weeks. The recorded commitment of participants during the seven-week supplier selection phase was 9% of the total; 1% of the total was spent during the week in which the project group reached its commitment decision.

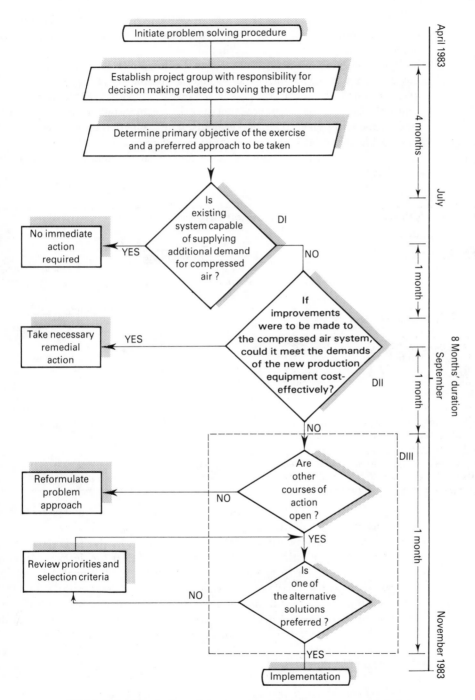

Exhibit 7.4 *Simple flow chart mapping the three main areas of decision.*

The different patterns of commitment of the group depicted in Exhibit 7.2 tend to support the view that purchasing and top management only adopt temporary roles in the decision-making process.

The considerable commitment made to the initial phases of the exercise is not only indicative of the technical and managerial complexity of the compressed air system problem. It may also suggest a somewhat misplaced preoccupation with technical issues – these being those that the membership would probably feel most comfortable with, given their backgrounds. The evaluation criteria which were generated (see Exhibit 7.5) show an implicit high regard for technical considerations. Yet, the group did recognize that the project carried some major managerial as well as technical risks.

Exhibit 7.5   Relative Importance of Selection Criteria

SELECTION CRITERIA	Members of the Decision-Making Group				
	Importance attached to each criterion (ranked)†				AVERAGE RANKING
	General Manager	Area Technical Manager	Production Manager	Works Engineering Services Manager	
Purchase price (incl. installation costs)	5	4	6	2	4.25
Operational power cost	3	2	5	1	2.75
Manufacturer's reputation	1	3	2	3	2.25
Reliability	4	1	1	5	2.75
Maintenance cost	6	6½	3	4	4.875
Delivery time	2	5	4	6	4.25
Estimated supervision costs	8	6½	8	8	7.625
Space requirements	10	10	9	10	9.75
Compressor weight	9	9	10	9	9.25
Contract terms	7	8	7	7	7.25

† Participants ranked the criteria (in order of ascendance) according to the importance they attach to them in evaluating alternative suppliers.

The compressed air system had evolved in a haphazard and incremental fashion as demands in finishing and handling changed. Unfortunately, its development had been poorly documented. Consequently, the TSE spent many hours surveying the existing network of pipes to estimate usage, leakage, demand cycles, etc. With the help of the DE he estimated the additional demand for compressed air which the plant expansion would create. Their estimate of 2,000 CFM ($\pm 10\%$) was derived from a study of existing operations and the load they placed on the compressed air system. Given that the additional plant would do 'more of the same', it did not seem unreasonable to extrapolate from the basis of existing operations. One of the potential suppliers who conducted his own survey and forecast of loading arrived at a figure of 1850 CFM which seemed to vindicate the internal estimate.

The job of estimating the real usage of compressed air was made very difficult and time consuming by the numerous leaks in the distribution pipework; many of which could be heard and not seen because of the sheer congestion of piping and machinery. The TSE designed and conducted an experiment to determine the leakage volume. The results confirmed the DE's expectations that, irrespective of loading at any one time, the compressed air system was losing up to 15% of the delivery volume in leakage. The energy which was lost in this way cost the firm in the region of £25,000 p.a. to produce. The PM was little surprised to discover the extent of the leakage problem. His supervisors frequently complained that the operating pressure of the compressed air system was too low at the finishing bay (the most distant point from the compressor house) to make the handling gear operate effectively. This finding exposed plant maintenance to considerable criticism. It did much to support the PM's view that works engineering services, and particularly maintenance, should be under his control since it was becoming a major constraint on the level of operating efficiency the plant was able to achieve. This issue often raised its head during the work of the project group. It seemed to focus attention on the covert conflicts of interest that existed between the PM and the WESM.

Whatever decision was taken about the preferred way to provide the additional compressed air supply, an extension to the distribution network would still be required. One of the first matters the project group dealt with was the installation of the new pipework. The works engineering services department took on board the task of designing the compressed air network, it being an integral part of its work on developing the layout of the new plant. The installation of the pipework was to be put out to tender, possibly to become part of the building services contract which was to be awarded. This part of the plant expansion was overseen by one of the other project groups. The membership of this group included the Works Engineering Services Manager, the Purchasing Manager and the Production Manager.

The project group delegated responsibility for routine buying decisions to the purchasing department. It was tentatively agreed at an early point that the purchase of the piping, control valves, handling gear and ancillary equipment might be dealt with by the standard ordering procedure that was in place. Such items were already being bought periodically from known suppliers to meet maintenance requirements. On these occasions the purchasing process was initiated by a maintenance fitter or engineer who would raise an order request specifying the item needed, a preferred supplier, delivery requirements and an estimated price. The buyer would confirm those details and place an order. The Purchasing Manager was confident that the routine ordering procedure would cope if technical services and/or works engineering services could provide in the near future a clear statement of what was required, to what specifications and in what quantities. One of his buyers had used the ATM's preliminary draft of the proposed network to estimate the total cost of this part of the project. It was expected to be in the region of £20,000. He felt that the size of the orders he could be placing might make it worth while re-evaluating possible alternative suppliers. The project group agreed that should this be feasible, a technical input would be required. It expected the purchase of the handling gear to be an involved process for which technical support was also needed.

Many of the attributes of the project group participants which impinged on the decision-making process were intangible and incapable of being measured or described in simple terms. The expression of authority, sociability, optimism, dependability, enthusiasm, diligence, loyalty, aggression, honour, reliability, and many other behavioural traits, was observed during the decision-making process. The effects of these traits on the behaviour of the decision-making group were extremely complex and difficult to unravel. They frequently represented the poorly judged response of a protagonist to a wrongly interpreted, or ill-defined remark or gesture made by other participants in the exercise, for instance: on several occasions, the PM's dismissive, and aggressively disrespectful attitude to the opinions of what he considered to be the 'technically naive and incompetent' sales engineers of a particular supplier, unwittingly created conflict within the project group. He felt the supplier should be excluded from further participation in the exercise. As he commented '. . . I've got more than enough to do with my time than listen to the ramblings of two young rambos who didn't know what they were talking about, or even care that they couldn't disguise it'. The PM was careful to point out that the supplier was a market leader and had supplied the firm in the past. Indeed, it had proved to be very good on its delivery and servicing contract. It had also provided, free of charge, an estimate of the compressed air demand which the operation of the new plant would create. He felt it might be a mistake to exclude the supplier at such an early stage of the process. Perhaps the PM could relieve the pressure on him to process information about potential suppliers by making use of the advisory services of purchasing research?

The most senior member of the project group, the General Manager, was seen to play a central role in its decision-making activities. He also exerted considerable influence within the group, especially at the point of taking decisions II and III. Despite this, the final outcomes on both occasions were largely the result of having attained a consensus of group opinion on most of the important issues. The General Manager was not seen to be free to take the decisions on his own, on the basis of his analysis of the situation, his personal goals or political motives. He was too shrewd to have wanted to anyway. In many respects, he was constrained by the abilities, attitudes, perceptions, responsibilites, preferences, social affiliation and goals of what were, in terms of absolute authority, really his subordinates. The plant director, in setting the terms of reference of the project group, had, in theory, enabled the diffusion of decision-making responsibility throughout the group membership. In practice, he had set up a mechanism to facilitate communications across functions and the exchange of specialist information and expertise.

Intra-Organization Contact

The General Manager's main points of contact with other members of staff involved in the exercise were through the other protagonists with whom he exchanged information on several matters: this excludes one occasion on which he directly requested information on the distribution network of compressed air piping from the Chief Development Engineer. The communications network shown in Exhibit 7.6 portrays the flow of information recorded by the author during the period September–October 1983, corresponding to the supplier selection phase of the decision process. It shows the central positions of the other participants. The relative authority and responsibility accorded to each participant's position within the organization is indicated by the distance from the central position, marked 1.

Exhibit 7.6 shows that the Production Manager, the Area Technical Manager, and the Works Engineering Services Manager had used, respectively 14, 12 and 12 channels of communication to provide and receive information about the compressed air project. The General Manager had used nine channels, eight of which enabled the exchange of information from other members of the project group to himself, and vice versa. Exhibit 7.7 is derived from the information contained in the communications network. It shows that in terms of the use of inter- and intra-departmental channels of communications, the Production Department was by far the most prolific; the Purchasing Department making relatively little use of them. However, when the data is corrected for the number of departmental staff participating in the exercise (that is, (a)/(b)), the pattern of usage alters.

Via the two main gatekeepers of the project group, that is, 2 and 3, then, through their subordinates 16 and 11 (also gatekeepers), the General Manager was known to have the potential to be in contact with each of the 19 members of staff contributing to the project. Six points of contact were used by suppliers and other external agencies to initiate a flow of information. Each of the suppliers listed in Exhibit 7.8 utilized these channels, but to various degrees.

It became clear that the Production Manager and the Area Technical Manager had been delegated the task of answering many of the technical/engineering questions that had arisen. The General Manager was then presented with summaries of the findings of the work undertaken in this way. On three occasions, the subordinates of these managers (11 and 16) made detailed presentations of the results of their work to the project group as a whole, but directed to the General Manager, in particular. Consequently, by reviewing the brief summaries of extensive background work, the General Manager was able to reduce his commitment to the compressed air project, and redirect it to other similar projects with which he was involved.

The nature of the communications network which was established was, to some extent, predetermined by the information needs of the protagonists. The patterns of communication activity which the group exhibited and the delegation of tasks within it, were both seen to have an influence on its decision-making behaviour.

The decision to expand the manufacturing capacity of the plant and the subsequent decision to purchase additional compressed air equipment, became a source of political capital for the Production Manager and the Works Engineering Services Manager. The political consequences of the decision were a source of

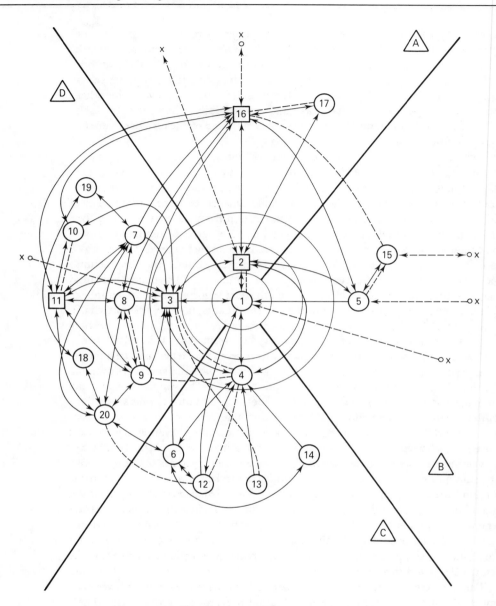

Exhibit 7.6   *Communications network (key given in Appendix 7.2).*

Exhibit 7.7   *Inter- and intra-departmental channels of communications.*

Department	No. of channels used		(a)	No. of participants from department (b)	(a)/(b)
	Inter	Intra			
Production	16	35	51	9	5.7
Area Technical Services	17	6	23	3	7.7
Works Engineering Services	10	14	24	5	4.8
Purchasing	5	3	8	2	4

some conflict within the project group, as these managers struggled to win initiatives. The source of the conflict was mainly the uncertainty surrounding which of these departments would be responsible for the upkeep of the new equipment once it had been installed: Production or Works Engineering Services.

The main issue concerned the redistribution of manpower resources which would need to be effected if the departments were to cope separately with the additional workload. Additional concern was shown for the dilution of control and authority, which was expected to accompany any departmental expansion. It would affect, not only the authority and status of the managers involved, but also the way in which the power invested in them could be exercised. Clearly, the three areas of concern had significant implications for productivity levels.

As things stood at present, the production department was responsible for the maintenance of the production line, with works engineering services providing the necessary maintenance expertise and resources. The Production Manager had been unhappy about this arrangement for some time. On two occasions recently, a machine breakdown had brought No. 1 line to a halt. The production department had notified WES some time prior to the breakdown of the need to have a look at the machine during the Sunday evening downtime period, but, because of other commitments, WES had not been able to make the inspection that might have prevented the breakdown. Situations like these were difficult to resolve, but the Production Manager felt that if works engineering services were to be put under his direct control then production downtime would be minimized, if not eradicated altogether.

Participants did strive to influence their peers to obtain benefits for themselves. Examples of this were noted where the Production Manager and the Works Engineering Services Manager jostled verbally with each other to obtain the most favourable vantage point from which to make a case for their departments. The Production Manager was able to make profitable use of the priority placed by top management on the direct manufacturing functions.

Selection Criteria

Appendix 7.3 gives details of the criteria which were used by the decision-making group to evaluate and compare alternative suppliers and their products. The focus

Exhibit 7.8   Analysis of Contact between Suppliers and Group Members during June to October 1983

SUPPLIERS (Disguised)	No. of visits made	Man-hours involved	Personnel involved	ATM		
				Meeting	Phone call	Letter
WP	0	N/A	Sales Manager	0	1	2
WS	0	N/A	Application Engineer	0	0	3
NY	0	N/A	Director and Sales Manager	0	0	0
IR	2	8	Divisional Manager	1	2	3
HD	0	N/A	Area Sales Engineer	0	0	1
BW	2		Production Sales Manager	1	6	3
AC	3	10	Area Sales Manager	2	4	6
AB	2	6	Installation & Sales Manager	1	3	3
TOTAL	9	28		5	16	20

of the criteria was predetermined to a great extent by the results of the preliminary problem-solving exercise, on which the precipitating decisions (Exhibit 7.2) were based. Exhibits 7.10 and 7.11 (in Appendix 7.4) display the overtly rational analysis of the preferred alternative suppliers, which was conducted as an initial screening exercise.† They show that the alternative suppliers, on this occasion, were accorded very similar evaluations. Consequently, less tangible criteria such as the depth of the empathy between the supplier's representatives and members of the decision-making group assumed considerable importance. Where suppliers had become involved in the preliminary stages of the exercise, perhaps by offering technical assistance with some aspects of the problem, they were seen to acquire the potential to pre-empt the sale. The practical import of this empathy emerges in the negotiating arena where social factors may consitute the just noticeable difference. Four of the potential suppliers were not evaluated as in Appendix 7.4, largely because of the lack of interest generated within the group. The quality of the contact these suppliers had established with the Area Technical Manager or the Production Manager proved to be the decisive influence.

Exhibit 7.11 (Appendix 7.4) displays the data that was provided when members of the project group were asked to rank the selection criteria according to their relative importance to the evaluation of alternative suppliers. Using the Spearman Rank Correlation Coefficient (Rs) to test, at the 5% level of significance, between all combinations of members, it was established that the two

† The responsibility for formal vendor assessment is located in the purchasing department. A major exception is in the case of technically complex capital goods in which the users, influencers and deciders may also be consulted.

Exhibit 7.8 *continued*

PM			GM			WESM		
Meeting	*Phone call*	*Letter*	*Meeting*	*Phone call*	*Letter*	*Meeting*	*Phone call*	*Letter*
0	0	0	0	0	1	0	0	0
0	0	1	0	1	1	0	0	0
0	0	1	0	0	0	0	0	0
1	1	1	0	0	1	0	0	0
0	0	0	0	0	1	0	0	1
1	0	0	0	1	1	1	1	0
1	1	1	0	0	0	0	1	0
1	0	0	0	0	1	0	0	1
4	2	4	0	2	6	1	2	2

sets of ranked data for each combination were positively correlated, that is, the ranks set by member A were not independent of those set by member B. It was concluded that the protagonists share similar perceptions of the selection criteria and the needs to be satisfied by each supplier. It is reasonable to expect this to be so in the case of a coherent decision-making group. It is interesting to note that based on the average ranking of the selection criteria, manufacturer's reputation becomes the most important.

The differences in the ranking of the criteria may be represented by the functional interests held by each of the group members. However, it is also fair to say that the differences indicate that, to some extent, other motives such as interdepartmental political considerations, may influence their importance.

Sources of Information

Exhibit 7.9 displays the data obtained when the protagonists were requested to indicate the relative importance of sources of information to them, during July 1983, when decision I was being taken; and during October 1984, when decision III was about to be taken. The Rank Spearman Correlation Coefficient (R_s) was used to test, at the 5% level of significance, if the ranks assigned during period A (July 1983) were independent of those assigned during period B (October 1984). This was found to be the case for the Area Technical Manager, the Production Manager and the Works Engineering Services Manager, indicating that their perception of the importance of each source of information altered during the intervening period. A positive correlation was found to exist between the ranks

Exhibit 7.9   Relative Importance of Sources of Information (Ranked in Order of Ascendance) to each Group Member during July 1983, when Decision I was Being Taken; and during October 1983 when Decision III was About to be Taken

| | Members of decision-making group | | | |
Source	Production Manager	Area Technical Manager	W. Eng. S. Manager	General Manager
Previous personal experience	2 (1)	1 (2)	1 (3)	1 (3)
Published journals, trade magazines	4 (5)	5 (5)	5 (5)	4 (5)
Internal company reports	3 (4)	2 (4)	3 (4)	2 (4)
Other members of staff	1 (2)	4 (3)	2 (1)	5 (1)
Potential suppliers	5 (3)	3 (1)	4 (2)	3 (2)

given on the two occasions by the General Manager. This indicates that his opinion on the importance of the given information sources did not alter significantly during the intervening period. Of some interest is the change in the ranking accorded by the protagonists to the importance of information provided by potential suppliers. The early involvement of potential suppliers was seen to influence the flow of information between the members of the project group and suppliers. In this way, the relative importance of the sources of information was altered.

Inter-Organizational Contact

Exhibit 7.8 summarizes the data collected by the author on the level of contact established between potential suppliers and members of the decision-making group, during the period June to October 1983. Most of the contact, in the form of meetings, telephone calls, and letters, was established between the group members and four suppliers: 90% of the telephone calls, all the meetings and 70% of the letters exchanged took place between the group and these suppliers. It is worth noting that the suppliers, which had established a high level of contact with the decision-making group, had made an effort to become involved at an early stage in the problem-solving phase of the exercise. It was concluded that in this way they had helped to create within the group, not only an awareness of their products and capabilities, but also favourable attitudes towards these character-istics. The degree of buyer–seller interaction was seen to be an important influence on the decision-making behaviour of the group, especially during the latter stages of the exercise.

Conclusion

In many respects this preliminary documentation of the study is anecdotal in nature. However, the considerable amount of qualitative and quantitative data which was gathered was best organized in terms of a description of the work of the project group as the author observed it.

Some evidence is provided to support the belief that where capital investment decisions are a main source of business for a firm, it should focus its marketing strategies and segmentation procedures on two areas of concern:

(1) The need to become involved in the customer's preliminary problem-solving exercise.

(2) The need to determine the important characteristics of the customer's decision-making process, and of the members of any decision-making group which is established.

This is, of course, what would be expected in a new-buy scenario, where the participants' perceived risk and information requirements are high. However, three further conclusions may tentatively be drawn. Firstly, in the context of the problem-solving associated with capital investment plans, a supplier's salesforce may also unwittingly play a gatekeeping role. Secondly, the profile of salesforce skills will vary at different stages of the decision process: technical skills may predominate initially; negotiating skills latterly. And thirdly, the strategic role of the salesforce must match the professionalism of purchasing management.

Appendix 7.2   Key to Exhibit 7.6

The process of communication can be broken down into four constituent elements: the message; the medium; the communicator; and the recipient. In this case, in about 60% of the occasions on which information was communicated, the medium used was oral; the other 40% used mainly written reports, articles or memoranda. The communication network plots the flow of information recorded by the researcher during the one-month period of gestation, which passed prior to reaching a point at which a choice of supplier could be made. During a structured interview, participants were asked to list the names of those individuals from whom they had requested, or to whom they had provided information, in relation to the compressed air system project, during the month in question. At the time, no data was able to be collected on who initiated the communication, or on the quality and quantity of information which was exchanged. Arrow heads indicate the direction of the flow of information. Other symbols are indicative of the following:

◄----►   Two-way exchange of information.

------   Recorded social meetings during this period, for instance: at lunch; or where participants shared recreational interests outwith their working environment.

←−−−−○ x   Flow of information from outside agencies – mainly vendors. Sixteen initiated two other forms of outside contact; with advisory agencies such as The British Compressed Air Society; and with individuals in another manufacturing plant who had recently been involved in the decision to purchase £100,000 worth of compressed air equipment.

A   Area Technical Services.

B   Purchasing.

C   Works Engineering Services.

D   Production.

Individuals Involved are Indicated as Follows:

1. General Manager
2. Area Technical Manager
3. Production Manager
4. Works Engineering Services Manager
5. Purchasing Manager
6. Senior Plant Maintenance Manager
7. Manufacturing Plant Superintendent
8. Electrical Plant Superintendent
9. Hydraulic & General Services Superintendent
10. Senior Design Draughtsman
11. Design Engineer
12. Chief Development Engineer
13. Methods Engineer
14. Process Planning Coordinator
15. Purchasing Officer
16. Technical Services Engineer
17. Technical Development Engineer
18. Production Control Superintendent
19. Senior Foreman, Hydraulic and General Services
20. Maintenance Foreman

Appendix 7.3

The criteria listed below were used to evaluate potential suppliers and their machines. Only those machines which satisfied the basic technical requirements of the specific application (that is, could deliver 1,000 CFM of compressed air at 100 psig) were evaluated using the criteria.

(1) *Manufacturer's reputation*   This is the extent to which the engineers were familiar with the manufacturer and his product; their past experience of dealing with the manufacturer and of using his products; the extent to

which the manufacturer and his product appealed to the engineers; and the credibility of the claims manufacturers made about their products, especially with respect to their purchasing price and technical performance reliability.

(2) *Power cost* A high degree of overall efficiency gives a low specific power consumption. This is one of the most important criteria as the annual power costs of a 1,000 CFM compressor can exceed the purchase price by as much as 50%.

(3) *Reliability* It is essential to minimize the production time lost because of compressor failure. The compressor must be seen to be capable of withstanding the continual heavy duty operation which will be required of it. Good inertial balance, low vibration, correct materials, high manufacturing quality of component parts and minimum operating temperatures, increase reliability. Spares availability and good after-sales service, although not directly related to the reliability of a machine, can help to reduce the production time lost if the machine does break down. Guarantees of performance and reliability may be negotiable.

(4) *Maintenance cost* Simple, easily replaceable and moderately priced wearing parts make maintenance work by own personnel possible and reduce maintenance costs.

(5) *Delivery time* The installation of the compressor was planned to occur one calendar month prior to commissioning the new production equipment. This was to allow plant engineers time to test the new pneumatic equipment, and make any necessary alterations to this equipment and to the existing compressed air system. Therefore, there was a delivery restriction of about 12 to 14 weeks, allowing a further two weeks for installing and commissioning the compressor.

(6) *Supervision costs* Automatic lubrication, automatic condensate draining of after and intercooler, reliable safety and regulating devices, all make continuous manual supervision unnecessary, thereby reducing supervision costs.

The sum of the financial burdens associated with criteria (2), (4) and (6) gives the total operating cost of the compressor. However, at this stage of the exercise, only criterion (2) can be computed with any degree of accuracy.

(7) *Price* The purchasing price (including installation costs) is an important selection criterion, but it was considered with respect to the extent to which criteria (1) to (5) are satisfied by each manufacturer and his compressor. Discounts on the list price may be negotiable, but only in the context of the overall package, of which price is only one element.

Additional criteria which were considered are as follows:

(8) *Space requirement* Factory floor space costs money. Therefore, a compact compressor design saves floor space and building volume.

(9) *Compressor weight*   A minimized machine weight and good inertial balance overcome the effect of vibration and thereby reduce the foundation costs associated with installing the compressor.

(10) *Contract terms*   In response to a request for a quotation, most of the short list of preferred suppliers provided provisional tender documentation giving details of such items as terms of payment, standard conditions of

Appendix 7.4

Exhibit 7.10   Selected Compressors

Compressor model	Type	Delivery pressure (PSIG)	Compressor speed (RPM)	Coolant rate (litre/s)	Rated CFM	Rated shaft HP
XLE H7-IR	Recip. 2 stage	100	750	1.30	1,049	201
ER5E-AC	Recip. 2 stage	100	970	2.2	1,095	240
VM1000-BW	Recip. 2 stage	100	750	1.30	1,115	220
RA 270W-BW	Screw	100	—	2.50	1,150	270

Note   These compressors do not represent all the 1,000 CFM, reciprocating or screw compressors on the market. The selection given here includes those considered best able to meet the criteria that were established and the application requirements of the particular situation.

Exhibit 7.11   Product Rating Index

Compressor model	Purchase price app.[†]	Power cost per annum[‡]	Installation costs (appx)	Delivery req. wks	Space required[§]
					Ranked
XLE H7-IR	£18,200	£26,415	£2,000	14	1
ER5E-AC	£17,500	£31,570	£1,500	14	2
VH28-APEB	£17,500	£25,575	£1,500	10	3
VM1000-BW	£16,500	£28,935	£1,500	12	4
RA270W-BW	£20,000	£37,295	£ 800	10	5

† This price is approximate but includes the cost of aftercooler, air inlet filter, all interconnecting wiring and pipework assembled, motor starting and control panel, and the cost of service engineer to install and commission the compressor.
‡ The power cost per annum is calculated using the power consumption of each drive motor given in Exhibit 7.10.

contractual agreement, guarantee of performance and dispatch, etc. An evaluation of the offers was conducted by the purchasing department. Ultimately, the details of each offer would be the subject of negotiation, the variable elements being related principally with performance and service guarantees, but also with price and delivery considerations.

Exhibit 7.10   *continued*

Net shipping weight (kg)	Floor area (m²)	Noise level (db)	Motor & mounting	Compressor specific power consumption HP/100 CFM	Motor shaft HP	Motor' specific power consumption HP/100 CFM
3,725	3.2	85	Flanged Induction Motor	19.16	251	23.95
3,496	3.7	73	''	21.90	300	27.95
4,530	4.8	85	''	19.73	275	24.66
3,000	6.4	77	Direct Coupling	23.48	338	29.35

Exhibit 7.11   *continued*

Maintenance & supervision costs¶	Vibration level¶	Weight§ Ranked	Comments on the manufacturer's reputation
High	High	4	Good relationship with this manufacturer and his products, have a good reputation.
High	High	2	Little contact with this supplier. No past experience of him or his products.
High	High	3	Very good relationship with this manufacturer. Excellent past service from his compressors. Useful advice on solving this problem.
High	High	5	No contact with this supplier, but his products have a good reputation.
Medium	Low	1	As above.

§ These characteristics are ranked in order of ascendence, as given in Exhibit 7.10.
¶ It was impossible to quantify these characteristics accurately. However, it was useful to indicate, in comparative terms, what could be expected from each machine throughout its lifetime in terms of these characteristics.

CASE 8

Southern Precision Engineering
Organizational Buying Behaviour/Personal Selling

Douglas T. Brownlie
Glasgow Business School, University of Glasgow

Case History

Southern Precision Engineering (SPE) was founded in 1968 by Dave Southern and his brother Geoff. Both had served in the RAF during the Second World War: Geoff as a senior aircraft engineer, involved in the development of hydraulic and mechanical subsystems for the undercarriages of bomber aircraft, including the Lancaster and Wellington; and Dave as an airframe fitter and inspection technician.

In the years following the end of the war, Dave moved to a precision engineering contractor in the aircraft and airframes sector. In addition to specialist precision engineering work, the firm also manufactured aircraft accessory equipment, including landing gears, propellors, gearboxes and hydraulic power control equipment. Dave rapidly established himself as a first class fitter, machineman and quality control inspector. So much so, that he found himself occupying the works manager's post after only three years as a production superintendent and four years as the production manager. Geoff pursued his design interests as a member of the airframe design team of a firm engaged in the design, development and manufacture of light aircraft for passenger carrying and military training.

The brothers had started SPE as a private limited company some 14 years after their halcyon days in the RAF. It was a venture they had often speculated about during their occasional flights of fancy in their local on the odd Friday evening.

The reality happened all too suddenly. Dave unexpectedly discovered that nine months after being appointed works manager, the firm had been bought out by a foreign producer who had decided to close the factory and replace its output of manufactured goods with imports. Finding himself suddenly unemployed, but with a cash settlement of almost one year's salary, Dave wondered what he should now be planning to do with the rest of his life and harked after the good old days in the RAF.

Events moved very quickly and Dave found himself on the telephone to his brother to postpone the Friday evening get-together they had planned for tomorrow. He told Geoff of the intriguing telephone conversation he had just had with Michel DuBois, the MD of the French firm that had made him redundant. Apparently, DuBois was in the throes of disposing of the factory's assets. He had just offered Dave an asset lot which consisted of a cleverly mixed bag of precision machine tools and well-worn standard machining equipment with some ancillary inspection gear. He had agreed with DuBois that the lot was being offered at an 'interesting' discount to what might currently be its nominal secondhand value; but he would not be convinced until he had had the time to inspect the machines and to consult his maintenance schedules and production planning and control records. DuBois respected the wisdom of his prudence and offered to meet both of Dave's requirements tomorrow evening. Nevertheless, the offer would be subject to the conditions that Dave made his decision within 72 hours of having seen the lot; and, that if affirmative, a deposit of £10,000 was made, pending completion of a deal within 21 days.

The rapid developments in his brother's life left Geoff feeling both excited and uneasy. He was not sure whether to counsel caution, encouragement, or both. Clearly, he felt, Dave should at least accept DuBois's invitation to inspect the machines and to talk in more detail about the deal and its conditions. But, in conversation with his brother, Geoff could not contain his sanguine nature and was soon enthusiastically speculating that if the machines were sound, Dave should go ahead and that he would join him to set up the firm they had often dreamt of.

After a successful meeting with DuBois, the brothers agreed that the logic of the proposed move seemed to be becoming irrefutable. They had access to a vast network of contacts, not only in the aircraft manufacturing industry, but also in the subcontracting firms which were currently under great pressure from a bullish aerospace industry to provide much sought-after precision engineered parts and components. They believed they possessed the credibility, experience and skills required to offer a specialist design, engineering and manufacturing service to both OEM and subcontracting clients. They would also be able to hand-pick a team of skilled machinemen and engineers from the 60 DuBois had just laid off.

The brothers spent a hectic three weeks raising support for the venture from within their own families, as well as from their bank managers and even potential clients. Between the two of them, they managed to finance SPE on a shoestring by remortgaging their houses, investing most of their savings and raising frightening bank overdraft facilities. They also negotiated a 10-year bank loan which matched the brothers' equity stake of £75,000. Thanks to a guaranteed mortgage which the local development council arranged with commendable speed, the brothers began negotiating the purchase of a small workshop.

In their previous guises, Geoff and Dave had dealt with various subcontractors on many occasions over the years. In the early days of SPE, Geoff and Dave came to rely on these and other subcontractors to push business in their direction whenever possible. This sometimes happened because the length of a subcontractor's order book precluded him from being able to meet the delivery requirement of a client's bid specification. It was not an option many subcontractors preferred to take. Not only did it deny them revenue, but they feared it would also put at risk their long-term client relationships.

Subcontractors were careful to preserve the grounds for goodwill and loyalty. They spent much time and money building lasting relationships, largely as a hedge against the cyclical fortunes of subcontracting, which would inevitably move into the buyer's market phase; but as Geoff and Dave knew from their days in client firms, subcontractors could not afford to endanger these relationships by accepting contracts for which they did not have the capacity to fulfil their delivery requirements – despite what they may have led the client to believe in their proposal.

On several occasions, SPE was called upon to help a subcontractor out of a fix he had got himself into by feeling obliged to agree to do a quick favour for a valued client – a favour the subcontractor had little hope of delivering without letting someone else down because of heavy plant loading. This situation also arose as a result of a subcontractor bidding successfully for more contracts than he ever expected to win.

The fragmented and cyclical nature of the subcontracting industry made it difficult to judge the rate at which any firm could expect to convert bids into contracts. Although, as Geoff and Dave had observed, it was not unreasonable to expect conversion rates to increase in an industry with spare capacity in a bullish market phase, it was almost impossible to predict accurately not only the size of the change in the conversion rate, but also when the change was likely to come into effect.

On other occasions, subcontractors would negotiate with clients during the preliminary stages of the bidding process to obtain their agreement to farm-out specific parts of a contract to SPE. Whenever such agreement was reached, the subcontractor usually had to agree to accept the risk of involving a third party. This meant carrying the burden of managing SPE's involvement and ensuring that the client's specified quality control procedures and documentation routines were adhered to. The OEM, or the main subcontractor, would always provide the detailed technical specifications, including dimensions, tolerances, and performance standards, as well as the British Standards quality assurance and inspection procedures to which SPE was contractually bound to adhere. They would also always supply the necessary raw materials, usually in the form of titanium, stainless steel, or aluminium ingots or forgings. In most cases, they also supplied the special jigs and fixtures that SPE would need to employ in the particular machining tasks for which it was responsible.

As a result of the way business came to SPE in the early days, SPE quickly became heavily involved in the machining to fine tolerances of small batches of non-critical aircraft components, such as the door hinges for mid-range commuter aircraft. Its willingness to do business at the eleventh hour, and its ability to make a first class job of it, earned SPE an enviable reputation for flexibility, reliability, quality, delivery, cost control and engineering precision. This reputation brought work to SPE from outwith the aerospace industry. Indeed, in the first three or four years of trading, up to 40% of its business came from outwith the aerospace industry in the form of jobs such as machining castings for car axles and blow-out preventers.

Since most of its early work came as a result of referrals, SPE had never felt the need to sell its services actively or to build its reputation. Indeed, Geoff and Dave had often congratulated themselves on spending little, if anything, on any form of sales, publicity or marketing. It was of much temporary comfort to them that clients usually made the first approach, either by means of direct contact, or through the grapevine of indirect contacts.

For everyone involved in SPE, the first six years of business were very demanding, but rewarding. It seemed that SPE's ability to take on small precision engineering contracts on a jobbing or small batch basis, with very little notice, and with a guarantee of first rate work, provided a service for which there was a firm demand. Indeed, in trade circles close to the brothers, SPE came to be known as 'Ever Ready', in recognition of its flexibility and willingness to help.

Geoff and Dave found themselves working very hard just to keep the firm's growth under control. The intricacies of cash flow management, capitalization and profitability were new to them. But they were happy to see SPE grow and measured the success of their efforts by this yardstick alone in the days before becoming accountancy literate. It was their policy from the outset to reinvest SPE profits to finance the procurement of additional machine tools.

At the end of SPE's first year of business it was employing 16 skilled engineers and machinemen and had achieved a turnover of £250,000. By April 1974, it had 82 employees and a turnover for the year in the region of £1.5 million. With such a rate of expansion, Geoff and Dave found that by 1972 they had no option but to seize the opportunity that had come their way to move from their original workshop in Coventry to a purpose-built unit on a newly reclaimed industrial site in the central Birmingham district. SPE's new premises had been built to accommodate 110 men. The firm has yet to utilize more then 75% of its capacity.

To help finance the expansion, the brothers brought Dave's son, Philip, into the business in 1972 as the Finance Director. He had several years' experience in both accounting and marketing positions in various firms in the mechanical engineering industry. He was presently the managing director of a light engineering firm turning over almost £20 million per annum from the manufacture of chain hoists. By negotiating an equity state in SPE, Philip provided a much needed capital injection of around £100,000 which helped finance the purchase of new plant and equipment.

The industry's outlook for continued growth in 1974–75 was not as confident as it had been in 1973. However, a string of small but lucrative contracts was about to be agreed that would at least ensure that the workshop's order book looked reasonably healthy for up to 18 months ahead. Even so, Geoff found himself giving increasing credence to rumours that were circulating in the trade that the next 12 months would see a bearish market. He felt sure that the economic effects of the recent oil supply crisis would have major repercussions for the airline industry. He could see it leading to escalating fuel costs, falling load factors and lower operating margins. These factors could force airlines out of business, or, at best, persuade them to postpone new aircraft purchases. In such circumstances, Geoff thought a depressed market looked likely.

Dave took a more positive view of developments. He agreed that airline fuel costs would rise and margins would probably fall, but he did not expect these events to have an immediate impact on the demand for subcontracted precision engineering services. The typically long lead time between ordering and delivering aircraft meant that orders had by now already been placed for aircraft that would not become operational for another five to ten years. This should, he felt, provide a partial shelter for subcontractors for at least two or three years, by which time airlines may have regained sufficient confidence to continue to replace ageing fleets of noisy and uneconomical aircraft. It was made all the more possible by virtue of the heavy penalty clauses included in aircraft procurement contracts as a means of protecting manufacturers from the late cancellations of orders.

Dave speculated that the shelter would only really work for those subcontractors whose services were of a sufficiently specialist nature that OEMs would still prefer to buy rather than make, since it would not be feasible for them to develop an in-house capability – even where they had spare capacity available. He took the view that in the longer term rising fuel costs would force airlines to drive OEMs towards aircraft designs that used the latest fuel saving technology. Dave did not think it unreasonable to expect the bolder operators to continue to invest in fuel-efficient aircraft in expectation of the cyclical upturn in market fortunes, which he thought would surely come. Indeed, the large international carriers might feel there to be strategic advantage in continuing to place orders for new and replacement aircraft throughout the downturn.

The brothers felt a crisis approaching and with it the need for some urgently needed but very difficult decision taking. They were beginning to suspect that SPE's reputation was becoming one for picking up small parts of contracts that needed to be done well and quickly. If it was true, the brothers agreed it did not augur well for SPE. Furthermore, on several occasions the firm had encountered short-term cash flow difficulties. They suspected the major cause of these difficulties to be SPE's third- and often fourth-party link to the OEM, which seemed to delay further payment being made for work done. The difficulty of managing SPE's cash was exacerbated by the largely piecemeal and unpredictable way that business came to SPE.

The enthusiasm and confidence of Geoff and Dave's early efforts seemed to be wearing thin. They were finding it almost impossible to plan ahead and saw little future growth and prosperity coming their way if they persisted in developing SPE along its current lines. Given that it was only a matter of months before the demand for subcontracting services began to soften, Geoff and Dave agreed that SPE was faced with four strategic options:

(1) Close the workshop now while the market was still prosperous and there was still a reasonable chance to realize a respectable price on the firm's assets.

(2) Do nothing, so effectively postponing the grim day of reckoning, by continuing to take business in fits and starts, in what is likely to become an overcrowded market.

(3) Enter the supply chain of another sector of manufacturing industry which also has a need for precision engineered parts and components, for example, automotive, consumer durables, electrical machines, electronics and mechanical engineering.

(4) Take a positive hand in promoting SPE's reputation, especially with OEMs and their major subcontractors. Only by doing so, does SPE appear to have any chance of being specified on the OEM bid lists as a preferred specialist subcontractor.

Intuitively, the brothers preferred the last option. However, it was with some regret that they realized that an indifference to marketing, which had previously been a source of pride, would become a burden as they considered what needed to be done to raise SPE's visibility with OEMs and their major subcontractors.

Geoff and Dave had come to expect that new customers would continue to beat a path to their door as SPE's reputation for engineering excellence spread. But, the success of the course of action they were now contemplating seemed to demand more than a passive reliance on word-of-mouth communications. Clearly, SPE needed to accelerate the spread of its reputation in specific directions if it was to have any hope of making an impact on the OEMs in the near future. Dave stated their problem succinctly. In his view, they needed to answer five questions: What should they be saying? To whom? At what point in time? Via what channels? With what effects? The brothers felt the new world of marketing beckoning them onwards.

Geoff believed they had the raw material of an effective promotional campaign, that is, a good reputation. Therefore, what they really needed to decide was how much they could afford to spend and on what? On reflection, the firm's reputation did seem to be concentrated in a small circle of friends and acquaintances in other subcontractors, many of whom had passed business to SPE. It worried Geoff that SPE had not had any direct impact on OEMs and on the wider circle of subcontractors. Had they let inexpensive opportunities to build goodwill and credibility pass them by, he thought?

The more Geoff and Dave pondered the future of SPE, the more they became convinced that the firm's prosperity was closely linked to that of the airlines and the aircraft manufacturers. Their reasons for being in the business in the first place owed as much to their love of aircraft engineering as to their desire to seize an opportunity to base a money-making venture on their experience and connections in the industry. It was with some reluctance but much resolve, that the brothers concluded that they must take their firm's reputation to the OEMs and their major subcontractors in the aircraft industry.

The brothers began actively to seek publicity in the trade press. They obtained entries in relevant trade directories and occasionally placed direct response ads. in selected journals, spending upwards of £5,000 p.a. in this way in the years 1975 to 1978. Dave commissioned the first of a possible series of glossy leaflets which described SPE's skills and achievements and gave client endorsements. The leaflet was designed so that the text could be updated to reflect changes in SPE's portfolio of successfully completed contracts. An enclosing envelope was also commissioned. It introduced the brothers and gave details such as the firm's address, telephone numbers and its approval numbers. Dave also prepared a covering letter to be sent with the leaflet and envelope in response to all enquiries received from the ads.

Geoff had two technical articles published in the trade's technical journals. He used these articles as the basis of a mailshot to selected people in the OEMs and several major subcontractors. In the letter he referred to the article briefly and related it to SPE's track record for engineering precision, reliability and flexibility. The letter was followed by a telephone call to answer any general questions the respondent might have as a result of the mailshot. But the main purpose of the call was to arrange an appointment for Geoff and Dave to visit the respondent's plant to discuss his business and to establish if SPE's technical skills and experience could be of any value to him.

So, the brothers proceeded to build awareness and recognition of SPE's capabilities in precision engineering among the OEMs and their major subcontractors. This they did on a shoestring budget of about £30,000 spread over the first three years of SPE's marketing renaissance.

It was not for another 20 months that Geoff and Dave's early promotional efforts really paid off. Until then they had only managed to keep SPE's workshop operating at pre-1973 levels of activity with work from referrals and overcommitted subcontractors. However, this work did bring with it several small contracts for the machining of critical but more sophisticated and valuable aircraft components such as engine hanger brackets.

On 19 January 1976 Dave received the enquiry letter shown in Exhibit 8.1. A major subcontractor to the world's leading aircraft manufacturers, National Aerospace, had invited SPE to participate in the bidding for part of a contract it had won to supply the main landing mounting for the new twin-seater trainer aircraft that one of its customers was planning to launch in 1981.

The brothers could hardly contain their excitement. Was this the breakthrough they had waited so long for? It was the first hard evidence that SPE was gaining recognition as a precision engineering subcontractor in its own right. Although the contract was potentially very large, it would also be demanding of both technical and managerial skills. Dave suspected there to be no more than about eight competing subcontractors with the resources, skills and track record

Exhibit 8.1   Initial Enquiry from National Aerospace

SPE Ltd   18 January 1976
Legge Lane
Birmingham

For the attention of Messrs Southern

Dear Sirs

In conjunction with a landing gear project currently under development we will shortly
have a requirement for the precision machining of aluminium outer cylinder struts. This
is highly specialised work for which several contractors have gained approval over the
years. We have written to all qualified contractors regarding our requirements. But, we
are also keen to give new contractors the opportunity to participate and would like to
know more about the capabilities of SPE.

We are not yet at the stage of requesting a formal proposal. The position is one of
judging contractor interest in the work.

National Aerospace will supply the subcontractor with the necessary raw material in the
form of aluminium ingots. It will also provide general and detailed engineering drawings.
The contractor will then engineer the strut design to our performance specification. A
copy of the design specification accompanies this letter.

A technical code of practice is in place for the British Standards quality assurance,
inspection and testing procedures that apply in all such civil aviation work. A 100%
inspection regime is mandatory. Qualified contractors have already been approved on
the grounds that their quality assurance, inspection and testing procedures have been
shown to satisfy British Standards requirements. New contractors must obtain
approval. This requires them to demonstrate that their systems and skills will enable
them to adhere to the set procedures which govern landing gear quality assurance,
inspection and testing routines and the associated documentation. We expect that your
previous work will have required you to demonstrate the ability to satisfy the conditions
of some of these procedures.

We anticipate that by September 1977 we will be ready to receive the first batch of 40
struts. In the first instance we will agree a contract for the supply of 400 struts, to be
delivered in monthly intervals on specified days, in batches of 40. There is the prospect
that a longer term supply agreement may be reached.

We trust that this general information will indicate the type of operation we are looking
for. Should you feel able to assist please provide details of your forward capacity
commitment along with your brochure and if possible samples of similar work currently
being processed by SPE. This will allow us to prepare a more comprehensive request for
you to submit quotations against.

Yours faithfully

D Briggs
Purchasing Manager

necessary to tackle the job. Geoff was sure there would be much prestige to be gained by SPE by successfully completing such a job. The brothers decided that SPE had to do everything in its power to try to obtain the business.

National Aerospace (NA) had been one of the leading UK suppliers of mechanical subsystems to the aircraft industry since before the brothers first entered the RAF. With a 1977 turnover of about £100 million, NA was now one of three UK firms supplying about 70% of all mechanical subsystems to UK aircraft manufacturers. At one stage, Geoff was involved as an RAF engineer in a development project that NA was working on for the RAF's new bomber at the time, the Wellington. Dave recalled that he had often been involved in the inspection, maintenance and repair of the firm's early landing gears. As an airframe design engineer, Geoff added that he had also been responsible for drawing up the detailed functional or performance specifications for landing gear components that were supplied to subcontractors such as NA, who would then engineer the design and manufacture it. All in all, the brothers felt they knew a lot about NA.

A week after receiving the letter from NA, Dave replied with the fairly standard letter shown in Exhibit 8.2. He was pleased to be able to inform NA of SPE's list of approvals. In the absence of more detailed information he could not be sure of the precise loading the contract would place on workshop capacity. Geoff reckoned it could account for anything between 20% and 50% of available monthly workshop capacity. The exact proportion would obviously depend on the man-hours required to machine and inspect each strut. Dave thought it might be a good idea to produce a test strut in the near future using soft tooling. This would at least allow them to give more specific answers to NA's questions about future plant loading and ultimately costings.

A quick glance at the order book for 1977 as it then stood showed that even if all currently prospective contracts became firm orders, SPE would still have sufficient capacity to meet the delivery requirements of the NA contract.

Over the years SPE had machined some 160 non-critical parts for a wide range of aircraft. The brothers assembled a sample of SPE's best work for NA to evaluate. It consisted of three more sophisticated, but non-critical parts and the three critical parts it had so far machined. The engineering of each of them had also involved a sequence of machining operations and detailed specifications which Geoff and Dave considered would bear comparison with those of the NA contract.

In many respects, the prospect of participating in the bidding for the NA contract was the biggest opportunity that had yet come SPE's way. In view of this, when nothing had been heard from NA after four weeks, Dave decided to follow up his letter with a telephone call. At the time he made the call Mr Briggs was out of the country, but he was told by his assistant manager that Mr Briggs was planning to visit SPE in the near future with a senior production manager and a technical services engineer.

Dave was encouraged by the news. He felt confident in the view that since Briggs would take the trouble to visit the workshop with two of his senior colleagues in tow, NA must be considering SPE to be a serious contender. Even

Exhibit 8.2   SPE's Initial Response to the Enquiry

25 January 1976

National Aerospace Ltd
High Wycombe

Dear Sir

Thank you for your letter concerning your landing gear project.

As requested, we send you information about our Company and the precision machining services we offer to the aircraft manufacturing industry. You will see that SPE has already obtained the British Standards approvals it requires to participate as a qualified contractor. We will also deliver to your factory a representative selection of the aircraft components we have engineered and manufactured. We believe they demonstrate our ability to work to fine tolerances and keep tight delivery schedules. We would be very willing to have you and your colleagues visit our workshop to inspect our facilities as well as some of the other aircraft parts and components we have engineered.

From the brief description provided it would seem that your requirements fall within our capability. We look forward to hearing further from you in due course.

Yours faithfully

David Southern
Managing Director

---

so, he could not help wondering why NA should choose to be demonstrative at such an early stage of the competitive bidding procedure. How have the other competing subcontractors responded to the invitation, he thought? What price does NA have in mind? How does it conduct its relationships with subcontractors on projects such as this one? Would NA supply the special tooling that would be used or was it to be manufactured? Dave was sure these questions and others like them would be answered when the NA team visited the workshop.

Several days after Dave's telephone call, the party from NA arrived unannounced at the SPE workshop. In the absence of both Dave and Geoff, Philip (who had only five minutes previously arrived at SPE to pick up some papers) spent almost three hours showing the party SPE's facilities and explaining its capabilities and expertise as best he could. The NA team seemed to be impressed by what they had seen; but since Philip could not answer the more technical questions, he also believed they were a bit frustrated – particularly the production manager, who seemed to be the senior man. He was keen to have answers to several questions of engineering and technical detail. Quality control and delivery were the issues he put to the top of the agenda. He also seemed ready to stipulate that SPE must produce a test strut if it was to have any chance of producing a realistic proposal.

Philip was relieved to be able to say that Geoff and Dave had already planned to do just that. When pressed to describe their plan in some detail and the present stage of its advancement, he could only say that in principle SPE would be prepared to produce the test strut as a gesture of goodwill and commitment to the project. But, he added, it remained to be settled who would bear the cost of the materials and the tooling that would be involved in the exercise.

Sensing a gentle prodding of NA's position on this question, Mr Briggs made it clear that it was not yet NA's policy to underwrite the costs to subcontractors of participating in the bidding. For the subcontractor the first stage in the bidding process was, he felt, one of self-selection on the basis of being willing and able to sustain the costs of participation. If successful, these costs could be recouped; if not, they could be sunk, or recouped on another occasion when the bidder was successful. On the other hand, Briggs continued, the production of the hard tooling would involve substantial costs which NA would ultimately have to bear, whether NA itself, or the winning subcontractor was responsible for it. However, NA was not yet in a position to negotiate on any aspect of the proposed contract.

At this point, both parties agreed that the meeting had probably achieved all it could in the absence of Dave and Geoff.

On their return, Dave and Geoff were surprised and disappointed by Philip's news, not so much by NA's hawkish stance on the issue of who should bear the cost of producing a test strut. In his previous job, Geoff would probably have expressed similar views to Briggs. Nevertheless, there could be grounds for some flexibility on the issue at a much later stage in the bidding.

Their surprise and disappointment was more attributable to the apparently underhand way Briggs appeared to have chosen to conduct the firm's business. The brothers would not have expected the senior professional staff of such a large and experienced firm to act in this way, particularly towards a subcontractor that they might have to work closely with at some future date. Their behaviour was not likely to encourage the trust and confidence on which a lasting and mutually beneficial business relationship was based. Clearly, the hit and run tactic had served NA's purpose of expediting a preliminary vendor evaluation. However, Geoff and Dave felt it had put SPE at a distinct disadvantage, when all they expected was a short phone call in order to know when to keep their diaries free. After all, how were they to know when the NA team was likely to visit the workshop? They certainly could not afford to wait around holding their collective breath until Briggs and his henchmen decided it was convenient to visit SPE!

In short, feelings in SPE were running high as a result of the incident. So much so that Geoff and Dave temporarily forgot how much they really wanted the NA business and began to consider other possible sources of business for 1978–79.

On reflection, the phone call which Geoff decided to make to Briggs during the heat of the moment was timely. Briggs obviously did not expect such a direct and forthright expression of dissatisfaction as Geoff provided. As a result of it, an apology was forthcoming. The brothers were also invited to the NA plant to meet the other members of the NA team and to discuss the detailed technical issues that were outstanding.

The meeting with the NA technical team passed off without major incident. Geoff and Dave were able to display their combined wealth of technical expertise and experience in precision aircraft engineering to the apparent satisfaction of the NA team. Some time was devoted to the question of who was to manufacture the special tooling that would be needed for the production of the struts. Until the meeting NA had been somewhat ambivalent about this matter. The brothers were very keen to influence NA in its make or buy decision. In their view, the manufacture of the tooling was as potentially lucrative as the strut contract. At the meeting, Briggs gave the clear impression that the NA project team would be looking for suggestions from bidders on the subject of the special tooling. He knew that NA was prepared to make the tooling itself then lend it to the successful subcontractor for the duration of the contract.

The brothers left the meeting with the feeling that, given a reasonable price, NA would much rather subcontract the manufacture of the special tooling. Given what appeared to be a very busy factory, Dave speculated that the manufacture of the special tooling would probably have little but nuisance value for NA. Some anecdotal support for this view had already been provided by an ex-colleague of Geoff's, who was now working in one of the NA design teams. At a recent meeting he had been boasting of NA's buoyant position. Apparently the main factory was working three shifts and looked like doing so for the foreseeable future. A rumour was also circulating the main plant that plans for a factory extension were about to be discussed with shop stewards. NA had recently begun working on four major contracts for airliner undercarriage assemblies. Three more were in the pipeline, in addition to the landing gear project that SPE was seeking some part of.

Six weeks after the meeting, Dave received a letter from Briggs formally inviting SPE to submit, in the first instance, a fully costed proposal for the supply of 240 struts in 12 monthly batches of 20. The delivery schedule was to begin six months after the contract had been finalized. The letter also invited SPE to cost the development of the special tooling. After much deliberation, Geoff and Dave replied within the stipulated 21 days with the letter contained in Exhibit 8.3.

The brothers were not entirely surprised when several weeks later, they were invited to meet the full NA project team in late June. Although the invitation did not disclose a venue, it did say that the director in charge of the landing gear project would be present, in addition to Briggs and the senior production manager whom they had already met. The purpose of the meeting was stated to be the 'clarification of areas of doubt' in the SPE proposal. To Dave and Geoff, this letter was tantamount to an invitation to negotiate on NA's terms. Dave and Geoff looked to the meeting with some apprehension. They wondered what they could possibly do to bring the outcome of the expected negotiating encounter more within their control?

Exhibit 8.3   SPE's Reply to NA's RFP

April 1976

Mr D Briggs
Purchasing Manager
National Aerospace Ltd
Crawley

Dear Mr Briggs

NA Request for Proposal 2974

It was with pleasure that we received your invitation to participate in the bidding for contract 2974. Our proposal is enclosed.

We are confident that we can meet all terms and conditions of your request for a total price of £498,300.

In our view, the contract involves two distinct pieces of work. Firstly, the development of the special tooling. And, secondly, the production of the outer cylinder struts.

Based on our past experience, we estimate that the development of the special tooling will cost £99,200. Our calculations are based on an hourly rate of £19. It represents the direct labour charge, overhead, G & A and profit. Procurement research indicates that a materials cost of £45,000 is a realistic estimate. It includes a 10% handling charge.

Our test run shows that the machining of the struts should take 100 hours per strut. In accordance with your instruction, the attached account breaks down the total cost for this part of the contract which is £399,100.

If this proposal is successful, SPE will be able to begin developing the special tooling in August of this year. This work will be completed six weeks prior to implementing our production schedule for the struts, which will provide delivery of the first batch of 20 struts to your plant at 10.00 am on March 11th, 1977. Delivery will thereafter proceed as stated in your RFP.

We thank you for the opportunity to do business.

Yours sincerely

David Southern
Managing Director
Southern Precision Engineering Ltd

Exhibit 8.3 (continued) Outer Cylinder Strut Contract Cost Breakdown

	(£)
240 structs @ 100 hours per strut : 24,000 hours	
Direct labour cost at £3.50 per hour	84,000
Overhead (250%)	210,000
TOTAL COST TO SPE	294,000
General and Administrative expenses (18%)	53,000
Sub Total	347,000
Profit margin (15%)	52,100
TOTAL COST FOR STRUTS	399,100
COST OF SPECIAL TOOLING	99,200
TOTAL CONTRACT COST	£498,300

CASE 9
Weighill Hotel, Glasgow †
Marketing Information Systems

David Buchanan
Loughborough University Business School

Introduction

The Weighill Hotel, Glasgow, was one of about 1,750 Weighill Hotels around the world, and one of over 60 in Europe. In 1985, there were 18 Weighill Hotels in Britain. Weighill Hotels' policy was to maintain high standards of accommodation. Teams were sent regularly to inspect properties to ensure that standards were being achieved. The chain began in America in the early 1950s; market research in 1979 showed that the Weighill sign was the third most widely recognized trademark in America after Coca Cola and MacDonald's.

In the mid-1960s, Weighill Hotels introduced one of the industry's first computerized reservations systems, and probably one of the world's largest privately owned computerized communications systems. It connected all their hotels around the world by satellite links through a computer centre in America. This system could confirm an advance reservation at any other Weighill Hotel in the world in seconds, free.

In 1986, Weighill Hotels employed around 1,700 people in its British properties and had a head office in England. The British operations were run by a Vice President – UK, who reported to the parent company in Canada. Reporting to the Vice President were four directors responsible for Personnel, Operations, Sales and Marketing, and Finance. The general managers of the British properties

†The research for this case was assisted by a grant from the Economic and Social Research Council, number F00232151.

Information for this study was collected during 1985 and 1986, and was updated in 1987. It is not the intention of this account to reflect current circumstances and policies within the company. Quotations reported from conversations with individual managers and members of staff reflect personal experiences and opinions. These should not be seen as representing current management views or company policies.

reported to the Operations Director. The Finance Director was responsible for management and financial accounting, security and risk management, and for management services. The management services manager was responsible for identifying and installing appropriate computer systems for all the company's properties in Britain.

The Glasgow property opened in 1982 in the central business district. It had 296 bedrooms, 10 meeting rooms, 6 suites, a split level restaurant, 2 bars, banqueting rooms and conference facilities for 800 delegates. The kitchen served around 1,200 meals a day on average, excluding banqueting work, and could on occasion serve 2,500 meals in one day. The main competition came from three other similar city hotels, and from two at Glasgow airport. The hotel employed a staff of about 250, of whom 230 were employed full time.

The restaurant was divided into a quick service coffee shop, a buffet, and the French à la carte restaurant. The property also had a shop, and a leisure club with a swimming pool, squash courts, sauna, sun beds and a gymnasium. The lounge bar was at the front of the hotel, and the cocktail bar overlooked the swimming pool.

The Weighill Hotel, Glasgow, was the 'revenue flagship' of the company in Britain. About 60% of revenue and 75% of profit came from room sales, the rest coming mainly from food and beverages. The property had a large beverage turnover compared with the other Weighill Hotels in Britain. The hotel's business by room nights was divided, approximately, 65% from the 'business' market, 20% holiday, conference and leisure, and 15% air crews.

The 'business' element, mainly men on expense accounts, generated about 80% of room revenue. Discounts were offered to companies with repeat business. A typical discount could be around 12% to 15%, but could rise to 45%. Discounts on leisure tours and airline crew deals could rise to 65%. As a rough indication of the significance of the business component of the hotel's business, on a daily revenue of, say, £20,000, only about £2,000 was paid in cash.

The property was a 'busy' one, with a high occupancy rate. Market share analyses put the property ahead of the main competition. On a typical night in 1985, with occupancy over 95%, revenue could be over £20,000, with roughly £13,000 from room sales, £4,500 from food, £3,000 from beverages, and a further £1,000 to £2,000 from use of telephones, the leisure club, laundry, and television films. Revenue was dependent on occupancy rate, on the scope and level of discounting, and on the extent to which guests used the hotel's facilities.

The organization structure, in outline, is shown in Exhibit 9.1.

The accountant was also the systems manager, responsible for the computer systems, for ensuring that staff at all levels used them effectively, and for liaison with suppliers. Most of the staff had been introduced to computing for the first time when they joined the company. In 1982 when the property opened, there were two members of staff with previous computing experience, and both were in 1985 still in key positions with respect to the running of the hotel's systems.

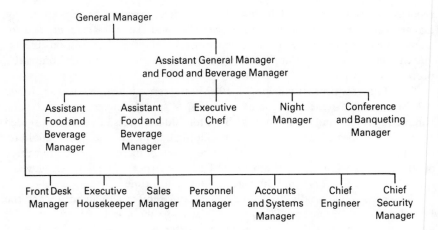

Exhibit 9.1   *Company organization structure.*

Computer Systems

The hotel had two main computer systems. Micos was the 'front desk' system handling reservations, customer billing and hotel accounts, and produced management information. Remanco processed customer orders and bills in the three restaurants, two bars, and room service.

There were eight other systems. 'Telectron' monitored consumption from the private 'minibars' in each room. 'Weighfax' was an in-house teletext service. 'Reservex' was the international reservations system. A computerized switchboard logged telephone calls. 'Bytex' monitored charges incurred by guests using the television film service. 'Uniqey' produced reprogrammable door keys for the electronic locks. There was a programmable controller for heating and air conditioning equipment, and two microcomputers for cost control, market sector analysis, payroll, word processing and revenue accounting.

These systems were of necessity bought from different specialist suppliers. No one supplier provided a comprehensive system, and most individual vendors had no desire to make their products compatible with those of others. Management wanted to establish system links where there were clear advantages, such as overcoming the need to rekey output from Remanco into Micos, to complete customer accounts. Technical constraints had prevented these developments.

All these systems, with the exceptions of the microcomputers, and the energy control system, were concerned with improving the service which hotel staff gave to guests. Despite their pervasive use throughout the hotel, the systems were used in a way that made them as unobtrusive as possible as far as guests were concerned. As one manager explained:

'These systems have not made staff redundant. The critical thing for us is that having computers does not run the hotel. You can imagine a busy checkout where you have got 160 businessmen and the computer goes down at the front desk – suddenly they are left with nothing. There is no information on the guests or rooms or anything else. There are backup systems, but there is no point in blaming the computer. Social skills are needed to cope with that, and to combat anything that gives an indication it is computerized. Frankly, guests do not want that. All they are interested in is the service.'

Another manager commented, forcefully,:

'The worst thing in the world I ever hear is someone telling a customer, it's the computer, I'm sorry I can't . . . The customer is not interested.'

The hotel's main computer system, Micos, had been operating since the hotel opened. It had eight terminals – three at the front desk, for printing bills, one in accounts, one in housekeeping, two in reservations and one for the telephonists. Micos produced accounting and management information through the 'night audit' package, which took about three hours to run, each evening, during the night shift.

Remanco handled food and beverage sales, and was basically a computerized cash register, with three terminals in the restaurants, two in the bars, one for room service, and one in the processor room for system programming and maintenance. At the end of each day, Remanco amalgamated sales, then calculated revenues from breakfasts, lunches and dinners.

When a customer order was taken, the waiter went to a Remanco terminal and entered the order codes for the food and beverages required. Orders were then automatically printed out in either the kitchen or one of the bars. Unless a guest asked for something special, this reduced the personal contact between waiting staff, and kitchen and bar staff.

Problems arose in the restaurant at breakfast, where guests could work through the fast buffet service and coffee and leave before their order had been keyed into a terminal. Much the same happened in the cocktail bar when it was busy. Staff, however, wanted the systems improved, not removed, and felt that the benefits outweighed the problems.

The minibars, monitored by Telectron, also caused problems when used incorrectly. Each bar held drinks in plastic trays which when removed broke a contact and registered a charge against that room number. The printed list had to be rekeyed into Micos to update each guest's account. Guests could, however, pull out a tray to inspect the contents without consuming the item, and thus still be charged. The computer system also controlled a message light system in each room, and the nightly automatic defrosting procedure.

The computerized switchboard and call logging system had generated substantial revenue for the property by producing an accurate record of guests' use of the telephones, reducing the discussion and argument between receptionist and guest that used to occur at check-out time when guests might dispute the size of the bill. The record of calls made from each telephone also helped management to deal with queries and problems which could arise after guests had left the property.

The corporate systems manager was responsible for developing future plans with an annual, centrally controlled, equipment budget. Management in Glasgow felt that they were not consulted over systems developments; but general managers were invited to comment on decisions, the development of microcomputer systems involved users extensively, and staff in some (but from necessity not all) properties were consulted. Central decisions meant standardization of systems across properties, which had several benefits for management and staff.

From an accounting perspective, the costs of the systems were difficult to justify. One manager argued that, 'there is nothing to say that these computer systems are more cost-effective than manual systems'. They had streamlined hotel administration and had reduced some costs, but they were intended to provide a better service to guests. Their main advantages were thus customer and market related, and qualitative.

The speed of the front desk system gave receptionists more time to talk to guests. The computerized reservations and billing system reduced errors. The restaurant system gave staff more time to spend with customers who got accurate and readable bills. These systems gave staff in the public eye opportunities to improve the quality of personal service. One manager said:

> 'I think any guest who sees the finished product has got to think it is better than a manual system. With a bill that has a breakdown of every charge guests can also say, 'that £2.40 for a cocktail was not me'. And I think it is definitely a winner with the guests because they can see the quality of the product that we are presenting to them. It is clean and tidy and neat and precise because it is right.'

Quality of personal service was the main competitive advantage that one hotel could have over another comparable property, given similar locations, and cost and price structures. So although systems benefits were intangible, they were strategically important to business success.

Management information was also central to competitive advantage. This was based on the daily report generated by the night audit package, but other systems also produced regular performance reports. These systems gave management performance feedback that was not available with conventional manual systems. The information had improved decision making on different levels and time scales. It helped management to identify trends, and to respond accordingly, and also helped to make daily operational decisions more effectively.

Senior management were interested in the information which indicated how well the business as a whole was performing, cost control and future planning. One manager commented:

> 'I personally have been involved in appreciating and getting a fuller understanding of more of our own in-house computing, that gives us all the up-to-date daily information on all sales aspects, payroll, cost, food and beverage, stocks. That is the main area that I personally use. All our own front of house, front desk operation is controlled here. That gives us all our reservations, check in, customer billing and city ledger.

I think what I have personally achieved is a quick and accurate way of running my business, of controlling costs and also planning my business ahead. We are very firm believers in forecasting. If you get your forecasting right, your costs should come in line.'

Most managers saw opportunities to develop personal expertise, job satisfaction and career prospects, as well as improving organizational effectiveness through these computing applications. The restaurant managers were, however, critical about the way in which the system slowed down waiting staff, and front desk management wanted to be able to call up a guest history from the database, and use that information to greet guests arriving in reception. Asked what advice he would give to other managers introducing similar systems, one manager said:

'You can't do enough training. Management and those involved have to be fully conversant with the system and what they expect to get out of it. I think management have got to feel happy and confident and are aware of what to expect and what not to expect. I think you've got to keep professionally updating more than you might do otherwise. We've spent a lot of time and money on training, but it is worth it.'

All heads of department in the hotel received a copy of the same daily report and other information which identified the performance of the property as a whole and of their individual sections of the business. The efforts of the management team thus became more closely coordinated through access to regular, shared performance information, discussed at regular management team meetings. The main customer billing system, Micos, and the staff who ran it, acquired a central coordinating role for the key functions in the hotel. Staff were generally able to find or confirm information about guests and rooms through a Micos terminal, rather than through the member of the staff of another department.

The purpose of the night audit package was to produce a day-end balance, and a series of management reports, analysing the hotel's business, including 'no shows', cancellations, check-outs, room changes, daily revenue, and invoiced accounts. The package also produced a 'room rate and letting analysis' which showed the number of rooms sold, complimentary rooms, rooms vacant and out of order, percentage occupancy, number of guests, potential revenue, actual revenue and revenue variance. The final printout was an account for each guest.

A senior manager assessed this information in the following terms:

'I think that interpreting profit and loss has been very much improved. It has meant that I have been able to involve many more people in the hotel because they all have the same information and they all have it very quickly. All the heads of departments have got the same information and it is easier to get everyone to interpret it the same way. Everybody is aware, they can see things happen, they can see trends, and you can develop from that into your sales and marketing strategy for the following three months. All that information is so useful in ringing alarm bells, or spotting potential opportunities. The sales manager sees something, I see it, and everyone is thinking along the same lines. Personally, that is the biggest single benefit to me.'

Another senior manager explained that:

'I find the most useful part of that information is our future reservations. It gives us a breakdown of singles and twins over the next six months, or a year. It can also show me peaks and valleys, days of the week, it gives me a breakdown by market sector – so I know the kinds of business I am getting in, which helps the sales department to make decisions on what to sell, when to sell, when to be rate aggressive, when to be soft on rates. So to me that is invaluable information.'

Another senior manager commented:

'What I think these systems do is make us more professional as a management team. I think that managers have become more efficient as individuals and are probably motivated more because they feel happier with that information. For example, our beverage sales here are very high, and quite complex because of the number of outlets. To get all that information and to get a true result was quite a lot of work, but now we are seeing something for that work and we feel confident that the result is accurate.

So I think that management probably feel more confident and therefore I like to think that they are more motivated towards achieving results. We do not hide anything. All our heads of departments know exactly how our business is doing. We have a profit and loss meeting every month and everyone has to explain their departmental ups and downs. That is another thing that is important today. People are given the job and encouraged to run it as if it was their business. Therefore, it is important that the information we give them is accurate and up to date.'

The reservations manager got a weekly printout showing bookings for the next six weeks. The reservations section prepared forecasts as well as handling current bookings. They monitored events taking place in the city which would create demand for accommodation, and which should therefore trigger advertising if the hotel had vacant rooms.

When a customer telephoned a reservation, the receptionist completed a 'reservation card'. These cards were kept in order of arrival dates and the information they carried was keyed into Micos. Guests were asked to confirm their reservations in writing, if there was time, and to cite either a credit card number or the name of the organization to which the account should be sent. Any changes to reservations were also keyed into Micos which produced a daily 'expected arrivals list'.

Micos was used to hold other guest information, such as VIP details. If a honeymoon couple was expected, a half bottle of champagne was put in their room. The daily arrivals list showed this information along with the room rate, and any other information about the guest useful to the housekeeping staff. This printout also indicated cancellations.

The reservations manager also produced a booking forecast, for all heads of departments, for the next ten days. This could show, for example, large group bookings, suite bookings, tourist groups and air crews, specials such as guests wanting roll-away beds for children, guests in wheelchairs who wanted rooms near lifts, and so on. The reservations manager also got an analysis of group arrivals over the next month, and contacted companies that had made the bookings to confirm them, as the cancellation risk for these bookings was high.

The computer helped to monitor the 'business mix'; it might not have been appropriate, for example, to have business conferences in the hotel at the same time as tourist groups. As one manager pointed out, 'one of the advantages of this system is that it lets you see when you can afford to take some, and when not'. Micos thus enabled management to monitor reservations much more closely than with a manual system.

The receptionists at the front desk, who also used Micos, had to present a friendly, sociable image to the guests. Their terminals were kept below the desk and out of direct sight of guests. When a guest checked in, the receptionist keyed their reservation number into Micos to get the room number, which could be allocated automatically, then cut the guest a key to that room using the Uniqey system. When a guest checked out, the receptionist called the Micos checkout screen and entered the guest's room number. The system then took the receptionist through a series of prompts designed to ensure that breakfast and telephone charges had been added. Micos then printed an itemized bill, significantly faster than producing such a bill manually.

A manager explained the advantages of this front desk system:

'The speed, the efficiency, the product for the guests which is really of a vey high standard. The old fashioned way – and people here come up and say, "I'm going to have breakfast and my room number is 221. Prepare my bill" – well that is all done so we just say "OK". And then he comes and asks for his bill and we call it up right way. It is clean and easy to work with. You are not messing around with huge pieces of paper, pencils and rubbers and things like that.'

However, while the system created time for staff to socialize more with guests, the check-in and check-out operations were completed very quickly. This created other problems, as one manager pointed out:

'The guest, once he has checked in, does not see us again until he checks out. We have no keys, we have a message light that goes on in the room. There is no reason for him to come back to the desk other than to pay his bill. So from a service point of view, you never really get to know your guests unless they are very regular. To check in takes three minutes.

I think it depends on the degree of computerization you take a hotel to, as to what you are trying to create. We are charging £60 a night here which is a lot of money. For that the argument has to be, what sort of service are we providing? We are frightfully efficient. But does the guest want something more than just efficiency? We get so many lonely men that travel who really quite like to have a chat, or come down and see the girls. . . it is all part of their routine, and we dismiss that. We have an express check-out facility, so they do not even need to go to the desk. They can just disappear. In this property it suits us because it is a businessman's hotel. But you could not put this level of computerization in a family hotel in Bournemouth, for example, where it would just die.'

That manager concluded, 'the guests really are certainly not secondary, but they are not as important as they were with the manual system, and the time you have to spend is of course not the same'.

The Remanco order and billing system was used throughout the three restaurants and two bars, and also by room service. It was used in similar ways in the restaurants and bars, but its implications for the work of staff were different.

In the restaurants, each waitress had a personal key to 'sign on' at the start of each shift, and to raise bills against customer orders. Guests sometimes 'played' with the terminals, but they could not get into the system without a key. As the waitress keyed an order using codes for each dish, the order was printed out automatically in the kitchen. This meant that the chef had a clear printout of each order, showing who keyed it at what time, rather than a hastily handwritten note. The accurate and itemized bills reduced mistakes, and reduced contact between restaurant and kitchen staff, which in turn reduced the arguments that typify relationships between chefs and waitresses.

One main implication of Remanco for the waitresses was that it turned them into cashiers. In a traditional restaurant, there was a cashier at the door, the waitress wrote out the customer's check and presented it to the guest who could either pay the cashier, or give the money to the waitress to clear with the cashier. The responsibility of the restaurant staff had thus increased in this respect. However, this did mean that some 'untrained' guests headed for the door when their meal was over, expecting to find a cashier on the way out.

The main advantage of Remanco for waitresses was that it reduced direct contact with kitchen staff. They no longer had to remember item prices, and they did not have to add up guests' bills. One problem, however, was that the codes changed monthly, as the menus changed.

One restaurant manager felt that the need to learn and remember these item codes slowed down service significantly, and that a simpler, and faster, system would have been more appropriate. In his opinion, 'the system was designed for an accountant, not for someone who works in a restaurant'. Another difficulty arose from the limitations of the modifier codes. There was for example no modifier for potatoes, so waitresses still had to go to the kitchen to tell the chefs whether guests wanted jacket or sauté. A guest might not want thousand island dressing on his prawns, or want breakfast without sausages, and so on. The system software did allow for the inclusion of additional modifiers, but a proliferation of such codes would have added to the learning difficulties. The system could take a long time to print out an itemized bill, which annoyed waitresses when the restaurant was busy, and at breakfast time when many guests were in a hurry.

On the one hand, waitresses had to learn a large number of codes, but on the other hand, there were not enough codes and modifiers to cope with the variety of customer requests. Guests received detailed and accurately added bills, but these could take time to print, and delayed guests who might have pressing appointments. But if the order information was simplified, management would not get the same degree of accurate and detailed sales and cost information from the system.

The lounge and cocktail bars also used Remanco. Here, staff and management felt that the routines and disciplines involved in its use were too slow for a fast bar service. The waitresses, however, felt that the benefits outweighed the disadvantages. Some managers, however, were not as positive in their attitudes to this system.

As in the restaurants, a cocktail waitress, say, took an order from a group at a table and then headed not for the bar but for a Remanco terminal. (Some guests complained on occasion that this indicated lack of service.) She then instructed the terminal to 'open' the table, and keyed in the table number, the number of guests, and the codes for the drinks they had ordered. Each drink had a four-digit code and the waitress did not have to remember the price. The order then printed out on a terminal behind the bar, where the barman prepared the order.

On a busy night, the computer response and the printer speed were slow, and when the bar was crowded, 'the system falls apart, really', in the words of one manager. Waitresses often found it quicker to give their orders directly to the barman (who keyed it himself) than to stand in a queue to key the order into a terminal. The system also required them to carry large numbers of copies of checks around with them during the shift, as well as handling their own money. When the system crashed, waitresses used manual bills, but this was also slow, and error prone because the waitresses had to learn, quickly, the current prices.

If the hotel wanted to launch a special promotion of, say, a particular brand of scotch whisky, or a new dish in the restaurant, the item code and price had to be keyed into Remanco during the night shift, when the system was not in use. On one occasion when prices were adjusted, errors were introduced, and orders were printed out in the wrong areas (meals ordered in a restaurant should print out in the kitchen, for example, and not in the cocktail bar). And as in the restaurants, the terminals in the bars had modifiers to indicate special customer requirements, but not enough to cover the variety of orders (sweet or dry white wine or sherry; with or without ice; Martini, Cinzano and Campari used the same code).

A waitress might have to strike up to 25 keys, depending on the nature of the order and how it was to be paid, just to serve an order, and get a bill printed and settled.

The information captured in the restaurants and bars by the Remanco system was used nightly to update guest accounts, and to prepare hotel accounts and management information. Some of the detailed operating features of the system created frustrating problems for the night audit staff, however, who were responsible for reconciling the figures:

'Our main problem at the moment is that if somebody in the restaurant has a bottle of wine and pays for the meal on the room and the wine by cash, in Remanco it will only come up as one bill, with the last method of payment. So it might have been a £22 bill. We are looking for an £11 charge, and we see a £22 cash bill. We don't know where the £11 has come from. So we have to find the reference number, go back to the waitress's [manually prepared] analysis sheet, look for the final copy of the bill, and see how it was paid off.

The other thing is the totals. It takes about twenty minutes to take off a departmental total. The consolidation sheet for each department balances with Remanco, and then Micos balances with the consolidation sheet. But we can't check that the consolidation sheets balance from Remanco until we are actually running the audit, so we are going on their word as being right, and most times it is. It is Remanco that can be wrong, because if someone pays it off to a different table number, for example the restaurants use table numbers 1 to 199, if somebody in the restaurant pays off a bill to table 299, that revenue will come up in the cocktail bar, although we have actually received it in the restaurant.

It means it's great fun. You'll balance your departments, but it's great fun trying to work out your breakdown at the end of the night. It's ridiculous for such a computerized effort, and at the end you are thinking of a number and doubling it. There are nights when we can't even get the revenue to balance. It says that cash and charge – we have so much and we have two printouts come off Remanco, the cash generator and an item generator. 'Cash' breaks it down into cash and charge, and 'item' breaks it down into beverage, food and cigars. So obviously both of those should balance. I've seen nights when they don't. So for that I haven't found an explanation yet.

We are going to have a problem when the American tours start in July, as they always have split bills. They are allowed something like £19, and they usually pay their bills in cash. Now those bills are coming out to £25, and they have only £19 posted. Although we know that it's probably cash, we still have to go through every single one of them and check them, which is crazy. You are doing far too much manual work when you've got a computer which should be able to do it for you.'

Management felt that there were gaps in the information provided by the systems. The daily report was prepared manually from information extracted from the two main systems, Micos and Remanco. Reservations forecasts were prepared manually from information extracted from Micos (if they were to go beyond the reporting of actual future bookings then human judgement was clearly required). The market sector analysis from Micos was translated manually on to another analysis sheet so that more useful comparisons could be made over the financial year to date, and with previous years – using information not stored by the systems. Information on individual customer histories was also not stored.

And as one manager explained:

> 'The main disadvantage of Micos is that it really does not tell me who is giving me business. The information that I want, I have to extract manually. I want to know how many room nights that company bought over the last six months, and Micos cannot tell me. I want individual credit records, and the system can't give me that either. My main bugbear is that the information is in there but I can't get at it. I would like to know how our business breaks down company by company, and who our top twenty customers are. It is embarrassing when customers tell me that they have spent £10,000 here last month and I have no way of knowing whether that is correct or not.'

Records of items used could be inaccurate when the order cancelling or 'voiding' procedure had not been carried out correctly, cancelling one item before ordering the new one. This procedure was easy to forget in a busy restaurant. Waitresses in a hurry could either make errors in entering customer orders, or use the 'open food' keys to deal with unusual requests. This meant that sales and stock records were inaccurate. Restaurant management in this property felt that the primary aim of the waitresses was to look after customers, not to generate accurate accounting and management information. That opinion was not necessarily shared by other company managers. There was, however, potential conflict between the use of the system to provide customer service on the one hand, and to generate appropriate management information on the other.

CASE 10

Deckgard

Marketing Orientation/Marketing Information Systems

N. Craig Smith

Cranfield School of Management

Paul Ettinger

European Institute of Business Administration (INSEAD)

Case History

An intriguing sight greeted Eddie Edwards, Marketing Manager at Marine Coatings, when he got back from lunch. Eddie had recently joined Marine and was eager to prove himself in his new position. A major priority was acquainting himself with Marine's products and technology, particularly as his Managing Director had asked him to submit his ideas on the product range proposed for 1987, the following year. He was currently reviewing Deckgard, a product only recently launched by Marine and not selling as well as expected. Earlier in the week he had asked Carole O'Connell, Product Manager for deck coatings, to dig out some data on the market for deck coatings from the firm's database. The computer printout had clearly arrived, for Carole, although not short, was hidden from view by a pile of paper at the side of her desk which Eddie estimated must have been five feet high!

As Eddie got closer to Carole's desk he could also see a second pile of computer printout, probably less than two inches high, on the desk. Carole, at last noticing Eddie, asked: 'Well, guess which is our market then?'

Eddie had suggested to Carole that she request a listing of ships with a likely requirement for Deckgard and a listing of those more likely to choose the conventional formulation. He rested his hand on the much larger pile which then wobbled precariously. Carole shook her head slowly and gently tapped the pile on her desk.

Marine Coatings

Marine Coatings is a division within CSE Coatings, a subsidiary of a large UK chemicals company with a turnover of around £1,000 million. CSE had played a vital role in supporting the group during the restructuring of its bulk chemicals operations in the 1970s. The contribution from the profitable Marine division had been particularly important. The other divisions within CSE are:

- Protective Coatings – producing paints for applications such as factories or oil refineries.

- Powder Coatings – serving a relatively new technology involving a baking process where the paint is supplied in a powder form. Applications include automotive components, domestic appliances, and general industrial use in, for example, the coating of parking meters.

- Coil Coatings – for coating steel coil used in the manufacture of, for example, domestic appliances.

- Packaging Coatings – for coating packaging products such as Coca Cola cans.

CSE has a turnover of around £350 million and employs over 6,000 people worldwide. It has a healthy operating profit of £23 million. Marine Coatings produces a large part of CSE's turnover and profits. Yet large though it undoubtedly is, CSE is dwarfed by some of its competitors. It is eighth largest in the world paint industry in volume terms, with ICI, the world leader, producing more than four times CSE's volume. CSE's strategy is to exploit its global strengths to dominate niches within the overall paint market. It largely ignores the two largest sectors in the paint market: automotive and decorative products.

Marine Coatings is the largest supplier of paint to the marine market in the world, with associates and subsidiaries in 32 countries. It has served the world's merchant fleet for over 100 years and has more than 30% of the total world market for marine paint. This has been achieved through in-depth knowledge and awareness of the marine market coupled with extensive investment both in world-wide distribution and R and D. Marine's product range covers most ship coating requirements; for internal and external use, above and below the water level, and cosmetic as well as highly specialized treatments such as anti-fouling paints (designed to prevent barnacles and weeds from attaching to the underwater hull of a vessel). Marine's products are used in new construction, maintenance and repair (in dry dock), and for on-board maintenance.

Marine has a sophisticated marketing information system which includes a computerized database. This carries information on all ships in the world of over 4,000 dead weight tons. It is a unique record of the coating treatments of around 7,000 vessels going back more than 15 years. The global representation of Marine allows it to have inspectors in every dry dock who will note the coating treatments and requirements of any vessel which comes in for maintenance and repair. Marine's competitors, such as Total Marine Flexoline, are unable to match this capability.

Deckgard

Deckgard is a primer for the treatment of ship decks, machinery and fittings, topsides and superstructures. It is a product for on-board maintenance, to be applied by the crew while the vessel is in service. The on-board maintenance market for deck coatings is about 40 million litres, of which cosmetic coatings constitute 75% and primers the remainder. In 1984 Marine had launched Deckprime, the first primer specifically intended for use during on-board maintenance. Prior to this, primers used in new construction and dry dock maintenance and repair had been employed. They were not very effective when applied in service because surfaces for treatment could not be adequately prepared. Deckprime overcame this problem and was far easier to use. As an 'all in one' it required only one coat, rather than the two coats required by the general purpose primer. Marine was very successful with Deckprime by focusing on user requirements in this way. Deckgard was a follow-up to Deckprime. The key properties of the two products are shown in Exhibit 10.1.

Exhibit 10.1   Key Properties of Marine Coatings' On-board Maintenance Primers

	Deckprime	*Deckgard*
In service anticorrosion performance	* *	* * * *
Applicable by brush or roller	x	x
Applicable to hand prepared surfaces	x	x
Single coat protection	x	x
Recommended for the repair of		
— alkyd†	x	x
— chlorinated rubber†	x	x
— vinyl‡		x
— epoxy‡		x
coatings		
Overcoatable with		
— alkyd†	x	x
— chlorinated rubber†	x	x
— vinyl‡		x
— epoxy‡		x
— polyurethane‡		x
finishes		
Approved for contact with foodstuffs	x	x
Suitable for use on all above water areas	x	x
Chemically resistant		x
Abrasion resistant		x

† Standard maintenance systems.
‡ High performance systems.

Marine's product literature describes Deckgard as a 'high performance surface tolerant epoxy primer for the maintenance of epoxy, coal tar epoxy and pitch urethane systems'. High performance systems have extended corrosion protection; Deckgard is intended for vessels employing this system from construction. Marine's Deckprime was a conventional primer for use on the standard maintenance systems. Deckgard's surface tolerant qualities enable it to achieve excellent surface wetting and adhesion to rusted surfaces. Once applied it is tough, flexible and chemically resistant, offering far greater corrosion protection in comparison with standard maintenance systems. In keeping with Marine's positioning in the marketplace, Deckgard is a high quality product with prices to match (see Exhibit 10.2). This extract from the product literature highlights Deckgard's benefits:

'Deckgard: the on-board primer for the maintenance of high performance systems
- surface tolerant – reduced preparation costs
- simple, rapid application – time saved
- single high build coat – reduced maintenance costs
Extended corrosion protection that's simple and cost effective!'

Deckgard had been launched in response to the earlier launch of similar products by the competition. Marine's expertise in R and D had enabled it to respond fairly quickly with a product that was technically little different in performance to the competition, although the competition were making greater claims for their products. Flexoline, in particular, was claiming that its product, Flexomastic, could be used with high performance and standard maintenance systems, providing superior performance in either case. Marine's technical people had found that the adhesion qualities of high performance primers were not

---

Exhibit 10.2 Pricing and Profitability

	Volume solids (%)	Specification	Typical net price per litre (£)	Typical net price per m² (£)	Relative gross contribution per m² (£)
General purpose primer	40	2 × 40μ†	1.50	0.30	50
Deckprime	41	1 × 75μ	1.88	0.35	50
Deckgard	80	1 × 120μ	4.72	0.71	100‡
Totomastic	86	1 × 200μ	4.00	0.93	
(by Total Marine)			–5.00	–1.16	
Flexomastic	90	1 × 125μ	4.00	0.56	
(by Flexoline)			–5.00	–0.70	

† μ denotes thickness.
‡ Deckgard earns twice the gross contribution per square metre coated of either Deckprime or Marine's general purpose primer.

optimum when applied to standard systems. However, Flexomastic was known to be selling well.

The Market

Shipping is a highly competitive business. Accordingly, ship owners have to run a tight ship! They are anxious to minimize all operating costs, including mainten-ance and repair. On average, a vessel will go in for dry dock maintenance and repair every two to two-and-a-half years. The costs for this are quite considerable, with dry-docking alone costing around £10,000 a day. Clearly, owners are keen to avoid too frequent stops for maintenance and repair because of these costs and because the vessel is out of service.

On-board maintenance can reduce the requirement for dry dock maintenance and repair. However, this is carried out by the ship's crew under the direction of their master. It is, as a consequence, fairly unsophisticated and not monitored by ship owners. So while ship owners wish to improve the serviceability of their vessels they are not prepared to spend a lot.

What Next?

Eddie had suspected that Deckgard had been inadequately promoted. There had not been a major launch event, nor had there been any advertising. Product literature had been sent out to Marine associates and subsidiaries worldwide but they were not stocking Deckgard. Despite having what appeared to be a good product, without distribution, sales were inevitably negligible. However, the two piles of computer printout suggested a more serious problem: less than 5% of ships used high performance maintenance systems. The market for Deckgard was confined to the small listing which was on Carole's desk.

CASE 11
Independent Bookshop Limited
Segmentation and Targeting

Howard Lyons
Sheffield Business School, Sheffield City Polytechnic

Introduction

The Independent Bookshop has been trading since 1979. The main goal is the provision and promotion of radical and alternative books for individuals and groups in the Sheffield area. The emphasis has been on retail trade, but a library supply service has been developed and sales to other institutions are increasing.

The IB also has a firm commitment to its organization as a workers' cooperative and to providing working conditions and staff training and responsibility in line with the goals of the cooperative movement.

Given this, financial planning is not aimed at profit making but at 'breaking even' while increasing trained staff and stock levels in order to improve the service provided.

Between 1980 and 1985, stock levels were increased from £9,512 to £26,218 (up 275%) and sales went up from £32,366 to £91,510 (282%). Staff numbers went up from one full-timer to three full-timers and a part-timer. Given that there is a period during which new staff members require to be trained, there is a similar underlying trend: turnover has steadily increased in line with stock and staff increases. Given the lack of external capital, this has had to be the result of careful forward planning – aiming always at as much growth as is consistent with breaking even. After minor losses in the early years, covered by private loans, the IB made a small profit in 1985.

The potential for further growth at the present premises in Glossop Road is limited by their out-of-centre location, a decline in the rate of growth of the student market (on which the site makes the IB over-reliant) and the limited usable sales space. Further constraints are lack of working capital and consequent cash flow and staffing difficulties in a highly seasonal trade. The move to Surrey Street

135

and associated financial arrangements are designed to overcome this and enable the IB to achieve the potential growth indicated by market conditions.

Sheffield is under-supplied with bookshops: on national averages, there would be 40. The Yorkshire/North-East area population buys fewer books per head than the national average, with a crucial gap in the middle ranges which seems ripe for exploitation. Of particular relevance to the IB, sales of radical and alternative books are below average, despite demographic counter-indications.

The IB's current sales are highest in quality fiction and poetry (including black, feminist and gay writers), sexual politics and politics. 'Caring' subjects, for example health and psychology, with an emphasis on alternative perspectives, also feature highly. Political newspapers, magazines and journals – most not available elsewhere – are high sellers and develop their readers as regular customers. Greetings cards and postcards have a higher profit margin than books and, again, because the ranges carried are not those most widely available, attract customers to the shop.

No other bookseller in Sheffield carries the same range of book subjects in similar depth. Where there is substantial overlap, it tends to be with only one or two other shops, and with different shops for different subjects. Though 'IB type' customers do not form a homogeneous group, they do tend to be regular book buyers with varying, overlapping constellations of interests, for example politics, Third World and environment; environment, vegetarian cookery and health; health, sexual politics, feminist literature. At the IB, such a customer finds a selection of books better than, or at least equal to, any other shop in a particular area and, most importantly, a much better browse overall. This combination is what tempts regular buyers to buy more, at the expense of other variable spending.

The IB's future strategy is based on maximizing the potential of the new site to attract existing customers more frequently and to gain new 'IB type' customers who will also increase their book buying. Central to this are worker training, a high standard of stock control and maintenance, and excellent customer service. There will be a certain amount of general publicity accompanying the new shop launch, but at the same time and in the future, there will be targeting of identified groups. Library sales will be maintained at a constant level, a declining percentage, due to the higher costs of this end of the market. Increased emphasis will be put on institutional sales, both as an area of potential growth and as a way of increasing awareness of radical/alternative book availability. Mail order and Asian mother tongue books are other areas to be investigated in the longer term.

The shop itself has been professionally designed to provide a welcoming environment and to make the best possible use of location and space within the constraints of its listed building status.

Growth to Date

The Independent Bookshop Limited has been trading since August 1979. Since then, its turnover has risen from £32,000 in the first full year of trading to £91,000 in 1985.

This growth has been achieved by:

(1) Development and consolidation of the IB's reputation as the only source
of books and pamphlets appealing to the sizeable minorities in Sheffield
and South Yorkshire interested in community issues, radical politics and a
wide range of alternatives in, for example, health care, good quality fiction
and poetry. These three categories currently account for about 50% of
turnover.

    Such development has been achieved by anticipating and responding
to the needs of local groups and placing a high emphasis on good customer
service.

(2) Development of a library supply service. The IB is currently sole supplier
of new books from 34 publishers to Sheffield City Libraries Department.
This accounts for 25% of annual turnover.

(3) The stocking of a selected range of university and polytechnic course
books, mainly in the areas of English literature, politics and sociology.
This accounts for 12–15% of annual turnover.

Overcoming Present Constraints

The move to new, city centre premises and changes in finance and staffing policy
being undertaken by the IB are designed to overcome a number of factors that
would otherwise constrain future growth.

(1) *Market* There is a declining growth rate in the student market for both
course books and general reading, to which the shop, by virtue of its
location, was originally geared. This is due to the drop in recent years in
the real value of student grants and to a shift in emphasis in higher
education from humanities towards technical subjects.

(2) *Site* The IB is in an out-of-centre site, with few neighbouring attractions
such as other shopping/leisure facilities and a resulting dearth of passing
trade. Students and local residents apart, customers have to make a
deliberate journey to use the shop.

(3) *Premises* The retail area at Glossop Road is being used at close to its
maximum stockholding capacity. Expansion there would have required
structural works not economically justified in the light of the above.

(4) *Finance and staffing* For some considerable time, the nearest the shop had
to capital was a bank overdraft facility. Interest repayments inevitably
meant running much harder to stand still. This resulted in insufficient
funds for adequate publicity and exaggerated cash flow difficulties. Market
and site further exacerbated the summer slump which is endemic to the
book trade and the result was inability to maintain sufficient staff to
undertake skilled work in busier periods. It is anticipated that with the
recent financial support from the Council and an 18-month holiday on
loan repayments, this problem will no longer haunt the IB in Surrey
Street.

Current Sales Strategy

(1) *Stocking*   It has been the shop's policy to stock reasonably priced
materials within the subject ranges it covers, for example politics,
women's studies, quality fiction, poetry, health care, etc. In practice, that
means that 99% of retail stock at any one time consists of paperbacks
(currently those under £10) and pamphlets.

  The proportion of pamphlets stocked has declined in recent years
because of changes in supply and market, and, because of their price
(average unit cost £1.10) they represent a relatively small proportion of
turnover (1.9%) while occupying a disproportionately large share of
potential shelf space (*c.* 10%). It is intended to reduce shelf space devoted
to pamphlets and place greater emphasis on stocking fast selling books
available at the usual trade discount from the regular trade suppliers.

(2) *Publicity*   This is currently tackled in several ways:

  (a) *Advertising*   In national magazines, for example *New Socialist* and
Spare Rib; in local papers, mainly the student press but also from
time to time in the *Star* in conjunction with a publisher.

  (b) *Approaches to academics*   Each year lecturers are asked to give to the
IB lists of recommended course books. Each year, more and more
lecturers have not only furnished IB with such information but have
specifically recommended its services to their students. The lecturers
approached have been those whose course lists would fit easily into IB
stocking policy.

  (c) *Bookstalls*   These are provided both for major national events that
take place in Sheffield (Critical Social Policy Conferences, 1983 and
1986; History Workshop Journal Conference, 1982; Conference of
Socialist Economists, 1986; trade union conferences) and for more
local events (the series of readings by well-known authors arranged by
the city libraries; Broomhall Carnival; Leadmill events; meetings of a
multitude of local campaign organizations).

    Books are also supplied on a sale or return basis to community
groups from as far afield as Doncaster and Mansfield for them to sell
at their meetings/events. Publicity material (leaflets, bookmarks, etc.)
accompanies these loans.

  (d) *Book launches*   The shop has organized book launches in Sheffield by
publishers such as Pluto Press and Longman. These generate good
media publicity, especially when, as with the Longman launch of a
volume of South African stories, the book is a topical one. They also
improve IB's standing with publishers.

  (e) *Book fairs*   In October 1985 the IB ran a successful 'Third World
and Multicultural Book Fair' in conjunction with the City Education
Department. An estimated 500 people attended and, again, good
media publicity was generated nationally and locally, both in the press
and on radio.

Current Sales Analysis

It has recently become possible to produce a detailed analysis of over-the-counter sales (73% of gross sales) with the acquisition of a computerized till.

Results for a 10-week period from 14 April 1986 to 23 June 1986 are shown in Exhibit 11.1.

Exhibit 11.1 *Highest selling sections.*

Section	% of Takings	% of Transactions	% of Shelf space	Average transaction (£)
1. Fiction	15.48	10.16	12.95	3.29
2. Sexual politics	13.84	5.84	6.16	5.11
3. Politics†	8.20	5.10	9.56	3.47
4. Cards	6.91	24.61	N/A	0.60
5. International	5.35	2.43	7.03	4.75
6. Psychology	4.07	2.04	2.15	4.30
7. Magazines	3.87	10.32	N/A	0.90
8. Health	3.28	1.69	3.08	4.17
9. Poetry	2.75	1.73	3.08	3.45
10. Newspapers (Political)	2.63	12.18	N/A	0.46

† Includes sociology and economics.
N/A indicates space not suitable for book display.

Exhibit 11.2 *Lowest selling sections.*

Section	% of Takings	% of Transactions	% of Shelf space	Average transaction (£)
1. Reference	0.03	0.02	0.02	3.50
2. Prose	0.14	0.10	1.23	3.15
3. Anarchism	0.19	0.08	0.30	5.12
4. Sci-Tech	0.22	0.10	0.69	4.66
5. Caribbean lit.	0.35	0.26	0.61	2.90
6. Art	0.43	0.20	0.20	4.59
7. Music	0.45	0.20	0.61	4.80
8. Trade unions	0.52	0.32	1.23	3.47
9. Rights advice	0.57	0.26	0.61	4.65
10. Media	0.66	0.38	1.23	3.68

Exhibit 11.3 *Sections with highest number of transactions.*

Section	% of Transactions
1. Cards	24.61
2. Newspapers	12.18
3. Magazines	10.32
4. Fiction	10.16
5. Sexual politics	5.84
6. Politics	5.10
7. Pamphlets	3.76
8. Remainders	2.78
9. International	2.43
10. Psychology	2.04

The main conclusions to be drawn from Exhibits 11.1 to 11.3 are:

(1) Within the context of the shop's policy of stocking moderately priced books, price plays a secondary role in determining whether or not a book sells. It is clear from Exhibits 11.1 and 11.2 that the average prices of the highest and lowest selling sections are very similar, for example while the second lowest selling section, Anarchism, averages out at £5.12 per unit, this is only £0.01 higher than the second highest section, Sexual politics.

(2) Customer motivation, based on the shop's known specializations in certain subjects, is probably the most important factor. Thus, Sexual politics, although the second highest priced section, generates the second highest proportion of turnover.

(3) Low priced items such as cards, papers and magazines, which have the highest number of customer transactions of any sections, obviously play an important part in attracting customers who might not necessarily be attracted to a bookshop that did not stock these ranges.

The Market for Books in Sheffield

A survey of book purchasing habits by region suggests that frequency of purchase in Yorkshire is lower than the national average and that the proportion of those who rarely, if ever, purchase a book is correspondingly high (Exhibit 11.4).

Exhibit 11.4 *Book buying rates.*

Frequency of purchase	UK average (%)	Yorks/North-East (%)
1. Once a week or more	4	4
2. Once every 2/3 weeks	5	4
3. Once per month	11	6
4. Once very 2/3 months	16	14
5. Once every 6 months	14	12
6. Once a year	11	11
7. Less than once a year/never	38	49

No specific survey is available for Sheffield/South Yorkshire, but there is no reason to suppose that there would be any significant variant from Exhibit 11.4.

In terms of Sheffield's population (537,557) this implies some 270,000 people will purchase books each year at an average of 4.2 books each.

A 1984 survey by 'Euromonitor' of the main sources of purchase for individual book buyers offers the breakdown shown in Exhibit 11.5.

Based on these figures, the total annual book sales for Sheffield would be 1,134,000 books, of which at least 249,500 are likely to be purchased from specialist bookshops. Comparison with the national average indicates that there is room for growth.

For all specialist bookshops, including the IB, the most significant group of customers is probably the fourth (Exhibit 11.4), those currently buying a book

Exhibit 11.5 *Sources of book purchases.*

Source	% of Purchases
1. Specialist Bookshop	22
2. W.H. Smith	19
3. Book Club	11
4. Newsagent	12

once every two to three months. They already make enough purchases for book buying to have a foothold in their leisure spending and increased promotion and exposure should seek to capitalize on this. Lifting them into the third group – once a month purchasers – where there is the greatest proportional difference from the national average – would make a major difference to local sales. This can only be helped by the fact that Whitaker's most recent figures show average book prices falling slightly after a five-year period of steady increases.

Sales are nearest the national average in the top two groups and present IB sales are heavily skewed toward this higher purchasing end of the market. Many customers are recognized 'regulars' and most buy more than one publication per visit. These people, and others like them who may be attracted to a more convenient site, form a pool of confirmed book buyers where improved stock control and maintenance (and thus availability of titles) should result in increased sales.

The Surrey Street site is well placed to attract groups who may be assumed likely to fall into these high or potentially high buying groups, being convenient not only for the Polytechnic, but for employees of the Town Hall, particularly the Social Services Department, and the MSC building, and for users of the Central Library.

It is not anticipated that the IB (or any other specialist bookshop) would benefit in the short term from increased buying at the bottom end of the scale, as infrequent purchases are more likely to be made from newsagents or to be 'own label' books from multiple retailers. There has been some speculation in the book trade that increased sales of such 'own label' books for young children may, in the long term, lead to increased book purchases from traditional sources for and by older children and teenagers.

A further indication of potential for growth is a Federation of Radical Booksellers' survey which estimated the UK radical book market as approximately £10 million. On a purely population basis, the Sheffield conurbation could expect to account for approximately £100,000 of this. Despite being the leading stockist of such titles, the IB in the last trading year reached only approximately 40% of this figure in this sector.

Bookshops in Sheffield

Financial projections call for an increase in market share by the IB of from 1% to 2% in the first year of trading at the new site, assuming a static market. As indicated, though, there is actually room for general growth in the book trade in Sheffield.

To gain this increased share of potentially increased sales, the IB will be promoting its own current specialities, participating in trade-wide promotions (for example book weeks) as applicable, and, to varying degrees, competing with other large and/or centrally located shops for proportions of specific segments of the general market. These shops are: Hartley Seed; Bowes & Bowes; Methodist Bookshop; Applebaums; and, to a lesser extent, Hudsons Bookshop, located in the Polytechnic Union.

Information on sales breakdowns in these shops is naturally not available, but a survey of their stockholdings has been undertaken and the results considered in relation to the IB's present and intended practice and sales. Book subject categories fall into three groups: those not stocked by the IB; those where the IB specializes and can already be considered to lead the market locally; and broad areas of overlap.

Subjects Not Stocked by the IB

Some areas stocked by other shops are excluded from the IB as a matter of positive policy, for example royalty, religion and mysticism, militaria. Other areas are given no priority by the IB and are, thus, almost wholly excluded in practice, for example hobbies and sport, business, study guides. Finally, there are academic fields where no or very few texts are stocked, for example the sciences, commerce, law, most foreign languages. Taken together, these areas account for a substantial portion of the shelf space in competing bookshops, as shown in Exhibit 11.6.

Exhibit 11.6   *Subjects not stocked by the IB.*

Shop	% of Shelf space
Hartley Seed	55
Bowes & Bowes	35
Methodist Bookshop	45
Applebaums	55
Hudsons	60

The differing percentages in Exhibit 11.6 largely depend on the degree to which the other shops themselves specialize. Hudsons stocks little beyond polytechnic texts. The others all give 20–25% of shelf space to a common core of books not stocked by the IB. Beyond that, Hartley Seed have a large university-oriented academic section (comprising half of the above 55%) and a major HMSO/Ordnance Survey Department. The Methodist Bookshop and Applebaums each devote about 20% of their shelf space to religion/mysticism. Bowes & Bowes is the least specialized and has not developed an absolute superiority in any particular area, but does have strengths in hobby books, travel and study guides.

The IB does not intend major changes in its policies in relation to the above areas, but will be adding small sections with an emphasis complementary to existing stock, for example organic gardening. Direct competition with other shops will be negligible.

Areas of IB Specialization

In these 'radical' categories, the IB carries more titles than any other Sheffield shop. Exhibit 11.7 shows the approximate percentage of shelf space given over to these areas by the various shops.

Exhibit 11.7 *IB specializations – stockholding.*

Section	IB	H. Seed	As a % of shelf space in: Bowes	M'dist	A'baums	Hudsons
Politics	10.0	1.0	N/A†	2.0	N/A	8.0
International	7.0	N/A	N/A	N/A	N/A	1.5
Sexual politics	14.0	0.5	2.0	N/A	N/A	1.5
Trades unions	0.5	N/A	N/A	N/A	N/A	N/A
Rights advice	0.5	N/A	N/A	N/A	N/A	N/A
Environment/rad. science	0.5	N/A	N/A	N/A	N/A	N/A

† N/A does not indicate that there is no overlap with IB stock – there may be some titles, but they are not shelved together and thus cannot be evaluated. Nor does this suggest an attempt to target interested customer groups.

As can be seen, in Exhibit 11.7 the main competition in these areas is from the academic bookshops. However, while Hartley Seed's 1% and Hudsons 8% are approximately equal to the IB's 10% (politics), stocking policies are quite different. The former tends to have mostly multiple copies of texts, often large and expensive, while the IB has smaller numbers of some of these and a far wider range of cheaper titles, appealing not just to students, but to academics, activists and the general public interested in particular issues. As an extreme example, no other shop was observed to have more than half-a-dozen inexpensive titles by Marx and Engels. The IB has over 30.

Exhibit 11.8 gives an estimate of the percentage of other shops' titles which the IB already stocks.

Exhibit 11.8 *IB specializations – % of other shops' stock held by IB.*

Section	H. Seed	Bowes	M'dist	A'baums	Hudsons
Politics	30	N/A	75	N/A	75
International	N/A	N/A	N/A	N/A	60
Sexual politics	100	100	N/A	N/A	100

Broad Areas of Overlap

Exhibit 11.9 shows the approximate percentages of shelf space currently given to major subject categories carried in significant numbers by both the IB and the majority of other Sheffield bookshops.

These topics have been divided into three groups, as shown in Exhibit 11.9.

In media/arts, cookery, and health, the IB is at present on the lower end of the scale of percentage shelf space and anticipates expanding. The amount of direct competition with other shops will be limited by a continued emphasis on 'alternative' titles. IB's cookery selections emphasize the inexpensive,

Exhibit 11.9 *Areas of overlap – stockholding.*

Section	IB	H. Seed	Bowes	M'dist	A'baums	Hudsons
			As a % of shelf space in:			
Media/arts	1.5	1.0	10.0	3.0	N/A	3.0
Cookery	3.0	2.0	8.0	5.0	8.0	N/A
Health	3.0	1.0	8.0	3.0	8.0	N/A
Education	2.0	2.0	N/A	0.5	N/A	4.0
Comm/soc. work	0.5	0.5	N/A	0.5	N/A	3.0
Psychology	2.0	0.5	N/A	0.5	N/A	3.0
Travel	0.5	7.0	12.0	5.0	3.0	5.0
Humour	1.0	1.0	4.0	1.0	3.0	0.5
Biography	0.5	2.5	1.5	1.5	N/A	N/A
Poetry/drama/prose	7.0	1.0	2.0	1.0	N/A	N/A
Adult fiction	13.0	18.0	14.0	15.0	20.0	10.0
Children's	1.5	10.0	5.0	20.0	N/A	N/A

vegetarian/vegan diets, and foreign foods. The media and arts sections will be expanded with a continued stress on critique of popular culture as opposed to book-of-the-film titles and glossy art books. Here, the major potential competition is with Hudsons, but, as with politics in the 'IB specializations', the stock is mainly course related. In health, there is overlap in the areas of fitness and books dealing with specific conditions. Again, however, the IB has a better range at the lower end of the price scale and a greater emphasis on self-help and feminist/socialist perspectives while the other shops' health sections include beauty/grooming, etc.

In education, psychology, and community and social work, the main emphasis of the IB is to provide an alternative perspective for students and practitioners and information/advice for consumers. As with politics, other shops' stock is largely student course books and, where aimed at the general public, a higher percentage of multiple copies of currently popular titles.

The remaining categories – travel, humour, biography, non-fiction literature, adult fiction, and children's books – represent the areas where the IB will be most directly in competition with other shops and where there will be the greatest dependence on passing trade to increase turnover.

One perspective on the degree of overlap here is shown by Exhibit 11.10 which indicates the percentages of titles stocked by other shops which are also held by the IB.

Many of the titles which do not overlap are in sub-areas which the IB does not intend to stock, for example stately home guides (in travel) or biographies of Conservative personalities. The literature sections will not have the number of multiple copies that academic shops do. Within adult fiction, there will be a continued emphasis on quality paperbacks with a significant percentage of stock and sales coming from minority interest titles – African, Caribbean, feminist and gay writers – rather than the mass market paperbacks that form a large part of other shops' stock.

In children's books, the IB cannot begin to compete with the variety of titles stocked by Hartley Seed and the Methodist Bookshop, perhaps even within the

Exhibit 11.10 *Areas of overlap – other shops' titles also held by IB.*

	H. Seed	Bowes	M'dist	A'baums	Hudsons
Media/arts	5.0	1.0	15.0	N/A	30.0
Cookery	10.0	10.0	20.0	40.0	N/A
Health	12.0	30.0	30.0	20.0	N/A
Education	12.0	N/A	20.0	N/A	25.0
Comm/soc. work	15.0	N/A	15.0	N/A	35.0
Psychology	15.0	N/A	15.0	15.0	35.0
Travel	0.5	5.0	40.0	30.0	100.0
Humour	1.0	40.0	10.0	50.0	60.0
Biography	12.0	25.0	25.0	30.0	N/A
Poetry/drama/prose	20.0	20.0	50.0	N/A	50.0
Adult fiction	35.0	40.0	40.0	25.0	95.0
Children's	5.0	30.0	15.0	N/A	N/A

range of titles IB would wish to stock. However, by increasing stockholding and adding a teenage section, while carefully selecting books that are non-racist and non-sexist, it should be possible to increase the amount of passing trade and the number of loyal customers. The aim is to offer parents and others who wish to buy gift books or to bring children in to choose their own books, an adequate and well-presented selection, along with an implicit guarantee that purchases won't offend. As the shop has been designed for wheelchair access, it will also offer the most accessible children's section to parents with pushchairs.

Looking at overlap from the opposite direction, there has also been consideration of the percentage of IB sales coming from books stocked by the IB as a result of a policy commitment to provide a range of titles on the subject and from the perspectives represented; and, within that figure, the percentage of IB sales coming from titles not available elsewhere locally.

Exhibit 11.11 shows estimated figures, based on the survey of competitors' stocks and IB sales figures for the same 10-week period used in earlier exhibits. Subject areas have been more broadly defined than in Exhibits 11.1 to 11.3 so that, for example 'Anarchism', evaluated separately for sales rate tables, has been added to 'Politics'.

In summary then, the IB's retail sales breakdown is roughly as follows:

43% exclusive
35% overlapping   78% radical/alternative
                   22% general

The Federation of Radical Booksellers' survey estimate of the UK radical book market as approximately £100 million used a definition which does not exactly align with either of the figures above, as the 78% radical/alternative includes a wider range of 'caring' (as opposed to narrowly 'political') titles and the 43% exclusive leaves out some radical titles carried as a small percentage of other shops' stock. It is estimated, rather, to cover about 60–65% of IB retail sales.

Based on retail sales of approximately £65,000 for the last complete year on the present site, this comes to just over £42,000 (at 65%) of the £100,000 that would represent the national average market for radical books. This suggests

Exhibit 11.11 *Percentage of IB sales reflecting policy commitment.*

	Retail sales		
Subject	% of IB sales	% to which IB committed	% exclusive to IB
Politics	10.6	10.6	6.4
International	7.8	7.8	5.1
Sexual politics	13.8	13.8	5.1
Trade unions	0.5	0.5	0.5
Rights advice	0.5	0.5	0.5
Environment/nukes/sci-tech	2.0	2.0	1.0
Media/arts	1.6	1.6	1.4
Cookery	1.7	1.5	—
Health	4.0	4.0	1.2
Education	0.8	0.8	0.1
Comm/soc. work	1.9	1.9	0.3
Psychology	4.0	4.0	1.2
Travel	0.6	0.5	—
Humour	0.6	0.5	—
Biography	0.9	0.6	—
Poetry/drama/prose	5.2	2.6	0.3
Adult fiction	18.0	9.0	5.0
Children's	2.0	2.0	—
Pamphlets	2.0	2.0	2.0
Periodicals	7.4	7.1	4.1
Remainders/misc.	5.4	4.3	5.1
	91.3	77.6	39.3
Non-book merchandise	7.6		
	98.9		

potential growth in this sector of 240% by effectively reaching the kind of customers who are already buying radical books in other places. This does not take account of the urban nature, history and political orientation of the area, which ought to be more than sufficient to offset any depressive effect of falling slightly below national trends in book buying generally.

Within the 35% overlap, it is important to note that this merely implies that at least one other Sheffield shop stocks a title. Reference back to the analysis of other shops' stock shows that while there is real competition with particular shops in a few areas (for example cookery/Applebaums), in the IB's strongest areas, it is the combined small stocks of four or five shops which fail to challenge the IB's depth of coverage.

Given its present stocking, reputation among existing customers and unique knowledge of many of the small publishers and much of the stock involved, the IB is best placed to take advantage of this expansion potential. This is further supplemented by its policy of stocking a large number of newspapers, magazines and journals unavailable elsewhere in the city. The periodicals' overlap is accounted for by only three popular titles. These do draw in customers on a regular basis who go on to use the IB for all of their book buying.

Though it is certainly expected that some of the projected increase in market share will come from the sale of general books and non-book merchandise to passing trade, the above figures suggest it could be achieved within the radical portion of trading and still leave that sector below the national level.

Future Marketing Strategy

Our first and foremost aim is to establish a basic bookshop service at Surrey Street. The IB will be moving there with two workers who have only a cursory knowledge of the running of the shop. It is not until they are trained that the company can hope to 'blossom forth'. For this period, IB has a holiday on loan repayments.

It is difficult to generalize about IB's customers (except possibly age range). One interest group does not necessarily identify with the aims of another. An overall publicity campaign, therefore, would expend a considerable amount of energy and resources while unlikely to produce results. What IB must constantly bear in mind is that it is a specialist bookshop with 1% of the existing Sheffield market, aiming to double sales, largely via increased sales of specialized stock to an increased proportion of specific target groups.

Effective publicity does not mean blanket coverage of the Sheffield population but meticulous identification of segments of the market. This must go hand in hand with the physical appearance and general atmosphere of the shop, which will be conducive to browsing and attractive to the copious passing trade.

Establishment of the IB at Surrey Street

This can be seen in three distinct stages:

(1) *Initial shop launch*
   (a) Leaflets inserted in all books sold up to six weeks before the move. (This is being paid for by a publisher.)
   (b) Posters and leaflets will be mailed to account customers. Trade union channels will be used to reach their members, including those who are also part of professional target groups.
   (c) Poster and leaflet campaign in the vicinity of the shop and targeted to relevant institutions.
   (d) Advertising in radical press and local student press.
   (e) Local press advertising, depending on cost and publisher participation.
   (f) Press releases to local radio, television and newspapers.
   (g) A formal shop opening with entertainment and a guest star, aimed at both individual customers and media publicity.

(2) *The first 18 months*

There will be a concentration on maintaining stock levels, customer order service, training the new workers and maximizing the efficiency of all existing work practices.

(a) *Stock*   The bulk of the increase in stock will be expansion of the existing sections, particularly fiction and children's books. However, this does not mean that the IB will be carrying stock that is indistinguishable from any other mainstream bookshop. All the IB expansions will be with their radical specialization in mind. It is also anticipated that most of the initial increase in sales will result from a combination of IB's excellent customer service, improved siting and much increased passing trade.

(b) *Media advertising*   The IB will continue to advertise in the national magazines and newspapers that it sells and at local events such as the Sheffield Show and Sheffield Festival.

(c) *Book launches*   The IB will organize regular book launches (hopefully, one every six weeks, depending on publisher schedules). Book launches are a particularly effective form of promotion: the authors attract their own targeted audience, the publishers pay any costs, and they frequently attract media attention.

(d) *Students*   The IB will continue to invite specific academics to submit their course lists for it to stock, although the move, occurring mid-October, will disrupt the service offered for the first and, sadly, most lucrative term of the academic year beginning 1986. Current sales to students can be broken down as follows:

Polytechnic   — £2,500
University   — £7,500

£10,000   — Course books
£ 1,000   — Radical/general

£11,000   — Sales to students

It is expected that the proportion of radical/general reading sales to course book sales will at best remain static.

Some course book sales to university students will undoubtedly be lost to Hartley Seed, but this will be compensated for by moving to a site which is more accessible to students at the various polytechnic sites (particularly Pond Street, Psalter Lane and Totley). The main competition here will be from Hudsons, but IB's strength, in terms of its specialities, lies in its stocking of a wider range of complementary books which will be used to attract trade and build continuing custom.

(e) *Library sales*   Sales to the Sheffield City Libraries Department generate a significant proportion of the shop's sales (currently 25%). However, they have a depressive effect on profit margin due to the compulsory 10% discount and the cost in workers' time in servicing the books ready for library use. There is no loss in granting 30 days' credit as books are normally special ordered, making turnaround equal to, or better than, average for shelf stocks. The goal will be to maintain library sales as a constant figure though a decreasing percentage of sales.

(f) *Institutional sales* Sales to other local authority and voluntary agencies, mainly in Sheffield and South Yorkshire, accounted for 5.5% of turnover in the last financial year. This figure is continuing to rise and IB aims at least to double sales. This area is a very attractive one as such sales do not require a discount or servicing. Again, they are mainly special orders and thus have a turnaround equal to or shorter than shelf stock.

The IB intends to increase its efficiency in supplying such orders and eventually target potential institutional customers systematically and actively promote itself via personal representation and mailings. As in other areas, the shop's strength lies in its ability and willingness to supply books not easily available at other bookshops.

(3) *After the first 18 months*

Once the two new workers are partially trained and all workers, therefore, will have the time and capacity to take initiatives, the IB will be able to devote itself to expanding its sales through targeted promotion.

(a) *Section promotion* Potential buyers will be identified and approached. The IB intends to do sales talks and exhibitions to as many groups as possible. IB will give priority to the following existing sections via this type of promotion:

Children's books	Playgroups, nursery schools, teachers.
Young adults' books	Schools, youth groups, teachers, youth workers.
Gay and feminist fiction/sexual politics	Women's groups, men's groups, gay groups.
Media books	Film societies, photography groups.
Trade union/Labour Movement history and practice	Trade unions, political groups, adult education.
Health books	Self-help groups, practitioners, professional organizations.

As new sections are researched and stocked, they will also require this type of promotion.

(b) *Mail order* The IB intends to develop a mail order service of use to organizations and individuals, particularly those outside Sheffield or with mobility problems.

(c) *Institutional sales and course books*   At this point, IB will be increasing individual representations from the shop to targeted organizations and academics with follow-up personal contact by phone or visit.

(d) *Ethnic minority groups*   There are presently some 17,000 people of New Commonwealth/Pakistan origin resident in Sheffield. There is no readily available information as to their book-buying habits and requirements. However, no city centre bookshop caters for these communities. The I & I Bookshop (formerly in London Road, currently seeking new premises) serves the Afro-Caribbean community, but there is no comparable outlet for books in Asian languages.

   The IB intends to work with the advice of the City Libraries' Multi-cultural Support Unit and the Sheffield Council for Racial Equality to quantify this market with a view to stocking relevant publications. This would be done in line with the shop's existing policies, for example probably quality children's books and adult fiction and politics, but not genre fiction or religious texts.

(e) *General promotion*   The IB will continue to work with other interested organizations for the promotion of its stock. These include Sheffield Libraries Arts Department, Sheffield Centre for Contemporary Popular Culture, the Crucible, worker/writer groups. The IB will also take part in general trade promotions where these are consistent with stocking.

Shop Promotion at Surrey Street

While the IB specializes in certain areas, it is important that it should not appear in any way elitist or deterring to prospective new customers or casual passing trade.

   Considerable thought has been given to planning and design of the shop's physical appearance (with expert advice) as a bright, informal and lively place rather than the more traditional 'tomb of knowledge' image.

Exterior

The status of 67–69 Surrey Street as a listed building does not allow much window space on the Surrey Street side of the building. The IB will be able to lower the level of existing windows some 18 inches and it will use them to provide a view into the shop rather than for window display. The window display area will be created on the gable wall end where traditional shop windows will be installed either side of the main door.

   Pub-type signs and possibly neon lighting on the interior of the windows will help attract attention to the shop from Surrey Street.

   The planned redevelopment of Tudor Square as a pedestrian area will improve the position considerably as the shop will front on to this area.

Interior

The emphasis will be on a bright, informal atmosphere created by the use of lighting, decor and music – which has proved a popular feature of the present shop.

Political newspapers and magazines will be sited near the door to attract customers. Though newspapers are sold at cost price, stocking them is advantageous because they are not available elsewhere and attract regular customers from IB's target markets for books. Magazines, with a 25% margin, make some contribution to profit and also attract regular customers.

Non-net goods (those whose price is not set by Net Book Agreement) like cards, stationery and wrapping paper will also be sited near the door to attract customers. These goods represent virtually the only opportunity for increasing mark-ups and are thus also important in themselves. It is anticipated that increased range, better display and the move to a site with more passing trade will enable these sales to be increased from approximately 7% of retail takings to 12½%.

There will be a 'Children's Corner' where adult customers will be able to leave their children to play or look at books or, alternatively, browse with them in a more relaxed atmosphere than is usually possible in shops.

There will be wheelchair access into and throughout the bookshop.

Opening hours

Opening hours will be geared to needs of the city centre shoppers and workers. The shop will open from 9.30 to 5.30 p.m. Monday to Saturday, with late opening to 8 p.m. on Wednesdays in the run-up to Christmas 1986 and beyond, if proven demand exists.

Service

The IB has always placed strong emphasis on personal service to the individual customer, and willingness to answer enquiries rapidly and helpfully will continue to be emphasized in staff training. The shop is currently able to order any book not in stock which is in print in Britain (which includes many US books with UK distribution agreements). This service will continue to be offered and will be maintained as a priority.

Pricing

Retail book prices in the United Kingdom are fixed by the Net Book Agreement. The bookshop's room for manoeuvre in this area is, therefore, non-existent. It is intended to maintain the shop's present policy of stocking relatively low priced books (mainly paperbacks), with an initial ceiling of £10.

The growth in trade and a resulting improvement in bargaining position will enable the bookshop to negotiate higher discounts from publishers.

Profit margins will also be improved by increased emphasis on the sale of non-net goods (cards, general stationery) whose retail prices are not fixed.

Contingency Plans

Sales will continue to be regularly monitored and set against costs. Should the IB, despite all its planning, experience and efforts, fall below IB's expected sales targets or spend more than its expected budget in general, it would need to prioritize the most profitable area of work and cut its costs.

Initially, costs could be cut by putting all efforts into the most profitable area of work, namely over-the-counter sales. Stocking policies would be amended so that IB's range would be cut and greater emphasis placed on maintaining stocks of titles with the fastest turnover and largest profit margins. This would not mean altering the overall policies of the shop but concentrating on better selling radical titles. This would require the maintenance of an excellent customer order service for less popular titles.

If retail trade in general is not producing sufficient income, resources would be diverted towards promoting further growth among institutions – the Polytechnic Library appears to be fertile ground.

To anticipate which particular area of work may falter and then anticipate its solution would require a book!

PART 3

Managing the Marketing Mix

Case 12	**British Aerospace Warton**	158
	New Product Development	
Case 13	**INFORAK**	168
	New Product Development	
Case 14	**MIT Tractors**	187
	Pricing Policy	
Case 15	**POK Electronic Systems**	190
	Pricing Policy	
Case 16	**Kilroy Products**	196
	Advertising Management	
Case 17	**The Langport Building Society**	201
	Advertising Management	
Case 18	**AVIS Rent-a-Car Limited**	207
	Distribution Management	
Case 19	**Scottish Express International**	216
	Physical Distribution/Marketing Information Systems	
Case 20	**Bartels Paperbacks**	225
	Marketing Mix Strategies	
Case 21	**Strathspey Ski Centre**	232
	Marketing Mix Strategies	
Case 22	**Auto-Main**	246
	Marketing Mix Strategies	
Case 23	**The Anglo-Saxon Artist Limited**	255
	Marketing Mix Strategies	

Conceptually, there are only two tasks in creating an effective marketing mix. First, the organization must determine which specific target market it will serve. Second, it must specify the mix of marketing variables that will best serve each target market. The latter task, however, requires that the organization determine or predict how target markets will respond to different levels of expenditure for each of the variables in the mix. Consumers' reactions can vary greatly from market to market and within the same market over time. Thus, although the idea of creating a marketing mix is simple to state, it requires complex decisions and careful planning. A company may choose to imitate competitors, find a new approach, or experiment to determine what is the best mix to offer. Regardless of the approach, those variables controlled by the organization and those outside its direct sphere must be considered. Particularly important is the performance of the entire marketing mix in the marketplace, not just the effectiveness of any one aspect such as a specific price or a particular marketing communication strategy.

Marketing managers who use the concept of the marketing mix can achieve a high degree of integration and a coordinated marketing position that should substantially improve marketing performance. When the marketing mix is incorporated into an organization's framework, it helps managers understand the complex and interrelated nature of their marketing effort. It offers a conceptual plan by which management can test and devise marketing approaches. The marketing mix is the logical basis for designing strategies that meet the needs of both specific target markets and the organization itself.

The importance of monitoring and controlling the marketing effort should not be underestimated, for it is fundamental to a marketing orientation. In the search to create the most satisfying marketing mix, managers confront many difficulties. First, they lack data on expected costs and revenues emanating from different possible mixes. Second, the interaction among the various ingredients of the mix and its acceptance in the marketplace cannot be accurately measured. Third, there are multiple and sometimes conflicting goals among the different units of an organization, and yet they must join to achieve an effective mix. Finally, the marketing mix cannot be adjusted continuously or altered to satisfy every possible target market, for that is simply too costly.

Blending the components into an effective marketing mix requires trade-offs among the product, pricing, distribution and communication elements, as well as among the variables that make up each of them.

The degree of control that management can achieve over the four components of the marketing mix varies by industry, product type and market conditions. Product, pricing, distribution and communication are controllable variables that can be matched to consumers' needs while satisfying the organization's objectives. But remember that each marketing mix is unique and must be accommodated to environmental, competitive and market factors – variables that largely remain outside management's control.

A product policy should be developed that addresses what types of products to offer and how to group individual products to take advantage of marketing strategy commonalities in reaching targeted markets. Product decisions provide the foundation and the rationale for designing entire marketing programmes. Brand identity and packaging are major product decisions, particularly for consumer product companies.

New products provide new life for otherwise ageing organizations and propel entrepreneurs to the top of new industries. The rate of new product introductions varies across industries, but new and better ways to serve needs and wants are ultimately introduced in all industries. Introducing a product can mean moving into an industry leadership position. New product development is an outgrowth of an overall business strategy.

In both profit and non-profit organizations, prices may be an active or inactive element within an overall marketing strategy. The first step in the pricing process is to set prices with attention to their effects on the overall product line, the promotional programme and distribution relationships. The role assigned to price in the marketing programme should be consistent with decisions about other marketing mix variables.

Price strategies are the guidelines and policies used to guide pricing decisions effectively to match target market conditions.

A central part of the advertising mission is communicating with specific audiences. A well-developed marketing strategy guides decisions concerning who the target audiences for the advertising programme should be. To be effective, advertising aimed at supporting the marketing strategy for a company's products (services) must ultimately influence buyer purchase decisions (sales). Successful advertising requires fresh and interesting ways to communicate selling points to target audiences. The advertising copy and layout should translate these selling points into an advertising presentation. Developing a media strategy is complicated by the fact that many different vehicles are available. Together, the media mix and media schedule decisions form a media plan. It serves as a blueprint for implementing the delivery of an advertising campaign. Alternative tests of advertising effectiveness have been developed because different types of objectives are set for advertising – communication objectives and sales objectives.

Firms rarely rely on only one of the four tools of promotion – advertising, sales promotion, publicity and personal selling. Each tool has particular strengths and weaknesses. The challenge for marketing management is to combine these tools in a way that will take advantage of their strengths and avoid their weaknesses.

Channels of distribution exist because of the advantages they offer in specialization of functions and because of the transactional efficiencies they provide to manufacturers and end-users. In selecting a channel of distribution strategy, a company seeks the best means of reaching its target markets. The selection of a channel is often influenced by management's estimate of the channel's ability to meet marketing objectives, its costs, its availability, and the time required for its development, as well as by control considerations and legal constraints.

The difficulties of managing physical distribution as an integrated system are compounded by the various levels that exist in many systems. The impact that physical distribution management can have on profits is increasingly recognized in companies where major benefits are obtained by managing an integrated system of activities for satisfying customers at efficient cost levels.

A company's marketing process must consist of an integrated strategy aimed at providing customer satisfaction. To develop such a strategy, a firm uses demand-influencing variables that together constitute the marketing mix.

The purpose of the *British Aerospace Warton* case is to draw student's attention to the role of users in the development and marketing of new industrial products, and to acquaint them with the marketing and strategic problems which arise when such user-initiated innovation is pursued.

The *INFORAK* case also deals with the new product development process. This case examines the market niche which such a new product might fill, looks at the developmental operations of the company, and examines the profitability of the venture. The central issues in the case are related to pricing policy, marketing research, product-positioning strategy, marketing strategy development and selling strategy problems.

The *MIT Tractors* case is designed to familiarize students with possible pricing objectives and strategies, as well as to dispel the myth that pricing decisions are tactical in nature and to assert their strategic implications. The case also demonstrates the possible application of the buy – response approach to pricing research.

The *POK Electronic Systems* case allows for a comparison of 'skimming' versus 'penetration' pricing in new product introductions. This case shows the relevance of demand, competition and cost factors in pricing decisions.

The *Kilroy Products* case deals with decision-making issues related to the development of a promotional strategy, in particular with regard to the design of an advertising campaign. It shows the relevance of the copy strategy, illustrative techniques and design principles in advertising decisions, as well as the implications of using different media scheduling strategies. The case also introduces other critical decision factors, such as 'cost per thousand', advertising effectiveness measurement, selection of push strategy techniques and post-testing procedures.

The *Langport Building Society* case enables the student to assess whether the advertising and the nature of communication presented in a sector of the financial industry is relevant to the market segment selected. This case suggests some possible methods of allocating advertising budgets and indicates what should be the main elements of an advertising plan.

The *AVIS Rent-a-Car* case is designed to familiarize the student with franchising as a vertical-marketing system, as well as to demonstrate some of the advantages and disadvantages of franchising for both the franchisor and franchisee.

The *Scottish Express International* case has a focus on the key features of physical distribution management. This case deals with the interface relationship between the introduction of a marketing information system and physical distribution decisions. The resulting effects of the new management system on performance measurement, product mix decisions and pricing policy are also analysed.

The *Bartels Paperbacks* case is designed to introduce the student to the concept of marketing opportunity analysis, as well as to show the relationship between portfolio analysis and the development of marketing mix strategies. Special emphasis is focused on the implementation of a marketing research plan, product mix strategies and marketing communication strategies.

The *Strathspey Ski Centre* case was developed in order to introduce the student to the different stages of the new project development process in the leisure industry. It presents and discusses many factors involved in the design of marketing mix strategies. The case shows the importance of analysing demand patterns and market trends. It also allows students to prepare an advertising budget in practical terms, as well as to develop a promotional strategy. Finally, the case is also designed to introduce students to the many implications of designing a distribution strategy in the services sector.

The *Auto-Main* case deals with the application, development and implementation of marketing mix strategies in a small business situation. This case involves the design of marketing research, segmentation, targeting and positioning, product policy, new product development, branding, pricing, promotion and after-sales programmes.

Finally, the *Anglo-Saxon Artist Limited* case deals with the situation of a firm that faces a very high (or over) demand, in the short term, that cannot be satisfied. The issue is, therefore, what should be the company's marketing policy in these circumstances. The case introduces students to the concept of demarketing and shows that a company's marketing policy affects its customers, distributors and agents. Students have to consider: customers' reactions; dealers' reactions; whether the promotional policy is really the key issue and what should the company do in the short term and long term, to alleviate its marketing problems. Other important marketing factors discussed in the case include the role of the marketing department, pricing policy, distribution strategy, analysis of competition and the marketing planning process.

CASE 12

British Aerospace Warton
New Product Development

Gordon Foxall
Birmingham Business School, University of Birmingham

Brian Johnston
Strathclyde Business School, University of Strathclyde

Introduction

British Aerospace Warton unit is located in Lancashire, England. Warton Unit is part of the company's Military Aircraft Division and employs almost 16,000 people. The unit was established in 1945 and is primarily responsible for the design, production and marketing of small combat aircraft as well as providing defence support services to overseas customers: the division employs 1,800 people outside the United Kingdom. Warton is Europe's most experienced combat aircraft research, development, production and flight test organization, and has produced such famous names as the Canberra, Lightning, Tornado and Jaguar. On the civil aviation side Warton unit is involved, with the Civil Aircraft Division of British Aerospace (BAe), in the manufacture of the Airbus range of aircraft along with French, German and Spanish companies. The nature of BAe's business is such that the company is a world leader in many aspects of advanced manufacturing techniques, not only in the aviation/aerospace industry but also in general engineering processes.

The production techniques employed within the company range from traditional methods such as milling, turning and drilling, to more novel processes such as honeycomb core carving and water-jet cutting of carbon-fibre composites. These functions are performed largely by craftsmen in the manufacturing process. The production process is of the batch type, and does not provide the benefits of long, stable, mass-production runs. Instead, Warton unit manufactures relatively small quantities of a large number and variety of parts in a given time period. The negative factors associated with this type of production include high volumes of work-in-process and inventory, and their related costs; low machine utilization and flexibility of operation, and poor response times. These factors, which have the effect of increasing labour costs, have inspired the development of various production techniques and the introduction of greater control over the entire manufacturing process. Until recently, however, while the application of sophisticated machine tools was cost-effective, the addition of further automation to activities such as material handling and storage, and large-scale application of computer control to batch production techniques had not proved to be economically efficient. British Aerospace, like other companies in 'batch industries', had been waiting for the advent of suitable technology that can apply the characteristics associated with mass production to batch processing in a cost-effective manner.

Numerical Control

British Aerospace has, in the past, introduced numerical control technology to its production process whenever it was found to be cost-effective. Numerical control (NC) was first applied to production in the early 1950s. NC or 'stand-alone' machines are used to produce high-variety/low-volume workpieces. Workpieces are machined in small batches, with the ability to output as many as 300 various part numbers per annum. The advantages of such machines are many: they are extremely flexible; engineering changes are easily incorporated and tooling requires minimal 'downtime', that is, the time between the changing of jigs and fixtures, and machining procedures, is greatly reduced. Early NC machines used punched cards or magnetic tape as their programmed input, but this was greatly improved with the introduction of paper tape as a medium. Numerical control, as a substitute for traditional machining methods, provides better, faster and more accurate control over machining functions. Warton Division has implemented numerical control technology over a wide range of production processes. An example of this is the Molins cell, which has been in operation for several years, and is used to machine small aluminium alloy parts.

Although NC proved efficient and effective compared to manual methods, as the number of NC machines in use increases, so do the problems associated with this technology. For example, a large number of programs is required. The control and management of the generation and issue of such programs has proved to be a particularly complex procedure, and unreliability of tape readers becomes a significant source of errors and resulting costs of scrap.

It was recognized that improved productivity and quality would require better NC techniques and it was generally accepted that computer technology was the only way of meeting the ever-increasing demands for such complex machining operations. Thus, Direct Numerical Control (DNC) evolved. This technology, first developed in 1968, represented a comprehensive automated control system with the ability to communicate with various machine tools by means of a wide range of controllers. The step-up from NC to DNC within BAe meant not only the replacement of the paper tape as the input medium by a direct computer link to the machine tool but also use of the computer for control of schedules, tracking of material and data availability, the collection of shop floor operating data, etc. DNC facilitates efficient machine tool shop management.

To complement these manufacturing procedures BAe Warton had been utilizing purchased or internally developed systems such as computer-aided design, numerical control programming, and production planning and control to help produce a series of fully intergrated systems capable of controlling all aspects of design and production. However, while this coordinated approach provides greater efficiency, BAe still encountered the common problems of inflexibility and low machine utilization found in batch production. A corporate plan was introduced which envisaged a number of projects running more or less simultaneously with a time scale allotted to each: the first was the implementation of a flexible manufacturing system for the small machined part facility which began in mid-1983 and is due for completion in mid-1987. Other projects include a sheet metal flexible manufacturing system, an integrated carbon fibre facility, automated assembly facilities and development of further DNC applications.

An Early Joint Venture

Warton's experience with DNC began with a joint venture agreement involving a British control system manufacturer on the development of a fairly sophisticated first-generation system, including shop management features as well as part program downloading. The companies had equal input to the project and engineers from both companies were responsible for the production of software.

The objective of the venture was to produce software for an operational DNC system, for in-house use by both companies and for commercial exploitation within a wider market. The major problem was that, though the machining facilities were similar, there were several different, and incompatible types of numerical controllers involved. Consequently, a standardized system needed to be developed to integrate all machines: the solution was a generalized post processor (BAeGen) which could deliver instructions, either directly or via an interface, to each machine. British Aerospace has 33 machines in use on this network system, mainly used in the profiling of large alloy billets. While this DNC system was the first large-scale operation undertaken by BAe, it is now being superseded by a more advanced system developed from the small machined parts Flexible Manufacturing Systems (FMS) facility at Preston. The project was conducted on an informal basis, the result of which was that BAe's partner marketed the resulting software product alone despite BAe's central involvement in the project. Thus, BAe received no financial reward for its efforts and, in fact, the company ultimately had to buy the software for use in this first generation DNC system.

However, the experience of this venture has given Warton management a valuable insight into the technicalities of, and problems involved in collaboration with other types of company outside their extensive aerospace collaboration experience. In reality, this can be a very complex procedure in terms of, first, the legalities of agreements and contracts; secondly, the delicate process of collaboration itself; thirdly, the opportunities for diversification via exploitation. Management at Warton were concerned that any future joint agreements with outside partners would be approached with full consideration of all the possible factors necessary to protect the division's (and the company's) intellectual property rights to the design and development of any product resulting from such agreements.

The Business Development Group

It was due in part to the need to protect the rights of the company to its products that the Business Development Group (BDG) was set up at Warton. Headed by Mr Tony Guest, the BDG has as its central aim the commercial exploitation of new product ideas which are internally generated. The group is responsible for the following:

(1) The identification of new products and processes within Warton which exhibit potential for successful marketing.

(2) The protection of the company's property rights through patents and copyrights.

(3) The identification, where appropriate, of firms which will further develop, produce and market the products and the negotiation with such firms of licensing arrangements and royalty payments.

(4) The control of the resulting arrangements.

In short, the Business Development Group acts first to create a commercial awareness throughout Warton Division and actively seeks out any potential prospects for commercial exploitation that arise internally. Subsequently, the BDG acts as a watchdog over the development of marketable projects right through to their commercial launch as products. This is no small task in an organization of the magnitude of Warton, where a large number of diverse activities and production processes occur continually. The main problem areas for the group are the setting of group rules for negotiations with other companies and the protection of property rights. In cases where an outside manufacturer cannot be found to develop further and market a product that is generated internally, the BDG will itself undertake the task of assessing possible markets for the product. Finally, the BDG would locate an external company capable of producing and/or marketing the innovation successfully. Overall, the work of the BDG is designed to give management a sound legal and technical operating basis from which the company can seek to commercialize any promising projects that emerge from within the division.

Flexible Manufacturing Systems

British Aerospace has identified a very large number of internal manufacturing applications for what can be described as Flexible Manufacturing Systems (FMS), but which are more accurately called Advanced Manufacturing Technology (AMT): this means the application of computer-based automation to production, covering recently introduced processes as well as traditional techniques. The utilization of this advanced technology within British Aerospace is seen as a logical progression from what has been achieved in past years in NC and DNC systems.

As a first step in this development, Mr Brian Entwistle, chief electronics engineer, introduced what was known as the BCA concept, the British Aerospace Control Architecture. This modular concept basically meant that systems software was designed or organized in modules which could be interchanged with each other, the different modules having different practical applications. Thus, available software could be transferred between different functions and linked with other systems for varying applications. This novel idea implied the introduction of control systems that were not available at the time. As a result of this concept, the initial idea for the application of flexible manufacturing systems technology emerged. Mr Guest, as head of the Business Development Group, was in a position to provide the impetus for commercial development of any products resulting from the FMS project. Mr Brian Phillipson, with responsibility for manufacturing systems, completed the control system development team.

The belief that advanced manufacturing technology was a necessary progression in a bid to bring the benefits long associated with mass production to batch processing was reflected right across British Aerospace. The corporate development plan was based on the realization that, while different departments within the company possessed various specialist skills, no single section of the organization could be a master in all aspects of the business. The need for a well-organized, corporate approach to the task was realized at the outset due to the considerable development costs involved. Within this overall plan, which has a life of 10 to 15 years, each site in the organization has assumed responsibility for development in different areas. Warton unit has the lead role in a number of 'early' projects within the schedule, the first of these being the application of flexible manufacturing systems technology to the small machined parts production function at Warton.

The resulting control system in its completed state is expected to have three main payoffs: firstly, to the small parts facility itself; secondly, to produce technology that can be implemented by other departments and divisions within British Aerospace; and finally, as a marketable product for application outside BAe. Other projects in which Warton Division has lead responsibility are in the areas of sheet metal, carbon fibre and some assembly processes. FMS and DNC projects in other divisions within BAe had also commenced before December 1984.

Small Machined Parts Facility

The small machined parts process at Warton facilitates the machining of a wide range of components from aluminium, steel and titanium materials. This unit comprises 18 CNC machining centres giving a capability of 26 spindles which can be run constantly. Prior to the introduction of the flexible manufacturing system, the production of small aluminium parts was achieved by the use of a Molins NC cell, incorporating automatic cutter change from magazines and automatic pallet transfer, a system first developed in the 1960s which is being replaced by a machine called Automax, developed by BAe and a machine tool manufacturer. A somewhat similar facility for machining of small steel and titanium components was installed about six years ago and is based on ten Japanese-made Mitsui-Seili, semi-automated machining centres. Thus Automax and Mitsui comprise the basis of the small machined parts facility. These machines represent a 'one-step' improvement in technology to the Molins cell in that they permit not only automated parts delivery/removal and tool replacement, but have additional features such as a sophisticated system for controlling machining conditions, that is, speeds and feeds, and a probing feature that monitors and compensates for cutter and workpiece dimensions. When combined with other features of the flexible manufacturing system, these improvements make it possible for Warton to undertake the automated machining of over 1,000 different components with reduced manufacturing costs, greater flexibility and control over all aspects of the manufacturing process. Other facilities involved in this system include automatic inspection and parts finishing machines, cutter regrinding machines, automated stores, and electrically controlled transporters which follow a buried wire track for movement of components and tools.

Systems that support and complement the main production processes have also benefited from the advance in technology within the small parts department. For example, computer-aided design and manufacture (CAD/CAM) has been incorporated into the function which ranges from the use of computers to perform isolated calculations, to the ability of a system to compile a bill of materials for instance, for production planning and control, and extensive integration of the design geometry process from drawing through production engineering to NC part programming. The small parts function, therefore, possessed the basic structure from which automation by computer of the entire process was a logical step, resulting in improved efficiency and productivity by reducing the time involved in the total production process.

As a first step in the development plan for small parts FMS, BAe management set out some overall objectives for the project. They were: (1) to implement small parts FMS on time and on cost; (2) to design control systems for maximum read across to other FMS projects; and (3) to realize commercial opportunities.

A specification for the FMS control system was drawn up, covering the functional and other aspects of the required system, from its operation through to contingencies in the event of failure of parts of the system. This task took some six months to complete during which time BAe invited some leading hardware and software producers to participate in the activity. The specification was put out for general tender but no one company could bid to supply the system as a whole. By taking the best features of the various systems offered by bidders, Warton management felt that they could succeed in their task. It was soon discovered, however, that much of the technology involved in the various bids had not yet been developed. Feeling that the requirements set out in the FMS specification could be reasonably achieved, and within the capabilities of available technology, the development team considered the options open to them with regard to initiating such a system.

The options available were as follows:

- To go it alone – build up internal resources, develop the system alone and market it from within the company.

- To use subcontractors for development work, then either market the system in collaboration with the subcontractor or alone.

- To pursue a collaborative venture in which development costs would be shared, after which the system is marketed jointly or some form of licensing is undertaken.

The first potential course of action considered was that of building up the required human and capital resources within BAe, without outside involvement in the project, and to market the product directly. By following this course Warton would be in a position to maintain full control of all aspects of the project and would reap all available benefits through marketing the resulting system. On the negative side, the development team noted the high level of demand for the limited in-house resources available at Warton and recognized the considerable task of obtaining the necessary capital and human resources within such a short development time period, causing possible delays in the overall time scales. The danger was also expressed that a rather insular viewpoint might result without some input from an external source. Management also considered that their lack of experience and organization in the marketing field, together with limited knowledge of the market, was a further negative factor in the 'go it alone' option.

The second option considered was to employ subcontractors for the development work; the division would then have the choice of undertaking the marketing activities itself, or achieving them under a licensing agreement with the subcontractors. This option provided the advantage that overall control would remain within Warton, whose personnel could oversee the various subcontractors engaged. However, the unit risked the loss of intellectual property rights to the project and it would also be, to some extent, dependent on the subcontractors for completion of the project. To coordinate the development would require a considerable workload for Warton personnel and could undermine their prime activities. High costs could also be incurred in respect of management workload and the rates charged by subcontractors. A further disadvantage would be that, by locating licensees to market the products, BAe would miss out on valuable practical marketing experience, which could be beneficial to the company for future innovative developments within the field. There would also be more opportunities for subcontractors to enter the market at an early stage as competitors, thereby diminishing BAe's market lead in this technology.

A third course of action examined by Warton management was of a joint development venture, involving one or more partners. The major factor against this option was that there would need to be a compromise of objectives with the partner(s). However, the favourable aspects appeared to outweigh this potential problem: BAe would be able to share the development costs while drawing from a wider knowledge and resource base. There was a higher probability of success in achieving all the goals set, particularly in the planned time scales. While profits from the venture would be shared, BAe felt that it would benefit from this arrangement in that a partner's marketing experience and organization would enhance its image and credibility and the knowledge gained could be retained only by the partners.

Each option was considered carefully and the decision was made to look for a suitable partnership that could meet the BAe criteria and the objectives of the FMS project.

Type of Partner

Warton Division had considerable experience of collaboration with other producers in the past, in developing military and civil aircraft such as the Tornado and the Airbus. However, in general, Warton was new to setting up a joint venture with another company; with the unfavourable outcome of the earlier agreement on the DNC project still in their minds, the FMS development team studied all aspects of such a venture in order to avoid a similar situation.

The form of collaboration was assessed in terms of number of partners preferred, size of company, nature of the collaboration, and scope of work that the partner(s) might undertake. Other factors such as commitment, security and balance of relationship were taken into consideration and it was decided that BAe would seek a single partner of similar size who would make an equal contribution to the project, would be willing to undertake a long-term commitment, establish close links with BAe and be prepared to market the resulting system on a formal joint basis. Potential partners were considered in such areas as controller manufacturers, computer/electronics manufacturers, machine tool manufacturers and systems/software houses. Other considerations were also assessed such as experience and commitment, available expertise in commercial and technical areas, and the ability to support and influence the project.

The partner finally chosen would have to provide considerable experience in all aspects of control system implementation, including hardware and software, and stretching from R & D to support activities. Thus, a number of specialist companies were excluded as it was felt that they could not provide a sufficient span of skills. Overall commitment to the venture was necessary and the partner would be required to offer strengths that would complement those of BAe as well as having similar goals and need for success of the project. The team agreed that multinational companies would not be able to offer these qualities and so this reduced the list further. Finally, one company was chosen which best fitted the overall requirements of the development team, a company that offered both software and hardware skills, experience of marketing ability, and a wide range of technical skills and resources. That company was the Electrical Projects Division of General Electric Company of England (GEC). At approximately the same time as BAe was considering the issues involved with its FMS project, GEC Electrical Projects Division had begun to consider certain aspects of manufacturing automation, and was beginning to draw the same conclusions as BAe regarding the need for development of a new type of FMS control system.

GEC FAST

GEC Electrical Projects Limited, part of the GEC group of companies, is concerned with the design, supply, installation and commissioning of major capital project systems within a variety of industries including electrical and mechanical installations for such areas as dockyards, oil rigs, airports, steel works and deep shaft mining. As an extension to these activities, a decision was taken by GEC Electrical Projects management to investigate the area of factory automation.

GEC FAST (Factory Automation System Technology) was established in 1980 as a division within the GEC Electrical Projects Company to develop a business in the field of factory automation projects, an area identified as having considerable commercial potential. To help establish GEC FAST a number of small companies were acquired with expertise in the fields of business systems, production control systems and robotic equipment manufacture, as well as various software packages. After two or three years, during which a number of consultancy and feasibility projects were undertaken, the group undertook, as an initial large FMS project, to develop a flexible assembly system at GEC's Kidsgrove plant where printed circuit boards were produced. This was seen as being an opportunity for FAST to develop the type of software which would be needed if the company were to achieve a more rapid growth in FMS projects, and an opportunity to establish a significant 'reference' project to aid marketing. GEC was still in the early definition stage of this project when it was approached by BAe.

Negotiations

The first step in negotiations towards a joint-venture agreement came in the form of general discussions with GEC management at the end of 1983, on an informal but highly confidential basis. Even at this level, it became increasingly apparent that collaboration offered very exciting possibilities. There was a need to progress to a more detailed level of negotiation and, with this in mind, a joint study of the proposed project was commissioned, to be completed by the late spring of 1984. If the results proved to be favourable, then an official agreement would be produced and finalized by that summer.

In drafting the agreement, following a very positive outcome of the joint study, a number of problems were encountered. Both companies, eager to protect their interests in the project, sought to ensure that a bona fide legal document was drawn up. The technical aspects of uniting two companies of the magnitude of GEC and BAe proved considerable, and a lengthy period of time was spent by the legal departments of both companies in completing the required documents. There was the risk that an agreement of this type might contravene European Commission competition laws. There was also the added complication that, following an abortive takeover bid of BAe by Thorn EMI, there was intense speculation about a possible GEC bid for the Aerospace group. Negotiations, meanwhile, progressed between management on both sides to decide what level of human and capital resources should be provided by each company. Only when issues such as these were resolved, could attention switch to the project itself.

The agreement was officially signed on 18 December 1984. The two companies agreed to collaborate in the design, development and marketing of a range of advanced manufacturing control systems. Almost £5 million would be spent over a two- to three-year period in order to develop and apply general-purpose computer programs and electronic hardware to control a range of computerized manufacturing equipment for use in both assembly work and the production of engineering components. Software of this type did not exist at that time.

The joint venture was to be run by a supervisory board and management committee of representatives from both companies. GEC FAST comprises some 30 staff, mainly engineering based. Not all were involved in the venture, but they were complemented by other staff within GEC Electrical Projects Systems departments. GEC FAST took responsibility for lead marketing on the venture's products and appointed a marketing manager while BAe had responsibility for the technical direction, and Mr Brian Entwistle was appointed Technical Manager. The BAe resources were provided from the FMS Control Systems department at Warton and the Manufacturing Systems department at Preston.

Early in 1985, shortly after the public announcement of the venture, the development team found that already, a number of companies were expressing interest in buying the system – a system which, at this stage, did not exist. However, this gave an indication of the potential volume of future demand for the technology and also helped, to some extent, in the assessment of likely markets for the product.

Acknowledgements

This case study was written as part of an investigation supported by a grant to the first author from the Economic and Social Research Council, London, under its Competitiveness of British Industry Initiative. In addition, the authors thank the executives of British Aerospace, Warton, and GEC FAST for their help and Janet Tierney and Frank Murphy for assistance at the initial stages of the research. The case has appeared in the *Journal of Marketing Management* and the authors are grateful to the editor, Professor M.J. Baker, for permission to reproduce it.

CASE 13
INFORAK
New Product Development

Luiz Moutinho
Glasgow Business School, University of Glasgow

Introduction

This business plan sets out the case for the establishment of a sole trader company, INFORAK, in spring 1988. Under the proposal, display racks carrying tourist leaflets would be placed in 80 hotel foyers in Edinburgh and 30 in Glasgow premises. Although the exact design and size of the racks is a matter that will be part of the research programme with hoteliers, for present purposes it is assumed that each rack, which would be freestanding, will contain 54 leaflets.

The management of the racks would be the responsibility of INFORAK. The racks would be provided free of charge to hotels, with advertisers paying for display of their brochures.

A similar scheme has been operating for seven years in London, where there are over 600 racks, and the same company, 'Brochure Distribution', began a similar operation in Birmingham in 1986. The company felt that with the relative concentration of accommodation in Edinburgh and Glasgow, there might be a case for a similar scheme in Scotland.

Michael Ambrose, the founder of INFORAK, was conscious of all the future difficulties related to his new venture. In particular, he was concerned about the profitability issue involved in the launching of this new service, its positioning strategy, pricing, selling and other marketing strategies to be implemented. He was also encountering some problems in defining the type of marketing research study which would provide him with accurate information in order to improve his decision-making 'batting average'.

The Concept of INFORAK

Scottish visitor attractions clearly need to promote their facility to both tourists (British and overseas) and local people. They do this in various ways including advertising in the press and Tourist Board brochures, and by distributing their leaflets through Tourist Information Centres. They may also attempt to distribute copies of their brochures through hotels and other outlets, but this is generally carried on in a haphazard fashion, and depends on the proprietor of the attraction having the time to visit the various outlets, and on the outlets themselves effectively displaying the brochure.

The proposed concept would for the first time ensure the effective display of attraction brochures in hotels (and could at a later stage be extended to guest houses, caravan parks and libraries). The scheme would get brochures into local residents' and tourists' hands in the places where they congregate, and provide visitor attractions with a whole new method of publicity. A similar scheme has operated in London since 1979.

Operation of the Scheme

(1) The company would obtain the agreement of hotel owners/managers, guest house proprietors, etc., to locate a brochure rack at a suitable point on the premises, normally the reception area. The rack would be provided free of charge!

 The rack would be stocked with leaflets from visitor attractions, and other businesses, for example, coach tours, entertainment programmes, major shops, etc., subscribing to the scheme, and, most important, would be *regularly restocked*, depending on demand at the particular location.

(2) From the 'host premises' point of view, the advantages of the scheme are:
 (a) A smart rack, regularly stocked with information on attractions, which will be of interest to guests. The hotel is thus providing an extra service at no cost.
 (b) Removal of situation where certain brochures are displayed in a haphazard fashion.
 (c) No responsibility for stocking the rack – this would be taken care of by the company.

(3) Attraction owners and others wishing to use this method of promotion, would pay a monthly fee for exposure in all racks in the scheme in a given area (*initially* this will be Edinburgh). The fee will depend on the number of racks in the scheme, but clearly quantities of brochures required will depend on the popularity of a particular visitor attraction or service.

 For the business using the service, the advantages are:
 (a) Brochure distribution to interested customers who make the choice to select a particular leaflet.

(b) An assurance that brochures delivered will be effectively displayed,
and that racks will be regularly restocked (weekly in peak periods).

(c) A method of distributing brochures without any worries for the
advertiser – one delivery to the company, ensures regular coverage in
all racks for an agreed period.

(d) A cost-effective method of promotion.

(4) Initially, racks will be placed in Edinburgh accommodation (the target
would be at least 100 – roughly one-third of the possible total).
Subsequently, it would be the intention to extend the scheme to more
premises in Edinburgh and to provide coverage in Glasgow and possibly
other key locations in Central Scotland (Ayr, Stirling, St Andrew's, etc.).
The racks would display leaflets for attractions and services within a
radius of approximately 50 miles (the likely maximum distance for a day
trip). Thus, in Edinburgh the visitor might find leaflets for places in
Stirling, East Lothian, Fife, The Borders and Glasgow, as well as the
capital itself.

The larger attractions such as the National Trust, the King's Theatre and
Edinburgh Crystal employ either internal staff or casual staff to distribute
brochures, but in other cases distribution appears to be a relatively random
process which is undertaken in different ways from year to year. Exhibit 13.1
gives distribution figures.

Exhibit 13.1 *Brochure distribution figures.*

Attraction	Brochures p.a.
National Trust	1.5 million
King's Theatre	200,000
Royal Lyceum Theatre	18,000 per show
National Gallery of Modern Art	150,000
Edinburgh Crystal	500,000
Royal Observatory	1,000 in hotel folders

The King's Theatre currently distributes around 200,000 brochures a year
and some of these organizations distribute through such channels as libraries,
museums and local tourist offices.

None of the organizations places its own racks in hotels or other outlets, with
the exception of Edinburgh Crystal, which will provide a rack if none is available.
Apart from this, all organizations simply use whatever is available – either racks
provided by the hotels, or tables in lobbies and lounges.

INFORAK – What Business Is It In?

INFORAK is in the business of:

• helping hoteliers to provide a better information service to their guests and
with much less 'hassle' to hotel staff than is generally the case at the
moment, when information is not always to hand;

- helping visitor attractions, shops, coach-tour operators, car-hire companies and other companies (for example banks, British Telecom, shipping agencies), effectively and in controlled ways, which requires no management input from the advertiser, to distribute their brochures to visitors in main Edinburgh and Glasgow hotels.

INFORAK – What Industry Is It In, and What Are Its Characteristics?

INFORAK will be part of the tourist industry in Scotland, and more specifically of the 'information provision industry' within the overall tourism scene in Scotland. Tourism expenditure in Scotland in 1986 was estimated at £1,520 million. By 1991, estimates suggest that expenditure is likely to increase by between 10% and 25%, most of the growth being accounted for by spending by overseas visitors.†

Edinburgh, and increasingly Glasgow, are important places on a Scottish holiday, particularly for overseas visitors, with 57% of overseas visitors including overnight stays in Edinburgh as part of their trip to Scotland, and 23% Glasgow‡ (by comparison, the whole of the Highland area accounts for just 28%, with areas such as Argyll, Dumfries and Galloway accounting for 3%–6% each).

In both Edinburgh and Glasgow, there is more of a propensity for tourists to use hotel accommodation (as distinct from self-catering and staying with friends and relatives), than in other parts of Scotland: 40% of holidaymakers in Edinburgh and 35% in Glasgow used hotels, compared with a Scottish average of 23%.§

Thus, there appear to be prospects of growth for the overall tourist industry in Scotland, and Edinburgh and Glasgow are clearly resilient parts of the overall picture. The opening in recent years of a number of major new hotels in cities would seem to confirm this.

There has been a growth in the number of visitor attractions in Scotland – and many others have been much improved to provide a more exciting visitor experience. The Scottish Tourist Board is keen to assist this sector of the industry, and has indicated that 'the development of new, and improvement to existing, visitor attractions' is a high priority for its capital grant-aid scheme.† As examples, a Whisky Heritage Centre is to open in Edinburgh High Street in Spring 1988, and in 1989 a 'Jorvik'-type experience, recreating the smells and noise of sixteenth-century Edinburgh, will also open nearby.

If there has been a growth in the tourist industry in general, and the number of visitor attractions', there has also been a growth in the production of promotional leaflets to draw visitors to the turnstile, a growth in advertising and promotion opportunities for attractions, but also an awareness by proprietors of

---

† *Source*: Scottish Tourist Board Business Plan, 1987.
‡ *Source*: STB, Profile of Overseas Visitors to Scotland, 1985.
§ *Source*: STB, Accommodation used by Holidaymakers in Scotland.

these attractions that they will need to promote their business if they are to draw more visitors, or even maintain market share. Many attractions have recently decided to produce leaflets for the first time, others to change from black and white to more striking full colour material. It is only in the past two years that the Ancient Monuments Directorate has produced a leaflet to promote the buildings in its care, and it wasn't until 1986 that a brochure was specifically printed for Edinburgh Castle. Similarly, the National Trust for Scotland began producing a colour leaflet to promote all its properties in 1984; Peter Anderson Mill in Galashiels started to produce a leaflet for tourists (as distinct from a catalogue) in 1985; the examples are endless.

Who Will Be the Customers of INFORAK?

(1) *Hotels*

For the scheme to work for the advertisers, racks must be located in a number of hotels. In Edinburgh there are 100 hotels listed in the Scottish Tourist Board's '*Where to Stay*', and in Glasgow, 45. There are also over 100 guest houses in the capital city, but only 13 in Glasgow. Initially, at least, the appeal of the scheme to the advertisers is likely to be that the stands are located in the larger hotels, many of which have a number of facilities beyond simply bedrooms, which may draw potential visitors into the establishment (for example bar, restaurant, meeting rooms, shops, car-hire office, etc.).

For the purposes of the profit and loss account and cash flow projections, it has been assumed that the establishments participating would have a standard rack, which would be made available at no cost. However, it may be that certain more 'up-market' hotels might like a 'bespoke' rack, particularly adapted to their design requirements. All hotels are concerned that the rack should be of a style and quality appropriate to their decor and furnishings – particularly those that have recently undergone refurbishment or decoration. INFORAK has the intention to investigate this issue among other problems in a market research study to be carried out between December 1987 and January 1988.

Samples of the cover letters sent to potential clients and distribution outlets (hotels), as well as the questionnaire applied to the hotel industry are shown in Exhibits 13.6, 13.7 and 13.8, respectively.

(2) *Attractions, shops, coach-tours and others who will display in racks*

With regard to advertisers, the scheme is likely to be of interest to a business situated in either Edinburgh or Glasgow, or which is within approximately 40 miles or 1 hour's drive of either centre.† This area is shown in the map presented in Exhibit 13.2.

---

† Research by the English Tourist Board suggests that one hour is the maximum driving time tourists are prepared to drive from their holiday base to a visitor attraction.

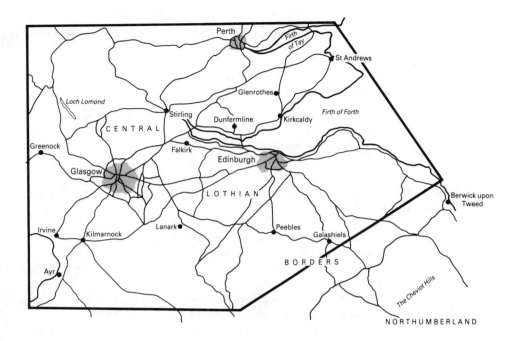

Exhibit 13.2 *Area from which advertisers will be drawn.*

There is also a broad threshold in terms of the size of the attraction (which could be measured in terms of visitor numbers and brochures produced) below which the INFORAK scheme would simply be too costly. Based on the knowledge of attractions, and that the scheme will have a proposed price of approx. £80 p.c.m., and a likely brochure requirement of 30,000–60,000 per year, the company's intention is to target the following customers:

(1) *Visitor attractions* With at least 10,000 visitors per year if located in Edinburgh and Glasgow, and 20,000 if outwith these two cities.† Where the attraction also has a major retail element (a distillery, glass works, etc.), it may be possible to drop the threshold figure.

(2) *Large car hire companies*

(3) *Chauffeur-driven tours* Companies providing a personalized, 'expensive' service.

(4) *Entertainments* Main theatres, orchestras, festivals.

(5) *Transport/tours* Local and national (Scottish) companies.

(6) *Shops* This is more difficult to assess, but an awareness of those retail outlets which already produce publicity material for distribution to visitors has suggested a possible list.

(7) *Miscellaneous* This consists of companies providing various services to visitors, for example banks, travel agents, British Telecom.

NB No eating places will be included in racks, as these would compete directly with hotel facilities.

Bearing in mind the criteria in (1)–(7) above, the list of possible advertisers to be approached includes:

in Edinburgh area	64
in Glasgow Area	43
outwith Edinburgh/Glasgow area	53

INFORAK — What are the Benefits of the Service for the Customers?

(1) *For the hotels accepting the racks, the benefits are as follows*:
   (a) *An enhanced visitor service* (which might result in more return business), as hotels are able to provide improved and more extensive information for their guests.
   (b) *Convenience* The scheme will involve no management by the hotel, as restocking will be regularly carried out by INFORAK.
   (c) *More efficient use of staff* Present reception staff would be freed from many time-consuming enquiries, and thus better able to deal with mainstream matters, for example checking in and out of guests.

(2) *For visitor attractions the benefits are more extensive*, and also vary to some extent, dependent on the particular advertiser.
   (a) *Easy to take part in* The scheme involves one delivery of brochures to a central point, after which INFORAK takes on all management.
   (b) *'Peace of mind'* Advertisers need not worry and can be confident that brochures will always be on display (unlike other schemes where there is no guarantee of display and brochures are kept in boxes in cupboards!)
   (c) *No lengthy commitment* Advertisers can advertise for a length of time to suit their needs, from one month upwards. This also gives them an opportunity to 'try' the scheme for a short period before making a decision on longer exposure.
   (d) *Easy to assess* Monthly reports on brochure usage will be provided to advertisers, as part of the service.
   (e) *'Status and credibility'* In some cases an attraction, etc., may achieve increased status by being featured in an attractive rack in an up-market hotel.
   (f) *Cost saving* For the few larger companies, either employing someone regularly or occasionally to distribute their brochures to hotels, there will be cost savings in using the scheme.

(g) *Gaining a new outlet for brochures*   For attractions where those involved are aware of the importance of hotels, but have not had the staff resource to distribute, the scheme will provide a whole new method of distribution for their material.

What is the Competition for INFORAK?

(1) *Hotels*   For hotels, the 'competition' with INFORAK – postulated at this stage as a free service, is for the hotels simply to carry on doing what they have always done to provide information. This might include accepting brochures which happen to be delivered and displaying them in various ways (occasionally in a rack, but more often on tables, or shelves, or attached to a display board).

(2) *Attractions, etc.*   In the broadest sense, the competition is any promotional activity that an attraction might take part in to gain more visitors. This could include anything from attending a travel trade workshop, to erecting signposting on nearby main roads, or advertising in the press or tourist guides. However, in most cases, an attraction or shop will examine it more narrowly by asking 'How can I reach visitors staying in Edinburgh and Glasgow?'

Exhibit 13.3 introduces an analysis of INFORAK's competitors. From this it will be seen that there are various distribution services, at a substantially lower price than that proposed for INFORAK (approximately £80 for 110 racks). In order to compare this with the other services, which are quoted per '000, let us assume that 25 leaflets are taken from each of the 110 racks, each month; this would give a total of 2,750 brochures distributed or about 2.9p per copy (however, this is a conservative estimate of leaflets taken up and the cost of each INFORAK brochure could be lower).

INFORAK must distinguish itself from other distribution services and the use of the Scottish Travel Centre, by the quality of its service (the benefits referred to earlier). It will definitely not attempt to compete with these in terms of its price.

The bedroom packs provided by the 'Landmark Trust' (for 1988 in Edinburgh only, but they may expand to Glasgow) is perhaps greater direct competition, since although it is a very different service, like INFORAK, it has a high element of management and control. For some smaller businesses, there may be a choice of spending £600 with 'Landmark' or INFORAK, but larger businesses may well participate in both schemes. The particular advantages of 'INFORAK' compared to 'Landmark' are that with INFORAK, visitors can actually take a brochure of interest, which it may be argued is more likely to lead to conversion to business than a leaflet which is read in a folder, but cannot be taken away as is the case with 'Landmark'. In addition, 'INFORAK'. provides flexibility of price depending on length of display, whereas 'Landmark' offers a 'one-off' price only.

Exhibit 13.3　INFORAK – Competitive Analysis

	Some other costs of brochure distribution/display	
	Cost	*Display*
Scottish Travel Centre, Edinburgh (Tourist Office)	£10 per 200 copies of a brochure (5p per copy)	Will display for a period in racks in the centre, but due to space constraint can't guarantee extended display.
Time Out magazine distribution service to various locations in Edinburgh (during Festival period only)	£18 per '000, (1.8p per copy)	Will drop off brochures at locations such as pubs, restaurants, 'Fringe venues' along with the magazine *Time Out*. Brochures will compete with many others, no formal display facility.
A Glasgow distribution service	£12 per '000, (1.2p per copy)	Will take on leaflet delivery if provided with list of drop-off points. No guarantee that places will accept leaflets or that they will actually be displayed.
Edinburgh Arts & Entertainment Limited	A5 size to 300 outlets in Edinburgh. £4.35 per '000, (0.04p per copy)	Venues mainly community centres, clubs, theatres, service designed for arts organizations but will take other brochures. No guarantee of display, and no racks.
Landmark Trust (Edinburgh)	£595 for 16,000 leaflets to be placed in 16,000 folders, (3.7p per copy)	Individual leaflets are placed in a pack with approx. 30 others and placed in hotal bedrooms Edinburgh to be used for reference by guests (i.e. leaflet cannot be removed).

Position in the Market

'INFORAK' will fill a niche that exists in the market at the moment. Many hotels are aware that they are not providing effective information. In many cases they have the resources and ability to obtain a display rack but would find it quite difficult to obtain a good range of tourist brochures and then to maintain stocks.

For advertisers, 'INFORAK' will fill a niche left by other distribution opportunities currently available in Edinburgh, by being the only service to get brochures into visitors' hands in city hotels, but where there is a guarantee of constant display.

In the light of the niche that has been recognized, and the emphasis on quality service for advertisers, the pricing of the product will not be based on 'costs plus'. Rather, it will be determined by what it is felt the market will take.

Price/Cost

In general, tourist attractions would expect to pay, while hosts would expect to receive the services free. There are some exceptions to this where hotels may indicate that they would be prepared to pay a 'reasonable price' for a service of this kind, particularly if the rack is purpose-built.

The fact that no one would comment on prices probably reflects the newness of the concept, and the fact that distribution and management of brochures is not regarded a *major* problem by those involved.

During the first year of operation, estimated fixed costs amount to £27,530, while the estimated total variable costs are £14,182 (total costs = £41,712). Sales revenue is forecasted at £50,000, representing a charge of £0.7356 per slot per month, amounting to £80.91 per month for 110 rack slots or £971 per year for 110 rack slots. The company expects that 20% of the potential customers will be using INFORAK only during the high season. Two cash flow forecasts (one related to a likely scenario and the other to a lower level of inflow) are presented in Exhibits 13.4 and 13.5.

Acknowledgement

The author wishes to express his gratitude to the Managing Director of INFORAK, Mr Michael Ambrose, for providing a substantial amount of information which made possible the development of this case study.

Exhibit 13.4   Cash Flow Forecast – April 1988–March 1989 – Likely Scenario

	Total 1988–89	April 1988	May	June
INCOME				
1. Grant (Scottish Tourist Board)	3,453	0	1,151	1,151
2. Sales (Inc. VAT)	48,124	0	1,421	3,535
3. Loans	4,000	4,000	0	0
4. Owner's Capital	4,000	4,000	0	0
5. Payment for VAT by Customs & Excise	1,689	0	0	0
	61,266	8,000	2,572	4,686
EXPENDITURE				
6. Stock/Materials – Racks	19,857	6,619	6,619	6,619
7. Wages – Part-time Distribution Staff	4,290	357	357	357
8. Salaries	4,039	336	336	336
9. Rent and Rates	2,600	216	216	216
10. Insurances	345	115	0	0
11. Heating and Lighting	330	0	0	55
12. Property Maintenance	0	0	0	0
13. Repairs to Plant	0	0	0	0
14. Postages	490	50	50	35
15. Telephone	460	92	0	0
16. Stationery	213	0	0	213
17. Audit and Accounts	230	0	0	0
18. Advertising	1,210	0	865	86
19. Office Equipment	1,630	0	1,286	0
20. Vehicle Lease Purchase	2,716	1,099	147	147
21. Travel Expenses – Part-time Staff	1,775	0	162	162
Travel Expenses – Proprietor	1,514	160	150	120
22. Proprietor's Remuneration	12,000	1,000	1,000	1,000
23. VAT (Payment to Customs & Excise)	3,674	0	0	0
24. Loan Charge	200	0	0	50
TOTAL	57,573	10,044	11,188	9,396
BALANCE BROUGHT FORWARD	0	0	– 2,044	– 10,660
BALANCE CARRIED FORWARD	0	– 2,044	– 10,660	– 15,370

Exhibit 13.4 *continued*

July	August	Sept	Oct	Nov	Dec	Jan 1989	Feb	March
1,151	0	0	0	0	0	0	0	0
4,812	5,091	4,956	4,999	4,863	4,652	4,576	4,643	4,576
0	0	0	0	0	0	0	0	0
0	0	0	0	0	0	0	0	0
1,689	0	0	0	0	0	0	0	0
7,652	5,091	4,956	4,999	4,863	4,652	4,576	4,643	4,576
0	0	0	0	0	0	0	0	0
357	357	357	357	357	357	357	357	363
336	336	336	336	336	336	336	336	343
216	216	216	216	216	216	216	216	224
0	115	0	0	0	115	0	0	0
0	55	0	55	0	75	0	90	0
0	0	0	0	0	0	0	0	0
0	0	0	0	0	0	0	0	0
35	35	35	35	35	45	45	45	45
178	0	0	87	0	0	103	0	0
0	0	0	0	0	0	0	0	0
0	0	0	0	0	0	0	0	230
0	0	0	58	86	0	0	0	115
344	0	0	0	0	0	0	0	0
147	147	147	147	147	147	147	147	147
161	161	161	161	161	161	161	161	161
116	100	100	110	140	140	140	120	110
1,000	1,000	1,000	1,000	1,000	1,000	1,000	1,000	1,000
0	0	0	1,882	0	0	1,792	0	0
0	0	50	0	0	50	0	0	50
2,890	2,522	2,403	4,444	2,478	2,642	4,298	2,472	
−15,370	−10,608	−8,036	−5,483	−4,928	−2,543	−533	−255	
−10,608	−8,036	−5,483	−4,928	−2,543	−533	−255		

Exhibit 13.5   Cash Flow Forecast – April 1988–March 1989 – Lower Level of Inflow

	Total 1988–89	April 1988	May	June
INCOME				
1. Grant (Scottish Tourist Board)	3,453	0	1,151	1,151
2. Sales (Inc. VAT)	46,933	0	677	2,859
3. Loans	4,000	4,000	0	0
4. Owner's Capital	4,000	4,000	0	0
5. Payment for VAT by Customs & Excise	1,689	0	0	0
	60,075	8,000	1,828	4,010
EXPENDITURE				
6. Stock/Materials – Racks	19,857	6,619	6,619	6,619
7. Wages – Part-time Distribution Staff	4,290	357	357	357
8. Salaries	4,039	336	336	336
9. Rent and Rates	2,600	216	216	216
10. Insurances	345	115	0	0
11. Heating and Lighting	330	0	0	55
12. Property Maintenance	0	0	0	0
13. Repairs to Plant	0	0	0	0
14. Postages	490	50	50	35
15. Telephones	460	92	0	0
16. Stationery	213	0	0	213
17. Audit and Accounts	230	0	0	0
18. Advertising	1,210	0	865	86
19. Office Equipment	1,630	0	1,286	0
20. Vehicle Lease Purchase	2,716	1,099	147	147
21. Travel Expenses – Part-time Staff	1,775	0	162	162
Travel Expenses – Proprietor	1,514	160	150	120
22. Proprietor's Remuneration	12,000	1,000	1,000	1,000
23. VAT (Payment to Customs & Excise)	3,674	0	0	0
24. Loan Charge	200	0	0	50
TOTAL	57,573	10,044	11,188	9,396
BALANCE BROUGHT FORWARD	0	0	– 2,004	– 11,364
BALANCE CARRIED FORWARD	57,573	– 2,004	– 11,364	– 16,750

Exhibit 13.5 *continued*

July	August	Sept	Oct	Nov	Dec	Jan 1989	Feb	March
1,151	0	0	0	0	0	0	0	0
4,745	5,024	4,956	4,999	4,889	4,812	4,711	4,711	4,550
0	0	0	0	0	0	0	0	0
0	0	0	0	0	0	0	0	0
1,689	0	0	0	0	0	0	0	0
7,585	5,024	4,956	4,999	4,889	4,812	4,711	4,711	4,550
0	0	0	0	0	0	0	0	0
357	357	357	357	357	357	357	357	363
336	336	336	336	336	336	336	336	343
216	216	216	216	216	216	216	216	224
0	115	0	0	0	115	0	0	0
0	55	0	55	0	75	0	90	0
0	0	0	0	0	0	0	0	0
0	0	0	0	0	0	0	0	0
35	35	35	35	35	45	45	45	45
178	0	0	87	0	0	103	0	0
0	0	0	0	0	0	0	0	0
0	0	0	0	0	0	0	0	230
0	0	0	58	86	0	0	0	115
344	0	0	0	0	0	0	0	0
147	147	147	147	147	147	147	147	147
161	161	162	161	161	161	162	161	161
116	100	100	110	140	140	140	120	118
1,000	1,000	1,000	1,000	1,000	1,000	1,000	1,000	1,000
0	0	0	1,882	0	0	1,792	0	0
0	0	50	0	0	50	0	0	50
2,890	2,522	2,403	4,444	2,478	2,642	4,298	2,472	2,796
− 16,750	− 12,055	− 9,553	− 7,000	− 6,445	− 4,034	− 1,864	− 1,451	788
− 12,055	− 9,553	− 7,000	− 6,445	− 4,034	− 1,864	− 1,451	788	2,542

Exhibit 13.6   Sample of Cover Letter Sent to Potential Clients

Name
Company
Address 1
Address 2
Address 3

Dear

This is to introduce INFORAK, a new company which will start operating in May 1988, and which I believe will provide a helpful new distribution service for your publicity leaflets.

INFORAK removes the 'hassle', staff resource and cost of distributing your brochures to 80 key hotels in Edinburgh and 30 in Glasgow. One delivery of brochures is all that is needed to INFORAK, who then ensure that your brochure is on show for an agreed period in display racks, each containing 54 leaflets, in hotel foyers (see photo).

INFORAK will give you the peace of mind of knowing that your leaflet is always 'up front', and you have no need to check with the hotel on the latest stock situation. It also gets your brochure into an attractive rack in a key location in the hotel, where it is visible and likely to be picked up, rather than on a table or shelf where your leaflet makes less impact.

You will be able to measure usage too, as regular reports will give you an indication of brochure uptake.

As I am keen to get your views on the new proposal, I would be grateful if you would spare me ten minutes within the next month.

I will telephone you to arrange a convenient time. I look forward to meeting you.

Yours sincerely

Michael Ambrose
Director

Exhibit 13.7 Sample of the Cover Letter Sent to Potential Distribution Outlets (Hotels)

Name
Hotel Name
Address 1
Address 2
Address 3

Dear

This is to introduce INFORAK, a new company which will start operating in May 1988, and which will provide a tourist information service, which I believe could benefit your hotel guests.

The scheme would provide a free-standing display-rack of the kind indicated on the attached photo, for the reception area of your hotel foyer, and INFORAK would regularly restock the rack with tourist brochures. The rack indicated would be provided free of charge, but more individually designed models could be made available for a small fee.

If you and your staff are regularly asked questions by guests about places to visit, where to buy certain goods, and the availability of tours, and sometimes have difficulty in giving comprehensive and accurate answers, then INFORAK will help. The display rack will contain 54 leaflets for all sorts of services and facilities of interest to your guests, which are located within one hour's journey-time of your hotel.

If you currently provide information for your guests, but have difficulty in getting hold of all the leaflets you require, or of obtaining top-up supplies, then INFORAK will help, as racks will always be kept tidy and restocked, with an INFORAK employee visiting once a week at busier periods to do this. Your staff need have no worries about obtaining leaflets – INFORAK will take care of all that.

If your information leaflets are currently laid out on shelves, counters or table tops, INFORAK will enhance the quality of the display with its attractive and visible rack.

As I am keen to get your views on the new proposal, I would be grateful if you could spare me ten minutes within the next month, to discuss it further.

I will telephone you to arrange a convenient time. I look forward to meeting you.

Yours sincerely

Michael Ambrose
Director

Exhibit 13.8   A Sample of Questionnaire Supplied to Potential Distribution Outlets (Hotels)

QUESTIONNAIRE A

HOTEL NAME . . . .

HOTEL ADDRESS . . . .

. . . .

. . . .

TELEPHONE NUMBER . . . .

PERSON CONTACTED . . . .

HOTEL CLASSIFICATION . . . .

1. How do you provide information on places to visit, shops, towns, car-hire, etc., at the moment?

(a) (i) RACK   Yes ☐   go to (a) (ii)

                                                               No ☐

(a) (ii) If YES, please describe size and style of rack

. . . .

. . . .

(b) Brochures fixed to a notice board in a public area.   Yes ☐

                                                                     No ☐

(c) Brochures laid out on a table, counter, or shelf in a public area   Yes ☐

                                                                       No ☐

(d) 'Welcome Pack' in bedroom   Yes ☐

                                                                     No ☐

(e) 'In-house' video   Yes ☐

                                                                     No ☐

(f) Nothing at all   Yes ☐

                                                                     No ☐

(g) Other

Please specify . . . .

. . . .

Exhibit 13.8 *continued*

2. If you have some information leaflets at present, how do you obtain them?

(a) Manager contacts attractions, shops, etc., when leaflets needed — Yes ☐

No ☐

(b) Reception staff contact attractions, shops, etc., when leaflets needed — Yes ☐

No ☐

(c) Porter contacts attractions, shops, etc., when leaflets needed — Yes ☐

No ☐

(d) Brochures are dropped off by attractions, shops, etc., without being requested

Yes ☐

No ☐

(e) Other (please specify) ....

....

3. Do you control the range and stock of leaflets available to your guests, or is it a question of what is made available to you?

Please specify ....

....

4. Would you welcome the installation of a display rack in your HOTEL (SHOW PHOTO/MODEL), containing 54 leaflets on places to visit, go shopping, towns, etc. within 1 hour of this hotel? The rack would be topped up regularly by INFORAK. There would be no charge for the rack.

Yes ☐

No ☐

Unsure ☐

If NO or UNSURE please give reasons ....

....

5. If NO or UNSURE in Q4 would you consider a personalized stand to your own design specification (but with INFORAK providing leaflets and regular 'topping-up')?

Yes ☐

No ☐

If YES please specify type of design requirements ....

....

Exhibit 13.8 *continued*

6. If YES to Q5 would you be prepared to pay for the cost of a personalized rack

Yes ☐

No ☐

7. Would you accept a prototype rack in your hotel for an experimental period?

Yes ☐

No ☐

8. Do you wish to make any comments about the scheme? . . . .
. . . .

Thank you for answering these questions.

CASE 14
MIT Tractors
Pricing Policy

Douglas T. Brownlie
Glasgow Business School, University of Glasgow

In 1987, the MIT tractor company entered its fourth year of manufacturing and marketing a basic four-wheel-drive overland jeep called the *Little Shifter*. Since its introduction, the company had been selling the vehicle in the United Kingdom through a network of 8 distributing agents and 12 franchised dealers. The latter also acted as sole distributors of the firm's core product, its line of agricultural tractors.

In line with the company's aim to target the jeep at what it thought to be a very price sensitive UK market, its very competitive retail price of £4,799 in the introductory year had only ever risen in line with retail inflation, at an annual rate of 5%. The product was marketed as a no-frills, but reliable and tough working vehicle that would appeal to farmers, estate managers and land owners.

As a result of mounting feedback from its dealership network, MIT has recently become sensitive to the growing market potential for an up-market version of its jeep. Seeking to react quickly to this business opportunity the company has designed the *King Shifter*. Based on the chassis and engine of the Little Shifter, the new vehicle incorporates modifications of the suspension assembly, transmission, interior decoration, fittings and body finish thought to be consistent with customer perceptions of quality. The underlying marketing theme was being geared to encourage and exploit the evolving cult status of such vehicles and their associations with a young, successful, leisure-oriented and trend-setting, but well-heeled and independent lifestyle.

The Director of Marketing is about to advise the board of the price he believes MIT should set to dealers and end customers for the King Shifter. He and his team normally have the authority to take strategic marketing decisions where their budgetary implications are at least manageable, if not known. On this occasion, however, the MIT board looks likely to set what it will consider to be a conservative target return-on-assets (ROA) of 10%, as an average to be achieved

187

over the first three years of the project. This is consistent with the hurdle rate used by the board on all MIT capital investments. Furthermore, it would not be unreasonable to expect the board's target ROA to increase dramatically in later years.

The Director of Marketing, Tony Edwards, has before him an executive summary of the factors he must consider in coming to his decision on price. This summary is reproduced in Exhibit 14.1. What price policy and strategy would you recommend that Mr Edwards set for the launch of the King Shifter? Compare and contrast possible cost and market-based pricing approaches that Mr Edwards might use.

Exhibit 14.1   Executive Summary of Price Considerations

(1) At current levels of productivity, the company has enough manufacturing capacity to produce up to 5,000 units per year of the new model.

(2) To exceed this quota by more than 20%, is expected to require investing in new plant capacity.

(3) The Director of Manufacturing is known to favour a production planning volume of 5,000 units in year one, building to full capacity in year two.

(4) The Director of Finance accepts the logic of economies of scale in production, but he will express some caution on the grounds that economies of scale in marketing may not be forthcoming if the selling-in process proves difficult. He will also stress the working capital implications of large stocks of finished goods and work-in-progress.

(5) The Total Fixed Costs (TFC) of producing and marketing the King Shifter are estimated at £5 million. This includes selling and promotional expenses, which are budgeted to account for about 10% and 15% of TFC respectively.

(6) The Total Variable Costs (TVC) are estimated at £5,000 per unit, 90% of which is accounted for by direct labour (50%) and direct materials (40%) (direct costs plus manufacturing overheads plus trade discounts and commissions).

(7) It is expected that assets of about £40 million would be employed during the first year of the launch of the King Shifter.

(8) The leading competitor of the three already in the market is producing a high-quality overland jeep which is currently retailing at £7,000. The competitor charges its dealers £5,600 per vehicle and is expecting to sell about 6,000 vehicles this year. It is estimated that the competitor's net profit margin is about £450 per vehicle. An estimated return on assets (ROA) of 5% is being achieved.

(9) At a recent trade show, the King Shifter model on display received very favourable reviews, 70% of the enquirers interviewed noting that the King Shifter seemed better designed and fitted than competing models. *Ad hoc* pricing research was conducted at the trade show on the firm's behalf. The buy-response technique was applied to a sample of non-owners/users of jeeps. The data collected was used to plot the buy-response curve of Exhibit 14.2, which shows the price above which the propensity to purchase might fall off.

(10) A group of industry analysts often used by the MIT board has projected 1988 sales of leisure-oriented jeeps at 12,000 units. This represents an expected growth rate of 40% on 1987 sales. A 50% average rate of growth is thought likely to persist into the early 1990s as younger car owners switch to status-giving vehicles and new market segments continue to evolve.

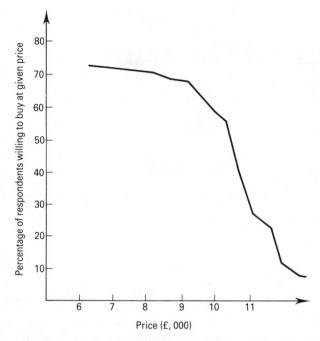

Exhibit 14.2 *Customer Response to Various Price Points.*

CASE 15
POK Electronic Systems
Pricing Policy

Luiz Moutinho
Glasgow Business School, University of Glasgow

Introduction

In July 1982, POK Electronic Systems faced a major pricing decision with respect to its new teleconferencing system. 'We're really excited here at POK Electronic Systems', exclaimed Mr Paul Kruger, the founder and president of POK Electronic Systems. 'We've made a most significant technological breakthrough in telecommunication systems.' He went on to explain that the marketing plan for 1983 for this product was now his major area of concern, and that what price to charge was the marketing question that was giving him the most difficulty.

Company History

POK Electronic Systems was founded in Glasgow, Scotland, in 1977 by Mr Kruger. Prior to that time Mr Kruger had been a senior lecturer in electrical engineering at one of the local universities. Mr Kruger founded POKES to manufacture and market products making use of some of the electronic inventions he had developed while at the university. Sales were made mostly to the car industry and the military. Sales grew from £200,000 in 1978 to £14 million in 1981. Profits in 1981 were £2.6 million.

The Teleconferencing System Project

During the last four years, Mr Kruger had been trying to reduce the company's dependency on government and auto-manufacturers' sales. One of the diversification projects to which he had committed research and development investment was the so-called TCS – teleconferencing system project. The objective of this project was to develop a system whereby a television picture, which could be displayed on a screen as big as 8 to 10 feet diagonally, could be used for small to medium-sized meetings and conferences within corporations and different types of institutions. By installing this system in different locations, executives are enabled to conduct their business meetings without having to move out of their offices. In the area of information technology, there is a growing trend towards the utilization of value added networks, such as the teleconferencing system. In late 1981, one of POKES's engineers made the necessary breakthrough. The rest of 1981 and the first few months of 1982 were spent producing working prototypes. Up until June 1982, POKES had invested £400,000 in the project.

Teleconferencing

Teleconferencing – a new concept in which meetings are conducted before a camera and relayed via satellite to video screens in several locations simultaneously – is changing the way a number of corporations and associations do business.

Teleconferencing will not replace the business meeting nor will it take the place of the rapport and personal interaction of businessmen and women meeting together. It's not a replacement, it's a complement, a supplement.

Clearly, something is afoot. In view of all the current activity, and the strong opinions about teleconferencing – pro and con – it seems necessary to attempt an informed assessment of the new medium.

Is teleconferencing here to stay, or merely the latest technological hula-hoop? Teleconferencing is not entirely new. The technology which permits satellite communications has been with us for almost 20 years. Only recently has it become economically feasible to use the technology on a mass scale.

The history of most new technologies follows a similar pattern. Initially, the new technology is too expensive and too bulky in size to be practical for anything other than large business, government and institutional use.

Pocket calculators, for instance, originally sold for many times their present cost. Computers were once huge in size and economically practical only for multimillion pound operations. Now they are priced within the reach of small businesses and households, and can fit on table tops.

Such is the consistent history of technological innovations. Being the first buyer of new technology is not necessarily the best position to be in.

The superlatives and underlying sense of excitement surrounding teleconferencing today have a familiar ring. In the 1950s and early 1960s, similar words were used to tout Closed Circuit Television (CCTV) as the next great advance in business meetings.

'Users in every part of the country report savings in travel and other expenses', said an RCA executive at that time, 'when television has been utilized to bring together their staffs in regular conventions or for special occasions such as the kick-off of a new product. They also have lauded the effectiveness and impact that results when meetings are televised to remote locations, thus enabling field men to receive the "word" direct and simultaneously from top management rather than secondhand from travelling teams. . . .'

Even the term 'teleconference' was first used in reference to CCTV. As early as 1952, CCTV was being used for a variety of events: heavyweight prize fights, the Metropolitan Opera, Broadway shows, medical and educational seminars, fund raising, government and trade association meetings, stockholders' meetings, new product introductions, press conferences, dealer and salesmen meetings.

CCTV did not gain wide acceptance for broadcasts beyond special events primarily because it was not cost-effective. The cost of telephone land line transmission was expensive, and satellite transmission was limited and financially prohibitive at that time as well.

AT&T's Picturephone – telephones that transmit both voices and the faces of callers – is another example of communications technology that did not gain the mass acceptance first predicted for it.

Originally introduced and demonstrated at the 1964 World's Fair, Picturephone was launched with great fanfare. In 1970, the company predicted that by 1975 the service would have 70,000 sets in use in 30 cities. By the 1980s, AT&T speculated, Picturephones would be widely used by business and the general public, replacing some forms of transportation.

The analysts were wrong. Picturephone as originally conceived was a commercial failure, not because of its technology, but because of its high cost. 'Cost, and cost alone', was the problem, said former AT&T Chairman John De Butts in an interview. 'Those sets each costs us a bundle to manufacture. Don't forget that a Picturephone has everything in it that the camera in a TV studio has, along with all the works that are in your home TV receiver – all in a compact desktop unit.'

Initially, AT&T concentrated on selling the service to businesses, institutions and other large customers in a few major cities, including New York, Washington, San Francisco, Chicago, and Pittsburgh; but the installation charges proved higher than most firms would pay, and not enough subscribers signed up to establish a practical network.

With new technologies, history has shown that caution is a wise and necessary response.

The new telecommunications technology permits teleconferencing to be offered to large businesses and associations as a cost-effective tool that delivers more for less and in less time. This is the reason why big business and associations are the prime movers behind the early use of teleconferencing.

It appears that every company or association that has had the teleconferencing experience has nothing but praise for it. Most users report time and money saved, ease and effectiveness of presentation, and a dramatic increase in the number of participants reached.

In October 1980, Symposiums International (SI), a Los Angeles based medical educational company, used the HiNet system to reach thousands of nurses in 77 cities. Noel Reede, President of SI, said the teleconference was an outstanding success. 'During one four-hour period we were able to put a distinguished team of doctors and nurses in front of thousands of nursing specialists, giving them the opportunity to learn the latest techniques in emergency nursing from some of the medical profession's top performers.

'The introduction of our promotion was a smashing success', said Daniel McMaken of North American Van Lines. The HiNet Communications concept gave us the opportunity to announce our new programme to our agent family without the expense of either touring the country to visit a number of locations with a small entourage of corporate personnel, or bringing the agents together at a single location for a two-hour presentation.

'We have to figure out the right formula to make teleconferencing profitable for all parties', says Gary Badoud, president of VideoNet, and the man who almost single-handedly started the rapid growth of satellite video teleconferencing.

Because of the tremendous savings teleconferencing offers the corporate world, Badoud says, trying to stop teleconferencing at this point would be 'like putting your shoulder to a glacier'.

Teleconferencing System Designed for World Use

A teleconferencing system designed to meet worldwide transmission standards has been developed by Compression Labs Inc., San José, California. Called REMBRANDT, the system offers full-motion video teleconferencing on bandwidths that give users a choice of picture quality and transmission cost.

International teleconferencing is possible because the system offers conversion between National Television Standards Code video used in the United States, Canada and Japan, and Phased Alternative Line video used in Europe, South America, the Middle and Far East.

The system also offers RGB, the worldwide video standard for graphics that are of high quality.

Additional features include higher resolution graphics and video switching for Simulvision, an option that allows the display of two or more video images at the same time, and extended network line communications.

Compression Labs, a publicly held company, designs, manufactures and markets full-motion colour video teleconferencing systems for use by business, government, and other organizations.

Among its customers are AT&T Information Systems, ITT Europe, Sony Corp., US Telecom and Vitalink Communications.

Video Screen Television

Extra large screen television systems were not new. There were a number of companies who sold such systems both to the consumer and commercial (pubs, restaurants, discos, and so on) markets. Most current systems made use of a special magnifying lens that projected a regular small television picture on to a special screen. The result of this process is that the final picture lacked much of the brightness of the original small screen. As a result, the picture had to be viewed in a darkened room. There were some other video systems that did not use the magnifying process. These systems used special tubes, but also suffered from a lack of brightness.

POKES developed a system that was bright enough to be viewed in regular daylight on a screen up to 10 feet diagonal and this was complemented with an innovative multi-person audio system for teleconferencing. This process was protected by patent, and Mr Kruger thought it would take at least two to three years for any competitor to duplicate the results of the system.

A number of large and small corporations were active in this area. Admiral, GEC, RCA, Zenith Electronics, Sony and Philips were all thought to be working on developing large screen systems directed at the consumer market. Sony was rumoured to be ready to introduce a 60-inch diagonal screen system that would retail for about £2,000. A number of small companies were already producing similar systems although without the multi-person audio unit which was tailored for teleconferencing purposes. PRIMETECH, a small East Anglia company, claimed to have sold 3,500, 84-inch diagonal units in two years at a £3,000 price. SOLO Electronics claimed one-year sales of 4,000 50-inch diagonal units at prices from £1,000 to £2,000. Mr Kruger was adamant that none of these systems gave as bright a picture as POKES's and that no other company came up with the idea of applying the core system to the potential market area of the teleconferencing business. He estimated that about 10,000 large-screen systems were sold in 1981.

Cost Structure

Mr Kruger was analysing the possibility of using a well-known industrial distributor to market the new system. This move would permit POKES to minimize some marketing costs as well as to provide a wider market coverage since this particular distributor had a strong customer base, salesforce, and also provided after-sales service. Mr Kruger expected about 50% of the suggested final selling price to go for the distributor's margin. He expected that POKES's direct manufacturing costs would vary depending on the volume produced. Exhibit 15.1 presents these estimates. He expected direct labour costs to fall at higher production volumes due to the increased automation of the process and improved worker skills.

Exhibit 15.1   *Estimated production costs of POKES's teleconferencing system.*

	Volume		
	0–5,000	5,001–10,000	10,001–20,000
Raw materials	£400	£380	£350
Direct labour	£450	£400	£200
Total direct costs	£850	£780	£550

Material costs were expected to fall due to less waste due to automation. The equipment costs necessary to automate the product process were £50,000 to produce in the 0–5,000 unit range, an additional £30,000 to produce in the 5,001–10,000 unit range, and an additional £20,000 to produce in the 10,001–20,000 unit range. The useful life of this equipment was put at five years. Mr Kruger was sure that production costs were substantially below those of current competitors including Sony; such was the magnitude of POKES's technological breakthrough. Mr Kruger was unwilling to produce over 20,000 units a year in the first few years due to the limited cash resources of the company to support inventories, and so on.

Market Studies

Mr Kruger wanted to establish a position in the business market for his product. He felt that the long-run potential for this market was greater there than in the consumer market. With this end in mind he hired a small marketing research consulting firm based in London to undertake a business market study to determine the likely reaction to alternative final selling prices for the system. These consultants undertook extensive interviews with corporate executives of potential purchasing organizations, and examined the sales and pricing histories of similar competitive products. They concluded that: 'POKES's teleconferencing system would be highly price elastic across a range of prices from £2,000 to £5,000'. They went on to estimate the price elasticity of demand in this range to be between 2.5 and 4.0.

The Pricing Decision

Mr Kruger was considering a number of alternative final selling prices. 'I can see arguments for pricing in order to skim the market or to penetrate the market and gain a foothold in the future', he said.

CASE 16

Kilroy Products
Advertising Management

Luiz Moutinho
Glasgow Business School, University of Glasgow

Company Background

In 1960, Mike Wilson, a used car salesman, invented the first self-adhering body-side mouldings for the automotive industry. With major financial and moral support from the major automobile manufacturers, he established Custom Trim Products in 1965. The company developed into an international firm, and was sold in 1977 for an undisclosed amount.

With these newly acquired financial resources, Mike and his three sons established a company called Global Resources, based in Manchester, England. Its primary function was to seek out individuals holding valuable patents. The company would provide funds for all aspects of placing an individual product or service on the market.

In 1979, Global Resources became incorporated as Kilroy Products to produce and market adjustable bicycle handlebars. This first venture was a failure and losses exceeded £300,000.

With the company's financial resources being drained, they began to take a closer look at a product that one of the sons had invented. As an avid sportsman and hunter, Peter realized the need to protect his guns while hunting. By June of 1981, a vinyl gun cover was produced. The original prototype was very archaic in style and design, but it was functionable. The covers were named Gun Pals.

In 1984, Kilroy's gross sales were approximately £500,000: 90% of the sales were attributed to the sale of 50,000 Gun Pals, 7% from Gun Wrap, and the remaining 3% from holsters, duffle bags and back packs. Projected sales for 1985 were £750,000.

Introduction of Gun Pals

Gun Pals is a unique product and a technological breakthrough for the hunting industry. Its major feature is to protect firearms while hunting. They fit the gun like a glove and don't interfere with the working parts. There is no other similar product on the market.

Prior to the introduction, the three managers of the company, John, Peter and Matthew Wilson, initiated a market study to determine if there actually was a demand for this product. Some of the most prominent dealers and distributors in the industry were personally interviewed. Through this study, several important facts were discovered. Aside from protection, the potential buyers suggested camouflage colours to protect hunters from the keen eyesight of wild animals. Guns are not standardized in dimension and function, therefore, several models would have to be produced. The dealers informed them of the top 10 selling guns. Buyers felt consumers would pay anywhere between £5 and £80 for such a product. Most important, 100% of the interviewed sample felt the product would be a big seller.

Timing was a crucial factor. Hunting supply sales are at peak from September to March. They decided to introduce the product to the buyers at a major trade show to be held in January 1982. Ignorant to the hunting industry, and unable to produce in mass quantities, Kilroy displayed the Gun Pals at the show. Orders in the amount of £50,000 were placed at the show.

Pricing

Kilroy Products wanted to penetrate the market. Initially, a £19.95 retail price was established. Working backwards from this price, dealers would pay £14.95, and the price to jobbers was £9.95. At these prices, per unit profits were very low. Realizing that this profit margin did not allow for trade allowances, which were commonplace in the industry, the price was increased £2.00 across the board.

The first year in business was not profitable. The £300,000 earned in sales was insufficient to cover costs. As a result, prices were restructured. This entailed a 30% increase.

Market Potential and Strategies

In the United Kingdom and overseas markets, there are three ways for Kilroy to reach the ultimate consumer. The first is the formal distribution channel: manufacturer, to jobber, to dealer, to consumer – 10% of the consumers in the industry purchase through dealers. Jobbers selling through mail-order catalogues is the second method. One of the largest catalogue companies, HES, has a distribution of approximately 8 million – 25% of the consumers purchase through mail order. The final approach is mass merchandisers – 65% of the consumers purchase through these outlets.

Currently, 50% of Kilroy's sales are coming from mail-order jobbers, 45% from the formal channel, 5% from direct sale to consumers. Reaching the mass merchandisers is one of the company's future goals.

The managers of Kilroy feel that establishing a good communication flow with current and potential buyers is an extremely important issue in marketing the products they sell. They attend two trade shows per year, and frequently attend hunting trips sponsored by well-known companies in the industry.

Eight manufacturer representative groups represent Kilroy Products throughout the United Kingdom. They have no in-house salesforce. However, they provide a toll-free number to all customers for order placing, enquiries, questions or problems. Peter, the product's inventor, is responsible for all sales and marketing functions.

Other potential markets include law enforcement agencies, the military and foreign countries. Kilroy has received enquiries from all of the above. Several sales have been made, but nothing major.

The market for gun covers is very large. Kilroy has only captured a very small portion. For example, approximately 3 million guns are produced annually in the United Kingdom. Of course, not all guns made and sold need protection. However, if a consumer spends anywhere from £300 to £3,000 on a gun with which he intends to hunt, £25 is not an unrealistic amount to spend on protecting it – 50% of all Gun Pals are sold for a £400 to £600 rifle, known as a BSA CF2.

Competition

John, the company Chief Executive, feels there is no competition for Gun Pals: 'No one competes with us for protection'.

Protection is the product's major feature, however, it also camouflages the gun. Two other products on the market are designed to camouflage guns. The first is a masking tape that wraps around the gun. The disadvantage of using this product is that it is time consuming. After each application, one must clean the sticky residue off the gun, which in turn damages the gun's finish. The other product is a camouflage paint. It has similar disadvantages.

John is not ignorant of the competition. Sooner or later someone will try to copy the product. They are protected by a patent, which they are willing and ready to defend. Since the product is in the introduction stage, competition is not expected for another two years, although there are rumours that Barbour is planning to launch a line of gun slips and covers within a price range between £22.00 and £43.00. Also, another manufacturer – Beaver – is trying to tap the low end of the market by developing a line of gun bags which would sell at between £5.00 and £18.00.

Advertising

In an attempt to determine initial demand and advertising impact, Kilroy placed coded coupon advertisements in several trade and consumer publications. Enquiries were scattered, nevertheless, a certain level of awareness started to develop. Dealers began calling because consumers were asking for the product. They were successful in their pulling strategy.

Upon request, Kilroy provided a price sheet and a leaflet advertising the product. It was later observed that this ad. was too cluttered, colour reproduction was poor, and the person viewing the ad. was not really certain as to what was being sold. During 1982 £50,000 was spent on these ads.

Most of the advertising budget is spent in magazine advertisements. A combination of reach and frequency strategy is used. Consumer publications geared to sporting and hunting, such as *Air Gunner* (monthly) and *Shooting Times* (weekly), carry 75% of the magazine ads.; 25% of the ads. appear in trade publications such as *Sporting Gun*. Ads. appear in three different magazines per month, this amounts to 36 ads. per year. Most ads. are black and white and half-page in size. The ads. are designed to create awareness as well as to inform the reader. The 1985 advertising budget has been increased to £100,000.

R.S. Advertising, a Manchester based, four-star rated agency, handles Kilroy's advertising. R.S. is well known in the industry and has helped Kilroy in many areas. Many magazines have featured Gun Pals and Kilroy Products in their 'new product' sections, giving them needed publicity. Also, R.S. has been able to place Kilroy Products on the front cover of several magazines.

Packaging

The original package for Gun Pals was poorly designed. The appearance shared the same problems as the first advertisement. Another problem was that consumers were opening the boxes and removing the merchandise. Dealers were unable to distinguish which parts belonged to which boxes. Also, boxes became worn, creating a 'used' appearance.

In 1984, the package was redesigned. It now appears in a blister pack with a less cluttered message. An attractive feature is the cross-reference chart on the back of the package, which enables consumers to determine which part number is needed, as well as availability of other covers.

The actual cost per unit package was increased with the blister introduction. However, the machine purchased for packaging is 600% more effective, which reduced per unit labour costs significantly. The higher package supply cost will be balanced by the reduction in labour costs. Hence, per unit costs will remain the same.

One of the largest problems Kilroy faces is the significant drop in cash flow during the summer months. Since sales are slow most of the cash is tied up in inventory. Also, the company is uncertain as to which part number to manufacture and stock in inventory. Trend analysis is not a very valuable method because of the rapid growth rate. A possibility being considered is an incentive programme for buyers to order early or inform Kilroy about their orders early enough. Nevertheless, the company has established efficient inventory control, as one of its short-term goals.

Kilroy Products is looking forward to a profitable growth period. Its major advertising and marketing goal, which is supported by its strategies, is to increase consumer awarenesses.

The company possesses many strengths. There are adequate financial resources which have and will continue to permit the company to make any necessary capital investments. The company's managers are experienced in establishing businesses, and each one has a very defined role in specialized areas of the company. The company is very quality oriented and will not sacrifice quality for profit.

There are several observed and not so obvious weaknesses. It appears that many of the company's strategies were developed through trial and error. Perhaps better methods of research should be implemented. Family owned and operated businesses, in general, are very limited. Most of the ideas, strategies and planning are limited to the knowledge of a group of individuals having basically the same background. Since the company is privately held, there may be a lack of incentive to reinvest profits, limiting the company's potential because of personal goals.

All in all, the company's strengths appear to outweigh its weaknesses.

John, Peter and Matthew were concerned about the advertising copy and scheduling strategies to be used in future campaigns, as well as about the costs and overall effectiveness of Kilroy's advertising. Furthermore, they would like to plan specific push strategies to be implemented in order to capture dealers' cooperation.

CASE 17
The Langport Building Society
Advertising Management

Arthur Meidan and Tom Lloyd
School of Management and Economic Studies, University of Sheffield

Introduction

Mike Clark, the marketing manager for the Langport Building Society was engaged in planning an advertising campaign to attract depositors' funds to the Society. The Langport was an old-established society which, in spite of a soberly conservative image, had reached and held, with its £2,500 million assets a position just outside the top ten in order of size of building societies. The problem that faced it was the recurring one of shortage of funds to meet the demands for mortgages, even at the current borrowers interest rate of 14½%. It was calculated that a further £50 million in deposits was necessary to clear the waiting list of acceptable mortgage applications before the expected fall in interest rates, which the Government was being urged from all sides to initiate, brought about an increase in demand for mortgages.

The Board had decided, and Mike had concurred, that a new high interest share be instituted, paying a guaranteed 2½% above the standard Paid Up Share interest which was currently at 8¼%. The new share was provisionally named the Topshare for purposes of internal communications but the final decision on the name under which it was to be marketed had yet to be made.

There had been dissenting voices raised at the Board meeting. Most of the objections arose out of perennial deeply-felt concerns over the fundamental objectives of the Society but Mike was rather nettled by some contributions to preliminary discussions over the projected advertising campaign to launch the new share. One director had quoted a recent article to the effect that the Cranston Building Society, Langport's nearest rival, had a higher market share in terms of deposits but had a lower market share of advertising expenditure than did Langport. This led to comments on the tone of Langport's recent TV advertisements which seemed to portray both Langport's depositors and borrowers as seedy comic characters. There was clearly some indignation felt: 'Makes us look as if we are laundering the proceeds of petty crime!'; 'Should we be subsidizing self-indulgent out-of-work film directors?'; 'An insult to our members!', etc. Mike defended the TV advertisements. A respected consultant had advised that there was a trend among aspiring under-30s to regard 'bounded disreputableness' as rather chic. It was to reach this segment, under-represented among Langport members, that an experimental approach had been tried. Mike continued: 'I concede we may have been ahead of the times; innovators usually are! However, that same article pointed out that our branches are bringing in an average of over £9 million each in savings yearly compared with Cranston's average of £7.5 million. That seems to validate our overall strategy!' (See Langport and Cranston balance sheets in Exhibit 17.1 and demographic distribution of Langport depositors in Exhibit 17.2.)

Mike had been instructed to produce a Topshare advertising plan, designed to bring in £50 million extra deposits and he had started by considering the product as envisaged by the Board.

Exhibit 17.1   Current Langport Building Society Balance Sheet

Liabilities and reserves	*£'000*
Shares	2,211,354
Deposits and loans	257,150
Taxation and other liabilities	70,205
Deferred tax	2,834
General reserve	99,892
	2,641,435

Assets	
Mortgages	2,109,946
Investments and cash	494,465
Fixed assets	35,208
Other assets	1,816
	2,641,435

Investors' Balances, Liabilities and Reserves	*£'000*
Shares	2,624,194
Deposits and loans	599,587
Taxation and other liabilities	56,186
Deferred taxation	7,541
General reserve	128,007
Reserve for future taxation	37,135
	3,452,650

Assets	
Mortgages	2,109,946
Investments and cash	494,465
Fixed assets	35, 208
Other assets	1, 816
	2,641,435

Exhibit 17.2 *Results of an in-house sample survey of characteristics of Langport depositors compared with the population of England and Wales at large.*

	Langport depositors (%)	Population of UK (%)
Male	58	49
Female	42	51
Age groups		
15–24	16	19
25–34	10	18
35–44	11	15
45–54	18	16
55–64	21	14
65+	24	18
Socio-economic groups		
AB	15	13
C1	38	19
C2	37	34
DE	10	37

The Product

Topshares presented considerable attractions to depositors:

(1) The current interest rate of 10.75%, basic rate income tax paid with compounding half-yearly interest giving 11.04% provided return unbeatable in the building society field. Even though interest rates fell these shares would give a high yield relative to investments of comparable securities.

(2) Topshares combined high returns with high liquidity at a modest cost. Ninety days' notice was required for withdrawal but deposits could be withdrawn immediately at a penalty of 90 days' interest on the sum withdrawn. Indeed, for accounts with more than £5,000 left after the withdrawal, no penalty was imposed.

(3) The sober image and practices of Langport convey an impression of security to depositors.

(4) The rather low minimum deposit of £1,000 made it attractive to depositors with modest sums of long-term savings to invest. If anything, Topshares were too attractive to institutional investors and to reduce the burden of interest payments it was decided to limit the maximum investment in these shares to £50,000. Further, the shares term was limited to two years.

The Marketing Plan

Mike started drafting out the marketing plan for presentation to the Board. So far he had written:

Marketing Objectives

(1) To improve the volume of deposits into Langport.
(2) To position Langport clearly and competitively within the savings market.
(3) To encourage increased holdings among existing users.
(4) To decrease the rate of withdrawal.

Advertising Objectives

(1) To present Langport Topshares as an attractive investment for private individuals, and for organizations, with up to £50,000 to save by drawing attention to the highly competitive interest rate and assured liquidity.

At this point he stopped. What did they want the advertising not to do? Certainly they didn't want to alienate existing customers as the previous campaign had apparently done, but what other traps did they want to avoid?

His mind drifted to what was, for him, the more congenial task of thinking over concrete, specific details – £50 million, about equivalent to a fortnight's deposits. It could be done but it wouldn't be cheap. He reached for the current issue of *BRAD* and started jotting down notes.

	Circulation (in millions)	Cost per insertion
Daily Mail	(1.8)	SCC £90 run of week option (35 cm × 6 columns per page)
Daily Mirror	(3.2)	£29,700 fixed day (whole page) £28,000 2-day option
Guardian	(0.3)	£14,000 whole page
The Times	(0.2)	£10,304 whole page
Daily Telegraph	(1.3)	£20,607 whole page
Observer	(0.4)	£17,500 whole page
Sunday Times	(1.2)	£29,000 whole page
Sunday Telegraph	(0.75)	£15,200 whole page
Yorkshire Post	(0.3)	£3,089 whole page

(SCC = Standard Column Centimetre)

He thought for a moment. Past experience suggested that they would have to be good, or lucky, to raise £100 deposits per £1 advertising expenditure. He continued thinking: 'Assume 33⅓% decay per insertion.'

He turned the pages of *BRAD*, making notes:

Thames	Mon–Fri 5.40–10.40 30 seconds £12,400
	Non-pre-emptible fixed spots: 75% surcharge
	Possible packages at half basic rate
Anglia	5.25–10.25 £7,500 30 seconds non-pre-emptible
Channel 4	£5,000 ditto
Tyne Tees	£7,500 ditto

He continued musing: What was it that consultant said? Something about blinkers as far as advertising was concerned? What about an airship trailing a banner?. . . Be serious! He turned the pages: 'National Solusites 16-sheet display at 775 sites at major shopping areas or on main roads leading to them £27–34 thousand depending on time of year.'

He then turnend to NRS material and to other handbooks (see Exhibits 17.3 and 17.4).

He continued for some hours, making occasional phone calls. Deciding the final marketing name of the share was a problem but he had set in motion a brainstorming session to come up with a short-list of possible names for consideration. Now it was a matter of getting down to the number crunching. But not just yet: there were things that might have to be rethought. And there might be something that had been missed. For example, he kept thinking about an inter-jection overheard from a noisy good-humoured political argument in a corner of the staff restaurant that day: 'You are way behind the times! The proles are already bourgeoisified: 14% of privatization shares bought by individuals, not companies, were brought by DE people!'

Perhaps it was necessary to go back to basics, asking simple questions.

A pilot survey indicated that questions related to marital status might be too sensitive to allow for a satisfactory response rate and investigation of those variables was not proceeded with. Geographical distribution of depositors was outside the scope of the survey: adequate information on that score was already in the Society's records. Broadly speaking Langport was strong in the North, fairly strong in the industrial conurbations of the Midlands but significantly less strong in the South.

Exhibit 17.3 *Socio-economic aspects of newspaper readership.*

Newspapers	Percentage of readers who are ABC1	Percentage of ABC1 population who are readers
The Times	85	5
Daily Mail	56	18
Guardian	79	7
Daily Telegraph	81	16
Daily Mirror	24	18

Source: N.R.S.

Exhibit 17.4   Extracts from Mike's Jottings

Percentages for households reached by ITV is socio-economically identical with the percentage for total UK households.

(Source: BARB)

Personal income   Percentage of population with income > £10,000, by region

North	26.3	Rest of South-East	35.9
Yorkshire and Humberside	30.3	South-West	27.3
East Midlands	30.4	West Midlands	24.9
East Anglia	26.1	North-West	28.2
Greater London	29.4		

(Regional Trends)

Average personal income taking into account housing subsidies, etc.

Bottom quartile	£3,960 p.a.
Middle quartile	£6,920 p.a.
Top quartile	£15,450 p.a.

Top 1% has 6% of income; bottom 50% has 22.7% of income   (Social Trends)

Percentage of adult population with building society accounts 64%
1978   43%   1968   15%

Percentage of adult population with National Savings Bank accounts 7%
1978   18%   1968   37%

Percentage of adults with TSB accounts   12%
1978   17%   1968   18%

Percentage of adults reading national daily newspapers by region

Paper	North, Y & H	E & W Midlands	E. Anglia & SE	Greater London	SW & Wales	NW
Sun	23	30	27	30	28	18
Daily Mirror	25	30	21	24	22	26
Daily Mail	7	9	14	14	11	9
Daily Telegraph	3	5	9	7	7	5
Guardian	2	2	5	8	2	4
The Times	1	2	5	6	3	1

Commenting later on the probable validity of the survey, a newly appointed director with a strong statistical background said the survey was 'methodologically unsophisticated' but probably didn't seriously distort the overall picture.

CASE 18
Avis Rent-A-Car Limited
Distribution Management

Anthony W. Dnes
University of Buckingham

Introduction

Avis is a world-wide operation, initially established in 1946, in the United States, by Warren E. Avis who opened in Detroit with just three cars. Today it operates 3,500 locations in over 100 countries with an estimated fleet of 265,000 vehicles. Around 21,000 employees work in the international Avis system. Franchising was adopted early in the history of the US parent company.

Avis Rent-a-Car Limited was formed in 1965 to develop car rental in the United Kingdom. It did not adopt franchising until 1984. However, expansion through franchised outlets has been rapid and there are now 53 of these as well as 70 company-owned rental stations (1988). Company outlets are located at airports and disproportionately in the South-East of England. Avis hopes to add 25 franchisees a year together with a few directly owned outlets. Avis belongs to the British Franchise Association. There is also a franchisee association which was set up by Avis.

Strategic Issues

The company's current strategy is one of expansion into previously neglected local markets for car hire. According to data which Avis supplied for this case study, in 1986, out of a total UK rental market worth £275 million, Avis had an 11.5% share. However, the share was more like 30% for national business rentals, and just 2.5% for local business and leisure use. Of the total market, about two-thirds is local hire business which is mostly covered by small, local firms. Avis has decided that it wishes to increase its penetration of local markets and is using locally based entrepreneurs as franchisees to achieve this. Current marketing strategy is to alter the positioning of the Avis brand name. Rental fleets consist of cars and light vans. About 75% of any outlet's fleet will comprise cars.

Avis's policy is generally to seek franchisees who will operate single-use sites under its logo. Some motor dealers do operate a franchise as part of a larger operation and some franchisees find that they can most easily rent a site which is part of a service station. Multiple franchisees are not ruled out by Avis but the preference is for 'hands-on' franchisees, as this is expressed by Mr Tony Brewer, the Licensee Relations Manager. Avis prefers to have a large number of franchisees rather than have whole areas of the country tied up by one franchisee. The fear is that a large multiple franchisee would operate in a manner detrimental to the interests of Avis and of other franchisees.

Nature of the Franchise

Avis offers a full business-format franchise with manuals covering all operating, sales and administrative procedures. A computerized administrative system (Wizard) which links with centralized Avis reservations, is also being made available for franchisees. No financial assistance is given to franchisees and Avis in fact regards their independent ability to raise finance as an important part of the selection procedure. A finance scheme specially tailored to Avis franchisees has been developed by the National Westminister Bank and preferential leasing arrangements are available from major companies like Ford Motor Credit. Franchisees are directed to this. Avis can show its owned outlets as working models for franchisees.

Mr Brewer sees franchisees' obligations as honouring the franchise agreement, and maintaining service levels at least equal to those of the company-owned stations. In turn, he sees Avis as providing technical and product innovation, giving marketing and operational support, and using purchasing expertise to obtain good fleet and insurance deals for franchisees.

A franchisee essentially receives the rights to operate under the Avis brand name, to use centralized booking arrangements, and to participate in a system of one-way vehicle hire. The Avis franchise system is illustrated in Exhibit 18.1, where dotted lines are used to show trading links over which franchisees have free choice, and where arrowheads show the direction of sales. No product is sold by Avis. Franchisees may choose to use company supply lines to hire or to purchase vehicles from manufacturers, and in particular from the Ford Motor Company. The lease arrangements are particularly attractive with manufacturers being very keen to place their cars into hire fleets as a promotional device. The cars are leased for 10,000 miles over three to nine months. The boxes showing the rental market in Exhibit 18.1 show the segmentation of internationally and nationally generated rentals into business and leisure hirers in the approximate proportions in which these arise. In addition, the franchisees are shown to be more involved in local as opposed to international business. Strictly speaking, the franchisee is not free to choose whether to service any particular customer, as he must accept centrally

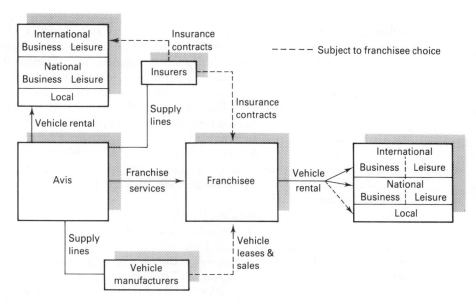

Exhibit 18.1   *Avis franchise system.*

booked and nationally negotiated hires and must service cars rented on the one-way systems.

The Franchise Relationship

Avis uses a written franchise agreement to clarify its relationship with franchisees. This specifies the marketing and operating support which is provided, the fees that are charged for franchise services, the monitoring of franchisee quality that Avis undertakes and the network systems in which the franchisee participates. It is a minimal agreement which does not try to legislate for every eventuality.

Essentially, the franchisee agrees to work to Avis operating standards, to participate in a system of one-way vehicle rental and to report his rental turnover (time and mileage plus collision-damage-waiver fees) at monthly intervals. He pays a sales royalty and a lump-sum initial franchise fee. In addition, the franchisee agrees to spend 2.5% of his time and mileage charges on local advertising; as part of this, standardized Yellow-Pages and telephone-directory entries must be placed.

Avis undertakes to promote the brand name nationally, to help the franchisee with vehicle and insurance procurement, to be available for consultation, and to supply all brand-name-specific displays, stationery and uniforms for the franchisee's use.

The franchisee always agrees upon an initial vehicle fleet and a plan for its growth when setting up with Avis. Hire rates are not fixed, however, for this would be illegal under UK competition law. The franchisee does abide by internal transfer prices for vehicles hired on the one-way system, under which they may be left at an outlet from which they did not originate and may then be used by the receiving station, preferably as a means to make a return journey. The renting company (Avis or a franchisee) must pay 60% of time and mileage charges to the owning company. This discourages a station from holding on to a one-way vehicle. The franchisee services vehicles which are in his area if required to do so by Avis or another franchisee, even if they are not his own; the franchisee is paid for such work at rates agreed from time to time.

The franchisee may leave Avis by giving six months' notice of his intention to do so. The franchisor's grounds for termination of the franchise agreement cover breach of any contractual term by the franchisee, the latter's insolvency and any case of substandard operation.

Apart from the written agreement the franchise relationship is subject to a number of understandings which have developed over time.

First, there is an expectation that the franchisor will undertake a significant amount of national advertising, although technically this is at the franchisor's discretion. In the 1986–87 financial year, £0.5 million was spent. The figure was reached by Avis using a task-and-method approach, where expenditure is set to meet certain advertising objectives (for example television exposure to be equal to that of rivals). The feeling at Avis is that large expenditures are required as part of a means of keeping good franchisees in the network and attracting new ones.

Secondly, there is an expectation held by the franchisor that franchisees will operate vehicles meeting Avis quality standards. This is the 'no-lemons principle', as Mr Brewer puts it, referring to the exclusion of cheap, low-quality cars from the business on this criterion. While the maintenance of standards is emphasized in the agreement, particular details of this kind are not spelt out and rely on a subsequent informal understanding.

Thirdly, it is accepted that Avis will take part in the selection of a franchisee's personnel. This is a strong addition to control over management appointments, which relates only to the managing director and operations manager, provided for in Section II of the agreement. Normally this involvement in selection arises when Avis offers the assistance of its district managers or franchising personnel to the franchisee.

Finally, it is understood that Avis vehicles may be used by a new franchisee at uncontrolled local rates until his business begins to be established. Then they may be used only at national Avis rates. This represents a little initial support for the franchisee and will be applied in a discretionary manner by Avis's regional managers. Franchisees confirmed the existence of this initial help.

Monitoring of the franchise network is fully integrated with that of company outlets. Daily conduct of the business is observed by district managers, on average about once a month in the case of franchisees. Apart from the requirement in the agreement for monthly performance reporting, copies of each day's rental agreements are sent into a franchisee's district office. For the first three months of operations copies also go to the head office in Hayes.

Mr Brewer feels that the agreement should not be continually quoted at franchisees but, rather, it should exist as a last resort to clarify issues in a business relationship. He would feel that the franchise department would be failing in its work if franchisees ever had to report one another over substandard operation. Mr Brewer claims that there are a few minor disagreements within the network over things like servicing transferred vehicles. Otherwise it is dispute free. There have been no terminations, contractual breaches or voluntary exits. In this last respect, it is important to note again that Avis makes it easy for a franchisee to leave after giving six months' notice of his intention.

The monitoring system is reinforced by the possibility of centralized complaints indirectly alerting Avis to under-reported rentals. Also, Avis claims to have a good idea of what business an outlet should produce. Underachievement would lead to investigation so that, again, honest reporting is encouraged.

Mr Brewer describes monitoring costs as very low for the franchised network relative to company outlets as so much daily supervision can be left to the franchisee.

Why Franchise?

Avis gains largely from an influx of entrepreneurial talent at the local level. Mr Brewer states that 'We will not just take on investors, as we need entrepreneurial participation'. The company's wish to expand into local markets requires that branches make efforts to drum up local business, for example, going out to local businessmen to establish new accounts. It is felt that this is most likely to happen when a branch is run by a financially committed franchisee. In addition, Mr Brewer can point to customer letters reporting service standards among franchisees which are at least as high as those achieved by Avis-owned outlets. Finally, capital-raising advantages are perceived: Avis sees franchising as a low-cost method of adding additional stations to the network.

Mr Brewer believes that Avis offers a huge brand-name advantage to franchisees: 'It is what we are selling'. In addition, central reservations and a national sales team which is active in the pursuit of company accounts both generate rental business for franchisees. The vehicle and insurance supply lines are also an advantage which Avis has to offer. Finally, the operating system used is held to keep costs to a minimum, which helps franchisees to weather better any demand recessions.

Fees and Returns

The agreement allows for a 10% royalty which is levied on turnover excluding sales tax (VAT in the United Kingdom). In addition, the lump-sum initial franchise fee stands at £15,000 in 1988. This figure may be negotiable in exceptional circumstances for a franchisee with an established rental site. The negotiation occurs for two reasons. First, Avis is keen to move its logo on to established sites as a matter of business strategy, as this aids expansion into local markets. Secondly, Avis's costs in starting up a franchisee are lower for an existing business. The start-up package includes such things as help with shopfitting, provision of uniforms, launch advertising, three-months' stationery require- ments, training and promotional materials. Avis does not aim to make a profit from the initial fee. Franchisees confirm that the initial fee is spent by Avis in starting them up in business. VAT is added to all fees paid to the franchisor and is claimed back by the franchisee.

Full set-up costs for a franchisee are in the region of £50,000. An example, of an Avis-supplied profit and loss projection, as a hypothetical fleet is built up to 26 cars and nine vans, is given as Exhibit 18.2. The Franchisee's income as a manager is included in costs. Fairly healthy operating profits are shown from the first year of operation. No longer term projections are available. It should be

Exhibit 18.2 Avis Profit and Loss Projection

Month	1	2	3	4	5	6
Revenue						
Cars	3,176	3,812	4,955	5,368	6,670	7,115
Vans	1,052	1,157	1,690	2,107	2,282	2,746
TOTAL	4,228	4,968	6,645	7,475	8,953	9,861
Vehicle Variables						
Maintenance	190	190	233	262	292	321
Insurance	416	489	654	736	881	971
Leasing charges	2,154	2,154	2,766	3,056	3,390	3,758
Road tax	108	108	133	150	167	183
TOTAL	2,868	2,941	3,786	4,205	4,730	5,234
Revenue Variables						
Fuel margin	(54)	(64)	(85)	(97)	(115)	(128)
PAI cost	67	79	105	117	141	155
Cleaning	40	40	40	40	40	40
Charge card fees	106	125	167	188	225	248
Commissions	36	43	57	64	77	84
Advertising	91	106	142	160	192	211
Licence fee	406	477	638	718	860	947
Doubtful accounts	14	17	23	26	31	34
TOTAL	706	823	1,087	1,216	1,450	1,592
Fixed Costs						
Salaries	1,944	1,944	1,944	1,944	1,944	1,944
Rent	625	625	625	625	625	625
Rates	167	167	167	167	167	167
Communications	18	24	39	45	54	61
Gen & admin	18	24	39	45	54	61
Light, heat & power	50	50	50	50	50	50
TOTAL	2,822	2,834	2,864	2,876	2,894	2,908
PROFIT/(LOSS)	(2,168)	(1,630)	(1,092)	(822)	(121)	128

remembered that fleets are expected to build up to higher levels in subsequent years. Also, capital costs do not feature in the appended projection.

Sales targets are not set as such but fleet projections do form part of the agreement. Mr Brewer believes that franchisees show better returns than would be common in the vehicle rental business. Avis is very happy with its overall UK profits which increased by about 350% between 1984 and 1987.

The Franchisees

Franchisees vary in their backgrounds and in the size of their businesses. Details of three of them are summarized in this section of the case. They are not named in what follows.

Exhibit 18.2 *continued*

7	8	9	10	11	12	TOTAL	%
8,004	9,338	10,482	11,435	11,911	12,387	94,652	73
3,198	3,198	3,943	4,429	4,429	4,429	34,659	27
11,202	12,536	14,425	15,864	16,340	16,816	129,312	100
365	408	437	481	496	510	4,185	3
1,103	1,234	1,420	1,562	1,609	1,656	12,733	10
4,292	4,730	5,211	5,831	6,035	6,322	49,699	38
208	233	250	275	283	292	2,392	2
5,968	6,606	7,319	8,150	8,423	8,780	69,009	53
(146)	(161)	(187)	(206)	(211)	(217)	(1,672)	(1)
175	198	227	249	257	265	2,035	2
40	40	40	40	40	40	480	0
282	315	363	399	411	423	3,251	3
96	107	124	136	140	144	1,108	1
240	268	309	340	350	360	2,769	2
1,076	1,204	1,386	1,524	1,570	1,615	12,422	10
38	43	49	54	56	58	443	0
1,802	2,014	2,310	2,536	2,612	2,688	20,837	16
1,944	1,944	1,944	1,944	1,944	1,944	23,328	18
625	625	625	625	625	625	7,500	6
167	167	167	167	167	167	2,000	2
70	70	72	86	85	88	712	1
70	70	72	86	85	88	712	1
50	50	50	50	50	50	600	0
2,926	2,926	2,930	2,958	2,956	2,962	34,852	27
506	990	1,866	2,220	2,349	2,387	4,614	4

All three operate from sites located on service stations in urban areas. They regard this as efficient. In two cases, the service stations belong to the franchisee who divides his time between his interests on the site. In the third case, the franchisee believes that the ready availability of vehicle services and the proximity to the motoring public are of benefit to him. Observation of such sites shows that the Avis brand name is not lost. Clearly though, shared sites fall short of Avis's ideal of a single-use site with an undiluted brand presence.

The three franchisees all emphasize the value of the brand name to them in explaining their decision to join Avis rather than go it alone. The brand name is thought to reassure the customer that he is buying a quality service with a full national back-up in terms of vehicle support and the availability of one-way hire. To the franchisee, this means that he is less dependent on price as a competitive instrument: higher perceived quality for hirers translates into better hire rates for the franchisee.

The central reservations system can generate as much as one-half or as little as one-tenth of a franchisee's business depending on his location. Locations in areas which attract tourists or businessmen from overseas tend to benefit most. The facility is seen as valuable by franchisees but is not emphasized to the same extent as the benefits of the brand name.

Company supply lines for vehicles and insurance are not as highly valued as Avis managers may think. The three franchisees all take at least one-half of their fleets on this basis but do not emphasize the benefits of the arrangement. The benefits are in terms of vehicle-lease charges and a saving of the franchisee's search and negotiation costs.

The franchisees believe that their personal investment in their businesses acts as a commitment-increasing device. They feel confident that Avis could not obtain the same level of local entrepreneurship by motivating employed managers with profit-sharing schemes. Franchisees typically have a high proportion of their personal wealth along with their reputation as businessmen sunk irretrievably into their franchised outlets. Not just failure, but lack of real success, would seriously jeopardize their futures. No employee has quite this incentive to be completely vigorous in building up business at the local level. Vigorous local entrepreneurship is what the franchisees believe they offer Avis – and this is of course what Avis is seeking in choosing expansion through a franchise network.

Because of the emphasis on brand-name effects, the franchisees' main expectation of Avis is that full efforts be made to develop the brand nationally. These efforts are expected to include multi-media advertising, the operation of a national sales team to promote contracts with major companies, and the more general support of an active marketing department.

None of the three franchisees has any serious grievance. Individuals speak of occasional gripes but of nothing more. Some network difficulties have arisen over payments for vehicles once they are in the one-way system. There are complaints that Avis is quick to charge a franchisee for vehicle recovery when he requests that a vehicle be sent back to him from the end of a one-way hire. However, payments from Avis have been relatively slow when a franchisee has recovered vehicles. One franchisee felt that he incurred high costs when attending to vehicles which belonged to other stations when these were in his area.

Franchisees speak of an easy-going relationship with Avis which is based on common interests. Avis has not been known to quote contractual clauses at any franchisee. Franchisees appear happy with their situation including their profitability: everyone interviewed expressed an intention to remain in the system.

Summary

The Avis franchise offers a brand name and a national rental network to franchisees. In return, Avis is able to draw on local entrepreneurship to develop local business by franchising. The development of local rental markets is Avis's principal current strategic goal. Franchisees are found to have a high level of commitment to developing the business. Avis's returns come mainly from a royalty which is levied on rental turnover. The single-use site does not materialize among franchisees, who commonly set up on service stations, and where this appears to be efficient, brand presence is not lost but may be diluted. Some fairly minor problems exist over fitting the franchised outlets in with the company stations. Overall, the current phase of Avis's development as a major UK vehicle-rental company is progressing successfully with growth in profitability and in the size of the network.

CASE 19
Scottish Express International
Physical Distribution/Marketing Information Systems

James McCalman
University of Glasgow Business School

Introduction

Scottish Express International (SEI) was one of the largest transport companies in Britain involved in the movement of freight both throughout the United Kingdom and internationally by road, sea and air. The company was a wholly owned subsidiary of the Laird Group of Companies and operated 12 international freight offices in the United Kingdom. The administrative head office was situated in Ayr on the west coast of Scotland, 45 miles from Glasgow. The company also operated a main sorting depot at Dundonald, Ayrshire. At the time of the case study the company employed 300 people and had a gross invoicing turnover of around £18 million per annum. Its main activities involved it in three separate areas of transport: international freight, which comprised air cargo, shipping and internationally routed road transport (TIR) was handled from 12 offices throughout the United Kingdom; the main domestic transport system, road haulage, operated from a central sorting depot at Dundonald and served all the other offices; there was also an aircraft handling division which operated at the main Scottish and UK airports.

Road Haulage

The road haulage division operated 70 freight vehicles which were able to generate an annual billing of £2.6 million. At the time of the study the division employed 78 drivers and warehousemen as well as subcontracting work to other road hauliers.

The collection or delivery of freight whether domestic or international was dealt with by the haulage division. Each office was linked via a domestic trunking service operating from the central sorting location. This system was originally established to cater for the domestic collection and delivery of air freight but from 1976 it became obvious to the firm that the movement of this air freight did not create enough volume traffic to justify the trunking operation. It was at this point that emphasis was placed upon gaining domestic freight to make the road transport operation viable.

The movement into the domestic road haulage area of transport was initiated as a direct result of the large losses being sustained in moving international freight to final destinations in the United Kingdom. These losses stemmed from vehicles being operated well under their full capacity, and the obvious solution was to incorporate the movement of domestic freight into the operation. This proved to be extremely successful and during 1983 the division began to break even. However, at this point SEI over-expanded its domestic operations. The major problem was that management information on the operation of routes was not accurate enough to identify immediate loss-making areas. As with the movement of international freight, the same mistakes appear to have been made with services operating well under their full capacity. However, this was not fully appreciated because of the lack of management information on route operations. Although during 1984 the revenue from domestic haulage consistently exceeded budget, the cost of operations also grew rapidly. It was felt that a computer-based accounting and management information system would provide the detailed information required on the profitability of specific delivery routes and local office depots.

Road Haulage Operations

For each movement of freight, one of the local offices opened a file and detailed the charges to the customer on an invoice. Details of SEI's fees and a charge for the use of the company's trucks were also included. This charge was credited to the haulage division. Where it was necessary for collected freight to be moved to another office for delivery, an agreed trucking charge was allocated from the freight file to the haulage division.

For each freight consignment, the local office would have three or four location collection vehicles available to move freight from the customer's premises to the local warehouse. The local office also had an evening trunker which moved freight to the main sorting centre at Dundonald. From here it was sorted for movement throughout the United Kingdom to the nearest suitable office from which delivery could be made.

Each freight consignment had a domestic roadline document assigned to it. The roadlines came in five part book sets and were designed to be prepared by clients. The roadline document was completed with details of the sender, consignee (recipient), where the invoice was to be sent, (if not to the sender), description of the goods and whether insurance cover was required. The customer then contacted his local SEI office which collected the freight and the four remaining parts of the roadline set. On arrival at the local warehouse, a copy of the roadline was retained by the originating depot and the goods were forwarded to the main sorting centre at Dundonald or direct to the consignee. Of the remaining three parts of the roadline, one was forwarded to Dundonald for pricing and from there to central accounts in Ayr for invoicing. The remaining two parts were carried with the goods, one as consignee receipt and the second as proof of delivery (POD) which was returned to the sort centre by the driver. One of the problems which arose out of this system was that proof of delivery copies were not always returned by drivers and it was hoped that the introduction of the new computerized system would address this problem by identifying those offices and drivers who did not return PODs.

The introduction of the latest computer technology took place mainly at the head office in Ayr, although a terminal was allocated to the main sorting centre office in Dundonald. The head office sought the computerization of its sales, purchasing and invoicing functions, with the latter being the prime concern. As such, the major part of the technical change introduced concerned the setting up of a computer room where roadline documents could be placed onto the computer, checked and then printed out as invoices to the customer. For this, three terminal screens were installed and two printers. Two screens were allocated to the sales team, one to purchasing and one to the sorting centre at Dundonald. Senior management were mostly located at the company's head office and were closely involved in the planning and implementation of the computerized system.

Past Experience with Computerization

SEI had operated a computerized invoicing system since 1983 and had already experienced a change in technology before the introduction of the present system. This had the obvious benefit of acquainting the operating staff with change and had involved the use of external bureaux that provided information to managers at SEI on performance. However, the use of these bureaux was not wholly beneficial for several reasons.

Firstly, the provision of monthly reports from one of the external bureaux proved to be too slow to allow any up-to-date analysis to take place. Management were always dealing with 'yesterday's news' which was not regarded as an efficient method of operation. One SEI director summed up the service provided by stating that, 'The information was pretty well dead by the time we got our hands on it'. Information returned to management at head office could be as much as one month out of date. What was required was a much more frequent service where weekly, or even daily, reports could be forthcoming on the operations of specific routes. It gradually became apparent to management that what was required was an internally operated system.

Secondly, the bureau system had operational and organizational difficulties which did not endear it to SEI management or staff. The kilogram weight of freight was not always entered into the terminal correctly by staff which 'messed up' the invoicing system. There were also problems caused by the fact that the software used by the external bureaux did not carry enough detail to meet the requirements of the company. SEI sought a more detailed analysis of the route allocation of revenue, for example allocation by destination depot.

The major problem with the previous computerized systems was the failure to provide management with accurate information on the performance of the road transport routes, at a pace that would allow them to take appropriate action. There was no method of measuring the level of success or failure of individual routes in monetary terms. Management firmly believed that they had the ability to solve problem areas within road haulage with adequate and current information. What handicapped the sustained profitability of the haulage division was an inadequate management information system. Without this, reactions to changes in the volume of freight were slow and pricing strategy had to be based at best on estimation.

Technology in Use

The computerized system introduced into SEI consisted of a financial costing system with a suite of application programs suitable to the company's needs. The system was installed by Weir Group Management Systems Limited in January 1985. The hardware consisted of a Data General Desktop Generation 20 system which contained a 156 kilobyte memory, 38 megabyte Winchester disk storage, seven visual display units (although Weir's only recommended three VDUs), two 160 CPS dot matrix printers and a 15 megabyte cartridge back-up unit. The total cost of the system amounted to £35,000.

The package installed was intended to meet SEI's requirements for sales invoicing, proof of delivery reconciliation, sales ledger, sales analysis and vehicle costing/cost ledger. The application would also make transport route/individual depot profitability calculations to aid management decision making. To give a more accurate analysis of the introduction of technical change it would be useful to examine the way in which each of SEI's requirements would be met by the computerized system.

The Proposed Changes to the System

SEI sought the installation of an in-house computer system which provided ready access to customer and vehicle details from a flexible enquiry system. The invitation to tender was drawn up for a combined hardware and software solution which would be suitable for a first time user. The initial physical requirements were for three screens and three high-speed printers to be based at the head office with the possibility of terminal access from local offices in the long term. The final system incorporated seven screens: three in the main office, two in the sales office, one in purchasing and one at the sorting centre at Dundonald.

The package developed had to satisfy the requirements of the following systems:

- Sales invoicing
- Proof of delivery reconciliation
- Sales ledger
- Sales analysis
- Vehicle costing
- Route/depot profitability

In the longer term, the package also had to be adaptable enough to integrate with a total financial ledger system, purchase and nominal ledger systems and expansion to include linking up with systems in the international freight forwarding division of the company.

Sales invoicing

The system was required to produce invoices and credit notes from the roadline document and produce composite invoices on a daily/weekly basis. Invoices had to be retainable in the system to provide automatic interface with sales ledger/sales analysis systems. Manual calculation of price would be replaced by automatic calculation based on kilogram weights and a tariff code, and by the application of standard discounts to regular customers. Manual override was also to be made available. The computer operators would enter the roadline details into the terminal at the rate of 300 per day. Once these had been entered they would be printed off as reports. These would then be checked against tape lists of roadline details prepared by staff at the sorting centre at Dundonald. Having checked the reports, staff would then generate invoices and have these printed out by the computer. This process was the main bulk use of computer time, and the main work of computer room staff who dealt with approximately 1,500 roadline documents from their branches every week which resulted in the creation of 1,000 invoices to customers.

The new computerized system allowed data entry which displayed the customer name and address by accessing master files from a specific customer code, checked customer credit limits and displayed appropriate warning messages where these were exceeded, calculated price by reference to tariff codes and discounts, and accumulated batch totals on the number of roadlines entered, kilogram weight and amounts. The output from the system took the form of invoices, customer credit notes and total reports. In addition, the system provided a transaction file of all roadlines for use in the proof of delivery reconciliation and sales analysis systems, as well as sales ledger posting details.

Proof of delivery reconciliation

On delivery of goods the customer signed a copy of the roadline which acts as proof of delivery (POD). These were returned to the Dundonald sorting office by the driver, and forwarded to the accounts office where they were batched on a daily basis. The PODs were filed in batches for subsequent reference by batch number. The new system was required to record batches and provide an index to the PODs. Where PODs were signed by a qualifying receipt, for example if they were damaged in transit, these 'qualified' PODs would be recorded by means of a flag field. This system would allow a list of PODs without roadline, a list of roadlines without PODs, and a list of PODs in numerical order showing both reference numbers.

The advantage of this system would be that it would allow PODs to be matched with invoices and, where these were missing, billing of the customer could be done via the POD. It also offered management the potential of being able to identify depots which consistently failed to return PODs and ultimately specific drivers who failed to return these. Staff at Dundonald would enter the roadline number they received from the driver's returned POD and this would be checked against the details appearing on the terminal. The terminal would then ask whether the POD had been qualified as a result of some inconsistency. Once a certain number of roadlines had been entered in this way they would be grouped together and allocated a batch number. All enquiries concerning a particular delivery would be dealt with by their roadline number which would indicate which batch they were filed under.

Sales ledger

The system was a multi-company, open item sales ledger with on-line customer files which held multiple addresses to enable statements to be sent to appropriate customer locations. It was integrated with sales invoicing and sales analysis. Customer statements were produced at period end or on request, and there was a facility for production of credit letters. The current status of a customer's account was accessible on-line with an optional printout facility. The system automatically cleared invoices and allocated cash at period end. The output from the system detailed statements, transaction records, outstanding balances and dates, and customer opening and closing balances.

The data entry process involved entering details of invoices and credit notes posted directly from the sales invoicing system. Cash payments were allocated directly against an invoice or a group of invoices and it was possible to have immediate access to the current status of a customer's account. The output from the sales ledger consisted of statements, audit trails (transactions processed during the period), aged debtor analysis (all outstanding customer balances by period), and a debtors' ledger (showing all transactions with opening and closing balances during the period).

Sales analysis

The objectives of sales analysis were to allow management the ability to examine the nature and volume of trade initiated by each depot, and to allow revenue to be apportioned to the depots and trunk route segments handling that freight. Both depots and trunk routes were regarded as profit centres. The trunk route profit centre comprised the distance between an originating depot and a destination depot. These routes were broken down into route segments.

All records were grouped and summarized using a six-digit tariff/route code taken from the roadline. A table was calculated for each origin/destination part of the code and the revenue percentages for each piece of freight apportioned by:

- origination depot
- origin/Dundonald
- Dundonald sorting
- Dundonald destination
- destination depot

The output from the sales analysis was first reported on freight revenue analysed by tariff code, and then reported on reapportioned revenue by depot/route segment. The sales analysis and vehicle costing figures needed to be examined both in terms of depots and routes, to enable management to determine depot and individual route profitability.

To ensure a fair allocation of revenue between the originating and destination depots, the procedure adopted to calculate the revenue apportionment was as follows:

(1) Obtain the total amount allocated to the freight consignment from the roadline document.

(2) Allocate the amount to each depot or route segment according to pre-determined percentages.

(3) Compare the amount allocated to the destination depot with the minimum and if necessary increase it to the minimum.

(4) Deduct the difference from the originating depot.

This analysis produced two main outputs for SEI management. First, reports on freight revenue analysed by the tariff code. Second, reports of reapportioned revenue analysed by depot/route segment.

Vehicle/costing

This system was able to collect costs as they related to particular vehicles, reapportion vehicle costs to associated depots or routes in relation to the use of the vehicle by that depot or route and combine vehicle costs with other costs to provide management information on operational costs. As with profit centres both the depot and route would be regarded as cost centres. Of the 70 goods vehicles, 35 were designated trunk route vehicles and details of each vehicle's mileage would be allocated to its particular depot/route. Identification was by the tariff code on the roadline. The benefits to management of vehicle costing would come in the form of monthly reports for the vehicle and its route/depot.

Cost information was gathered by vehicle, by depot/route segment and by group division. The analysis by vehicle examined fixed costs, such as depreciation, lease charges, insurance and vehicle hire, as well as variable costs, such as fuel, tyres and maintenance. Depot and route costs were detailed as subcontracted vehicle costs, wages, hire and maintenance of equipment, etc. The divisional analysis of costs examined wages/salaries and administrative overheads. The output from such an analysis came in the form of monthly reports on vehicle costing and a route/depot report to be used for examination of route/depot profitability.

Route/depot profitability

As part of the management information package, the introduction of the new system offered senior SEI management the ability to measure the profitability of routes/depots against their operating costs. Comparison of costs and revenues from the vehicle costing and sales analysis sections were made at route/depot level. Monthly statements were prepared showing costs/revenue by category, depot/route analysis and company analysis.

The system operated retained its nerve centre at the head office in Ayr, and it was from here that the information on routes and depots would be analysed by senior management and strategic decisions made on the company's operations. These decisions were arrived at using the analysis given by the new system to identify the problems that the previous system either could not point out, or was too slow in identifying. It must be stressed that the introduction of the new system was used to solve a particular problem.

Management Objectives

Previous studies have shown that different levels and functions within management hold different expectations with respect to computing technology and the criteria on which investment in new systems is based can be extremely varied with respect to their nature, precision and the time scale taken into account. There is also evidence to suggest that conventional cost justification approaches to investment appraisal are not relevant of these types of systems.

There can be little doubt that the introduction of technical change into this organization was the result of a senior management initiative to improve the flow of information to them. The fundamental basis of this was that they did not receive accurate data on the performance of the road haulage division in time to enable decisions to be made regarding its operation. However, another factor which encouraged the introduction of technical change was the use made of domestic road haulage by branch management. Road haulage had always been viewed as a service facility for the international freight division and as a result of this branch managers were prone to using this service without apportioning realistic revenues to the road haulage division for use of their domestic vehicles. Branch managers could mask the individual performance of their own branches by allocating a negligible amount to the road haulage division while keeping the bulk of the revenue from the movement of international freight for their own branch. In effect branches were using the domestic road haulage division to collect and deliver international freight without paying the full costs associated with this domestic movement. Branches appeared as profitable while domestic road haulage operated with high costs and low revenue.

SEI experienced problems in trying to match the system that it desired to a package being offered by the various companies approached. A prepackaged software program was not available and custom programming was too expensive and time consuming. The ultimate solution was a customized package which could fit management desires. The important point to note here was that the hardware offered took second place and was not as crucial to the purchasing decision. What mattered most was the capabilities of the software and whether it met the company's needs. This created serious repercussions when the system was finally operational in that the major problem area resulted from an inability on the part of the hardware to cope with the demands made of it.

As part of a long-term strategy, the introduction of the computerized system to the road haulage division was seen as a first step in linking up with the international freight division. Although the manual control method for the international side of the business was deemed to be a more than adequate means of organization, SEI management had consciously set out with the intention of networking their operations with the ultimate goal of having each local office linked to the head office via the computerized operation. This would have the added benefit of removing another area where lack of management information caused difficulties.

CASE 20
Bartels Paperbacks
Marketing Mix Strategies

Luiz Moutinho

Glasgow Business School, University of Glasgow

Introduction

In late August of 1978, armed with 200 cinder blocks, 500 board feet of shelving and 2,000 paperbacks, Peter Jones moved to Bradford, West Yorkshire, to start a business: thus began Bartels Paperbacks. Peter got the idea for a paperback exchange from a friend who had opened one a few years before. At the time, he was in graduate school for journalism. He worked at the store during the day, attended classes in the evening, and slept on the couch at night. Peter thought he would make a million pounds.

Although Peter has not yet made a million pounds, Bartels Paperbacks has grown to be one of the largest used paperback chains in the Yorkshire area. There are currently two locations: Emm Lane and Jacob's Well near the city centre. Another store in Huddersfield was sold in 1979, shortly after opening the Emm Lane store. Bartels carries more than 50,000 used books.

The Emm Lane Store

The Emm Lane store opened in August of 1979 with 4,000 books. Today, the same 400 square foot space contains 20,000 books with new trades coming in at a rate of nearly 100 per day. Since only about 1,000 books are sold every month, the Emm Lane store is practically doubling its stock each month.

The Jacob's Well Store

The Jacob's Well store originally opened in November of 1982 in an upstairs location. Since moving to a storefront location with 1,000 square feet of space in

August of 1984, sales have increased 300%. The store contains a little more than 30,000 books with new trades coming in at a rate of around 60 per day. Since about 1,500 books are sold every month, it appears that growth is minimal. Yet, the overflow of books coming into the Emm Lane store provides nearly 500 new books for Jacob's Well each month.

The Trade Concept

Bartels buys, sells and trades almost any paperback which is in good physical shape: recent fiction, mysteries, children's books, romances, science fiction, classics, biographies and non-fiction. Paperbacks are typically priced at one-half the cover price + 25 pence (for example a £4.95 new book would be £2.48 + 25 pence = £2.73 if bought used at Bartels Paperbacks).

The most unique concept that Bartels brings to the market is the idea of trading used paperbacks. Although the concept is essentially that of a two for one swap, Bartels has provided some refinements: Bartels gives credit in exchange for paperbacks. The customer receives 25% of the cover price in trade for paperbacks listed over £2.00; 20% of the cover price in trade for romance paperbacks; and 10% of the cover price in trade for all other paperbacks. The customer receives a credit slip when he or she brings in paperbacks to trade. Each time a paperback is selected, one-half of the cover price will be deducted from the credit slip. All the customer pays is 25 pence in cash for each paperback chosen, up to the limit of the credit. One caveat: science fiction paperbacks may only be bought with cash or with science fiction trade. However, science fiction is the only type of paperback for which cash will be given: science fiction books may receive either 25% of the cover in trade, or 10% of the cover in cash.

Bartels was founded on a simple philosophy: provide people with an opportunity to trade their used books and to purchase books at a reasonable price, and the business will take care of itself.

Although this philosophy provided for great growth, it did little to provide for a steady revenue stream and profit picture. Thus, this marketing analysis is designed to provide a means to improve that profit picture.

Marketing Overview

Marketing has been a neglected aspect of Bartels' business. The company has no cohesive marketing strategy. It does not provide any cohesive plan, control or organization to market its business. The single marketing strategy employed is: when the company has sufficient cash flow, then money is spend on marketing.

Although no unified marketing plan is in place, Bartels uses a committee approach to spend its few marketing pounds. The responsibility for determining where the money is to go is shared between the owner and the two divisional managers. The owner makes the final decision as to money spent to benefit both stores, but each manager has some discretion as to money spend in local support.

The Market

The company image possessed by Bartels is a 'small-town mum-and-dad shop' image. Bartels is not a 'high-tech' or 'glossy-slick' company with high power sales tactics. It is a low-key approach, with a comfortable atmosphere and little, if any, sales pressure. The company is concerned with customer satisfaction rather than pressure sales tactics.

Customer service is the most important component of Bartels. The employees of the company are continually assisting the customers in finding the books they need, reserving books for customers, and even referring customers to competitors who may have a special book. Bartels have even bought books from competitors and resold them at no profit to satisfy customers.

The two divisions have a relatively different clientele. The Emm Lane store consists of approximately 50% women, 25% men and 25% children. Also, the clientele of the Emm Lane store are typically affluent individuals with more than a passing interest in reading. The Jacob's Well store customer base consists of approximately 50% young adults, 25% older adults and 25% children. Repeat customers represent a majority of the business at both divisions.

Bartels offers customers a wide selection of books at a very reasonable price. Of the 50,000 books offered between the two locations, the selection is wide: children's books, classics, mystery, romance, science fiction, out-of-print paperbacks, recent fiction, biographies, non-fiction and poetry. This product mix is essential to the company because it offers a wide selection of books for its customers' varied interests. This also assists in maintaining the company's major goal of customer satisfaction.

Further, Bartels offers its products at very low prices because the company wanted to offer a reasonable price to its customers that would also provide the company with some revenue stream to continue its operations. The books are priced at one-half the cover price plus 25 pence. With the trade policy, as explained above, customers only pay 25 pence cash for each book they take out. This trading system provides two important functions: (1) it continually builds up the company's inventory; and (2) it provides cash by charging 25 pence for each book taken out. This pricing strategy and trading system is extremely important to the company because the low prices and trading system are the major factors in bringing in new customers and generating repeat sales.

Thus, Bartels has an excellent relationship with its suppliers because its suppliers are its customers. All inventory is built up by the trading system and the company's inventory has grown tremendously over the years.

Marketing Goals

Bartels' marketing goals are:

(1) To double the company's business by reaching more customers through generating more repeat sales, and by acquiring more new customers.

(2) To diversify the company's product line into used records, tapes, videos and books on tape.

(3) To continue to provide superior customer service and satisfaction.

The major factors in bringing in repeat customers are:

- low prices,
- unique trading system,
- excellent customer service, and
- convenience due to good location.

New customers are more difficult to find. Bartels does not have any assistance in promotions from any outside sources such as advertising agencies. However, advertisements are sometimes generated from other sources, such as the organizers of poetry readings held monthly at the Jacob's Well store.

Nor does Bartels use any marketing research. This lack of marketing research could be detrimental to the company because it is impossible to gauge the success of the current marketing policy. To develop a marketing strategy, it is critical to know the number of potential customers and the market mind share in order to implement the correct strategy.

Marketing Strategies

Customers The target markets of Bartels are mainly women and young adults (college students) since these markets represent the majority of the company's business.

Price Bartels keeps its prices very low to keep customers and provide for new customers and it also provides a trading system to offer its customers a different alternative for purchases.

Location The Emm Lane division's location in the city provides easy access for its customers. This division also enjoys a quality reputation in the city. The Jacob's Well division also offers an excellent location for its customers because it is on a main street and has excellent walking traffic. It is also near some colleges and a few years ago, the division moved from an upstairs location to the downstairs and this move provided an immediate increase in revenue of three times its previous business. Also, Bartels takes great advantage of its shelf utilization. It is extremely important for the customers to be able to get the books they need conveniently. All books are organized by category and by author in each category and the high-margin books get a full-cover display to catch the attention of the customer.

Promotion Bartels does not provide any cohesive, well-thought-out plan for promotions. A written facsimile of the trading policy is given to each customer. This provides an opportunity to understand better the policy, and serves as a reminder that Bartels takes in trades. The poetry readings which occur once a month at the Jacob's Well store are another avenue of generating good public relations. The poets put together their own leaflets and post them. The *Telegraph and Argus* has also mentioned Bartels as a place to listen to poetry in a number of articles. Further, the *Telegraph and Argus* contains a listing of happenings around town which also mention the poetry readings. Bartels also gives away gift certificates to local benefits, auctions and proms.

Advertising The company uses mostly leaflets that are posted at local establishments such as small retail shops and restaurants. They are also posted at only one of the nearby colleges (University of Bradford). The company also runs a once a month ad. in a local newspaper (the *Target*). An advertisement is run very infrequently in the University of Bradford newspaper. Also, Bartels runs a classified ad. every week in the *Telegraph and Argus* and in the *Yorkshire Post* in the Leeds area.

Product selection With 50,000 books, Bartels provides a wide range of books to satisfy all its customers' needs.

Product mix Having a single product line, used books, hampers Bartels' ability to provide a broader product mix to interest new customers and keep old customers. Exhibit 20.1 shows the BCG portfolio matrix as applied to Bartels' product mix.

Finally, adjustments are made to the marketing programme as the need occurs since there is a lack of an organized marketing plan and no stringent rules that must be followed. There is no measurement of the effectiveness of the marketing

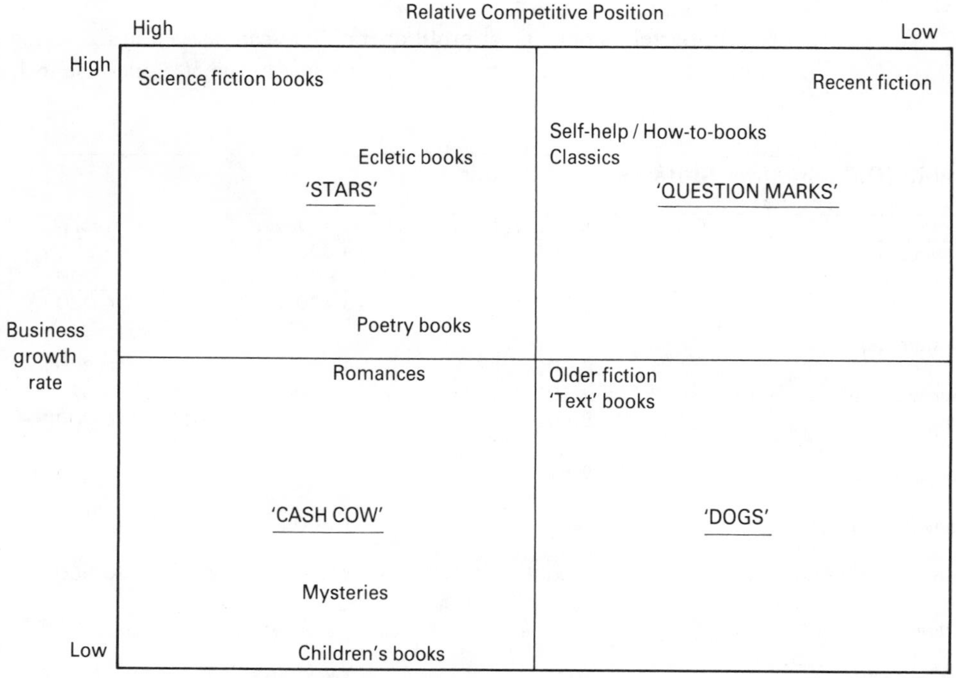

Exhibit 20.1 *BCG portfolio matrix.*

plan nor are there policies to evaluate performance, standards, or the monitoring of the marketing plan.

Competition   The competition facing Bartels consists mainly of used book stores, convenient-type stores, and major book store chains. In the convenience stores, impulse buying at the check-out counter accounts for the greatest competition for recent fiction. There are many major book chain outlets which also provide for competition in the recent fiction category. However, few have the breadth of product in the science fiction area. Further, out-of-print books and non-bestsellers are all but impossible to find at the major chains. Thus, the competition for older fiction is greatest among other used book stores. However, used book stores are few and far between.

Financials   The Emm Lane store contains 20,000 books. New trades are coming in at a rate of nearly 100 per day. Since only about 1,000 books are sold every month, the Emm Lane store is practically doubling its stock each month.

Sales have been growing at nearly 15% annually, but profits have continued to lag due to an increase in expenses of nearly 20% annually. Much of this is due to a new landlord who raised rents almost 50%.

The Jacob's Well store, since moving to a storefront location, has experienced a 300% increase in revenue. The store contains a little more than 30,000 books with new trades coming in at a rate of around 60 per day. Since about 1,500 books are sold every month, it appears that growth is minimal. Yet, the overflow of books coming into the Emm Lane store provides nearly 500 new books for Jacob's Well each month.

Overall, Bartels is not a great profit operation as can be seen in Exhibit 20.2. The Emm Lane store is showing a loss mainly due to the 50% increase in rent.

Exhibit 20.2   Income Statement for Bartels

	Emm Lane (£)	Jacob's Well (£)	Total (£)
Revenues	16,200	19,020	35,220
Cost of goods sold	300	900	1,200
Gross profit	15,900	18,120	34,020
Operating expenses:			
Rent	6,000	4,800	10,800
Administrative & general	2,100	2,520	4,620
Selling	8,400	9,600	18,000
Total expenses	16,500	16,920	33,420
Pre-tax income	(600)	1,200	600
Number of books sold/year	12,000	18,000	30,000
Average revenues/book (£)	1.35	1.06	1.17
Break-even (£)	16,500/0.982	16,920/0.953	33,420/0.966
	16,802	17,755	34,596

The only cost of goods borne by the company is from the science fiction books, since these are the only books purchased outright.

The trading system used by the company does not provide a sufficient amount of revenue and, due to the trading system, the company only averages £1.17 per book. Also, Bartels must bear a large amount of fixed costs and the company must sell at least £34,596 to break even. Due to the small amount of revenues generated by each book, Bartels must overcome its barrier of high fixed costs by generating enough revenue to cover its fixed costs and provide profits.

SWOT Analysis: The SWOT analysis is an assessment of both the internal and external environments of the company. The strengths and weaknesses of the company are analysed in the internal environment and the opportunities and threats of the company are analysed in the external environment. Exhibit 20.3 shows the SWOT analysis for Bartels.

Peter Jones was hoping that a turnaround strategy would bring a brighter future for Bartels.

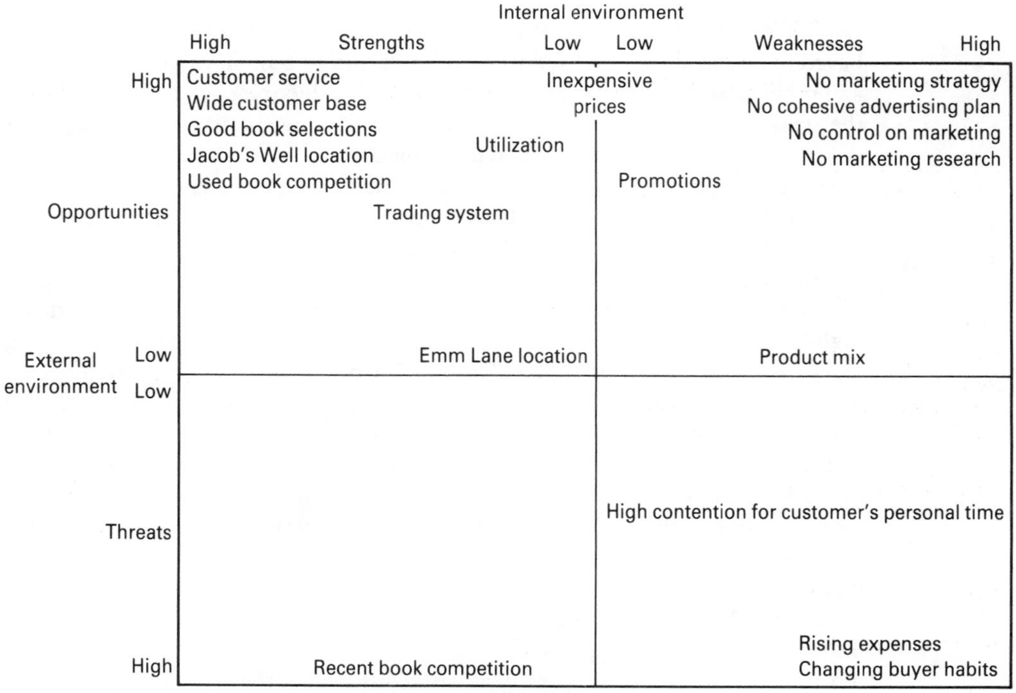

Exhibit 20.3 *SWOT analysis.*

CASE 21
Strathspey Ski Centre
Marketing Mix Strategies

Luiz Moutinho

Glasgow Business School, University of Glasgow

Case History

After a week's skiing at one of the prestigious resorts in the Highlands, Moira Thomson and Stephen Smith had arranged to meet to talk animatedly of their newly hatched plans to become partners in developing a new and different skiing haven in Scotland. It all started when Moira's former economics school classmate and other friends of long standing who shared an eight-person apartment during the week became disgusted with standing in lift queues, paying £15 daily for tickets, gulping down tasteless food in a crowded subterranean tavern and picking their way precariously across poorly maintained, and alternately icy and muddy, walkways. Also, their favourite chairlift had broken down twice during the week, forcing them to take to the intermediate slopes for most of each day.

Among the group that had skied together annually for more than a decade were a lawyer, the owner of an electronics firm, a stockbroker, a doctor, and two high-level executives, all of whom felt sanguine about the prospects of banding together, investing perhaps £40,000 to £80,000 of seed money each, and financing the remainder through loans and venture capital to launch their dream. The clincher of the deal was immediate availability of a friend and fellow skier's non-working property, covering 3,560 acres and contiguous on one side to abandoned timberland and on the other to a Forestry Commission area that happened to be marked, along with six or more other sites in the district, as a potential ski area. There were numerous creeks on the property, a trout stream and a sizeable river that was part of the property's boundary line.

Nature has endowed the region with magnificent mountain ranges offering unparalleled winter recreational potential. Of the four areas classified as 'major', most operate daily and a few only at weekends during the winter season. Major winter holiday areas include such destination resorts as Aviemore and Spey

Valley, Cairngorm, Lecht, Glenshee and Glencoe. Acreage for the proposed site is relatively isolated in the north-central part of Scotland, about an hour's drive from Inverness and Fort William (see Exhibit 21.1). An airport about 70 miles distant, served by one major and three regional airlines, is linked to the potential ski resort by a two-lane road that is well maintained. There are good bus and train links.

The project idea was discussed in a heated conversational manner among the potential development partners. Many important issues were raised through comments such as 'snow tractors cost £100,000', 'snowmaking systems would cost millions', 'chairlifts are over £400,000', and 'we'll have to contract for an environmental impact study – I hear they cost around £35,000'. When the subject of staffing arose, one of the corporate executives, a Glaswegian, remarked, 'I was told that the K.L. Leisure Group PLC – a top-notch organization – employs a salesforce of over 12 people and a marketing director and good staff to make it go!' Next day, their enthusiasm was undiminished and their audacious idea for the development of a ski resort spurred further deliberations.

Concerning the environmental impact issue, there was concern about the strict regulatory mood in Edinburgh and how their hopes of quick approval might be affected. The legislative climate within the newly appointed cabinet of the Scottish Office did not appear to be inclined towards making headway diluting the existing environmental strictures, easing regulations and making decisions that favoured development of this type of project. The so-called 'green lobby' was

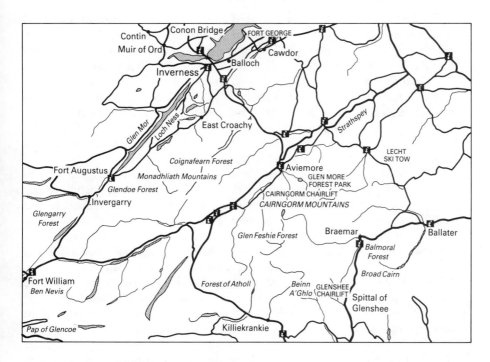

Exhibit 21.1 *Area map of the Strathspey Ski Centre location.*

perceived as having an increasingly important role concerning the preservation of present legislative framework for the protection of the environment. Nevertheless, the eager entrepreneurs believed that they could make an excellent case for their project and that little direct local opposition would materialize. Thinking of a suitable model after which to pattern their resort project they considered Aviemore. This famous ski resort, located 28 miles south of Inverness, was the epitome of popular ski areas in the United Kingdom. The group knew that starting to compare their project with Aviemore would be impossible, with its surface lift, chairlifts, runs, multiple excellent hotels and lodging facilities, restaurants and pubs, tennis courts, swimming pools, child care centre and many tourist shops. Also, Aviemore's ski school was renowned, and its ski touring trails abundant. 'Perhaps', the doctor intervened, 'we should consider another model, say, Lecht'? And so the brainstorming discussion went on.

The Stirling lawyer added a note of caution:

> 'In 1982 my wife and I, and our two children could visit Aviemore for a week's ski holiday and spend £450, including travelling expenses; next trip we'll spend about £1,200 for the same package. Transportation costs, lodging, and lift tickets have gone up faster than the consumer price index (CPI). I think we should act with caution and realize that only those with a moderate to high discretionary income will be able to afford it. Leisure time alone won't create the demand we want for the resort.'

What they would settle for provoked a lively discussion based on a spirited disagreement: slopes offering good skiing on terrain varying from broad, gentle glades, to steep chutes, perhaps 15 trails on about 800 acres, to start with. Stephen thought that three double chairlifts would be a good beginning. Soon they concluded that a lot more information was needed about break-even volume and about all the services required to create a well-planned, attractive and pleasant resort complex. Also, in their enthusiasm, they could not overlook the need to serve all ski levels – beginner, intermediate and advanced. And what other resort facilities, they asked themselves, would be required to attract summer visitors and tourists to help cover overhead costs? This was a separate issue.

The would-be partners believed that in addition to traditional ski-area services and activities, it could be desirable and hopefully profitable to include glider skiing as well. This would be for the few who possess both technique and endurance – courageous skiers who want that 'something extra' that only deep powder can offer, something that cannot be found at traditional ski resorts even when with this goal in mind, they hoped and needed the snowfall to be steady and substantial. Also, the slopes would need to be perfectly groomed.

For the past four years, three of the group had spent one of their two or three annual skiing holidays on mountainsides in Switzerland. Based on their experiences of having paid £950 each for a six-day package, they concluded, however, that only the upscale buffs would be prospects for glider skiing.

There was a consensus atmosphere within the group in relation to other specific aspects of the project. They knew that daytime temperatures in the area were usually comfortable, the snowfall was light and dry at that 1,150 foot elevation, and they could expect a good average of inches of powder throughout the season. And they were close enough for Aviemore and Lecht customers to start patronizing their ski resort. Also, they estimate there were 300 to 400 rooms available at nearby hotels and guest houses, as well as bed and breakfast accommodation within a 20 mile radius, to help cope with the visitor traffic until development begins at Strathspey Ski Centre. Strathspey Ski Centre was the tentative name submitted by Stephen, and quickly seconded by Moira Thomson. 'It sounds clean, fresh and fun', said one of the two corporate executives, 'and signifies what we plan to offer'. There was a common consent. The enthusiastic skiers cum entrepreneurs seemed determined to take the project further ahead but they were concerned about all the strategic issues they should consider before proceeding with the development of the idea. The stockbroker proposed then that a framework for a strengths–weaknesses, opportunities–threats analysis of the project should be developed by the group. They were also eager to discuss alternative design concepts for their product. Should they go 'luxurious' or 'utilitarian and economic'? What target markets should they consider? How could they assess and analyse market potential indices in those segments? How could they develop specific marketing mix programmes tailored to each target segment? The group then agreed that they had to seek advice and guidance from a marketing management expert.

The UK Skiing Market

In 1986 the total number of skiers in the United Kingdom aged 15+ who had skied on snow at least once in the last five years was 2.2 million. This figure indicates in broad terms the number of people in Britain who have ever skied. A more meaningful term to use in the analysis of the skiing market is 'regular participation in skiing'.

Exhibit 21.2 *Participation in skiing (1973–85).*

	Millions of people who take part in skiing regularly			Regular participants as a percentage of the total population		
	1973	1979	1985	1973	1979	1985
Adults	0.1	0.3	0.4	0.2	0.6	0.9
Children	0.1	0.1	0.1	0.6	1.0	1.2

Source: Leisure Consultant General Household Survey.

The definition of 'regular' is complex. Exhibit 21.2 refers to the number of people who took part in skiing in the most popular annual quarter for skiing activity in each of the years noted.

The trend shown is, overall, one of steady growth in skiing participation. The total of 500,000 participants in 1985 concurs with many travel trade estimates.

It is estimated that there is a core group of approximately 440,000 adults who ski on snow regularly (That is, at least once every two years).

Ski Clubs

Membership of ski clubs is one particular measure of participation in skiing. There are an estimated 250 ski clubs in the United Kingdom with approximately 51,000 members. The largest club is the Ski Club of Great Britain with, perhaps, 12,000 members resident in the United Kingdom. A list of the largest Scottish clubs would include the Aberdeen, Cairngorm and Bearsden Ski Clubs.

Dry Slope Skiing

Another sign of the increased popularity of skiing has been the growth in the number of dry ski slopes. There are now about 100 dry ski slopes in the United Kingdom, of which about 15 are major sites (for example Hillend in Edinburgh).

The Holiday Market (UK Skiing Visits Abroad)

The market is split into three principal components: packaged holidays, school ski groups and independently arranged holidays.

Estimates indicated that there were approximately 260,000 packaged skiing holidays sold to adults in the 1985/86 season. Exhibit 21.3 shows recent trends in packaged holiday sales.

Exhibit 21.3 highlights a picture of dramatic growth. Between 1978/79 and 1985/86 the number of packaged ski holidays sold rose by 126%.

Exhibit 21.3   *Estimated number of packaged skiing holidays 1978–86.*

	'000	Change year on year (%)	Index
1978/79	115.0		100
1979/80	141.5	+ 23	123
1980/81	171.4	+ 21	149
1981/82	181.8	+ 6	158
1982/83	185.0	+ 2	161
1983/84	207.0	+ 12	180
1984/85	234.0	+ 13	203
1985/86	260.0	+ 11	226

Source: Mintel based on trade estimates.

It is estimated from the trade press that, in addition, to packaged holidays 115,000 independent ski holidays and 150,000 school ski places were sold in 1985/86. This gives a combined total of 525,000 skiing holidays sold in 1985/86.

Broadly speaking that total number of skiing holidays sold in the last eight years has more than doubled from 250,000 in 1978/79 to 525,000 in 1985/86 (an increase of 110%).

The sales of skiing holidays – £170 million in 1985/86 are divided as follows:

	£ million
Skiing holidays abroad	
packaged (including schools)	130
independent	40

The Scottish Skiing Market

There appears to be general agreement that it is meaningful to talk of a 'Scottish' skiing market, that is, many UK residents, including Scots, generally confine their skiing to overseas winter holidays. There is a wide variety of estimates of the size of the Scottish skiing market: 50,000–60,000 regular skiers could be taken as a fairly conservative estimate of its current size. This compares with a total of about 440,000 UK skiers.

The most useful measure of the demand for skiing is skier days per annum. Information for two seasons – 1978/79 and 1985/86 is presented in Exhibit 21.4 to show market size and trends:

Exhibit 21.4 reveals that over the period 1978/79 to 1985/86 the total number of skier days rose by 64% from 335,000 to 549,000. In terms of market share there has been some change over the period, principally a drop in the market share held by Glenshee and Glencoe, and the emergence of Lecht to the point where it now holds 10% of the market.

Exhibit 21.4 *Demand for skiing.*

	1978/79		1985/86	
	No. of skier days	*Market share (%)*	*No. of skier days*	*Market share (%)*
Cairngorm	215,000	64	350,000	64
Glenshee	95,000	28	120,000	22
Glencoe	25,000	8	24,000	4
Lecht	(not started full operation)	—	55,000	10
Total	335,000		549,000	

Sources: 1978/79: RBL research study for the Scottish Tourist Board; 1985/86: Mackay Consultants research study for the Scottish Tourist Board.

The average compound growth rate in the total number of skier days over the period 1978/79 to 1985/86 is approximately 7% per annum. The annual increase at Cairngorm was also 7% – mirroring the overall growth rate.

The Mackay Consultants report (1986) estimated that the 1985/86 skiing season generated about £10 million of income for the local Spey Valley economy. This income generated the equivalent of about 280 full-time jobs on an annual basis, or 673 full-time jobs during the skiing season.

Similar estimates were also made for Glencoe as part of this study. Skiing at Glencoe provided a total local expenditure of about £375,000 in 1985/86. This generated the equivalent of approximately 11 full-time jobs on an annual basis, or 32 full-time jobs during the skiing season.

Market Forecasts

Any forecasts about the skiing market have to be set in an economic and social context. A wide variety of factors will influence future participation in skiing (either as a recreational or tourism activity). These factors include:

(1) An increase in holiday entitlement. Average holiday entitlement with pay has been steadily increasing since the 1960s. For example, in 1963, 97% of full-time manual employees had a basic entitlement of only two weeks, but by 1984, 80% had an entitlement of more than four weeks. It is anticipated that this trend will continue over coming years.

(2) The income of those in work has risen in real terms in recent years. This has given many people (especially those in the ABC1 socio-economic groups – the prime skiing market) an increase in their disposable income. This trend is likely to continue in the medium term.

(3) There had been a general trend for an increasing number of people to take more than one holiday each year. The proportion of adults taking two or more holidays a year increased from 18% in 1976 to 20% in 1984. This trend is expected to continue.

(4) There is a generally increased interest in fitness and health, although active participation in outdoor activities is still very low, for example only 1% of people aged 16 or over participated in rambling/hiking in 1983, while 2% participated in golf and 2% in cycling (General Household Survey, 1983).

(5) Children who learned to ski at school are coming on to the 'adult' market but because skiing is a relatively new sport, proportionately few people are dropping out of the older end of the market, that is, demography is favouring market growth.

Skiing is undoubtedly a growing sport/holiday activity. The popular BBC television programme 'Ski Sunday' which runs throughout the winter months attracts an average audience of 4 million viewers. The audience has grown from about 0.5 million when the programme first started nine years ago.

Ski magazines are also enjoying increased popularity. The two most popular publications are:

Ski Special – four monthly editions – circulation (1986) 45,000;
Ski Survey – five monthly editions – circulation (1986) 20,000.

There has also been a growth in the range of more specialist magazines produced for the serious skier, for example *Inside Edge* and *Skiing UK*.

The major holiday companies anticipate continuing growth in the skiing market. For the 1986/87 season Thomson (the market leader) increased the number of packaged holidays offered by 25% compared to the 1985/86 season. A number of other companies have also increased their holiday capacity significantly, for example Ski Sunmed increased its capacity by 20% for the 1986/87 season.

Neilson estimates that overall the packaged holiday market will grow by about 5% in 1986/87. This estimate appears slightly cautious given recent trends.

Ski holiday prices will remain competitive. While peak period prices for the 1985/86 season rose by around 7%, off peak prices remained static. These competitive prices, together with the increased media exposure being given to skiing, will broaden the base of the skiing market. It will attract people from a wider range of socio-economic backgrounds.

The market is expected to become increasingly segmented as different market niches are developed. Examples of two different market segments are group chalet holidays in upmarket Austrian resorts, and school skiing holidays in popular French resorts. Mintel predicts a growth in market volume through the development of market niches.

There are indications of a growth in the second ski holiday market (often short break holidays).

Skiing has become a very fashionable activity whose appeal is unlikely to diminish in the short to medium term.

There are a number of factors that will directly influence the future of the Scottish skiing market:

(1) The general increase in interest in skiing will have a positive influence on the Scottish market.

(2) HIDB surveys (1985) estimated that school children represented one-third of total skier days at the Scottish ski centres in 1984/85. The large number of Scottish school children participating in skiing will provide the Scottish market with a sound and probably increasing base. In an HIDB survey (1985) of 250 schools in Scotland a significant proportion of schools had ski clubs (68%) and, perhaps more importantly, a relatively high proportion of schools (41%) included skiing in the curriculum.

(3) The general increase in the number of people taking more than one holiday, together with the more specific trend towards second short break ski holidays will give Scottish skiing a good market opportunity.

(4) The various studies undertaken on Scottish skiing have all indicated that the prime market for Scottish skiing is Scotland itself and the North of England.

The total resident population (mid-1984) of Scotland and the northern half of England (as far south as Birmingham) is 28.6 million (51% of the UK population). Even a more restricted definition of Northern England (excluding the Midlands) gives a population total of 19.5 million (35% of the UK population).

These population figures give a crude indication of potential market size. If we restrict these figures to the second definition of the market area and only include the population aged 15–59/64 this reduces the population to 12.2 million. If all the skier days recorded in Scotland in 1985/86,

(549,000) were allocated to this population (12.2 million) it produces a figure of 0.05 skier days per head of population. Such a low figure indicates, albeit very broadly, the market potential. Although it is of course accepted that a definitive indicator of market potential would have to take into account factors such as personal income and lifestyle.

(5) The improved road network in Scotland will continue to encourage people to ski in Scotland. The development of the A9 has had a major impact on skiing at Cairngorm, particularly with regard to the growth in the day visit market.

(6) As the number of skiers staying overnight at ski centres increases, *après-ski* facilities would be expected to improve enhancing the overall attractiveness of ski holidays in Scotland.

As to future growth in the Scottish skiing market, it is felt that in the short to medium term (say the next five years) annual growth of approximately 5% is a realistic estimate. This assumes 'average' snow and weather conditions. This forecast could be exceeded if new ski runs were to be developed since long queuing times are presently dissuading many people from skiing.

Such an estimate can only be a short-term extrapolation based on an analysis of existing trends. There is no other meaningful way of assessing the skiing market.

Skiing is undoubtedly a growth activity or industry in Scotland. The annual rate of growth of demand, measured in skier days, has exceeded 10% in recent years. Many people involved with the industry feel that the demand would be even greater if there were more and better facilities in Scotland. At present there are four ski centres in Scotland, shown in Exhibit 21.5, and there are plans for others at Aonach Mor (near Fort William), Ben Wyvis and Drumochter, although it is unlikely that all of these will proceed. Exhibit 21.5 is reproduced from the National Planning Guidelines (by kind permission of the Scottish Development Department).

According to figures provided by the four ski centres, demand during the winter 1985/86 season was equivalent to 549,000 skier days, with the individual figures being:

Cairngorm	350,000
Glenshee	120,000
The Lecht	55,000
Glencoe	24,000

Cairngorm dominates the market with about a 64% share of the total number of skiers. The shares of the other three centres are Glenshee 22%, the Lecht 10% and Glencoe 4%. The figures will vary a little from year to year because of differing weather conditions and skiing seasons.

Programmes of improvement and/or expansion are underway at each of the four centres, although there are physical, environmental and planning constraints in some instances. As mentioned above, there are also plans for new facilities elsewhere in Scotland.

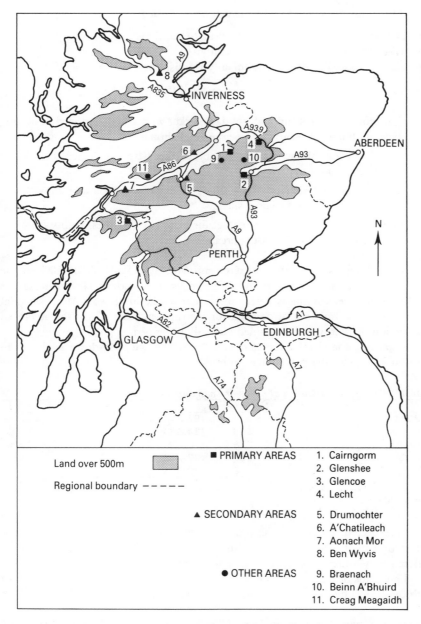

Exhibit 21.5 *National planning guidelines – 1984 skiing developments.*

Three distinct market segments can be identified:

- Day trips at weekends, by Scots, usually multi-visit.
- Weekend stay, mainly Scots, several visits.
- Holiday – weekend/weekday, mainly English, one visit per year.

The four skiing resorts tend to cater for different markets:

(1) Cairngorm – a weekend and holiday market with a high proportion of long stays, with a wide Scottish and large English market.

(2) Glenshee – a local day trip or weekend market with a wide Scottish catchment area.

(3) Glencoe – a predominantly local Glasgow day trip market attracting the more experienced and rugged skiers.

(4) The Lecht – a local day trip market for beginners/families mainly from Aberdeen and the surrounding area.

Most skiing is done on Saturdays and Sundays. Thus about 50% of the 350,000 skier days at Cairngorm were Saturdays and Sundays. Nevertheless, the quality of midweek skiing is a very important marketing factor. Also, potential exists for the stimulation of demand for instruction, particularly the advanced instruction market, which remained virtually untapped.

Regarding the characteristics of the skiers, the age breakdown is shown in Exhibit 21.6 (with the percentages in brackets).

Exhibit 21.6 *Age distribution of skiers at Cairngorm and Glencoe.*

	Cairngorm		Glencoe	
< 20	1,380	(52.2%)	212	(46.0%)
20 – 30	915	(34.6%)	194	(42.0%)
30 – 40	278	(10.5%)	35	(7.5%)
40 – 50	63	(2.4%)	13	(2.9%)
50 +	8	(0.3%)	7	(1.6%)
	2,644		461	

Source: Mackay Consultants.

As expected, young people under 30 years of age dominate. The Glencoe proportion in the 20–30 group is higher than that at Cairngorm, presumably reflecting the different types of skiing and facilities at the two centres.

The ratios of male to female skiers at Cairngorm and Glencoe are shown in Exhibit 21.7. The skiers' origin distribution is shown in Exhibit 21.8.

Exhibit 21.7 *Male/female distribution.*

	Cairngorm		Glencoe	
Males	1,756	(66.4%)	337	(73.2%)
Females	888	(33.6%)	124	(26.8%)

Source: Mackay Consultants.

These distributions are consistent with the market descriptions. Glencoe is very dependent on Scots, mainly day trips, whereas Cairngorm attracts large numbers of skiers from England. The numbers from overseas at both centres are very small.

Most skiers at Glencoe come from the Glasgow/Strathclyde area, whereas Cairngorm attracts a wider Scottish market.

On skiing standards, the skiers classified themselves as shown in Exhibit 21.9.

The results regarding the length of stay are shown in Exhibit 21.10.

Sources of information on skiing in Scotland used by skiers are given in Exhibit 21.11.

Exhibit 21.8 *Skiers' origin distribution.*

	Cairngorm		Glencoe	
Scotland	1,523	(57.6%)	405	(87.8%)
England	1,033	(39.1%)	45	(9.8%)
Wales	24	(0.9%)	1	(0.2%)
N. Ireland	23	(0.9%)	4	(0.9%)
Overseas	41	(1.5%)	6	(1.3%)
	2,644		461	

Source: Mackay Consultants.

Exhibit 21.9 *Skiers' self-concept.*

	Cairngorm		Glencoe	
Beginners	441	(16.7%)	44	(9.5%)
Intermediate	1,240	(47.0%)	237	(51.5%)
Advanced	839	(31.8%)	180	(39.0%)
Non-skier	118	(4.5%)	—	—
	2,638		461	

Source: Mackay Consultants.

Exhibit 21.10 *Skiers' length of stay.*

	Cairngorm		Glencoe	
Today only	561	(21.2%)	318	(69.0%)
Weekend	303	(11.5%)	83	(18.0%)
Longer	1,599	(60.5%)	30	(6.5%)
Friday–Sunday	135	(5.1%)	8	(1.7%)
Saturday–Monday	46	(1.7%)	22	(4.8%)
	2,644		461	

Exhibit 21.11 *Sources of information used by skiers.*

	Cairngorm		Glencoe	
Friends	319	(55.7%)	51	(83.6%)
Articles in papers	131	(22.9%)	6	(9.8%)
Ski Holiday Scotland	44	(7.7%)	—	—
Ski exhibition	8	(1.4%)	—	—
Other	71	(12.3%)	4	(6.6%)
	573		61	

Source: Mackay Consultants.

The breakdown by method of travel is shown in Exhibit 21.12.

Exhibit 21.12   *Skiers' method of travel.*

	Cairngorm		Glencoe	
Private car	1,959	(74.1%)	412	(90.3%)
Scheduled coach	60	(2.3%)	3	(0.7%)
Private coach	318	(12.0%)	38	(8.3%)
Rail to Aviemore	172	(6.5%)	—	—
Air to Inverness	52	(2.0%)	—	—
Other	83	(3.1%)	3	(0.7%)
	2,644		456	

Source: Mackay Consultants.

At Cairngorm the average expenditure per skier per day is £28.22.

Among expenditure categories, the most important are ski passes (£6.10), accommodation (£4.66), entertainment (£3.69) and meals off the hill (£3.34). Together these four categories account for just under two-thirds of total spending. Skiers staying in hotels spend a daily average of £39.46.

Average daily expenditure for day skiers is £18.19, compared with £30.92 for the longer stays. An obvious difference is the spending on accommodation, which accounts for £5.92 on average, and there is a difference of £2.59 in spending on meals off the hill. Day skiers spend £6.25 per day on ski passes, while longer stay skiers spend £6.06.

The Scottish average expenditure is £24.53, well below the figures for England, Wales and Northern Ireland (£33.36). Of course, virtually all of the non-Scottish skiers are longer stay visitors whereas many of the Scots are day skiers. However, the average spending of overseas skiers at £29.18 is surprisingly below that of the English, for example.

The Cairngorm Chairlift Company's estimates of demand in terms of skier days for the last few years can be presented as follows:

Season	1981/82	226,788
	1982/83	289,330
	1983/84	292,405
	1984/85	319,313
	1985/86	347,902

If we take the last figure and multiply that by the average daily expenditure at Cairngorm of £28.22 we get an overall expenditure figure of just over £9.8 million (£9,817,794 to be precise). In general terms, therefore, we can say that the winter 1985/86 skiing season generated about £10 million income for the local economy.

The facilities at Cairngorm during the 1985–86 season comprised four chairlifts, eleven tows, café/bar/shop/toilets at base, two cafés with toilets on the hill, plus ancillary facilities such as ski school, ski club hut, storage buildings, offices, etc.

The hill is thought to be overcrowded by 70% of skiers at Cairngorm. This reduces their enjoyment, the time they spend actually skiing and the overall value for money. There are also many complaints about the queues for the lifts and tows. Other comments related to the need for a larger beginners' area and for more advanced runs, as well as the need for higher capacity uplift to reduce queues.

For Glencoe the main expenditure category is ski passes which at £6.85 on average accounts for 44% of total spending. The day skiers at Glencoe account for 69% of the total, compared with 21% for Cairngorm, and this is a major factor in the differences in spending patterns. Day skiers at Glencoe spend an average of £7.11 per day on ski passes, while longer stay skiers spend £6.27.

The existing facilities at Glencoe include two chairlifts and five tows. There is a café on the hill but not at the base, and there are toilets at the base but not on the hill. There are also ski school and ski club huts.

CASE 22
Auto-Main
Marketing Mix Strategies

Luiz Moutinho

Glasgow Business School, University of Glasgow

Introduction

Auto-Main is a small, family-owned car-repair company, located in Barrhead, Scotland. Previously the company had been set up in Glasgow, but John and Maureen O'Hara decided to move it to Barrhead since they felt that there was a good potential market in the area to tap and far fewer competitors than in Glasgow. John O'Hara is a very experienced auto mechanic who had developed a mobile service in Glasgow, prior to coming to Barrhead, since the planning permission to build a garage was very difficult to obtain.

The company employs three qualified mechanics and two trainees, all under the supervision of John O'Hara. Auto-Main opens six days a week and is situated in the city centre, right in its main street, which could provide good visibility to the company. Nevertheless, there are parking restrictions and the main entrance/frontage of the shop is not very attractive in terms of making it more visible, informative and appealing to potential customers. John O'Hara is now planning to install an exterior canopy, painted in orange and black (the colours of the company) which also includes the company logo on both sides and its name on the front. Hopefully, the Auto-Main name, logo and colours will then be made more prominent, projecting into the main street so that they can be better seen by potential customers passing by.

The major strengths of Auto-Main can be summarized as follows: (1) good premises with large space available for future expansion; (2) good personalized service; (3) high-quality service provision; and (4) competitive advantage in auto-tuning.

The company's main weaknesses can be described as follows: (1) capital shortage; (2) limited manpower resources; (3) unattractive atmosphere and poor customer facilities; (4) less-than-ideal working conditions (lack of heating, bad ventilation and poor lighting); (5) underutilized working space; and (6) low market awareness.

The working area has not yet been divided into specific repair bays and the lack of general refurbishing, proper customer facilities and basic infrastructures seem to account for the low level of attractiveness of the premises.

Product and Pricing Policy

Auto-Main specializes in auto-tuning, full and engine service, clutch repair and brakes repair. Exhibit 22.1 introduces the product mix and price list of Auto-Main.

The company has been engaged in a controlled service expansion and is now studying different market opportunities for introducing new repair services.

In terms of contribution to total turnover and labour allocation, tuning services represent 34% on average (depending on the monthly cyclicality), full and engine service account for 20%, while general repairs, clutches, brakes and other service sales contribute the remainder of the turnover.

(AM) Auto-Main   OPEN 6 DAYS

41 CROSS ARTHURLIE STREET, BARRHEAD G78 1QU
Telephone: 041-880 7085

Hours: Mon. - Fri. 9am - 5.30p.m.
Saturday 9a.m. - 3.30p.m.

PRICE LIST EXAMPLES:—

ECONOMY TUNE-UP: WHILE—U—WAIT
Includes Labour + V.A.T.   **£12**

FULL SERVICE
inclusive of Service parts
Parts Labour + V.A.T.   **£46**

ENGINE SERVICE
Parts / Labour + V.A.T.
PLUS FREE TUNE-UP 4cyl s/carb.   **£34·50**

CLUTCHES:
Capri / Cortina   1.6cc £59.00
Cortina 2 litre £63.00
Fiesta 950/1.1 cc £72.00
Escort 1.3 MkIII £74.00
These are just a few examples of types and prices

BRAKES:

Cortina - Cavalier — Fiesta — Capri Ital,
Front or Rear Supplied/Fitted incl. V.A.T.   **£19**

SURE SPEEDY SERVICE ALWAYS

Exhibit 22.1   *Product mix and price list of Auto-Main.*

The average repair times for the different services provided are as follows:

	Minutes
Tune-up	30
Engine service	45
Full service	60
MOT	30

Total fixed (overhead) costs amount to £84,136 per year, while the average contribution margin is 60%. The gross profit margins by service rendered range from 50% in auto-tuning to 46% in full service. In terms of sales seasonality, Auto-Main has detected the following indices:

	Seasonal index
First quarter (January/February/March)	0.60
Second quarter (April/May/June)	1.50
Third quarter (July/August/September)	1.00
Fourth quarter (October/November/December)	1.20

The annual turnover of Auto-Main is £216,000. While the average selling price per repair job is £23.00, the average variable cost per repair job unit is £9.20. The company is planning to make a total investment of £45,000 over the next 12 months, regarding the acquisition of new equipment and tools, the programme for upgrading the premises and facilities, as well as the appropriations for the marketing budget.

The Market

The total number of cars in Scotland was 1,183,000 in 1984, while the total number of cars in the Strathclyde Region was 469,000 in the same year, representing 40% of the total in Scotland. The average car owner in Scotland can be characterized as a male individual aged between 25 and 45.

Car makes as proportions of totals for Scotland are broken down as follows:

(%)	
Ford	26
British Leyland	20
EEC	18
Japanese	12
Vauxhall	10
Talbot	6
Others	8 (6% foreign; 2% British)

Car ages as proportions of totals are represented as follows:

	(%)
Up to 2 years old	17
2–4 years	23
4–7 years	34
7–9 years	13
over 9 years	13

In terms of car insurance, the available figures indicate the following percentages:

	(%)
Fully comprehensive	64
Third party, fire and theft	24
Third party only	7

Regarding car maintenance, protection and appearance, 38% of cars are washed at least once per week, while 25% of motorists use automatic car washes more than three times in a year. Two-thirds of car owners have not used an automatic wash in the last year (1983).

The average repair bill paid by the average car owner in this market is £25.00.

Exhibit 22.2 shows the average expenditure on cars per year.

Exhibit 22.2 *Average expenditure on cars per year (£)*

	1980	1981	1982	1983	1984
Petrol	473	605	559	626	660
Servicing/repairs	160	151	111	211	146
Other running costs	208	213	226	244	251
TOTALS	841	969	896	1,081	1,057

Auto-Main's potential geographical market is based on the existing population in the Renfrew district and three additional areas: Newton Mearns, Beith and Kilbirnie. These geographical market boundaries can be seen in Exhibit 22.3, as illustrated by the shaded area.

Some of the relevant demographic and automobile-related statistics within this potential market are described in Exhibit 22.4. The three additional geographical areas (Newton Mearns, Beith and Kilbirnie), which are part of Auto-Main's potential market, have a total population of 33,491 persons, bringing the total population figure in the potential market for Auto-Main to 238,814 individuals. Auto-Main has set up the objective of attaining a 3% market share.

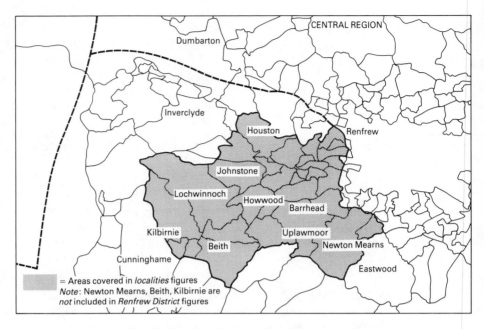

Exhibit 22.3   *Auto-Main's potential geographical market.*

Exhibit 22.4   Renfrew District: Population and Automobile-related Statistics

---

1. *Total population*:   205,323
2. *Sex*:   99,123 males
            106,200 females
3. *Age groups*:   16–24   15.2%
                25–34   13.9%
                35–44   12.6%
                45–60   19.7%
4. *Unemployment rate*:   13.3%
5. *Availability of car*:   49.5%
6. *Number of households*:   77,198
7. *Households with cars*:

	Number of households	Total number of individuals
One car	27,912	87,866
Two cars	6,317	22,722
Three or more cars	926	3,745
	35,155	114,333
Total number of cars 43,324		

Note   The percentages given or implied in items 3, 5 and 7 also apply to Newton Mearns, Beith and Kilbirnie.

Source: 1981 Census.

Customers

Auto-Main's typical customer can be characterized in demographic terms as follows: predominantly male, working class (C^1/C^2), living within a 10-mile radius, earning an average income of £6,000 to £10,000 and falling into the age bracket: 30–50 years old.

The age of the car is also considered to be an important segmentation variable, and a very large percentage of Auto-Main's customers have cars over three years old.

The average repair cycle for the average customer is 16 weeks and the average bill paid by the customer is £25.00. In general, customers prefer to pay in cash. In psychographic terms, Auto-Main has found that many of its customers are shiftworkers, a large proportion of customers like to take the car for repairs on Saturdays (almost as if it were a leisure activity), and many customers like just to stand there and watch the repair being done. Thirty-five per cent (35%) of the company's turnover is derived from repeat business and customer loyalty.

Word-of-mouth communication has been the most effective way to channel customers into Auto-Main, followed by the traffic flow generated by customers passing by due to the central location of the shop, and finally the market response generated from the advertisements placed in the local media.

Competition

Auto-Main has three major direct competitors (in terms of similar repair services provided) in its local market: C & M Motors, Briars and Mulholland, and Carlibar Motors, while the first of these companies is considered to be its strongest competitor. Another important competitor is the giant company, Kwik-Fit Euro, which has an outlet located just a few yards in distance from Auto-Main along the main street. Kwik-fit specializes in exhausts, tyres, suspension, batteries and radiator repairs, although some other additional services are also provided, such as brakes, clutches, steering and MOT testing. Kwit-Fit opens seven days a week and it also uses a fixed-price policy for servicing and lubrication. Kwik-Fit has been developing an aggressive pricing and best value policy, providing refunds if the customer finds the same quality product in stock locally at a lower price within seven days of purchase. These refunds can amount to more than the price difference found and claimed by the customer. Adding to this policy, Kwik-Fit has been stressing service attributes, such as quickness, friendliness, efficiency and 100% customer satisfaction in its advertising messages.

The three direct competitors are well established in the local market and they all carry similar product lines of auto-repairing.

The market awareness of these competing companies seems to be higher than Auto-Main's, but only due to the recent relocation of the company to this area and the opening of the repair shop in this market.

Auto-Main does not have much information available about its competitors' policies, strengths or weaknesses. In some cases, Auto-Main was able to collect information on sales volume regarding some of the competitors' services. For example, C & M carries out approximately 11 MOT repairs per day. The average price charged per MOT is £12.52 for approximately 30 minutes' work. The potential profits on MOT repairs are relatively high.

Since the opening of Auto-Main, John and Maureen O'Hara have been pursuing a fixed-price strategy (always conveyed in Auto-Main's advertising), which seems to provide the company with a clear differential advantage over the competitors, according to customer feedback collected by Auto-Main in order to assess customer satisfaction levels on a continuous basis. Auto-Main is also in the process of developing other competitive advantages, such as:

- service reliability/good quality
- quickness
- personalized service/friendliness
- no 'overselling'

Some of these competitive advantages that Auto-Main wants to pursue seem to bear a close resemblance to the marketing strategy which has been developed so far by Kwik-Fit, if one takes into account the necessary proportions (size and resources of the company, type of services provided, target market, repair job turnover and profit margin).

Marketing Activities

The marketing efforts carried out by Auto-Main evolve around three major activities: market research, pricing and advertising.

Market Research

John and Maureen O'Hara have been conducting informal surveys of their customers regarding the analysis of the sources of information used to select Auto-Main, perception of rendered services, overall customer satisfaction and attitudes towards the price policy. They were also able to characterize their target market in demographic and psychographic terms. The company has set up a data file which includes information on the customer's name, address and number of visits.

Pricing

Auto-Main has been pursuing a fixed-price policy in the provision of its repair services and so far the results seem promising.

Advertising

Auto-Main's advertising strategy is concentrated in the use of print media – two local newspapers (*Barrhead News* and *Paisley Express*). The copy strategy is mainly informative and developed around two basic USPs (unique selling propositions): auto-tuning and fixed price. One additional appeal, which is included in the message, relates to the quickness of the service (as seen in Exhibit 22.5 which shows a typical Auto-Main advertisement).

Auto-Main has also been placing advertisements in the *Motor Market Weekly* and is now considering the use of publicity by securing some editorial space in the local media through the development of some 'company stories and events' (for example by showing concern with the unemployment rate in the area and being willing to accept and train new employees, the opening of new improved premises and a charity raffle). Regarding other media utilized by the company, Auto-Main used promotional leaflets in the past, but the results of this effort were less than positive.

The Future

Auto-Main's long-term objective is to achieve a substantial penetration rate in the local market and increase the visibility of the company. To accomplish this,

Exhibit 22.5   *An illustration of a typical Auto-Main advertisement.*

Maureen and John O'Hara wanted to improve Auto-Main's marketing efforts, despite the limited financial and managerial resources available.

They wondered how much they should spend, what media would be most appropriate, what repair services would be best to promote and what efforts would be required to generate an effective marketing plan. Still, they know that marketing a small business which had all these internal and environmental constraints could be a very challenging and rewarding task.

CASE 23

The Anglo-Saxon Artist Limited
Marketing Mix Strategies

Arthur Meidan

School of Management and Economic Studies, University of Sheffield

Introduction

The Anglo-Saxon Artist Limited was a medium sized pottery firm that offered a very high quality and variety of distinctive designs. The products were sold in London and other major cities in the United Kingdom, mainly to tourists, through leading antique and artist dealer shops, at very competitive prices.

The company's marketing manager was John Stodart, who although he did not have any formal marketing education, was a member of the local branch of the Institute of Marketing and tried from time to time to attend various marketing management courses.

The Products

Anglo-Saxon's main 'asset' was a team of top pottery designers, June and Jim, who although originally from South America, were able – after studying at the Guildford School of Art – to combine very successfully the South American (Indian) motifs with traditional British designs in an *exceptional and unique* way. These designs, which were all hand-made and therefore virtually impossible to subcontract, made Anglo-Saxon's products in demand throughout the year and not just during the tourist season(s). Anglo-Saxon Artist Limited was distributing its products through independent agents that charged approximately 12.5% on top of the ex-factory prices. The retailers' mark-up was between 100% and 200% (or even more), depending mainly on the dealer's location.

The Distribution

John Stodart was very much interested to expand the sales and the profitability of Anglo-Saxon Artist Limited. He even has considered developing export contracts with dealers and antique shops in the Republic of Ireland and over the Channel, in the EEC. In addition, he wondered whether it would not be a good idea for Anglo-Saxon to open its own distribution outlets in London, Stratford-upon-Avon, Edinburgh, and some other selected locations, in order to 'save' the 'high retailers' margins for the firm, as well as having its own agents.

The catalogues were used by the retailers for the selection of pottery models that were then ordered via the agents. The retailers (antique dealers, etc.) used to give copies of these catalogues to many customers for future mail order from their own outlets. The catalogues themselves were quite expensive to produce, costing up to £5 per copy depending on the number of copies printed and the number of pages (models) included.

Frankly, J. Stodart found this an unreasonable expense; yet he felt that the retailers and dealers (as well as the agents) would find this unacceptable and would resist any introduction of a charge per catalogue. The marketing manager felt that a 'possible' way to economize on this promotional cost, would be to allocate a more limited total number of catalogues equally among the agents.

The Future Strategy

As demand was very high and could not be supplied, the management envisaged a manufacturing capacity expansion. However, because of financial and technical difficulties, it would take at least nine months until the production could be increased and the existing demand satisfied.

Faced with the above named problems, J. Stodart decided to ask for professional help. Through the local MSC (Manpower Services Commission) assistance to small firms, Mr Stodart obtained the services of a consultant, who advised the immediate introduction of a charging fee for the catalogues or, alternatively, the allocation of the existing number of copies equally among the distribution agents.

At the last Friday meeting with the agents, the marketing manager advised them about the new promotional arrangements (*re* catalogues), and apologized for the lack of products and inability to meet the demand. He concluded by saying that in approximately nine months, the financial and technical difficulties would be solved, and the production would increase at least two-fold.

The meeting was very stormy. All the 60 agents were against the change in the promotional policy, as this would negatively affect their relationships with the retailers.

After the meeting one of the agents summarized the present situation: 'Virtually all of us can obtain from this company only about 60% of all our orders. We all bring in good orders and a lot of business, week after week. Doesn't Anglo-Saxon have a marketing policy?'

PART 4

International Marketing

Case 24   **Massey-Ferguson–Agromet-Motoimport [Poland]**   262
International Marketing
Case 25   **Flexible Technology Limited**   284
International Marketing
Case 26   **Europack**   295
International Marketing

International marketing is being accepted increasingly as a way of life. The task of defining a company's environment, markets and competition is no longer limited by national boundaries. The expansion of international communication and shipping facilities has made the world a smaller marketplace. Multinational marketing is a complex form of international marketing that involves an organization engaged in marketing operations in many foreign countries. Many large multinational companies are becoming even more geocentric (world orientated). The geocentric assumption is that there are major differences from country to country and that these differences are important in the formulation of a national marketing plan, but at the same time there are important similarities among markets, and these similarities must be recognized to develop an effective integrated and coordinated international marketing plan that maximizes the profitability of a worldwide marketing effort.

The importance of international marketing is increasing as countries become more and more interdependent through international trade and direct investments. While markets may or may not be global, there is no question that competition is becoming global through mergers and acquisitions.

International marketing differs from domestic marketing mainly in that it involves different macro and task environments. Opinions vary on how to conduct an international marketing effort, dividing over the issue of uniformity across markets versus adaptation to local markets. Deciding whether or not to use global marketing hinges on legal issues as well as on cost savings and effectiveness in different environments.

Adjusting to a different culture is perhaps the greatest challenge confronting international marketers. The most important differences between domestic and international marketing relate to the environment of different nations. The social/cultural environment (language, social organization and religion, values, attitudes) is difficult to understand fully unless we are sensitive to marketing relativism (that is, that our assumptions tend to be unconsciously based on our own culture). The political and legal environment is often different in other countries than in our own, whether because of political instability, international politics, or the maze of laws and regulations that differ from country to country. It is also essential to analyse the level of economic progress and the existing infrastructure as well as the technology, distribution structures, competition and geography.

The four steps in international marketing are to analyse the macro and task environments, to determine which markets to enter, to select entry strategies and to design the marketing programme.

Determining which markets to enter involves two steps: preliminary strategic analysis and screening through matching company and country needs; and a more detailed study of how much adaptation is required in the marketing mix and the cost and revenue implications of such adaptation. Selecting one or more entry strategies means choosing among exporting (indirect or direct), joint ventures (for example licensing, management contracting, contract manufacturing and joint ownership), and the acquisition or creation of a wholly owned subsidiary.

The marketing programme must be designed to take into account all the unique aspects of the international setting. While a simple product-extension strategy may be selected, product adaptation or even product invention may be preferable.

Although the task of international marketing is similar to that at home, there are areas where significant differences arise that can have an important influence on the outcome of a marketing programme. These differences must be considered when developing alternative marketing strategies for foreign markets.

Companies that operate in one or more foreign markets must decide how much, if at all, to adapt their marketing mix to local conditions. At one extreme are companies that use a standardized marketing mix worldwide. Standardization of the product, advertising, distribution channels, and other elements of the marketing mix promises the lowest costs because no major changes have been introduced. At the other extreme is the idea of a customized marketing mix, where the producer adjusts the marketing mix elements to each target market, bearing more costs but hoping for a larger market share and return. Between these two extremes, many possibilities exist. Given the risk of international marketing, companies need a systematic way to make their international marketing decisions.

Because the risks and uncertainties are so high, marketing research is equally important (and probably more so) in foreign markets. Management can then determine whether there is an adequate market for the product and can decide how the product should be marketed. Marketers must examine each country completely in terms of the proposed products or services and not rely on an often-used axiom that if it sells or is successful in one country, it will surely sell in another. A product must be compatible with the environment in which it is used.

International promotion planning must take into account cultural differences such as customs, the meaning of colours and symbols, and the level of literacy. The use of media requires international adaptation because media availability varies from country to country. Media habits also vary by country. Every international advertiser must decide whether or not to extend, adapt or invent appeals, illustrations and copy for each national market

Regarding price policies, there is the issue of the terms of trade, which determine real selling prices and the division of such costs as insurance, documentation, packaging and freight between the buyer and seller.

A further aspect of price terms is the possible mixing of cash payments and goods in barter or in countertrading agreements. These forms of trading may involve straight barter, compensation deals, counterpurchase agreements or buy-back arrangements. Price competitiveness must also take into account the effect of changing relative currency values.

Distribution systems tend to be different in other countries. The international company must take a whole-channel view of the problem of distributing products to final consumers. There are striking differences in the numbers and types of middlemen, and in the size and character of retail units abroad. A major goal in distribution policy is to gain full market coverage, thus: (1) gaining the optimum volume of sales obtainable in each market; (2) searching a reasonable market share; and (3) attaining satisfactory market penetration. International marketing management must determine what can be done to improve marketing performance, effectiveness and efficiency.

Companies must also develop an effective organization for pursuing international marketing. Most firms start with an export department and graduate to an international division. The expansion of international operations has resulted in changed organizational structures for many businesses. Within this organizational adaptation, some selected organizational prototypes that have been used are the export management company (EMC), built-in export departments, separate export departments, the international division, regional management centres, the international headquarters company, worldwide product structures, worldwide geographic structures, the matrix organization, umbrella companies and the interglomerate (international conglomerate).

The future of international marketing looks bright. In fact, many experts see the day when there will be truly a 'world market'. While this day may be far into the future, the trends all appear to aim in that direction. This is why many firms are becoming more internationally minded and are in agreement that many marketing opportunities and challenges of the future lie in international marketing.

The *Massey-Ferguson–Agromet-Motoimport [Poland]* case provides an opportunity to investigate the role of the contractual joint venture arrangement as a vehicle for technical change. Many important issues are raised in the case, such as the role of a foreign trade enterprise, licensing and sub-licensing, use of trademarks, financing, production of components, organizational reporting, hierarchy networks and buy-back policies. The case does lend itself to the utilization of a role-playing format.

The *Flexible Technology Limited* case is aimed at getting students to analyse the difficulties faced by small firms in the electronics industry as they grow and recognize that markets for products in this industry operate at world levels. The case looks at factors, such as the timing of entry to the market, the development of product in the form of spin-off enterprise from foreign-owned multinationals, market specialization which enables large domestic and export shares to be achieved, and the potential available even to small firms in this industry.

The *Europack* case also deals with foreign market entry. The case analyses the different alternatives open to a company in how to service a foreign country. There is much that students can develop along the lines of positioning, corporate image and general effectiveness as expressed in sales. The case considers a portfolio of market entry opportunities being available to the company, as well as factors such as organizational structures, communication problems, salesforce management, competition effects, channels of distribution, product portfolio matrix, dumping and marginal pricing, performance criteria and sources of risk.

CASE 24

Massey-Ferguson–Agromet-Motoimport [Poland]†

International Marketing

Stanley J. Paliwoda

Faculty of Management, University of Calgary

Introduction

On the 12 September 1974, an industrial cooperation agreement (ICA, see Exhibit 24.1) was concluded between Massey-Ferguson-Perkins Limited, a British registered company and Agromet-Motoimport, the Polish Foreign Trade Enterprise (FTE) for agricultural machinery, on behalf of the Ursus Tractor Union (see Exhibit 24.7). At the time of signature, this was the largest contract ever to have been won in Eastern Europe by a British based company. Massey-Ferguson had been trading in a small way with Poland from the 1950s, but talks on a cooperation project only began in 1970, and quickened after the change of political regime in Poland in 1971, leading to the initialling of an agreement of industrial cooperation on the 23 August 1974, and its formal signature and acceptance one month later.

The initial proposal was for the licence of MF tractors and the refurbishing of the Ursus existing plant on a gradual basis to accommodate the new intended production lines. However, after the agreement had been signed and during the planning phase, it was decided by the Polish side that a new tractor plant should be built for these new production models. The agreement that was signed, therefore, was for the design, construction and operation of the world's largest tractor plant outside the USSR, for the licence to build 38 versions of eight basic tractor models in the range 38–75 h.p., together with three models of Perkins

†The preparation of this case was made possible by the cooperation of Massey-Ferguson Limited and by the financial support of the Leverhulme Trust. It was prepared by Stanley J. Paliwoda (Department of Management Sciences, UMIST) under the supervision of Professor Roy W. Hill at the National College of Agricultural Engineering, Cranfield Institute of Technology, in 1979. This case provides a basis for class discussion and is not presented as an illustration of either effective or ineffective handling of business problems.

Exhibit 24.1 Definitions of Industrial Cooperation

There is at present no internationally accepted definition of industrial cooperation, and so the following definitions are offered:

'Industrial cooperation in an East–West context denotes the economic relationships and activities arising from
- contracts extending over a number of years between partners belonging to different economic systems which go beyond the straightforward sale or purchase of goods and services to include a set of complementary or reciprocally matching operations (in production, in the development and transfer of technology, in marketing, etc.) and from
- contracts between such partners which have been identified as industrial cooperation contracts by governments in bilateral or multilateral agreements.'

UN Economic Commission for Europe, *Analytical Report on Industrial Cooperation among ECE countries*, Geneva 1973, p. 2.

'. . . a contractual economic relationship between two or more enterprises of different nationalities, extending over a longer period, whereby a community of interest is established for the purpose of complementary activities relating to the supply of licences and equipment, development of new technologies, the exchange of information on and the use of those technologies, production and marketing, with provision for the settlement in kind of whole or part of the obligations arising from co-operation activities.'

UN Economic Commission for Europe, TRADE/Ac.3/E.10., 15 October 1976.

'. . . industrial cooperation is generally understood to denote the economic relationships and activities arising from contracts extending over a long time period (typically five to ten years) between partners belonging to different economic systems, providing for reciprocal transfer of one or more commercial assets (such as technology, knowhow, capital, products, marketing and services), to meet specific objectives of the contracting parties. This relationship is usually one in which the Western partner has no equity interest . . .'

Jenelle Matheson, Paul McCarthy and Steven Flanders, 'Counter-Trade Practices in Eastern Europe', *East European Economies post-Helsinki*, A Compendium of Papers Submitted to the Joint Economic Committee, Congress of the United States, Washington DC: US Government Printing Office 1977, p. 1278.

'Industrial cooperation is defined by the following main characteristics:
(1) The cooperating parties are producers (trade organizations may act as intermediaries).
(2) Final products or knowhow or services are supplied according to technical specification and timetable agreed upon by the cooperating parties.
(3) The period of the cooperation is planned for several years.'

Polish Foreign Trade Research Institute, *Some Problems of Industrial Co-operation with Foreign Partners*, Warsaw 1977 p. 2.

(Exhibit 24.2) diesel engines for these tractors, with a plant capacity of 75,000 tractors and 90,000 engines annually. Under the terms of this agreement, MF contracted to purchase goods to the value of £165 million by the end of the 15-year contract period. These goods were to be mainly tractors and tractor components, engines and/or their components manufactured in Poland to MF designs and quality standards, but included a provision for unspecified goods which were sought by MF and could be provided by Polish industry. At the time of signing the contract, this particular provision was agreeable to MF since throughout the period from 1972 to 1975, it had been experiencing lost sales for failure to produce sufficient quantities to meet world demand. Evidence of this is provided by the 1975 Annual Report which cites worldwide industry production of tractors as having increased 45% in the period 1971 to 1975, a period of unprecedented growth in the farm industry of the Western world.

Massey-Ferguson's Background

Massey-Ferguson acquired its present trading name in 1958, five years after the Canadian company Massey-Harris had merged with Harry Ferguson Limited of the United Kingdom. The history of MF corporate growth has been built on a series of mergers and acquisitions (listed in Exhibit 24.2).

Daniel Massey was a farm equipment business started in 1830 and incorporated in 1847. The firm's international orientation began with the exhibition of Massey farm machinery at the Paris Exhibition in 1868. Headquarters were established in Toronto in 1879 and by 1883 yearly sales had reached $1 million. A London office was opened in 1887 and by 1890 European sales had reached US $125,000. Mergers with the A. Harris, Son and Co. and the A. Patterson-Wisner Co. in 1891 made the new Massey-Harris organization the largest company of its kind in the British Empire with a sales volume of about US $3 million and a full line of agricultural implements.

Massey-Ferguson was the first North American agricultural engineering company to enter international markets and its 1977 North American sales account for only 28% of its global sales, as against a percentage of approximately 75% for John Deere and International Harvester, after which it is the third largest farm equipment producer in the world. Although a Canadian company, MF earns only 8% of its worldwide turnover from Canada, and thus derives its income from being able to service its international network. Taking into account new licensees and associated companies, there are currently some 90 factories (see Exhibit 24.6) building the company's products in 30 countries, half of which are developing countries. This feature is both a strength and a weakness for MF. In 1977, International Harvester and John Deere concentrated roughly 75% of their sales in the more stable North American market while MF was pursuing sales in South America and the Third World: 70% of MF manufacturing takes place outside North America as against 20% for John Deere.

In 1978 MF built tractors in 19 different locations worldwide, and crawler tractors at four of these plants, but seven of these 19 plants are ones in which MF

Exhibit 24.2   Massey-Ferguson – Chronology of Mergers and Acquisitions

Date	Country	Acquisition/Merger	Products
Farm Machinery Group			
1953	UK	Harry Ferguson Ltd.	Tractors
1955	Australia	H.V. McKay-Harris Pty. Ltd.	Acquired control of implements manufacturer
1959	UK	Standard Motor Co.	Plants and facilities
1960	Italy	Landini	Tractors, crawlers
1961	India	TAFE (49%)	Tractors
1961	S. Africa	Sofim	Implements
1965	USA	Badger-Northland	Barn and forage equipment
1965	USA	Solar Aircraft	Plant and offices
1966	Australia	Crichton Industries Pty. Ltd.	Sugar cane harvesters
1966	Spain	Motor Iberica (37%)	Tractors, trucks, engines
1967	Brazil	Minuano SA	Implements
1969	Denmark	Lomgeskov Plovfebrik A/S	Ploughs and cultivators
1969	Argentina	Rheinstahl, Hanomag AG	Tractors
1969	Mexico	Ransomes	Implements
1970	W. Germany	Eicher GmbH	Tractors
1970	S. Africa	Slattery Group	Corn harvesters
Industrial and Construction Machinery Group			
1957	USA	Midwestern Industries	ICM loaders and backhoes
1960	Italy	Landini & Figli	Tractors and crawler tractors
1969	Italy	Simmel (33%)	Crawler track components
1970	W. Germany	Hanomag	Construction equipment
1972	Italy	Beltrami (50%)	ICM components
Engines Group			
1959	UK	F. Perkins Ltd.	Diesel engines
1968	Mexico	Motores Perkins SA	Diesel engines
1973	Mexico	Diesel Nacional SA (21%)	Diesel engines
1974	USA	White Motors	Engine plant

Source: MF Company Report (various)

has only a minority shareholding and thus would find any drastic rationalization hard, if not impossible, to implement.

The United Kingdom is the main manufacturing centre of MF tractors for export, which explains also why this industrial cooperation agreement with an ostensibly Canadian company, should be regarded as a British contract. Tractors are high technology items with very large economies of scale in production, which enables them to be shipped economically, due to a high value-to-weight ratio. In 1978, MF claimed a sales turnover of US $2,900 million and 20% of all farm tractor production in the West, but, at the same time, its overall market share in North America was declining, though North America still accounts for approximately 50% of MF research and development. MF is the world's largest producer of tractors, an activity which is still very much based in Britain, ever since the days of Harry Ferguson.

Massey-Ferguson and Eastern Europe

MF came to realize that the amount of business that could be generated in Eastern Europe, despite all efforts, was marginal. The interest was there but sales were few, and were often just single purchases by East European agricultural machinery research institutes which wanted machines to evaluate their technology content. An MF executive described the background as follows:

> 'We studied the markets. We knew something of their agriculture. We were quite convinced that we had products that were or should be acceptable in these markets and we continued, as any good business would, the pursuit of whatever trading opportunities there were, and the Polish project in a sense was the consequence of several years of that kind of cultivation of the possibilities.'

Two earlier events had influenced MF attitudes towards Eastern Europe. Firstly, the 10-year licensing agreements which MF had won in Yugoslavia in 1955 for tractors, combines and implements which had included lump sum payments for the drawings and documentation, royalty payments on the products manufactured, and substantial sales of the MF products to Yugoslavia. These agreements followed an earlier licensing arrangement made by Perkins for the manufacture of diesel engines which were suited to the MF tractors and combines. Secondly, there was the successful experience of the Fiat Company in an industrial cooperation agreement in the manufacture of saloon cars in Poland. To quote MF's Director of Special Operations:

> 'By the time the Poles started to talk to us, the Fiat project was already an undoubted success. . . . Barriers that previously existed were much reduced by the Fiat experience and they were able to apply the practical lessons learned from Fiat in negotiating the details of a contract with us.'

Massey Ferguson had already identified Poland and Romania as the most promising markets for agricultural machinery in Eastern Europe, in terms of the size of the markets, general lack of mechanization, and the number of horses still in use on the farms. With Romania, MF has initialled an industrial cooperation agreement in 1972 for the joint manufacture of wheel loaders, but despite the fact that this was the culmination of two years of negotiations, the agreement was never subsequently ratified. The cooperation agreement with Poland was different in that it was much larger in size, value and duration, and because of the degree of commitment given it by the Polish side. The Polish approach to the project was described by MF as a '. . . very bold, a very imaginative one'.

The Polish side came to Britain to talk to MF in 1970, a time when the company had been undergoing a massive expansion. The Poles wanted a new line of tractor which over time they could produce 100% for themselves. The initial reaction on the part of MF was very cool. There were two schools of thought in MF at the time: one, which said that the company should have nothing to do with licensing or selling MF designs and techology to Eastern Europe because of the dangers of future uncontrollable competition from such courses: the other, which realized the importance of the Fiat cooperation deal and anticipated that such a deal between Agromet-Motoimport and one of MF's competitors such as John Deere of Deutz, could pose a threat to the company.

On the question of MF's participation in a cooperation venture with Agromet-Motoimport, and the reasons leading to it, an MF executive said:

> 'In the early stages our motivation was not clearly defined except to feel that we ought to be doing something there but without seeing clearly how to do it. But we should certainly keep our ears open, we should always be seen to be interested, should always be ready to seize any opportunities that occurred because there was the uncomfortable feeling that these were huge markets; that the opportunities were there for somebody one of these days, which could then offer us a competitive threat in some kind of backdoor operation.'

MF was influenced in its decision by the favourable nature of a previous licensing operation in Yugoslavia which had terminated in 1965 in respect of tractors, combines and implements although the Perkins engine licence arrangements have been manufactured and updated. The licensing deal gave Yugoslavia a substantial industry built on the original transfer of knowhow from MF and a recent £30 million World Bank Loan has permitted further expansion of her tractor manufacturing capacity. Another factor which influenced MF was the undoubted very large domestic demand for tractors within Poland, which, coupled with MF's special buy-back relationship would contain the risk of future competition from Polish tractor exports at least for some time to come.

Opinion within MF continued to be divided: some, feeling that the project should proceed only with the MF trademark; others, feeling that MF should not be connected in any way with the end-product from Ursus. However, since MF was only prepared to license if it could control the exports of products resulting from this cooperation project, it was eventually decided that Agromet-Motoimport should incorporate the MF logo and trademark. In parallel with these conclusions, the Polish side would be allowed a free choice of tractor models including those then only available in prototype, such as the '500' series tractor, which was subsequently adopted for cooperation. However, in contrast to the offering proposed to the Poles by the West German firm Deutz, this was not a fully metric series but a compromise – 'soft' metrication it has been termed – since it involved the adaption of designs conceived in imperial sizes. The changeover to metrication was in the longer run inevitable for MF, and within the context of this cooperation agreement may have been an added bonus for the company, although this would certainly have added to the complexities of transmitting data and designs to Poland, since not only had the material to be translated into Polish but all sizes had also to be converted. Altogether there are 5,500 components to be made and although the volume of these components may vary, precision still remains of the essence.

Background to the Polish Tractor Industry (See Exhibit 24.7)

The original Ursus factory was founded in 1893 and sited in Ursus, 15 km from Warsaw, where farm machinery was produced until 1902 when the production of internal combustion engines began. By 1918, trucks and cross-country vehicles were being produced and in 1922 the production of agricultural tractors with internal combustion engines was started. In 1930–39, production was diverted to making trucks under licence to Fiat SpA, Italy and Berliet, France. Nationalization took place in 1937 and production was diverted to the production of military equipment. During the Second World War, however, the Nazis removed all the production machinery and installations, and then destroyed the factory buildings. It was later rebuilt and from 1947 until 1957 produced Lanz-Bulldog tractors, known as the C-45. About 750 were produced per month. In 1957, new production lines were being introduced which were not to be ready for production until 1959 and so in the interim period, production continued of the C-45 and also of the C-308 which was a small two-wheeled tractor with a linkage point for a trailer. This small tractor was not for agricultural use but more for gardens. Only 2,000 of the C-308 were produced, but it provided a suitable stop-gap between the old and the new production lines. In 1959, production lines were ready for the C-325 tractor which was introduced, and all the old lines were discontinued. In 1960, 6,400 C-325 tractors were produced, which when first introduced had a horse power of around 30.

Ursus, therefore, had a good tractor in the small range but nothing in the middle (40–65 h.p.) or large (c.80 h.p.) group. Industrial cooperation, therefore, was started in 1962 with the Zetor tractor factory in Czechoslovakia which had a 45 h.p. tractor. This led to further product modifications: the C-325 became the C-328, then C-330, then C-335, essentially the same small two-cylinder tractor but modernized and capable of now producing 45 h.p. In the middle range group, the C-4011 tractor was built in cooperation with Czechoslovakia. This model changed subsequently to being the C-350, C-355 and C-360A (a four cylinder tractor with four-wheel drive version). In the large size group, the C-380 was produced, again in cooperation with Czechoslovakia. This model became the C-385 and gave rise to the C-1201 and C-1204, all current production models. Cooperation with the Zetor plant in Czechoslovakia meant that Ursus was able to acquire Czech engines for her larger tractors, in exchange for tractor body parts.

During the 1970s the Ursus Mechanical Works underwent a major reorganization and merged with five smaller specialized factories which were producing tractor parts, to form the 'Ursus' tractor group or as officially known, the Tractor Industry Association. The plants concerned were:

Ostrow	radiators
Gorzow	steering kits
Wloclawek	brakes
Chelmno	clutches
Nisko	hydraulics

Ursus produced 58,000 tractors in 1977, mainly of the C-335 and the C-360, the C-335 being currently phased out. Over the period 1972–75, 33% of output was 35 h.p. tractors, 60% 55 h.p. tractors and 7% 85 h.p. tractors. Ursus production has grown from 38,700 units in 1970 to 57,600 units in 1975 and 58,800 units in 1976. The original plant produces 200 tractors per day in two eight-hour shifts with a workforce of 15,000 which compared with 80,000 tractors produced annually by 5,000 at Coventry shows that productivity is low. Tractors are very badly needed in Poland and so, consequently, production targets have to be met regardless of the conditions in which the factory is operating. The plant and machinery is old and so are the tractor designs. However, because of production targets it has always been inconceivable to halt production for re-tooling. Moreover, 25% of output is exported to the West for hard currency.

Ursus has its own Product Research and Development Centre and its own prototype workshop, working closely with the Agricultural Ministry Institute of Poznan, and the Ministry's Institute for Buildings, Mechanization and Electrification (IBMER) in Warsaw. (Exhibit 24.7). Ursus had developed its own new family of tractors, but this was rejected by the government anxious to introduce new technology and production methods into Poland. The proposal for a new plant was introduced at a later stage in the negotiations. It was decided first of all to introduce a new plant on a gradual basis and this MF was willing to do, but, upon further reflection, the Polish side did not consider this to be a practical proposal, and so the construction of a new plant became part of the project. As outlined in Exhibit 24.8 the MF tractors will cover the 38–75 h.p. range, there will be 15,000 Perkins engines available from Ursus each year for other applications in Poland, while the six cylinder Perkins engines manufactured under a separate agreement at the Andrychow engine plant in the South of Poland, will be used for the larger Ursus tractors, which will be further developed in conjunction with the Zetor tractor works of Czechoslovakia, as well as for other agricultural, industrial and marine applications. See Appendix 24.8 for a projection of the Polish tractor industry range until 1985.

Outline of the Industrial Cooperation Agreement

The 15-year agreement embodies the largest project in the Polish Government's 1976–81 Five-Year Plan in Poland, and comprises:

(1) A General Agreement, which outlines the objectives of the two partners and the method of arbitration.

(2) A Licence Agreement stipulating the rights of both parties, what is provided in manufacturing rights, and the extent of production line improvements that are to be conveyed. The licensing rights conferred by MF are for use in Poland only. There is a clause also which broaches the thorny problem of when is a new tractor also a new technology. It has

been agreed that where modifications have been made, these will be passed on to the Polish side, but where there is a new technology involved not subject to the present agreement then this could only be transferred under a separate agreement. The clause delineates what is meant by a new technology and it is generally understood to mean a new technological concept such as a hydraulic motor.

(3) An Industrial Cooperation Agreement which covers economic and commercial relations, how expenses are paid on both sides, the level of buy-back and also the pricing structure for goods bought by either side. The price basis is MF world prices, and either side offers discounts but the Polish discount is larger than the British discount to Poland because of the marketing and distribution costs which MF will incur with the Polish products.

(4) A Project Implementation Contract. This covers planning and schedule timetabling. MF is responsible for designing the new plant and supplying the technology; the Poles are completely responsible for the implementation of the contract. The contract involves the manufacture in Poland of 38 versions of the eight basic MF tractor models listed in Exhibit 24.7.

Features of the Industrial Cooperation Agreement

The Ursus project involves building and equipping, together with GKN, a new tractor plant alongside the old one. There is a certain amount of refurbishing but it is essentially a new tractor plant that is being created, where 70% of the volume of all the tractor components will be produced on site, with additional imputs coming from the other six newly expanded Ursus Union factories in Poland. Consequently, a high degree of detail is required. The proposed Ursus plant will be one of the largest tractor plants in the world, the area of the new buildings encompassing 2.7 million sq. ft and a site area of 3.6 million sq. ft which makes it larger than the British Leyland plant in Oxford or MF's own tractor plant at Banner Lane, Coventry (1.7 million sq. ft). MF has responsibility for the full planning details of the new plant, its commission, technology and quality of output. GKN has been awarded a separate contract for the construction of a new 75,000 ton foundry at Lublin and for the expansion of the existing foundry and forge at Ursus. A separate manufacturing plant was necessary to enable the present Ursus production to continue while the new plant was tooling-up, and allow for future scaling-down of the Ursus plant once the new plant comes into full production in 1985, when, all things being equal, production from the combined Ursus complex would be in the region of 58,000 Ursus tractors, 75,000 MF tractors and 15,000 Perkins engines, for other applications in Poland, per year.

MF gladly concedes the important role played by the British Government prior to the final signature of the contract. This role was mainly one of encouragement, but included also the offer of advantageous credits. The terms which the ECGD were able to offer then were very advantageous and were 'front-ended' so as to give MF an early return on the project. The financing terms were crucial to acceptance of the package. The Poles had talked among others to Deutz, International Harvester, and Fiat, but only Deutz was able to offer a competitive line of tractors together with an attractive financial package. Deutz products, unlike MF, were designed in metric sizes and would not require any conversion. However, the ECGD came back with a very tempting financial package at a time when Polish–West German relations had sunk to a very low level in 1974 over the political question of the repatriation of ethnic Germans in Poland.

The Polish side wanted a 'complete' tractor, a licence which was 'without holes', that is, all the inputs which MF used in manufacture had to be included in this transfer of technology. However, since MF brought out more than half the components used in its manufacturing plant at Banner Lane, Coventry, this request was received coolly and almost led to a breaking point between the two parties. Finally, a compromise was reached on the two greatest points of contention:

(1) A list was agreed of goods which it was felt would be unreasonable for MF to provide, for example rubber tyres. The understanding was reached that if the Polish side was lacking in any item in this list then they would have to acquire that technology for themselves, as it was not part of the contract. However, in separate negotiations with potential suppliers, the Polish side, eager to minimize the hard currency cost of these purchases, sought counterpurchase deals with its suppliers which proved to be a contributory factor in the three-year delay in the production schedule for which the Polish side was responsible.

(2) A further list of exclusions was all items presently made in Poland, and for which therefore it seemed reasonable to assume Poland already had the necessary manufacturing capability. The Poles would have to meet the problems of adapting these products to production requirements themselves.

However, these provisions were not entirely enforceable because of an escape clause which stated that if the Polish side was genuinely unable to achieve the required results by its own means, and was able to present a strong case in support of this, then MF would undertake to assist in solving the problem and, if essential, to provide the Poles with supplemental licences and knowhow. A number of licences were taken out by MF and sub-licensed to the Polish partner, but paid for by MF within the total negotiated licence fee. In this event, the Polish side did not talk to the licensors directly, but only through MF.

Financing

The financing of this particular deal was undertaken by a consortium led by Barclays Bank which arranged the first ECGD guaranteed loan in September 1974 for £127 million; and a second ECGD guaranteed loan for US $220 million in September 1978, also in connection with the Ursus project. (The engine project at Andrychow, negotiated with Perkins Engines Limited, is a separate project entirely from the Ursus project.) Generally, the project is a self-financing one because of the buy-back principle which allows Agromet-Motoimport to recoup the hard currency costs of the project. There is no fixed category of buy-back goods, only a certain level of buy-back which must be bought from Poland by 1989, and this can be from:

- MF products manufactured under licence;
- other Polish buy-back goods, a category which entails a much smaller commitment.

However, the Poles will pay financial compensation for any: '. . . disadvantageous factors encountered as a result of the product coming from Poland . . .'. Buy-back is an annual decision made on both sides taken on the basis of '. . . Our needs, their abilities . . .', which also reviews the price structures on both sides in the light of inflation. Once the Ursus MF plant is in full production it is hoped to have an annual setting of MF buy-back numbers with a monthly 'fine tuning'.

The shortage of foreign currency means that MF c.k.d. (completely knocked down) kits cannot be purchased. In fact, a smaller number has been bought by the Poles than was anticipated in the original 1974 plan, before the plant ran into tooling delays.

Although the projected handover of all planning documentation took place on schedule in accordance with the agreements, the project as a whole is now subject to an approximately three-year delay, mainly because the Poles have been placing orders for plant and equipment years later than anticipated. One factor causing this delay has been Poland's problems with its hard currency reserves. This factor has also caused substantial reductions in the quantities of c.k.d. kits imported by Poland from MF during the start-up phases of the project.

Organizational Framework for Cooperation

With regard to the day-to-day implementation of the contract in 1977/8 staff numbers vary, but there are nine resident Poles at director level from Agromet-Motoimport and Ursus staff who have been assigned to MF's Polish Project headquarters at Stoneleigh, Coventry, although the number of Polish visitors often varies between 10 and 40 per week. On the MF side, there are 83 members of the Polish Project in Coventry and two full-time based at Ursus, plus, of course, support staff such as secretaries and typists. Within the MF organizational structure, the Polish Project was originally incorporated within the Three 'A's'

Division – Africa, Asia and Australasia (including MF Special Operations, London, responsible for marketing in Comecon). The Polish Project still has its headquarters in Lucerne, Switzerland, but with corporate reorganization in 1978 disbanding the previous product and geographical groups, control passed to the Vice President – Planning and Business Development.

Initially, director-level meetings were held on a monthly basis but they are now – four years on – held once every two months, alternating between Warsaw and Coventry. A pattern of decision making has also been agreed upon:

(1) Preliminary screening. Polish directors from Ursus in Coventry will perhaps be able to solve the problems or at least reduce the possible alternatives for action.

(2) Secondary screening by telex. There is a direct telex link from Coventry to Agromet-Motoimport. There are two permanently based MF staff there who liaise with the Ursus factory and with Agromet-Motoimport, the Foreign Trade Enterprise.

(3) Plenary sessions, every two months, alternating between Warsaw and Coventry.

Marketing Organization

The development of international markets requires both time and money and the Polish side is markedly short of both, and this has been one of the motivating factors for cooperation on the Polish side. MF has accorded Agromet-Motoimport exclusive rights to sell licensed products in Poland for use in Poland, and non-exclusive rights to sell to most CMEA countries. Exports to all other countries will be channelled only through MF. Regarding the livery of Ursus produced MF tractors, it was finally agreed after negotiations lasting 18 months that within CMEA these tractors will be known as MF–Ursus tractors with MF livery, and for all other markets will be known only as MF tractors, with a small plate which is mandatory to indicate the country of origin.

Polish personnel are trained in service and parts and Agromet-Motoimport is supplied with sets of documentary information on distribution organizations and practices. The Polish side is responsible for all warranty claims on Polish-produced MF models.

The Future for Massey-Ferguson–Agromet-Motoimport Cooperation

There are two areas in which further cooperation could develop:

* Agricultural implements, such as drills and harrows.
* Industrial machinery which will base itself on the 75 h.p. MF tractor to be produced at Ursus.

In agricultural implements, MF actually buys many of its implements rather than making them, but as potential goods for buy-back MF points out that with implements there are not the same economies of scale as with tractors, that freight costs are heavy, and that the specialized requirements of local markets are a further constraining factor.

The Present Dilemma

In mid-1978 it became apparent that the costing of the new Ursus plant – now three years behind schedule – had been overtaken by inflation. This was due to two factors: two-figure Western inflation in 1975 and 1976; and the fact that the Polish side had placed orders for equipment years later than originally anticipated. The consequence was that the original 1974 agreement figure of £165 million buy-back by 1989 was insufficient to make this project self-financing for the Poles in respect of their hard currency expenditures. Agromet-Motoimport was therefore asking MF to agree to an increased buy-back of £310 million so that they could offset the Western purchases of machinery and equipment necessary to bring the new Ursus plant fully into production, and also extend the time period of MF's participation in the project. However, MF experience to date of buy-back has been one of difficulty although the situation is expected to improve once the new plant achieves production of MF designed components, but these production schedules are now three years behind. It has also been the case that other items of automotive component buy-back in which MF is interested have been subject to heavy demand from the rapidly growing Polish passenger car and bus industries and so have not been available on a regular basis.

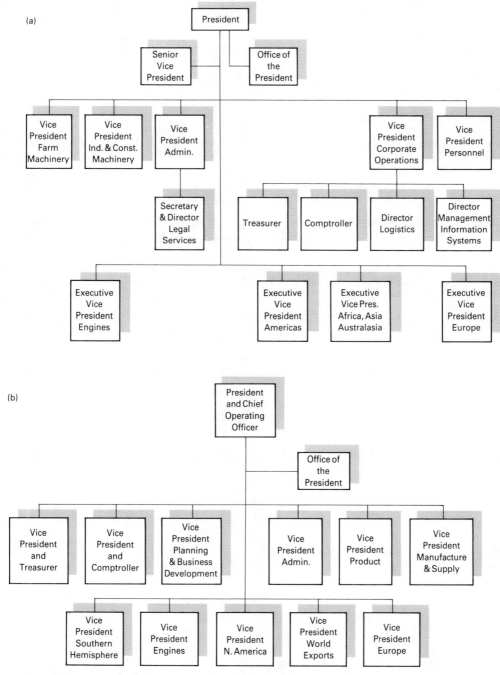

Exhibit 24.3 *Massey-Ferguson organizational structure: (a) pre-1978; (b) post-1978.*

Sources: MF Company Reports 1974 and 1978.

Exhibit 24.4 Massey-Ferguson: Sales Statistics (in millions of US dollars)

	1978* % of Amount Total	1978* ($)	1977* ($)	1976* ($)	1975* ($)	1974* ($)	1973* ($)	1972* ($)	1971 ($)	1970 ($)	1969 ($)
Net Sales By Markets											
North America											
Canada	6.4	188.7	193.5	213.2	184.0	142.4	100.2	85.8	69.1	65.2	79.9
United States	23.6	689.1	646.4	641.9	562.4	471.6	422.2	330.8	293.6	247.8	285.9
Total	30.0	877.8	839.9	855.1	746.4	614.0	522.4	416.6	362.7	313.0	365.8
Europe											
United Kingdom	11.5	336.3	274.4	225.4	211.6	157.5	146.8	128.9	116.2	114.3	106.1
West Germany	9.9	288.4	220.2	183.1	157.5	88.0	102.6	62.4	56.4	57.8	47.5
France	6.6	194.5	189.3	166.7	171.3	142.4	137.4	119.2	95.6	88.5	110.7
Italy	5.4	157.0	136.2	119.1	89.5	59.3	54.5	45.7	39.4	41.8	37.3
Scandinavia	3.8	110.6	102.7	90.4	86.9	56.1	45.6	42.3	41.3	39.7	34.7
Benelux	1.3	38.9	44.2	39.8	33.3	19.0	15.8	10.5	9.3	11.6	8.4
Spain	0.6	16.2	21.6	19.3	18.6	16.7	10.2	8.3	4.3	8.1	9.0
Austria	0.5	14.0	21.9	15.9	14.4	10.3	10.9	8.3	10.1	8.2	6.0
Other	1.6	47.9	42.9	30.5	30.4	17.5	16.1	14.3	13.9	14.0	11.5
Total	41.2	1,203.8	1,053.4	890.2	813.5	566.8	539.9	439.9	386.5	384.0	371.2
Latin America											
Brazil	8.9	260.4	277.1	403.6	363.1	213.3	164.5	121.5	76.4	58.8	43.0
Mexico	1.4	42.6	20.9	37.4	35.0	19.0	11.3	11.5	11.5	11.7	11.8
Argentina	1.2	34.0	109.2	72.6	51.7	51.1	29.2	15.5	10.1	9.6	3.8
Other	1.4	41.8	48.3	35.8	51.8	32.7	23.5	15.9	21.8	14.7	11.5
Total	12.9	378.8	455.5	549.4	501.6	316.1	228.5	164.4	119.8	94.8	70.1
Africa											
South Africa	2.7	80.5	76.5	73.0	99.2	70.2	45.5	43.6	44.7	38.0	38.9
Libya	0.5	13.6	14.6	14.8	28.9	19.0	11.4	7.7	4.2	0.6	3.4
Sudan	0.1	2.0	4.2	10.5	3.5	1.7	0.3	4.8	0.5	2.6	1.4
Other	2.4	69.6	73.1	51.3	63.9	36.1	26.4	21.5	27.5	27.5	24.3
Total	5.7	165.7	168.4	149.6	195.5	127.0	83.6	77.6	76.9	68.7	68.0

	%										
Asia											
Iran	1.0	30.8	10.1	38.5	15.5	0.8	0.3	0.1	0.2	0.1	0.9
Turkey	1.0	28.4	51.6	76.4	44.3	24.4	29.0	16.2	8.1	3.9	10.0
Pakistan	0.4	12.2	21.1	29.2	15.9	5.4	1.4	2.8	1.8	4.0	4.0
Japan	1.0	30.4	18.8	17.2	23.4	12.5	7.7	6.5	7.4	5.4	4.3
Other	3.3	95.5	65.2	44.6	48.4	25.2	19.1	17.8	23.3	20.1	19.8
Total	6.7	197.3	166.8	205.9	147.5	68.3	57.5	43.4	40.8	33.5	39.0
Australasia											
Total	3.5	102.1	121.3	121.5	108.8	92.4	74.3	50.5	42.6	43.9	55.3
Total	100.0	2,925.5	2,805.3	2,771.7	2,513.3	1,784.6	1,506.2	1,192.4	1,029.3	937.9	969.4
Net Sales By Quarters											
First	18.3	535.4	491.4	498.5	437.4	339.6	253.9	177.7	197.6	172.8	158.8
Second	26.5	776.6	660.9	713.6	604.1	434.1	359.2	287.8	256.4	249.7	248.2
Third	24.3	710.2	733.4	667.5	645.2	457.5	380.5	327.4	249.4	235.9	265.7
Fourth	30.9	903.3	919.6	892.1	826.6	553.4	512.6	399.5	325.9	279.5	296.7
Total	100.0	2,925.5	2,805.3	2,771.7	2,513.3	1,784.6	1,506.2	1,192.4	1,029.3	937.9	969.4
Net Sales By Products											
Farm & Industrial Machinery											
Tractors	38.6	1,128.3	1,178.2	1,171.5	1,020.5	674.4	575.5	474.2	396.0	331.0	339.6
Grain Harvesting	11.4	334.8	308.4	359.8	340.1	248.3	202.6	143.3	128.0	99.4	148.4
Hay Harvesting	1.8	51.5	61.2	52.8	51.2	39.6	37.1	28.5	29.3	26.1	30.1
Industrial Machines	5.9	173.5	146.4	147.6	129.9	120.3	119.3	104.9	84.7	89.5	89.9
Other Products	7.6	221.8	224.1	230.1	215.2	190.9	152.1	111.4	97.0	99.6	94.7
Parts	10.4	305.7	275.4	267.2	267.9	215.6	175.9	135.9	116.4	102.1	95.4
Total	75.7	2,215.6	2,193.7	2,229.0	2,024.8	1,489.1	1,262.5	998.2	851.4	747.7	798.1
Construction Machinery											
Machines	7.5	220.2	185.7	169.6	158.0	78.3	61.8	37.3	36.9	38.6	38.1
Parts	1.5	43.7	39.0	33.4	35.7	12.4	9.0	6.6	5.9	6.2	6.1
Total	9.0	263.9	224.7	203.0	193.7	90.7	70.8	43.9	42.8	44.8	44.2
Engines											
Engines	19.2	560.9	512.9	486.0	402.1	263.0	220.8	197.7	166.1	179.4	160.7
Deduct MF	(6.2)	(182.7)	(182.4)	(200.4)	(168.7)	(104.8)	(87.1)	(80.0)	(59.1)	(57.8)	(55.8)
Parts	2.3	67.8	56.4	54.1	61.4	46.6	39.2	32.6	28.1	23.8	22.2
Total (Net)	15.3	446.0	386.9	339.7	294.8	204.8	172.9	150.3	135.1	145.4	127.1
Total	100.0	2,925.5	2,805.3	2,771.7	2,513.3	1,784.6	1,506.2	1,192.4	1,029.3	937.9	969.4

*Settlement accounting: for 1972–78 only.
It is not practicable to restate individual years prior to 1972.

24.5   Massey-Ferguson: Financial Statistics (in millions of US dollars except where indicated)

		1978	1977	1976	1975	1974*
Summary of Operations						
Net sales	($)	2,925	2,805	2,772	2,513	1,785
Gross profit	($)	554	596	654	574	407
Net expenses (excluding interest)	($)	517	414	384	337	246
Interest expenses (net)	($)	187	151	101	99	57
Provision for Reorganization Expenses	($)	116				
(Loss) Profit before taxes, etc.	($)	(226)	31	169	138	104
Income taxes	($)	12	11	61	48	37
Finance subsidiaries and Associate Cos.	($)	21	13	10	9	7
Net (loss) income	($)	(257)	33	118	99	74
Dividends – Common	($)	4	19	18	13	15
– Preferred	($)	2	10	7	2	
(Loss) income retained	($)	(263)	4	93	84	59
Financial Condition						
Working capital	($)	430	697	732	626	507
Additions to fixed assets	($)	99	147	175	170	110
Depreciation and amortization	($)	77	69	54	45	35
Total assets	($)	2,547	2,594	2,305	1,997	1,620
Current ratio		1.3	1.6	1.8	1.8	1.7
Asset turnover ratio		1.2	1.1	1.2	1.3	1.1
Debt/equity ratio		2.1	1.2	0.9	1.0	0.9
Liabilities and Shareholders' Equity						
Current	($)	1,272	1,075	883	830	721
Other	($)	735	712	619	515	369
Shareholders' equity	($)	541	807	803	652	530
Return on closing equity	%	(47.5)	4	15	15	14
Per Cent Increase From Previous Year						
Sales	%	4.3	1.2	10.3	40.8	18.5
Cost of goods sold	%	7.3	4.4	9.2	40.7	18.9
As a Per Cent of Sales						
Cost of goods sold	%	81.1	78.8	76.4	77.1	77.2
Gross margin	%	18.9	21.2	23.6	22.9	22.8
Marketing, general and administrative	%	12.7	11.8	11.1	10.7	11.4
Engineering and product development	%	2.3	2.4	2.2	2.2	2.4
(Loss) Profit before Provision for Reorganization Expense, taxes, etc.	%	(5.1)	1.1	6.1	5.5	5.8
Provision for Reorganization Expense	%	4.0				
Net (Loss) income	%	(8.8)	1.2	4.3	3.9	4.1
Per Common Share ($US)						
Net sales	($)	160.27	153.71	151.87	137.71	97.80
(Loss), Income (after cumulative dividends on preferred shares)	($)	(14.53)	1.26	6.04	5.31	4.05
(Loss) Income retained	($)	(14.41)	0.20	5.07	4.62	3.23
Equity	($)	24.37	38.71	38.51	33.56	29.04
Toronto Stock Exchange quotes, High	($)	20¼	24⅛	32	18⅛	24⅜
($Canadian) Low	($)	9½	16⅛	16¾	12⅛	11½
Dividends declared ($Canadian)	($)	0.25	1.08	1.00	0.70	0.80
Dividends paid ($Canadian)	($)	0.25	1.08	1.00	0.90	0.80
Shareholders/Employees						
Employees		57,983	67,151	68,200	64,572	60,822
Shareholders – Common shares		31,353	30,619	31,039	35,844	35,541
– Preferred shares		11,370	10,208	10,620	5,046	
Common shares outstanding (thousands)		18,250	18,250	18,250	18,250	18,248
Preferred shares outstanding (thousands)		3,825	3,999	3,999	1,600	

*It was not practicable to include the impact of FASB 8 for years prior to 1974, which year includes the cumulative effect of all prior years.
Source: MF Company Report 1978.

Exhibit 24.6 Massey-Ferguson Manufacturing Plants and Facilities Worldwide

Farm and Industrial Machinery

Argentina
Massey-Ferguson Argentina S.A.
Rosario Plant (270,000 sq. ft) – agricultural
tractors.
San Lorenzo Plant (76,000 sq. ft) –
implements.

Australia
Massey-Ferguson (Australia) Limited
Bundaberg Plant (207,000 sq. ft) – sugar cane
harvesters, loaders, backhoes.
Sunshine (Melbourne) Plant (1,373,000 sq. ft)
– combines, implements

Brazil
Massey-Ferguson do Brasil S.A.
Canoas Plant (581,500 sq. ft) – combines,
implements, backhoes.
Sao Paulo Plant (389,000 sq. ft) – agricultural
and industrial tractors.

Canada
Massey-Ferguson Industries Limited
Brantford Locations
–Combine Plant (812,000 sq. ft) – combines,
combine cabs.
–Foundry (255,000 sq. ft) – grey iron
castings.
–Implement Plant (804,000 sq. ft) – plows,
mowers, rakes and other implements, combine
and tractor components.
–Steel Processing Plant (275,000 sq. ft) –
steel stampings.
Toronto Plant (1,835,000 sq. ft) – balers,
corn heads, forage harvesters, tractor cabs,
combine and tractor components.
Kanmet Ltd.
Cambridge Foundry (61,000 sq. ft) – grey iron
and nodular castings.

France
Massey-Ferguson S.A.
Beauvais Plant (932,000 sq. ft) – agricultural
tractors, tractor components.
Marquette Plant (1,155,000 sq. ft) –
combines, balers, tractor cabs, components
and grey iron castings.

Italy
Massey-Ferguson S.p.A.
Como Plant (115,000 sq. ft) – tractor
components.
Fabbrico Plant (380,000 sq. ft) – agricultural
wheel and crawler tractors.

Rhodesia
Rhoplow Limited
Bulawayo Plant (56,000 sq. ft) – animal draft
implements, hoes, peanut shellers.

South Africa
Massey-Ferguson (South Africa) Limited
Safim Manufacturing Limited
Vereeniging Plant (658,000 sq. ft) –
implements, tractor accessories and
attachments, industrial loaders, transport
systems.
Slattery Manufacturing (Proprietary) Limited
Potgietersrus Plant (216,000 sq. ft) –
harvesting machinery, implements, trailers.

United Kingdom
Massey-Ferguson (United Kingdom) Limited
Baginton Plant (312,000 sq. ft) – tractor
components.
Coventry Plant (1,517,700 sq. ft) –
agricultural and industrial tractors, axles,
gearboxes, other components.
Kilmarnock Plant (789,000 sq. ft) – combines,
combine tables, tractor accessories.
Knowsley Plant (304,000 sq. ft) – tractor-
backhoe-loaders.
Manchester Plant (511,000 sq. ft) – tractor
loaders, tractor-backhoe-loaders, 4-wheel-
drive agricultural tractors, tractor components.

United States
Massey-Ferguson Inc.
Des Moines Plant (570,000 sq. ft) – 4-wheel-
drive agricultural tractors, disc tillage
implements, tractor-backhoe-loaders.
Detroit Locations
–Southfield Plant (820,000 sq. ft) –
agricultural and industrial tractors, tractor-
backhoe-loaders.

Exhibit 24.6 *continued*

Farm and Industrial Machinery *continued*

–*Van Born Plant (497,000 sq. ft)* – tractor transmission and axle assemblies, hydraulic and power steering pumps, tractor components.

–*West Chicago Street Plant (314,000 sq. ft)* – tractor and combine transmission and axle components.

Badger Northland Inc.
Kaukauna Plant (267,000 sq. ft) – Badger Northland forage and feeding equipment; solid and liquid manure disposal systems, manure spreaders.

West Germany

Massey-Ferguson CmbH
Eschwege Plant (587,000 sq. ft) – roller chain, gearboxes, gears, hydraulic cylinders, combine axles, grey iron castings and other components.

Gebr. Eicher GmbH
Landau Plant (240,000 sq. ft) – tractors and implements.

Construction Machinery

Brazil

Massey-Ferguson do Brasil S.A.
Sorocaba Plant (147,000 sq. ft) – crawler tractors, tractor-backhoe-loaders.

Italy

Massey-Ferguson S.p.A.
Aprilia Plant (600,000 sq. ft) – crawler tractors, hydraulic excavators.
Ravenna Plant (110,000 sq. ft) – construction machinery components, hydraulic excavators.

West Germany

Massey-Ferguson-Hanomag Inc. & Co.
Hanover Plant (2,900,000 sq. ft) – wheel loaders and dozers, crawler tractors, compactors, tractor components.

Engines

Australia

Perkins Engines Australia Pty. Ltd.
Dandenong Plant (16,000 sq. ft) – industrial diesel engine assembly, engine reconditioning.

Brazil

Motores Perkins S.A.
Sao Bernardo Plant (259,000 sq. ft) – diesel engines.
Sao Paulo (Alvarengas) Plant (48,000 sq. ft) – diesel engines.

Progresso Metalfrit S.A.
Sao Paulo Foundry (97,000 sq. ft) – grey iron castings.

France

Perkins Industries S.A.
Genainville Plant (30,000 sq. ft) – agricultural diesel engine assembly, engine reconditioning.

United Kingdom

Perkins Engines Group Limited
Peterborough Locations
–*Eastfield Plant (1,828,000 sq. ft)* – diesel and gasoline engines, engine reconditioning.
–*Fletton Plant (198,000 sq. ft)* – diesel engines and engine components.
–*Walton Plant (166,000 sq. ft)* – engine components.

United States

Perkins Diesel Corporation
Canton Plant (587,000 sq. ft) – diesel engines.

Perkins Engines Inc.
Farmington Plant (40,000 sq. ft) – diesel engine assembly.

Associate Companies and Per Cent Owned

Argentina

Perkins Argentina S.A.I.C. 30%
Cordoba Plant (262,000 sq. ft) – diesel engines.

Brazil

Companhia Industrial de Peças para Automóveis 28%
Sao Paulo Plant (196,000 sq. ft) – forgings.

Piratininga, Implementos
Agricolas Ltda. 40%
Butia Plant (65,000 sq. ft) – farm implements.

Exhibit 24.6 *continued*

Associate Companies and Per Cent Owned *continued*

India
Tractors and Farm Equipment Limited 49%
 Madras Plant (193,000 sq. ft) – tractors and
 implements.

Italy
Simmel S.p.A. 33%
 Castelfranco Veneto Plant (380,000 sq. ft) –
 crawler tractor components.

Libya
Libyan Tractor Company 33⅓ %
 Ta Joura (Tripoli) Plant (118,400 sq ft) –
 tractors (under development).

Malawi
Agrimal (Malawi) Limited 20%
 Blantyre Plant (12,000 sq. ft) – hoes, animal
 draft equipment.

Mexico
Massey-Ferguson de Mexico S.A. 49%
 Queretaro Plant (145,000 sq. ft) – tractors.
 Naucalpan de Juarez Plant (58,000 sq. ft) –
 farm implements.
Motores Perkins S.A. 24%
 Tuloca Plant (153,000 sq. ft) – diesel engines.

Morocco
Compagnie Maghrebine de Materiels Agricoles et
Industriels S.A. 24%
 Casablanca Plant (54,000 sq. ft) – tractors.

Peru
Tractores Andinos S.A. 49%
 Trujillo Plant (70,000 sq. ft) – tractors.
Motores Diesel Andinos S.A. 24%
 Trujillo Plant (109,000 sq. ft) – diesel engines.

Spain
Motor Iberica S.A. 29%
 Barcelona Locations
 –Lopez Varela Plant (406,000 sq. ft) – tractor
 components.
 –Zona Franca Plant (779,000 sq. ft) – trucks
 and tractors.
 –Montcada Plant (196,000 sq. ft) – sheet-
 metal components.
 Madrid Locations
 –Avda. Aragon Plant (109,000 sq. ft) – diesel
 engine components.
 –Cuatro Vientos Plant (726,000 sq. ft) –
 diesel engines and trucks.

Other Locations
 –Corrales de Buelna Plant (207,000 sq. ft) –
 tractors and engine components.
 –Corrales de Buelna Foundry (528,000 sq. ft)
 – castings.
 –Noain Plant (187,000 sq. ft) – combines,
 balers, cornheads.
 –Ejea Plant (97,000 sq. ft) – farm implements.
 –Tauste Plant (16,000 sq. ft) – farm
 implements.

Other Massey-Ferguson and Perkins Companies

Canada
Perkins Engines Canada Limited
Rexdale

France
Moteurs Perkins S.A.
Saint-Denis

Italy
Motori Perkins S.p.A
Como

South Africa
Perkins Engines (Proprietary) Limited
Johannesburg

United Kingdom
Massey-Ferguson (Export) Limited
Coventry
Massey-Ferguson-Perkins Limited
London
Perkins Engines Limited
Peterborough

West Germany
Perkins Motoren GmbH
Kleinostheim

Licensee Locations

Farm and Industrial Machinery: Greece, India,
Iran, Japan, Kenya, Malaysia, Pakistan, Poland,
Portugal, Thailand, Turkey, Uruguay.

Construction Machinery: India

Engines: Greece, India, Iran, Pakistan, Poland,
Republic of Korea, Turkey, Uruguay, Yugoslavia

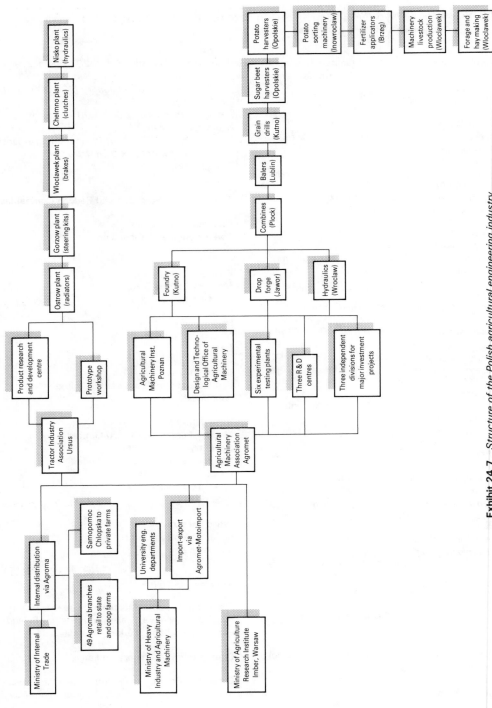

Exhibit 24.7   *Structure of the Polish agricultural engineering industry.*

Exhibit 24.8   A Projection of the Polish Tractor Industry Range until 1985

Group 1: 38 h.p.
Possible cooperation with a Western manufacturer, for example British Leyland.

Group 2: 38–75 h.p.
MF Models: The ICA specified 38 updated versions of the following models:

3 Cylinder	4 Cylinder
MF 133 38 h.p.	MF 165 62 h.p.
MF 135 46 h.p.	MF 168 69 h.p.
MF 148 49 h.p.	MF 185 75 h.p.
MF 152 49 h.p.	MF 188 75 h.p.

which in their currently updated versions comprise:

3 Cylinder	4 Cylinder
MF 235 38 h.p.	MF 265 60 h.p.
MF 255 47 h.p.	* MF 275 66 h.p.
MF 500 47 h.p.	MF 565 60 h.p.
	* MF 575 66 h.p.
	* MF 590 75 h.p.

The Polish versions of these models which may subsequently change, will be known as the 'PX' Series.

Ursus models:

2 Cylinder
C- 335 35 h.p.
C- 355 55 h.p. (being phased out)
C- 360 60 h.p.

Group 3: 80–120 h.p.

6 Cylinder Zetor Engine:
* C- 385   85 h.p.
C-1201 120 h.p.
* C-1204 120 h.p.

Development of this range is to continue with the Zetor Tractor Works of Czechoslovakia, but there is the possibility of using Perkins engines within this range.

Group 4: 120 h.p.
Possible cooperation with the USSR

* = 4 wheel drive option

Sources: These are unofficial figures, compiled from a number of different sources.

CASE 25
Flexible Technology Limited
International Marketing

James McCalman

Centre for Technical and Organizational Change, University of Glasgow
Business School

Introduction

Flexible Technology Limited, a subsidiary of Cambridge Electronics Industries, was a UK-owned company and the largest manufacturers of high-volume and high-technology flexible printed circuits in Britain. The company was based at Townhead, Rothesay on the Island of Bute on the west coast of Scotland, 30 miles from Glasgow. The company was established in 1980 by a founding team comprising three directors who had worked at IBM, Greenock, and a fourth who had sales links with the other three. At the time of the case study, Flexible Technology was wholly involved in the manufacture of the flexible circuits which were printed circuit boards that bend. These consisted of a layer of copper foil sandwiched between two thin layers of very high-temperature plastic with circuit access holes drilled through them.

Product and market awareness were seen as the key elements of the successful growth of the firm. Flexible Technology restricted itself to the high-quality, highly specialized end of the flexible circuit industry which was centred around defence equipment at home and in the United States. There was a conscious policy of not becoming involved in the high-volume, low-cost production of flexible circuits for major manufacturers of consumer products, such as washing machines and cars. Flexible Technology dealt more with space, avionics and weapons markets where profit margins were higher.

The background of the organization emphasized the development of a product idea originally conceived by a multinational computer manufacturer and its subsequent application by others including Flexible Technology. At the beginning of the 1970s it became apparent that quite a substantial market existed for the use of flexible circuits in commercial and industrial applications which were not being exploited by the multinational computer manufacturer. The advantages of these circuits were:

- simplified assembly of complex circuits;
- low mass and size where space and weight were important criteria in a product's make-up;
- reliability in applications where they were connecting constantly moving parts;
- low cost and ease of assembly for high-volume requirements.

It was not until 1979 that market opportunities and advances in technology made the setting up of a flexible circuit manufacturer feasible. By this time the UK market for this type of product was £5 million and was being supplied by four manufacturers. There were problems in the market, however, which encouraged the establishment of the company. Manufacturing lead times were long, prices were high and the level of product quality was poor leading to criticism of the quality of end-product.

This particular segment of the electronics industry was characterized by two main features. First, there was a lack of manufacturing capacity within the flexible circuit market which threatened the extension of user applications. Second, overpricing also discouraged further applications. These factors occurred at a time when technological advances in electronics-based products were creating market demand for flexible circuit manufacture. The market capacity and market demand are detailed in Exhibit 25.1 and emphasize the gap between what was or could be produced and the level of demand for this type of product.

Flexible Technology was established at a time of world recession and had the dubious benefit of not having anyone else about to invest in a purpose-built facility for the manufacture of specialized flexible circuits.

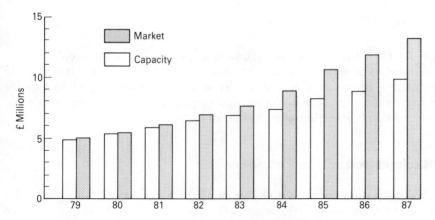

Exhibit 25.1 *UK market demand for flexible printed circuits 1979–87.*
Source: Flexible Technology company document, 1985.

A purpose-built facility was provided by the Highlands and Islands Development Board (HIDB) which also suscribed equity and provided the firm with loan capital. The venture capital organization, Investors in Industry (3i) also suscribed to the firm's equity as well as providing commercial loan capital. Other finance came from the four founders who contributed £64,000 of the £101,000 original share capital, ordinary shareholders, and the bank provided an overdraft facility to match the founders' capital input.

Production began in 1981 and in the intervening five years the company had captured 30% of the UK free market in flexible circuits. Exhibit 25.2 provides a breakdown of the level of sales and exports during the company's five years of existence. These figures emphasize a slow initial growth period of 18 months followed by a rapid increase in sales and export activity from 1984 onwards.

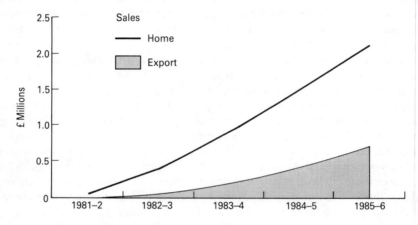

Exhibit 25.2   *Flexible Technology sales and exports 1981–86.*
Source: Flexible Technology company document, 1985.

By 1987, the company had grown to employ just over 100 people and had increased its manufacturing plant by taking over a storage facility next to the main plant. It is important to note that three of the nine positions were held by the founding members. The fourth left the company soon after the firm were taken over by Cambridge Electronics Industries in January 1986.

Background of the Founders

Flexible Technology was well aware that high technology start-ups required a founding team with interlocking skills that encompassed the needs of the business. The four founding members had experience in production, product and process development engineering and sales. Similarly, the Managing Director had been in a senior management position prior to setting up the firm and had gained valuable management experience.

The Managing Director had worked at IBM's Greenock facility from 1967 to 1977 before leaving to take up a senior management position with Thorn-EMI. This provided experience of managing a subsidiary operation with profit responsibility which produced results for Thorn-EMI. It also benefited the start-up when venture capital firms examined the track record of the entrepreneurs.

The level of technology transfer from the larger organization was fairly high as might be expected from the founders who had been closely involved in developing similar products within the larger firm. There were initial difficulties associated with leaving larger organizations, and these were identified as a 'hands off' approach to the new venture. This differs substantially from the experience of high-technology start-ups in the the United States.

This type of attitude to entrepreneurial drive may be an aspect that is peculiar to the setting up of British high-technology firms. Certainly, in the United States, the number of start-ups from the larger electronics firms which have become successful enterprises in their own right owes a lot to the breeding ground atmosphere in areas such as Silicon valley. In the United Kingdom, this policy appears to be frowned upon in preference to a distancing approach at the outset.

There were specific benefits which the background in larger organizations offered the entrepreneurs and which could be magnified for the rest of the industry. Apart from the obvious experience gained in the manufacturing processes and products that the new enterprise hoped to develop there were management lessons gained in larger firms.

Previous research into the factors likely to influence the success of new technology-based firms have noted some key variables which can be classified as common characteristics of the founding members. These characteristics were examined during the course of the case study to determine whether any of the key characteristics applied to Flexible Technology. Key characteristics of entrepreneurship in the electronics industry include the following:

- Strong entrepreneurial background
- High level of education
- Relatively young age of founders
- Technical background developmental as opposed to research oriented
- High achievement needs of entrepreneurs.

One of the benefits possessed by Flexible Technology was its Managing Director's continued achievement needs which drove the business onwards. This was combined with an awareness on the part of all the founders that to develop into new areas they would have to devolve some of their own power base within the company. For example, to allow the Managing Director to develop the company abroad it was felt necessary to bring in a manufacturing manager who would 'run the show' in his absence.

In summing up this section four key points emerge:

With respect to the entrepreneurs:

(1) The background of the founders reflected a high level of education and experience gained within the electronics industry with large organizations. There were specialists in the main business areas required by the firm.

(2) A desire to develop individual achievement aims whether financial, prestige or personal development oriented was the driving force in setting up the firm.

With respect to the firm:

(3) A product market gap was identified very early and acted as the impetus for start-up even during a worldwide economic recession. The entrepreneurs were not diverted from start-up because of the knowledge that the industry did not have enough capacity.

(4) Concentrated effort in the preproduction planning stage ensured the business and the entrepreneurs had enough capital, the correct equipment for most of the processes, and the right facilities to succeed.

Current Status of the Organization

This section describes the current position of Flexible Technology in terms of the company's financial position, the products manufactured and the development of the firm up to 1987. This included the takeover of the firm in 1986 by Cambridge Electronics Industries, a UK electronics conglomerate. Development factors indicate that the company had progressed steadily during its first two years of trading but from 1984 began to capture an increased share of the flexible circuit market both at home and abroad to a level where it became an attractive proposition for takeover.

From late 1984 through to June 1987 Flexible Technology had experienced a period of rapid market growth which coincided with developments in the end-markets for its products, and the end of economic recession which increased the flow of orders. The situation was so encouraging that the company had to turn business away in certain areas because it would have hampered the planned growth of the firm. This business was chiefly in the area of high-volume, low-cost manufacture of flexible circuits which was not a field the company wished to become involved in. As one manager pointed out, the company preferred to price itself out of this area of work to concentrate on high-quality production which was more profitable.

Exhibit 25.3 indicates the profitability, employment and growth of Flexible Technology and provides details of the financial progression of the firm.

In addition, the company had net assets of around 0.75 million and in 1986 had taken up an extra 6,000 square feet of manufacturing capacity in an adjoining facility. The reasons behind this level of success were a concentrated effort on the more specialized markets for flexible circuits, such as applications for the US Government's spacelab programme and the development of applications for military use both in the United Kingdom and the United States.

Flexible circuits were not as sophisticated as their rigid counterparts, the printed circuit board, but their main advantage was their pervasive use

Exhibit 25.3 *Flexible Technology performance indicators 1982–86.*

Year	Sales	Employment	Profit/loss
1982	£54,000	23	£111,000 (loss)
1983	£406,000	37	£23,000 (loss)
1984	£1.26 million	74	£115,000 (profit)
1985	£2.01 million	82	£383,000 (profit)
1986	£2.75 million	95	£531,000 (profit)
1987 forecast	£3.35 million	>100	£688,000 (profit)

throughout a multitude of end-user applications. Flexible circuits were used in washing machines, motor cars, orbiting space laboratories and satellites, defence weapons systems, military and commercial aircraft, computer disk files, computer control equipment and cellular radio.

It was Flexible Technology's desire to remain outwith the more consumer oriented area, such as washing machines, and deal with the more sophisticated, high-quality end of the market. Accordingly, as the company had progressed so had its customer base. A company document written at the end of 1985 noted that:

'As our technically more demanding clients have built up confidence in our ability to supply high quality British Standard approved circuits, so our earlier dependance on the smaller industrial user has diminished. They now represent 24% of our output while our military and computer customers have grown to account for 42% and 34% respectively.'

The production process was highly automated and wherever possible computer numerically controlled (CNC) machinery was used. The drilling of holes in the circuit, electroplating, photo resist exposure and laminating were all done using CNC machine tools. The process had continuously evolved since establishment. As one employee commented:

'We have been developing our processes for five years and you eventually find out what all the pitfalls are and modify them. For example, originally we used to have a lot of problems with simple things like putting a part in the equipment because the circuit would curl up. Somebody suddenly thought that we could put fibreglass round it to hold it in position.'

Advances in production came about as a result of experience and growth in the number of processes undertaken in-house. When the firm first started some of the production processes were carried out by subcontractors. This proved to be inadequate as the Managing Director explained:

'We didn't attempt to establish the whole of the process that we have today at the outset. My view was that we didn't want to bite off more than we could reasonably digest. We relied in the early days on some of our processes being performed by subcontractors and we learned very quickly that subcontractors don't perform the work as well as you would like, and certainly not as well as you are able to do because they have different requirements through keeping lots of different customers happy with one single process. So we had to augment our basic capability more quickly than had originally been envisaged by installing additional processes in fairly short order.'

This gave the firm the advantage of controlling the whole production process and not being reliant on subcontractors who might not be in a position to meet the demands placed on them. Flexible Technology had not paid any dividends to investors and had ploughed profits back into the firm in the form of new capital equipment. For example, in 1986 capital expenditure amounted to £380,000. It was one of the recognized mistakes of the company that it had not attempted to establish the whole manufacturing process in-house from the outset.

Firm Development

Flexible Technology had experienced some difficulty in making the transition from small start-up to medium sized firm in terms of alterations in management style and the production environment which it was believed suited an expanding firm. There were three particular problems that created difficulties which the firm had to respond to in order to maintain growth. The first concerned the acquisition of appropriate management skills for a growing firm. The second involved a movement away from management by founders to a more decentralized control. The third concerned the type of production activity on the shop floor which involved a change from what could be termed 'front to back' production responsibility on the part of operators to more formalized production line techniques.

The growth in size created its own problems on the production side. Having to train larger numbers obviously affected output. As the Managing Director noted:

'The manufacture of a flexible circuit involves up to 115 different operations. Now whilst the major operations are automated we are dealing with plastic film in some cases one-thousandth of an inch thick. Handling is a major problem, any creases in the copper start to cause defects. Inexperienced people don't know how to handle it, don't know how to load machines, and don't understand the machines' parameters. There is quite an extensive training period. The machines are capable of an output of two to three times their present level, but our people are not. What determines our growth is how fast we can hire, train and keep people.'

To get round these difficulties the company introduced greater specialization. However, the company had not totally abandoned the concept of 'front to back' training of staff, but pressures associated with growth meant that specialization appeared more appropriate.

One of the major factors in the company's growth was the attainment of BS 9000 which was a quality standard used by the Ministry of Defence for assessing the quality of military suppliers. Flexible Technology gained BS 9000 standard within two and a half years of setting up the business. Its ability to gain this certification rested on the standard of its products in comparison with other flexible circuit manufacturers. This again reflected the gap which existed in the flexible circuit market for high-quality products.

The question of building a company reputation for quality in the industry was important in Flexible Technology's development pattern. However, having established this reputation there was an awareness that overexpansion could place the firm in difficulties which might result in tarnishing a carefully nurtured set of industry standards. The Managing Director was willing to learn from the experience of others in the rigid printed circuit board industry about the problems of overtrading:

'The printed circuit board industry is littered with the corpses of companies who have bitten off more than they can chew. They have usually finished up overtrading. It takes years to build up a reputation and we don't always get it right, but you can lose it overnight so we are quite cautious in the sense of wishing to balance managing the business and managing the growth. If we left it to the market we'd be up and down. I don't refuse to bid against a plethora of enquiries but what we do is use the lead time to control when and if we are getting orders. By and large we get 90% of what we bid for.'

The presence of a large number of foreign-owned enterprises in the Scottish electronics industry can be presumed to create greater levels of benefit to the economy than those associated with direct employment gains. Of these benefits, the growth and development of an indigenous sector maintaining close links with foreign firms in this country might well provide an example of the presumed advantages linked to high levels of inward investment.

Previous research has tended to suggest that the creation of linkages between indigenous and foreign firms has not developed to levels that might have been expected. The low level of material input purchases emanating from foreign-owned companies to local suppliers, and the subsequent high import penetration suggests that these linkages are fairly weak. One key area of concern was to examine the linkages between the case study organization and foreign firms both at home and abroad. This concerned previous and current links, foreign firms with which Flexible Technology Limited was involved, the role played by electronics firms in Scotland in the development of the organization, and the company's experience in dealing with large multinational concerns.

Flexible Technology was not linked to the foreign sector in Scotland in terms of sales to electronics firms although around one-fifth of its business was with UK electronics firms based in Scotland. At the time of the study the percentage of sales taken up by exports stood at 56%. This had increased from 25% in 1985, and the prospects were for continued growth in export potential.

Market specialism, especially in the military area, meant that Flexible Technology was always going to be a highly export oriented firm. However, that had not prevented it from capturing a large share of the UK market for flexible circuits. This market was estimated to be around £13 million, of which Flexible Technology had 28%. The US market was estimated to be around £140 million which indicated the desire to become international with the United States being the major concern.

Although there were, and still are a large number of supplying firms in Scotland, there appears to be a tendency for a first and second division of indigenous electronics firms. The first division comprises those organizations that have quickly developed large-scale export markets having first secured a home base. The second division comprises those firms that are completely oriented towards the provision of goods for the home base, and in many cases the provision of goods for one large customer within that home base.

The difference between first and second division firms can be seen in the tendency for first division firms to become multinational in their own right, based on superior quality goods and product innovation.

Flexible Technology at the time of this study was considering seriously the possibility of opening up a second manufacturing plant on the eastern coast of the United States some time in 1988. The reasons for this were fairly straightforward, market potential in the United States was ten times that in the United Kingdom. Having captured around 30% of the UK market, the natural tendency was to internationalize. As one manager commented:

'We don't see ourselves getting much more out of the UK market in terms of market share. We are already the biggest in the UK market and what is left is the type of work that we don't want, the high volume stuff. Our main market is the military and the communications industry and what we will continue to do is expand into foreign military and communications markets. The scope in America and Europe means that there is no restricting factor in terms of sales. The only restriction is our ability to produce, capacity problems. We are looking at the possibility of having a duplicate plant in America and we are looking at whether to have a greenfield site, acquire an existing plant, or acquire an existing company.'

The opening of facilities in the United States was preferred to setting up another plant in the United Kingdom for two reasons. The first was obviously because the market would be in the United States. The second was related to finding the correct resources to copy the success made of the first venture. As the Managing Director explained:

'It is enormously tempting to do the same thing elsewhere in the UK. We basically funded our own growth and it would be tempting to go to someone and say, "Give us another £5 million and we'll do it all over again". But I just haven't got the management resources to do that. There aren't any in flex circuit manufacture. The biggest weakness Britain has as a manufacturing nation is that it doesn't really have good manufacturing management. It is re-doubled in the flex circuit market and our competitors have had very high rates of management turnover. Two of them to my certain knowledge are looking for managers.'

The development of the company stresses the benefits of large-scale multi-national presence in the economy and the potential that this brings for generating local companies with market potential beyond the United Kingdom. The product idea was generated within IBM but the market potential lay outwith the company, and it was the entrepreneurial drive of the founders who left the organization to develop the product potential in the military and communications markets. There were direct comparisons with some of the major electronics companies established in the United States whose founders had left companies, such as Texas Instruments, to set up in business for themselves.

Firms that maintain themselves as Scottish or UK oriented will survive by supplying one or two large customers, or a host of smaller customers, but the potential for growth is restricted by the actions of those customers. Breaking through that dependency into international markets is one of the key characteristics of the successful indigenous enterprises that currently exist in the Scottish electronics industry. Going international is likely to be a high-risk business, yet the potential for success is far greater. This rests on some very basic assumptions about the competitiveness of Scottish companies. One of these is obviously the drive to become larger, but there are some basic fundamentals that must also be in place.

Future Development of the Company

Having determined that the company was set up with the initial aim of developing a large export market for its goods, this section sets out how the founders believed the company would develop in the future.

There were two main features to the development of the company. One was that growth would continue in the manufacture of flexible circuits as Flexible Technology's only product area. The second has been noted as the internationalization of the firm. There were no desires to diversify the firm out of the successful manufacture of flexible circuits and management saw no reason for such diversification given that they were operating in a highly profitable market, kept pace with technological changes that applied to this market, and had further growth opportunities abroad. As one manager commented:

'The potential for profitable companies is tremendous in this market. It is not like the printed circuit board (PCB) industry as yet. It may become that way because I am sure that some of the multinationals are looking at flexible circuits and seeing it as a nice little number. The problem is that there are very few people worldwide with sufficient expertise to go into the business. Money or equipment are not the problems, it is expertise that is restricted. We are masters of our own destiny and we can only make a mess of it. It is like Everton going for the league championship, they could only lose it, they couldn't win it, they could only lose it. I say that as a Liverpool supporter who was hoping like hell that they would lose it.'

Given that the company was in such a strong position there seemed little incentive to look to other products for diversification of the company.

However, there were other factors that would influence the company's future development. The continued exports to the United States had opened up opportunities which the firm believed would be best served by setting up manufacturing facilities in the United States. As the Managing Director explained there were two reasons for this. One was linked to the need to be close to the market, the other was related to management of the company as it grew to what would eventually be saturation level:

> 'Electronics is becoming more and more capital intensive and it is also a global market. There are very few markets which you can serve nationally which means that you are competing on a global basis and mechanization, reduction in costs is endemic. . . . Since we have started to supply the US we have also started to receive unsolicited enquiries from US users, people like Honeywell and Applied Technology. Assuming we are successful with opening a plant on the east coast we will almost certainly consider opening a plant on the west coast and in Germany.'

There were other features of the company's development that would have to be addressed. One of these concerned the effects of growth on the the Rothesay plant. One manager explained what he felt had happened:

> 'We are going through a stage just now where things are slightly awkward. It is the old story that we have grown so fast that the disciplines need tightening. We have put in a few more overheads to tighten these disciplines. The discipline of material control for example, has been recorded on Kardex and has now been computerized. You can tolerate a certain amount of it but as the company grows bigger you can't afford to. The quality structure is creaking slightly and we have had to address that. There are now two people doing quality issues full-time whereas before I was doing it as a half-time job until February 1987.'

Quality issues had always been important to the company but as its size grew, and as it became more and more a specialized manufacturer of circuits costing in the region of £50, then quality became a vital issue. As one manager commented:

> 'You have to be a lot more careful because you are talking about a lot of money if you scrap one or two circuits at a time. We have to be stricter in the way we do things.'

The future for the company seemed to make management of the firm extremely bullish in their hopes that the company would continue to grow and would broaden its manufacturing horizons beyond Scotland. There appeared to be little reason to doubt that this would be the case. The purchase of the firm by Cambridge Electronics Industries in 1986, when the four original founders traded their Flexible Technology shareholding for Cambridge Electronics shares, seemed to confirm the long-term future of the firm.

CASE 26
Europack†
International Marketing

Stanley J. Paliwoda
Faculty of Management, University of Calgary

Introduction

Europack is a German packaging company which is experiencing problems with its operations in France, where the local packaging industry could be said to be mature and highly competitive. The focus is on the foreign sales subsidiary referred to elsewhere as the 'first preference of most firms' (Tookey, 1975).

French Sales Organization

Europack has a matrix organization and two product divisions: Frisch, which is vertically integrated and produces raw material and 'converts' it, that is, adds successive stages of value; the other – Rohr – is not able to produce its primary materials and has to buy these in, but because of the size and inflexibility of its plant and printing machinery, requires long production runs (see Exhibit 26.1).

Managers at Head Office confronted with declining sales and low profits from overseas markets have blamed their agents and sales subsidiary. The divisions themselves are concerned about the lack of growth and poor profitability from their business in France. The popular culprit has been the joint sales office, located in Paris. Questions were raised about the sales subsidiary: Was it a good idea to have a joint sales office? Would it be better for each division to have its own salesman working from home? Did the salesmen spend too long in the office? Were they energetic enough? Were they suited to the task? Were they sufficiently

† This case was prepared as a basis for class discussion rather than to illustrate either effective or ineffective handling of an administrative situation. The name of the company is fictitious and some of the details have been altered to protect the identity of the company.

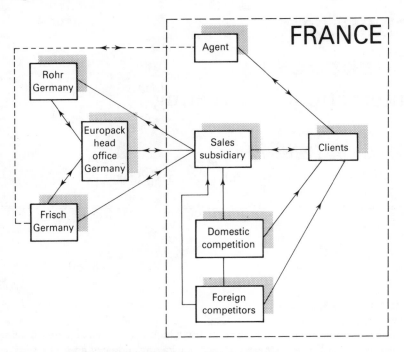

Exhibit 26.1 *Sales organization in France.*

well motivated as they did not receive commission? Being an organization that had many tasks to fulfil in selling, disseminating knowledge, ensuring post-purchase satisfaction and general troubleshooting, it was feared that sales commission may place an undue emphasis on only one of those activities. Did salesmen receive the back-up services which they required from the German parent? Were the language problems significant? Was there a problem which once identified could materially change for the better the fortunes of the sales subsidiary? The optimal situation is where the sales representative is a trusted information source backed up by a company that in the mind of the buyer is a reliable supplier. This combination raises a formidable barrier to competitors (Hakansson, 1982; Turnbull and Cunningham, 1981).

Firstly, this particular sales subsidiary is a curious hybrid representing divisions in the home country which are completely autonomous. Secondly, selling requirements for a product change over its life cycle. The industrial producer that has the wrong distributors for the stage the product is in may make the following observations of its distributors: 'They don't call on the right people ... they don't know how to sell the benefits of the product ... the distributor is mostly filling repeat telephone orders and delivery is too slow' (Hlavacek and McCuiston, 1983).

Thirdly, was the organization correct for that foreign market and level of business? The challenges to existing methods of distribution in industrial markets arise from:

- changes in size of distributors;
- changes in costs of maintaining a direct salesforce;
- changes in service requirements; and
- changes in products handled.

Against this, there is a trend taking place in industry of a shift from selling direct to marketing through distributors (Micham, 1980).

Corporate strategies depend upon customer requirements which are already to some extent known; together with established channels of distribution existing in that market; and customer expectations for delivery, levels of stocks and provision of services. However, a product which has certain comparative disadvantages may be preferred if an outstanding service is provided and service is a major influence on buying decisions. It is up to the firm, therefore, to make the final decision as to the level of commitment and investment it is prepared to make in that market in order to meet the needs and desires of its potential market. Therefore, as the level of sales in a market increases, the type of organization which is most economical will alter. At a certain level of turnover, the employment of a full-time representative will become feasible, where costs are no longer shared with other accounts. Finally, turnover can reach a level where an overseas base becomes the most economical way of marketing, when the work is sufficient to engage an office full time (Duguid and Jaques, 1981).

However, within the industry, new contact patterns are emerging also. Since packaging is a custom-designed recurrent purchase, customers need easy access to suppliers for design or delivery changes. Interviews with customers suggest that more and more of these contracts are being made directly between the customers and the factory where the goods are being made.

Packaging lines run at high speed and downtime are expensive and so foreign customers, just like domestic customers, need rapid and competent technical service. For other than minor problems this means bringing a specialist from Germany. In this respect the Paris sales office acts only as a channel of communication. The main role of the sales office is in the maintenance and development of customer relationships.

Industry Background

In sum, the packaging industry is mature with overcapacity in Europe. The flexible packaging industry has three basic raw materials – aluminium, resin and pulp. For use in flexible packaging these raw materials are converted into foil, plastic film and paper. They, in turn, can be used on their own or laminated with each other to make a great variety of packaging products. Final products range from simple plastic bags to special multi-layer films, for soup pouches, or coffee packaging. Flexible packaging is subject to a great variety of 'converting' processes. As well as being printed it can be formed, coated, embossed, lacquered, etc. The industry consists of the raw material producers; the foil, plastic film and paper manufacturers; and the converters, each with separate stages in the manufacturing cycle. The converters buy in manufactured film, foil or paper then 'convert' it by adding another level of value – added whether laminating, embossing, printing or lacquering, etc. Converters are therefore often more expensive than competitors who work from raw materials through to final product but retain their market niche through the provision of quality and service.

Frisch manufactures, converts and supplies plastic film especially polyvinyl chloride (PVC) and polyethylene (PE). Rohr is a converter specializing in the lamination of complex materials involving film, foil and paper.

Within each product-class of packaging, cross-substitution is taking place. Polypropylene (PP) for paper and PVC, polyester for glass, etc. Concentration of supply is another feature of certain sectors of the flexibles' packaging industry. To take the example of the PVC market, this is one where the market is a European one in terms of supply: France does not have its own domestic producer of either rigid PVC or oriented PVC which is used for film. Production, therefore, comes mainly from Italy and Germany with some production of PVC also from Britain, Italy being the market leader in Europe for PVC. For possible suppliers of oriented PVC film which is required for the production of the standard 'Sellotape' or 'Scotch' brand transparent adhesive tape, there are only three suppliers in Europe. In terms of competition, though, PVC faces competition, in sacks from PE, and in tapes from PP (transparent tape) and PE (recording tapes).

In 1980 the packaging industry experienced a massive shake-out but many sectors, including PVC, have remained relatively stagnant since. Where there is concentration of supply, however, it means that suppliers have to take a long-term view and cannot enter and leave a market at will. This becomes a strategic limitation once it is realized that growth prospects are limited for years ahead, that competition is bidding down already weak profit margins, and that currency fluctuations such as the French franc against the Deutschmark in the past two years have meant in effect a devaluation of 18%.

Given the small number of suppliers and customers in many of the subsegments, it is not surprising that close relationships develop, that special circumstances influence the choice of supplier and that suppliers seek to protect their positions by agreements between each other. Technology, though, can change relationships. Changes in materials and the arrival of new competitors work against such close relationships.

Background to Europack

Europack is an autonomous division within a diversified company. Corporate policy has been for subsidiaries to be set in competition with outside suppliers, and so while the overall volume of in-house supply has been greatly reduced, subsidiaries are still expected to act as supplier of last resort to the parent company if a suitable supplier cannot be found.

The sales office is responsible for representing the German parent's three autonomous divisions each of which has a different management structure and style. In Germany, there is little integration among them but in France, the activities of the company as a whole are handled collectively. Two of these divisions account for more than 90% of the sales in France.

However, its two main divisions had by now both grown considerably and evolved different strategies. This explains separate and different divisional approaches to the French market.

The different strategies pursued are best understood by comparing the profile of customers which each company has built up. Originally, both Rohr and Frisch employed commission agents in France. In 1968 Frisch was the first to change to a small sales office with a salaried salesman. Then from 1970 onwards Rohr and Frisch, as well as two other German subsidiaries and a Dutch subsidiary, combined to have one export sales office in France. This change coincided with major changes in the restructuring of all the parent company's packaging companies in Europe.

In the mid-1950s this group moved from an organization based on regional groupings to a system of product divisions. A similar reorganization took place in the packaging companies about 10 years later. This was when Europack became the holding company and coordinator of a number of European subsidiaries. This new organization felt the need to coordinate marketing efforts. Hence export activities, which had previously been the responsibility of each subsidiary, were reorganized and joint sales offices were formed in each of the key markets. These sales offices reported to the centre as well as to the companies whose products they were selling. The idea was to improve service by having one point of contact for customers, and to assist the subsidiaries' efforts to sell to those customers with several plants in Europe.

Since Europack already had two packaging subsidiaries in France it was natural to attach the export sales office to one of them and this was the original arrangement. The salesmen, recruited from both France and Germany, then divided their time between the products from the different exporting companies. As time passed, the number of salesmen decreased, and, since neither of the French subsidiaries had an ideal location, in 1980 the export sales office became a separate legal entity with its own office in Paris. A system involving commission was originally used to pay salaries and overheads, but this led to disputes over pricing and all expenses are now borne by the exporting companies.

By 1982 the Paris sales office was becoming established but just at this moment further structural change took place throughout the group which involved closures, sell-offs and management buy-outs, the central office to which the Paris sales office reported being greatly reduced in size.

The Two Product Divisions

Frisch has a larger and less concentrated business base in France than Rohr. It has 79 customers, the largest representing only 15% whereas Rohr has 24 customers with the largest representing 60%. Frisch has introduced new products so that 24% of sales are from markets developed in the last four years. Frisch's business is with local French customers and only a very small proportion with the group parent company. Relationships with customers are strong and about 50% of business comes from customers who source exclusively from Frisch. On the other hand, 60% of Rohr's business is with the group parent company and relationships with customers are less strong than those with Frisch.

Five multinational corporations account for 71% of Rohr's business in France; but multinationals account for only 2.6% of Frisch business in France. This has aroused the fear that because the multinationals' purchasing managers are able to exchange electronically international price comparisons for standard items purchased regularly within their groups, so consequently profit margins for Rohr on this business must be lower. Exhibit 26.2 shows customer profiles.

Exhibit 26.2   *Comparing customer profiles.*

		Rohr	Frisch
Growth	Growth in last 4 years	Decline	Stagnant
Concentration	Number of customers	24	79
	Largest customer (%)	60	15
	Top five customers (%)	80	62
Development of new markets	Business in new markets in last 4 years (%)	5	26
Type of customer	Business with multinational customers (%)	71	3
	Business with group parent company (%)	60	2
Strength of relationships	Business where company has 100%	10	50

Frisch has strong relationships with its customers because of its greater degree of specialization. It is one of a handful of European producers of PVC flexible films with the advantage that there are no French competitors for some of its films. It sells on an international basis specializing at three levels to Rohr's two. Rohr is technically able to meet a wider range of requirements than Frisch but not able to match it on profitability. Against its local competitors, Rohr is foreign with no particular competitive advantage.

Frisch has customers with special requirements that local competitors cannot easily meet, while Rohr has both more multinational customers and is subject more to local competition. This competitive weakness makes Rohr more vulnerable to price which is influenced also by currency exchange fluctuations.

Europack is able to invoice in DM only for those products which have few European suppliers. For the remainder, like everyone else, it invoices in Ffr. This again separates Rohr and Frisch.

Frisch is protected by receiving payments in its own currency. Rohr, with lower profit margins, is forced to accept payment in a currency which is weak against the Deutschmark which further weakens its competitive position.

Rohr's business in France can be split into two – the business with the group parent company and third-party business. Although business with the group parent company is with several different French subsidiaries, buying is handled centrally. For historical and protocol reasons, the Paris sales office is not involved. Since questions of managerial hierarchy are involved, negotiations take place directly with the German management who fly over specially to Paris. Thus the Paris sales office has little role to play in this relationship with group parent business or in crucial decisions about retaining or abandoning the business. The Rohr salesman at the Paris office is the main contact for the maintenance and development of third party business. Rohr is more expensive than local competitors for standard items, and so, most of this business has to be for specialized end-use applications, such as coffee packaging. Yet, the market for higher value-added for which a foreign supplier can effectively compete is limited.

Compared with Rohr, Frisch has had a flow of new products replacing those where business has been lost to competition. Frisch, whose customers are usually local companies, has benefited from a greater continuity of sales staff, and from the personal relationships that they have developed.

To summarize, the Paris sales office handles some administration and invoicing and acts as a two-way channel of communication. The sales staff maintain and develop business with existing customers. For new business they are dependent on innovations coming from Germany.

The overall strategy for the sales subsidiary is one of a mixed portfolio based more on volume criteria than specialization. This French strategy also serves to protect the company's domestic prices as well, for if discounts were to be offered once to domestic German clients, they will be asked for on subsequent occasions. Here, discounts are being used to buy up business in a market in which the longer term future is uncertain.

The Attitude of the French Sales Subsidiary Staff

Two salesmen plus the manager covered France for all product applications. The salesmen were each assigned to a product division and the manager's time was divided 80:20 between Frisch and Rohr. The manager's view was that sales staff must be available on call and so he tried to spend more time in the office than on the road. The Europack parent has few people able to converse in French which puts further pressure on the sales subsidiary staff. It is not possible for a prospective French client to speak to the German product division direct and discuss needs. This lack of linguistic ability meant also that the sales subsidiary had to carry tasks such as invoicing to French customers although this was provided as a support service by Head Office elsewhere in Europe.

Subsidiary personnel were complaining of frequent telephone calls from the product divisions to continually ask about progress made. The manager had just completed a five-page memo for his Managing Director on the development of his sales staff.

There were no formal reporting procedures organized into the communications system between parent and subsidiary aside from the annual planning and budgeting exercise. Sales were the most obvious form of tangible feedback but when these did not materialize in sufficient volume there was nothing to report, although the sales team were as busy as ever dividing their time between making contacts and making themselves available at the office for clients.

The Attitude of the German Head Office Management

They were unhappy about the performance of the French sales operation but frightened also of giving it too much latitude. Had there not been a need for volume production or had a more attractive market emerged elsewhere, it is doubtful whether they would be in France. When it came to controlling the sales subsidiary, the German management felt powerless, unable to comprehend what was happening and unable to motivate the sales subsidiary staff the way they could free agents. For this reason and also because free agents required less resources, this was actively being considered as an alternative form of market representation. The popular perception was that this failure was due to the laziness of the staff in Paris.

Conclusions

The sales subsidiary was found wanting on control and performance. Exports within a mature industry need both better distribution and lower costs than this sales subsidiary could provide. The question of image may even have been improved by the appointment of a local, well-connected agent. Image affects purchasing behaviour where xenophobia is present but, in buying from abroad, clients have anxieties also as to security of supply. Were this to arise, there are doubts about the availability of French speaking personnel within the organization able to assist.

Lower overheads on even a much-reduced volume of French business would still be acceptable to the parent company as it would eliminate much of the marginal business being pursued. Meanwhile, competitive pressures in the shape of new materials and new product-class competitors were working against close relationships and long-term profitability. The choices were either to move out of France and employ an agent instead; or to wait for the economic climate to improve.

PART 5

Non-Profit Marketing

Case 27 **The Scottish National Orchestra**   308
            Non-Profit Marketing
Case 28 **The Scottish Football League**   320
            Non-Profit Marketing

Non-profit marketing is a general term used to characterize the marketing challenges and practices of 'non-business' organizations. A broadened or generic concept of marketing views marketing as consisting of much more than simply business transactions. In this broadened context, marketing is defined as a human activity directed at satisfying needs and wants through exchange processes. Thus, the arena for marketing activities and application of marketing principles has been expanded to include non-business areas in society, including the marketing of persons, places, organizations and ideas. The main thrust of the broadened concept of marketing is that realistic marketing planning can enable non-business organizations to improve their operations.

Traditionally, non-profit organizations have been expertise-driven rather than customer-driven. Typically, these organizations are part of the 'voluntary action sector' which includes cultural, communal, charitable and active social change groups such as a symphony orchestra, art museum, church, child care cooperative or homeowner association. Or, a non-profit organization might be a government agency or political action group such as a department of social services, an independent school district, or a political party.

Non-profit organizations vary widely in their fundamental missions as well as the nature and scope of their resources and activities. In most cases, the economic dimensions and marketing functions of non-profit organizations have been underdeveloped. Yet, each non-profit organization must compete culturally, politically and economically to realize its mission and survive. Each non-profit organization must transform its ideals into causes, services and/or products that offer genuine value to its target publics – members, clients, audiences, donors, board members and the general community. These target publics voluntarily give their support and resources to sustain the non-profit organization. They are its markets and ultimately its consumers.

Marketing provides a perspective and framework which encourages non-profit organizations to consider their missions, problems and opportunities strategically, and to manage their activities carefully, responsively and effectively. Non-profit marketing focuses on building, facilitating and developing exchange relationships that enact an organization's mission, serve its publics and promote its viability. Marketing can be used both to attract resources and to manage action programmes.

Non-profit organizations vary widely in their grasp of marketing knowledge, the extent of their marketing orientation, the complexity of their market opportunities and problems, the scope of their formal marketing efforts, the sophistication of their marketing practices and the effectiveness of their marketing strategies.

A few years ago, there was relatively little sophisticated marketing in non-profit organizations. Some non-profit organizations even viewed marketing with great suspicion. But as the world changed, marketing has been applied more and more in non-profit organizations. Non-profit groups increasingly employ professional marketers and compete with business to obtain marketing expertise. It is a mistake to regard non-business marketing as totally different from business marketing. The basic marketing concepts and techniques are applicable to both, yet imagination is required to apply creatively to non-business areas the same managerial tools that are applied to business areas. Non-business marketing more often strives to achieve something other than stimulating demand. Multiple objectives (as opposed to profit) complicate marketing in non-profit organizations.

Non-profit organizations more often depend on a number of groups or 'publics', whereas business, even today, is considered primarily responsible to three groups (stockholders, employees and customers). Due to the high dependence of non-business organizations on a number of groups, environmental analysis may be more important for non-business organizations and the marketing activity of non-business organizations may be equally directed at several of their publics.

Non-business activity is more often socially sensitive and controversial and more subject to environmental constraints, such as legislation and public scrutiny.

The products of non-profit organizations are often services and more often intangible, especially the marketing of 'ideas'. Non-business organizations use advertising (versus marketing) more often than do business organizations. By definition, marketing requires an analysis of market needs and the coordination of product development and all other marketing variables to match those needs. Non-profit groups sometimes adopt promotion but not marketing.

Non-business organizations are more dependent on multiple publics than the typical business firm. Some non-profit organizations provide services to the general public, some to their members and some to carefully defined target groups. Most provide intangible services and information to their constituencies. In fact, non-profit organizations have three primary marketing tasks: resource attraction, resource allocation and persuasion. The concepts of the marketing mix – communication, distribution, pricing and product – are indeed applicable to these organizations.

'Strategic planning', 'strategic audits', 'portfolio management' and 'product line pruning', are familiar terms in the business sector, but they also have applicability for many non-profit organizations. These business concepts can be particularly useful to non-profit organizations that provide more than one service to their clientele. The first step in programme portfolio analysis is the classification of the organization's various offerings. Once programmes are classified, the implications for strategy resource allocation and direction of cash flow will often be obvious. The task of managing a multi-programme non-profit organization can be arduous. Such organizations must manage their programme portfolios in order to maximize effectiveness.

There is a growing demand for accountability in a sophisticated donor community. This provides the impetus for the adoption of well-known business concepts so that non-profit organizations may use their dwindling funds more effectively. Administrators and board directors of non-profit organizations will be faced with increasingly severe competition for time, money and management skills as the non-profit sector becomes more cost conscious. Perhaps the most significant change with non-business marketing is the absence of good measures of performance that can be used for control purposes. Non-business organizations do not have internally generated sales and profit figures to guide their activities and must find other ways to evaluate performance.

Marketing provides non-profit organizations with practical management perspectives and methods that can help them to become more strategically orientated, responsive, thorough and potentially more effective. Marketing is built on a premise of exchange management. The symphony produces and offers an aesthetic experience. The audience gives its attention, appreciation and money to share the experience. As such, there is an exchange of values and valued offerings, and there is a shared experience – a relationship emerging.

Marketing has developed frameworks and specific methods to study consumer publics and market dynamics; to translate an ideal or idea into a competitive offering; to design a comprehensive programme to promote, price and deliver the offering; to manage a realistic portfolio of programmes; to attract resources – donations, voluntary efforts, more earned income; and to evaluate, control and change organizational efforts appropriately and proactively. A marketing orientated non-profit organization can achieve a responsive sense of itself and its mission, a strategic perspective of its markets and offerings, a realistic set of objectives and programmes, and a strong probability of reaching its potential and ensuring its viability.

The adoption of a serious marketing perspective and competent marketing practice involves organizational development, strategic analysis and decision making, programming and market action, and constructive evaluation. Programmes should be predicated on sensitivity and responsiveness to consumer publics' values, needs, behaviours and desires, and on analyses of competitive factors.

At a strategic level, the marketing audit is an excellent framework to examine and formatively evaluate the non-profit organization's mission and management systems; its programme portfolio; its market and environmental dynamics; its competitive positions; and its marketing programmes, performance and potential.

Marketing has an active social orientation, a strong voluntary perspective and responsive managerial frameworks. As such, marketing can help the non-profit organization transform its ideals into competitive offerings, its offerings into responsive programmes and its programmes into consumer public service and economic viability.

Marketing will inevitably be applied more and more by non-profit organizations. Consequently, business students with formal marketing training will be employed increasingly by non-profit groups.

The *Scottish National Orchestra* case demonstrates that a non-profit-making organization has as much need as a commercial one to maintain efficient and effective management control, and that a formal and detailed strategy is vital. The case illustrates the difficulty associated with the introduction of marketing disciplines in an environment where they have not existed before. Several critical issues are raised in the case, such as marketing organization, targeting, product policy, marketing research, price strategy, promotional activity, sponsorship and financial implications.

The *Scottish Football League* case illustrates the difficulty of properly marketing a sport, especially at the League/Association level. The case helps students to appreciate the role of marketing and understand the breadth of marketing concepts when applied to a non-traditional situation. It provides students with an opportunity to develop suitable marketing policies, strategies and mix programmes. Some important marketing concepts and techniques are involved in the analysis of the case, such as marketing budgeting and sponsorship, segmentation and targeting, as well as promotional strategy.

CASE 27

The Scottish National Orchestra
Non-Profit Marketing

Matthew J. T. Caminer
Allied Distillers Limited

Introduction

The Scottish National Orchestra is Scotland's most distinguished professional orchestra, giving concerts and making recordings throughout Scotland and the rest of the United Kingdom, as well as making overseas tours. Like all British professional orchestras, the management of its affairs is dominated by financial matters, the problem being more one of survival than of growth.

The SNO has a considerable pedigree, dating back to 1885, is acknowledged to give performances of the highest artistic calibre, and has an enthusiastic following throughout Scotland. The management team is small and young, and upon it lies the burden of establishing a programme for the orchestra's development in the face of severe financial constraints.

Overview of the Situation

The General Administrator has the task of identifying and satisfying the marketing needs of the organization and relating them to its financial and organizational objectives. With no marketing background himself, and no marketing specialists in the management team, this task is made particularly difficult. The Scottish National Orchestra was innovative in being one of the first British arts organizations to introduce subscription tickets, but the general marketing environment is not progressive, and disciplined strategic planning has not been considered a prerequisite for the orchestra's continued success. The focus in arts management has been concentrated on the need to attract industrial sponsorship as a means of surviving, and to permit growth. This emphasis places a considerable burden on the General Administrator, leaving less time for management of longer term strategic issues, such as programme planning policy, the implications of Glasgow's new concert hall, and how best to take advantage of the city's nomination as European City of Culture 1990.

General Background

History

The SNO was founded in 1885, although it has only existed in its current, full-time form since 1950. Until that time, known as the Scottish Orchestra, it had operated on a part-time basis except for a short break during the First World War.

It is therefore an organization with a considerable history, and, in Scotland, its reputation is second to none in its field. It is very much part of the national establishment, and its professional excellence in public concerts and in the recording studio is recognized both at home and abroad.

Activities

The organization's activities are described in the annual report as 'to administer the Scottish National Orchestra which gives performances of symphonic, operatic and choral music. The subsidiary company, Scottish National Orchestra Society (Properties) Limited, is responsible for the operation of the SNO Centre.'

The activities thus described combine public performances, studio recordings (for broadcasting companies and the record industry), tours of the United Kingdom and overseas, participation in major festivals and the promotion of and participation in educational activities.

Although the orchestra's base is Glasgow, it is the nature of the Scottish population that, even when 'at home', a considerable amount of time is spent touring within Scotland, the winter subscription concert season from September to April being especially intensive.

The subsidiary company, SNO (Properties) Limited, owns and operates the SNO Centre, a refurbished church building in the West End of Glasgow. Although primarily used by the SNO itself as a rehearsal hall and recording studio, the Centre is also hired out to outside musical bodies when available. Since the early 1980s it has been a popular venue for small and medium size concerts.

The Organization

The organization comprises 92 players, all of them specialists on their chosen musical instruments. The board of directors includes members of the orchestra, representatives of outside bodies, several non-executive directors and two members of the full-time management team. The orchestra is managed by a small, professional team (organization chart: Exhibit 27.1).

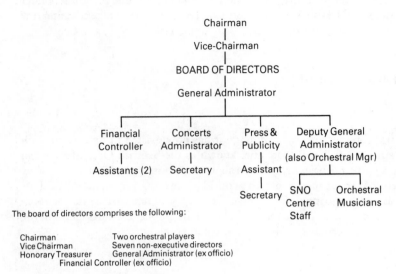

The board of directors comprises the following:

Chairman	Two orchestral players
Vice Chairman	Seven non-executive directors
Honorary Treasurer	General Administrator (ex officio)
Financial Controller (ex officio)	

Representatives of 13 Scottish Regions
Assessor for the Scottish Arts Council
Four Assessors for the Convention of Scottish Local Authorities

The full board meets twice a year, operational authority being delegated to the General Administrator and his staff

Exhibit 27.1   *Organizational structure of the SNO.*

The representative strength of the local authorities and the Scottish Arts Council on the board reflects the major sources of the orchestra's funds. Their concerns tend to dominate internal discussion, which is hardly surprising given the marginal financial basis upon which the orchestra operates. The presence on the board of a number of honorary directors provides necessary balance. These are individuals selected for their standing in Scottish industry, who are glad to share their expertise and experience with the orchestra's full-time management.

Given the nature of its activities, the playing members are indispensable: without changing the nature of the orchestra in a radical manner, the numbers and specialities involved could not be changed. Similarly, the supporting management team is so small and specialized that changes could not easily be made, except for equivalent replacements when required.

The musical profession is not well paid, either at the performing or management level; it is therefore insufficient to assume a 'professional' attitude and approach to work. Within the SNO, the prevailing atmosphere reflects vocation and dedication. A great deal of dedicated effort is the reason for the excellent artistic results, and in this respect, the players, management and staff are all of a high calibre. There is a little evidence of outmoded ideas and values, but the vibrant and innovative approach of the core management is proving to be a beneficial influence.

The work takes place in an environment that is constrained by exceptional financial hardships. The fact that the most lucrative work for orchestras and their players is to be found in London inevitably compounds these difficulties.

The Product

It is easy to describe the activities of the SNO. It is less easy to explain their nature, or to establish whether they represent a product or a service. For instance, the question is raised as to whether the SNO belongs to the serious music or the entertainment industry; whether it is a commercial organization or rather one performing a social service, and so on.

A clue may be found in an analysis of the work that it chooses to undertake. It is open to the SNO to perform *only* popular classics, or *only* 'highbrow', esoteric compositions – each type has its audience. There is a middle road, combining some of each type of music, and this policy is followed by most orchestras as a means of appealing to the broadest possible cross-section of the audience, thus filling seats and at the same time presenting an attractive proposition to potential industrial sponsors.

In the same way as an industrial company, therefore, the SNO has to make strategic choices of a very businesslike nature. This choice is dictated by the SNO's own strategy, described below. Its execution results in a mix of the elements described above, thus meeting all the commercial and organizational criteria for a well-balanced symphony orchestra.

Just as it was difficult to analyse the activities of the SNO, so it is unrealistic to suggest that there is such a thing as an average consumer (concert-goer, record-purchaser, radio listener, etc.) People's motives for going to concerts vary widely. These include an intellectual interest in music, a wish to enjoy music at a superficial level, the need to go out and be with other people, the need to support and identify with a national institution, whatever its nature, and the psychological need to be seen in the 'right' place on a particular night.

The SNO is musically capable of meeting all the needs at the narrow, musical end of the spectrum, and certainly covers all the other needs more than adequately. By the choice of repertoire within the context of the organizational strategy, the SNO could potentially confine itself to specific elements, but in fact takes the broader stance described above.

Organizational Strategy and Market Mission

These were described in the following terms by the General Administrator:

'The Scottish National Orchestra aims to be a leading contributor to the cultural life of Scotland. Within the harsh financial constraints of the classical music industry, we attempt to offer a well-balanced programme to the public, a realistic form of sponsorship for our supporters and a stable source of employment to our players. The appointment of Neeme Järvi as musical director has provided focus both musically and commercially, leading to improved audiences, increased sponsorship and extensive recording commitments. It is our intention that the SNO should continue to look outwards at the needs of the community which it serves. While it might be pleasant to indulge in programming of an esoteric nature, this would be impractical, and our strategy is to appeal to as broad a range of people as possible. Only thus can the orchestra expect to survive the financial hardships which will always be present as long as the current system of funding continues.'

Organizational Culture

The influence of finance on the orchestra is obviously of the greatest importance. The financial position is dealt with elsewhere, but everything is geared to doing as much as possible with as little money as possible. Thrift plays a major part; so does a concentration on excellence, without which the orchestra cannot survive. Whether artistic excellence has always been matched at a managerial and operational level is open to debate. The orchestra continued with the active participation of the same Musical Director, Sir Alexander Gibson, for 25 years until 1984. His influence affected the culture of the orchestra as much as the artistic policy and musical standards.

Many of the administrative staff have many years of service. They are supported by numerous very active part-time, volunteer workers throughout Scotland, who help in many small ways, such as manning stalls and hosting Friends' events. Their approach tends often to be non-innovative and conservative both musically ('We know what we like and we like what we know') and organizationally ('We've always done it this way').

The hard-core professional managers, however, are quite the opposite, striving towards excellence although frequently deprived of the resources with which to pay more than lip-service to such an approach. It is observed that their enthusiastic, hard working attitude has tended to rub off on to the older staff employees, thus bringing about a change of culture.

The SNO is only able to act as an independent organization up to a point: the funding of its activities is derived to a greater extent from public funds than from the paying public. To this extent, market needs and competition alone could never wholly dictate the nature of the product, the policies and strategies: this lack of freedom inevitably colours the culture of the SNO.

Three senior management figures, the Musical Director, the General Administrator and the Chairman, have quite distinct roles.

The Musical Director is responsible for the artistic policy of the orchestra. As well as choosing when and what he himself will conduct, he liaises with the Chief Guest Conductor to discuss his concerts. Up to a point he is involved in the remaining concerts, recordings, etc., and has a role in developing a plan several years into the future. Maestro Järvi drew attention to his frustration at having to be governed by commercial and box-office considerations rather than by artistic ones, when planning the season's programmes.

The General Administrator is responsible for booking artists, arranging programmes with them and ensuring that the musical content of the orchestra's life is properly constructed. He also handles the bulk of sponsorship seeking and is answerable to the board for all the activities of the orchestra. Many appointments are ultimately also his responsibility, although the Deputy General Administrator, who is also the Orchestral Manager, deals with the day-to-day aspects of such matters.

The role of the Chairman is less easy to define. He is involved more in providing an objective overview, at the same time undertaking a selective public relations function. This is particularly important with regard to the SNO's relationship with the Scottish Arts Council, the local authorities and the sponsors.

Environment

Cultural Environment

Reference has already been made to the broad nature of the product/service offered by the SNO. There is a strong influence of the changing social environment, one in which values have altered, tastes evolved and peoples' entertainment needs have become increasingly influenced by high unemployment.

Thus, when the SNO undertakes concerts in schools throughout Strathclyde Region, it is not simply fulfilling a cultural and educational need for today; it is also staking its claim to the interest and involvement of tomorrow's potential concert-goers, and thereby investing in the future.

It is not simply a question of musical tastes. People who do not think twice about spending £5 on a round of drinks in the pub complain about spending the same amount on a concert ticket. Television has contributed to the decline of all kinds of live entertainment, as have hi-fi systems and all the other leisure opportunities that have developed over the last 20 years.

It is in this environment that the orchestra seeks not only to sell tickets and records, to engage world-famous artists and to employ the best available players; but also to convince its funders, the Scottish Arts Council, the local authorities and its sponsors that by supporting the SNO they are engaged in a worthwhile undertaking.

Competitive Environment

In addition to the environmental factors described above, there exists a large amount of competition in Scotland. Glasgow, a city of nearly 1 million inhabitants, is home of not only the SNO but also the BBC Scottish Symphony Orchestra, Scottish Opera, Scottish Ballet and the Citizens' Theatre, all professional bodies of a high calibre. As well as these, many small professional and amateur organizations exist, all competing for the same finite audience.

Competition is not restricted to arts organizations. From a financial point of view, the ability of organizations like the SNO to obtain funds from public sources, principally the Scottish Arts Council, and from commercial sponsors, can make the difference between survival and collapse. Political factors influence both the total amount and the criteria for distribution of public funds; while the competition for industrial sponsorship is huge, not only from arts organizations, but also from the sports world and from charitable organizations. Furthermore, companies undertaking sponsorship are themselves subject to market forces which may effectively force them to discontinue some or all sponsorship.

Financial Environment

In recent years, it has become increasingly necessary for orchestras to build their entire existence upon the difficulty of surviving within the financial environment. Public money is a major factor in keeping arts organizations afloat, either through the Scottish Arts Council or through local authority funding. It is not possible automatically to expect these sources to increase, and very often the sums available remain static or even shrink.

The growth of sponsorship has led to a growth in professional sponsorship management and consultancies, chief among which is the Association for Business Sponsorship of the Arts. Whether sponsors really hope to gain commercial benefit from their sponsorship or are simply being altruistic is very difficult to determine. In the United States sponsorship can be written off against tax, but this is not so in the United Kingdom, making it hard to obtain support for what many people think of as a minority interest. Thus it is not only a problem of the competitive environment, but it is also a financial one because the industrial sponsor who was the mainstay of the organization's industrial sponsorship last year may not be in a position to provide any support at all this year.

Finance

Introduction

Exhibit 27.2 summarizes the profit and loss, and sources of income and expenditure for the SNO for the last three financial years. Reference was made earlier to the low pay of orchestral musicians. In 1985, the orchestra took a major financial risk by deciding that players should be more competitively paid. This resulted in a major deficit. In 1986, the situation was turned around, although not without drawing on funds from the Charitable Trust which provides fundamental capital support for the SNO.

Exhibit 27.2 Profit and Loss Statement 1984–1986

('000 Pounds)	1984	1985	1986
Turnover			
Concert receipts	459	465	522
Hire of orchestra	139	147	260
Broadcast/TV fees	75	130	65
Concert sponsorship	49	83	116
Recording sponsorship	28	19	48
Net gain on record sales	1	0	1
Corporate members/advertising	28	37	57
Total turnover	779	881	1,069
Other Operating Income			
Donations	42	38	43
Friends of the SNO	9	5	2
Gain on disposal of assets	2	0	0
Total other operating income	53	43	45
Operating Costs			
Salaries/subsistence	1,323	1,471	1,487
Artists' fees	103	130	177
Hall rental	80	97	95
Hire of music, instruments	21	25	27
Misc. concert charges	70	101	82
Recording costs	23	38	59
Programme printing	41	42	56
Depreciation	14	18	18
Printing & advertising	130	145	132
Transport & travel	69	71	73
Gala concert net proceeds	0	0	29
Total operating costs	1,874	2,139	2,235
Gross Deficit	1,041	1,214	1,123
Administration Expenses			
Office administration	201	203	272
Sponsorship consultants	4	4	2
Total administration expenses	205	207	274
Net Operating Deficit	1,246	1,421	1,396
Other Income			
Scottish Arts Council	926	996	1,251
Regional/district authorities	273	281	172
Interest received	5	5	7
Carnegie UK Trust	3	3	2
SNO Endowment Fund	50	0	48
Total other income	1,257	1,285	1,480
SNO Properties Surplus/(Deficit)	(2)	(5)	59
Surplus/(Deficit) For The Year	8	(141)	144

Sources of funds

The orchestra obtains its funds from four major sources: the Scottish Arts Council (40%), box office income (40%), sponsors (10%) and local authority grants (10%).

The SNO was one of the earliest organizations to import the subscription ticket concept from the United States. By selling a very high proportion of tickets for all the concerts in the season before the season starts, the system provides a guaranteed audience, certain income, as well as benefiting cash flow. Sales in this way range from 80% for the Edinburgh series to 95% for the Glasgow Thursday series.

As discussed above, the SNO is subject to political decisions which can quite radically affect the orchestra's welfare, often due to factors which are totally unrelated to the arts in Scotland. Thus, while the SNO is able to keep its head above water, an overnight change in government policy could cause an instant crisis.

Sponsorship represents a small proportion of the income, although the figure has improved dramatically in the last year. Some of the reasons for not obtaining sponsorship have already been explained. The SNO invests very little in formal fund-raising and sponsor-seeking activities, the General Administrator attracting sponsorship almost single-handed. Scottish Ballet, by contrast, employs a full-time sponsorship manager whose exclusive task it is to obtain sponsorship, both new and repeated. It reflects nothing but credit on the SNO that it succeeds as well as it does, but such an appointment must be a tempting alternative way of helping to guarantee the longevity of the organization.

Expenditure

Salaries represent by far the largest drain on the orchestra's resources. Many international artists are beyond the scope of the SNO. This presents a dilemma: without attracting international stars, there is a limit to the lucrative engagements that can become available as revenue sources. On the other hand, the engagement of expensive artists would result in an unacceptable financial drain. The SNO strikes a balance in this regard, tempting concert-goers with a satisfactory blend of artists.

The small organization, in terms of staff and property, means that the overheads are low in real terms, although they represent a drain that must constantly be kept in check.

Marketing

Marketing Orientation

The SNO is dedicated to the excellence of its product. Financial considerations influence how it uses that product. It is that excellence that ensures that all the financial sources described above can be maintained and put to the best possible use.

The SNO does not have a marketing department. There is, however, a press and publicity department, whose activities overlap with a number of marketing roles. Despite their lack of the specialist, professional marketing skills and disciplines needed to develop a strategy over time, the managerial flair of the individuals in the department goes some way towards remedying the problem.

Marketing Budget and Management

The marketing budget is set as part of the overall budget package, and is then broken down by the Press and Publicity Officer (Exhibit 27.3).

Exhibit 27.3 *A typical breakdown of the marketing budget expenditure.*

Activity	£	%
Subscription series brochures, summer proms series brochures, posters and street banners	79,200	60
Media advertising	39,600	30
Small advertising items, point-of-sale items, gift items, etc.	13,200	10
	132,000	100

The activities (Exhibit 27.3) are very much geared to selling subscription tickets, which is not so much a marketing activity as a financial necessity. There is a finite number of seats actually available for sale and given the high rate of pre-sale described above, it could be argued that there is no need for a formal marketing function.

The SNO will face a new situation once a new, purpose-built Glasgow concert hall has been constructed, to replace the old St Andrew's Hall destroyed by fire over 25 years ago. In a city of nearly 1 million inhabitants, there is little marketing challenge in filling a civic assembly hall holding an audience of only 1,216 people. Furthermore, the nomination of Glasgow as Cultural Capital of Europe in 1990 may be expected to provide the political and commercial stimulus to ensure that the replacement hall is completed swiftly. While it might have been imagined that the additional stimulus of 1990 and the potential availability of a hall holding an audience of 2,500 might already have been recognized as strategic opportunities, the fact is that the specialist professional marketing skills needed to exploit the situation are not currently available within the SNO.

Planning Processes

No formal marketing plan is produced by the SNO, nor is there a longer term company marketing strategy within which such a plan could operate. What marketing planning there is at the SNO is directed wholly at the subscription ticket scheme, takes place in the summer each year, and amounts to a project-planning exercise for the production and distribution of brochures by mail and in strategic distribution points (ticket offices, public libraries, etc.). Given that these are normally produced to specification and are distributed on time, the current system can be said to work very well.

Innovation

Within the United Kingdom, the SNO was a pioneer in the introduction of subscription tickets, and in the artistic sphere its Musica Nova festival of contemporary music every two years represents the breaking of new ground. It has nevertheless been felt that within the narrow confines of the SNO's activities, as described in the annual report, there appears to be little scope for further innovation. Marketing opportunities do, nevertheless, exist and these have only been exploited up to a point.

For instance, programmes bought for 50 pence by concert-goers, are traditionally a marketing province, and are frequently made into self-financing publications, the production costs being met entirely by advertising revenue, the cover price remaining a revenue source. For many years, the SNO has ignored this approach, and has considered the programmes to be a province of the Concerts' Manager. Expenditure and receipts from printing and advertising/cover price respectively have been treated as part of the income and expenditure outcome of a concert. As a result of this strategy, SNO concert programmes have either carried no advertising at all, or only that of some of the sponsors, for whom free advertising was part of the deal.

At its Glasgow concerts, the orchestra permits an outside organization to erect a stall selling albums and cassettes in direct competition with its own stall (see below). No fee is obtained for this activity which the SNO sees as offering a service to the public.

The SNO erects a stall on concert nights. In Glasgow, it is manned by members of the office staff who are traditionally paid a retainer for doing the task, and elsewhere by students in exchange for free tickets. The stall carries a full range of the orchestra's recordings, as well as an attractive range of advertising items (coffee mugs, aprons, pens, etc.). This is obviously an important source of income. The drain on potential sales of SNO recordings, due to circumstances mentioned above, is an example of this, and the possibilities for improvement of the somewhat unimaginative sales stall certainly do exist.

None of these three items in themselves would prove to be substantial sources of revenue, but given that the orchestra operates within a very small financial framework, such activities can in fact prove valuable.

Marketing Information

It has not been considered necessary to develop a marketing information system at the SNO. As indicated earlier, no research of any kind has been undertaken, whether *ad hoc* or omnibus, qualitative or quantitative, and no audit data has been bought. Given the very high proportion of subscription sales it has always been felt that the SNO audience was satisfied with the nature of the product, the music performed, the timing and whereabouts of concerts, the artists engaged and so forth. The current pattern of SNO activities has continued unchanged for many years, and little merit has been seen in investing the time and money needed to build up an audience profile and other details that would be included in a marketing information system, given the perceived limitations on the effectiveness of doing so.

Conclusion

The Scottish National Orchestra is a vibrant organization, whose performances are of the highest international standard, and whose management succeeds in maintaining a good balance of housekeeping and progress, against the pressures of a turbulent and challenging environment. The SNO provides a quality product, one with which its customers and funders are satisfied. Given the traditional nature of a symphony orchestra few opportunities are recognized for change or innovation, and within this scenario the SNO operates efficiently and achieves its objectives.

The greatest cause for anxiety remains the question of finance: the SNO's vulnerability to political change creates insecurity, but is beyond the management's control. At the same time, the exploitation of industrial sponsorship as a means of raising further finance is at an undeveloped stage and its full potential has still to be realized. There is, therefore, immense pressure on the General Administrator and his team.

Heavy investment in sophisticated marketing tools is a luxury that the SNO believes it cannot afford. Marketing planning and the development of marketing information systems are not considered to be business priorities, and management considers that the introduction of strategic marketing planning would not result in any significant improvement. Given the lack of professional marketing expertise within the management team, this may ultimately be considered the central long-term issue to be faced by the organization.

CASE 28
The Scottish Football League
Non-Profit Marketing

Gerard J. Shepherd
Reidvale Housing Association Limited

Luiz Moutinho
Glasgow Business School, University Of Glasgow

History

The Scottish Football League was formed at a meeting in Holton's Hotel, Glasgow, on 20 March 1890 with 10 clubs participating in the First Division: Abercorn, Cambuslang, Celtic, Cowlairs, Dumbarton, Hearts, Rangers, St Mirren, Third Lanark and Vale of Leven.

In season 1893/94 a Second Division was formed consisting of the following clubs: Dundee, Hibs, Morton, Motherwell, Northern Partick Thistle, Past Glasgow Athletic, St Bernards and Thistle, together with Cowlairs which had rejoined after having previously withdrawn in 1891/92.

Although the two divisions set-up was now well established, automatic promotion and relegation, as in existence today, was not operative, instead a voting procedure, adopted by the First Divison clubs, decided the promotion-relegation debate.

The First World War saw the abandonment of the Second Divison, not reinstated until the 1921/22 season. The same season saw the introduction of automatic promotion and relegation, much to the delight of Alloa the first club to be promoted under the new system.

Season 1923/24 saw the introduction of the Third Divison. With clubs unable to complete their fixtures its existence was somewhat short lived, financial constraints enforcing its abandonment midway through season 1925/26. The two league set-up remained until the end of season 1938/39, when the Second World War intervened and the League was consequently suspended.

It was not until the 1946/47 season that the League was re-established in an 'A', 'B' and 'C' divisional format. The same season saw the League Cup being introduced with Rangers FC 'thrashing' Aberdeen FC by four goals to nil at Hampden Park. The 'C' Divison was subsequently absorbed into 'B' Divison, resulting in a set-up which continued for about the next 20 years.

During the 1970s there had been frequent and lengthy discussions on restructuring Scottish League football to make it more competitive and therefore more attractive to the consumer. This restructuring finally materialized in 1975/76 with the now 38 clubs arranged into three divisions; a Premier, First and Second division consisting of 10, 14 and 14 clubs respectively. This format has continued until season 1986/87 whereby a transitional 12, 12, 14, formation had been agreed for two years with a return to the former system at the end of season 1987/88.

The League Cup was introduced in 1946/47 and except for the four seasons from 1977/78 to 1980/81, when it was organized on a straight knock-out basis, this competition has been structured in the form of mini leagues with the league winners then playing out the competition on a knock-out basis.

Both League Championship and League Cup come under the jurisdiction of the SFL which is run by a management committee of 12 members elected by the 38 clubs which up until 1986/87 recommended proposals to the clubs. Voting was on the basis of one vote per club with a two-thirds majority (that is, 26 clubs) required for a proposal to be carried.

The ten Premier Division clubs on average account for 70% of the total market on attendances yet on the basis of the one vote per club they have only 26% of the total vote. A fact that was the basis of the threatening and very damaging crisis at the SFL the outcome of which was, *inter alia*, a revamped voting system whereby the Premier Division clubs have four votes per club, the First Division clubs having two votes and the Second Division with one vote per club. The ramification of such a system is yet to be seen. Clearly the power base has shifted towards those clubs contributing more to the football scene but it remains to be seen whether those disconsolate clubs will remain loyal to the umbrella body and what is it they say about absolute power?

Alterations, additions or amendments to the Constitution and Rule of the League can only be taken at an annual or special general meeting and require a two-thirds majority before they can be declared competent. Any notice by member clubs proposing alterations to the Rules of the League must be submitted to the Secretary not later than 31 March in each year in the case of the Annual General Meeting or twenty-one days in the case of a Special General Meeting.

The normal day-to-day duties of the League are vested in the administration headed by the Secretary who is a paid official not permitted to vote at any meeting nor be connected with any League club. Some of the many duties unertaken by the administration include the compilation of League Championship and Cup matches and receiving all registration forms and contracts of service for players currently registered with the 38 member clubs.

The Product and its Price

Put simply the product is entertainment of the football variety packaged in two formats – League Championship and League Cup – and having lost 7 million spectators since 1945 the observer would quite rightly assert that league football was firmly encamped in the decline period of its product life cycle (PLC), as in the case of other entertainment products, such as the cinema. However, since about 1980 there has been a levelling of attendances at both league and cup matches, now around the 4 million figure. Indeed if the figures since 1980 are seen in isolation then attendances have perceptibly increased in successive years which may not indicate a resurgence but certainly a slowing down of the accelerating trend downwards. Although the fall off in sales has occurred throughout each division the Premier Division has fared less badly than the First and Second Divisions. This is perhaps just as well since the contribution made by the Premier Division accounts for some 70% of the total sales figure.

Marketing can be defined as a social process by which individuals and groups obtain what they need and want through creating and exchanging products of value with others. What needs are satisfied by the attendance at football matches? In the main it is those psychological human needs that are satisfied by allowing, for example, a vent for frustration and anger and an outlet for emotion and prejudices: the latter more apparent at specific grounds than others. Being associated with success in these modern times will also hold much attraction for individuals whose self-ambition and fulfilment have not been, or have only partly been attained – leading one to perceive that the market for football is situated at the lower end of the social scale.

The cost of admission to SFL matches depends on a number of variables: where the customer wishes to view the match (terracing, enclosures, etc.); the class of fixture being played (Premier, First Division, etc.); and the individual's age group (adult, child or pensioner). Since about 1960 the price of admission has almost doubled in real terms and it is hardly surprising that the substantial increase in the cost of the product coincided with, or perhaps even contributed to, the marked decline in consumers of the product, particularly in a period of economic recession. These price increases may have been an attempt to increase revenue to compensate for rising costs but it appears that the football industry either misjudged or overlooked a basic economic principle. Where an industry (or company) is in competition with other outlets for consumers, which football is, the demand for its product will most probably be price elastic: that is, price increases will reduce quantity demanded by a relatively greater amount such that revenue from gate receipts will fall and subsequently reduce the benefit from price increases. Price flexibility was introduced at the beginning of the 1981/82 season when admission prices set by the SFL were 'recommended' only and clubs could vary the price on the basis of how they saw the attractiveness of the fixture: a realization that the laws of supply and demand could vary from fixture to fixture.

Marketing Environment

Senior grade football in Scotland is an industry where the companies (the clubs) are competing against other sports, leisure activities and various forms of light entertainment for consumers. Consequent on this mutual dependency of clubs on each other for public support, the football industry in Scotland might well be considered a business where the clubs are simply branches of a parent or holding group: the SFL with its head office in Glasgow. Just as traditional industries evolve, develop and change their organization and structure in response to environmental factors such as closures, liquidations and new entrants, so also has the Scottish Football industry during its existence.

Analysing further the environmental constraints within which it operates, should enhance our understanding of the SFL and go somewhere in explaining its current standing within the industry.

Economic

The demise of heavy engineering in the West of Scotland has contributed unquestionably to the fall in revenue experienced by the affiliated League clubs. Traditionally, the 'Saturday Sanny' was content and affluent enough to satisfy his demand for professional top grade football, a 'passion' which filled the coffers of football clubs in the calm days of 10 million supporters annually. This loss, understandably, has filtered through to would-be sponsors and endorsers.

A constant sore point has been the iniquitous rating of sports stadia in Scotland – a system which is constantly being lobbied against by the League and as yet remains unresolved. Undoubtedly, the burden of rates exacerbates an already perilous financial position and its obscenity becomes more apparent when it is realized that Celtic FC paid last year in rates an amount equivalent to the aggregate of the last ten successive years of Watford FC's (affiliated to the English Football League) annual rates bill. Its continuation is becoming increasingly intolerable, as manifested in the vilifying debate between the Scottish Office and the League.

Legal – Safety of Sports Grounds Act 1975

The most recent significant piece of legislation enacted has been the Criminal Justice (Scotland) Act which, *inter alia*, outlawed the drinking of alcohol to, from and at sporting stadia. The 'Act' was designed primarily to ameliorate the 'hooligan' problem at football grounds. In this respect it has been successful but at the same time revenues at the turnstile have been lost: a fact the League accepts as an acceptable cost of improving the image of the game.

Political

Increasingly this area is becoming the most limiting constraint within football today. Currently, it would be true to say, Government views football as a causal factor in contributing to these less disciplined times. An assertion bitterly rejected by the League, countering that football is merely a reflection of a more general decline in social standards. This may be so but the Government has as a result of several very recent football 'incidents' requested the authorities (SFA, SFL, etc.) to 'put their house in order'. A consequence of this attitude has seen the enactment of the 'Safety at Sports Ground Act', which has perhaps gone excessively over the top in making safer the spectating of the sport with the additional safety costs being borne by the club; the case in point has been the 'policing' charges. It is a constant source of bewilderment to the League as to how the 'costing out' of police time is arrived at: £13.68 per hour (4 hours required).

With Britain repeatedly being placed low down on variously compiled 'national health' league tables, successive governments have laid great store in participation as opposed to spectating. 'Fit for life' campaigns and the like, have seen the Scottish Football Association (SFA) enjoying an expansionary period of time with the growth in football participation, the corollary of which is that attendances at games has suffered: the lifeblood of the professional game.

Marketing Orientation

When the subject 'marketing' was first broached with the Secretary Mr James Farry, the initial response was 'but we don't do marketing'. This erroneous contention, as it turns out, was more to do with semantics than facts.

While not carrying out specific demographic research on its market, the SFL does extract data from social research papers on the subjects (of which there are many) and also from the clubs themselves which they see as being more advantageously placed to carry out such work. Recent evidence of knowing the customer and supplying his needs has been the growth of 'executive' facilities, providing more than just a game of football. This area of growth is not seen as the panacea to football's malady but has helped to utilize overcapacity and at the same time ease the constant cash flow problem of those more enlightened clubs.

It has to be stressed that the SFL does not look to the executive market to reverse the decline of football but merely as a secondary source of revenue. It is towards the 'cloth cap brigade' and his family that the League angles its product, it is his money at the turnstiles, his 'boy' playing the game and his family spectating. This is where the market lies, not with the upper end of the market with 'quiche lorraine and side salad' thrown in. It is the 'punter' who in the past has provided the money and the talent for the long-term good of the game. The executive end of the market is only seen as marginal when compared to the income that can be derived from 30,000 or so fans turning out to watch.

Evidence of the SFL's thinking in terms of target market can be seen when we consider the sponsorship money being attracted: 'Fine Fare' supermarkets, 'Mitre' football products, and 'Skol' lager, all operating at the lower end of their respective markets. Further articulation of the marketing activities of the SFL can elicit its current marketing strategy.

Marketing Activities

Promotion

The SFL has on occasions allowed its product to be promoted in conjunction with another. A campaign whereby vouchers were enclosed with a particular brand of soap powder entitling the customer to attend a Premier Division League match of his/her choice is an example of the type of campaign periodically mounted. The pricing policy mentioned earlier is seen as another way of promoting a game where the fixture may prove less attractive than others.

Advertising

Earlier, the analysis of the product suggested it satisfied to a degree the consumer's psychological needs with its success in this area proving to appeal to a massive audience, albeit a dwindling one. Eager then to associate itself with the football industry are organizations wishing to communicate their product to that sector of the public. Football is seen as an ideal vehicle to promote/heighten awareness of a consumer product. A by-product and result of its broadly based consumer appeal is the ability of the League to negotiate deals whereby the 'coverage' of football is inextricably linked with some other product/service. Sponsorship as it is known provides the 'League' with its second major source of revenue and it would be true to say that the SFL's deal is not in advertising, but in advertising space by promoting very actively this type of relationship. Glossy brochures advertise to potential customers the benefits from being sponsors of its variously packaged products.

At the corporate level, the SFL does very little in terms of advertising, content to let clubs themselves entice their audience.

Publicity

It is in this area of the communications mix that the SFL excels, the evidence is the average daily newspaper/tabloid dedicating some two to four pages of news coverage exclusively to the product. Its manipulation of the press and TV ensures a stimulation of demand by planting commercially significant items of news, via those media, in its public/customer at a negligible cost. Specific personnel within the organization are entrusted with the task of briefing or 'leaking' the propaganda, generally steeped in controversy and intrigue. The League's awareness of the nuances of and benefits from good public relations has resulted in a specially designed room equipped with external communication lines and the ubiquitous 'bar' (the negligible cost). By gearing itself for this type of activity the League could be said to be running a very slick and effective public relations department and benefiting from it as a result.

Financial Information

By far, the main source of income to the SFL is derived from the 'Pool Promoters Association' (PPA). Royalties accruing from the copyrights of the Scottish Football League's fixtures provide about £1.6 million per annum. This represents 25% of a total figure based on 2¼% of the 'net turnover' of the PPA. Contracts are entered into for periods of between 8 and 10 years, both parties seeing this as particularly advantageous in terms of stability and future planning. Sponsorship, the second major source of revenue, is split between several of the products, the main areas being:

(1) *League Championship* This is currently being sponsored by Fine Fare supermarkets in the sum of £¼ million per year (£750,000 for the three-year deal expiring May 1988).

(2) *League Cup* This year it is being sponsored by Skol Lager providing some £150,000. The SFL has this sponsorship involvement since 1982. A new three-year deal has been signed involving a total sum of £600,000.

(3) *Footballs and sportswear* Mitre sportswear contributes £50,000 p.a. for the endorsement of its products by the SFL, as well as 1,000 'free' footballs worth £65,000 (total £115,000).

(4) *Scottish Football League Review* A glossy compendium of facts and figures for the enthusiast published by the League and sponsored by the Clydesdale Bank PLC, contributing about £50,000 p.a.

These inflows of cash are distributed to the member clubs at certain times of the year, after the running costs of the League (overheads, etc.) have been deducted. The basis of distribution, often a contentious issue, is such that the Premier Division receives the lion's share. The exact details of the system are rather convoluted and serve no purpose within the marketing context. Suffice to say that eight clubs in Scotland attract 69% of the total spectators to the game and that the basis of allocation is in no way reflective of this statistic.

From the Balance Sheet (Exhibit 28.1), the reader will observe that the 'Capital Account' sitting at £163,000 at 31 March 1985 is perhaps on the low side when you consider the size, complexity and responsibility of the body. This sum

Exhibit 28.1   The Scottish Football League Balance Sheet 31 March 1985.

	Note	£	*1984* £
Current Assets			
Sundry Debtors		84,335	253,055
Stock	7	1,518	1,640
Bank – Current Account		89,559	23,423
Deposits – Money Market and Building Society		880,000	765,000
Cash in Hand		624	49
		1,056,036	1,043,167
Current Liabilities			
Monetary Awards		541,025	389,025
Sundry Creditors		410,737	570,735
Taxation		—	—
		951,762	959,760
Net Current Assets		104,274	83,407
Fixed Assets	8	74,450	64,548
Deferred Taxation	9	(15,267)	(5,287)
		£163,457	£142,668
Capital Account			
Balance at 1st April, 1984		142,668	138,168
Surplus for year after taxation		20,789	4,500
Balance at 31st March, 1985		£163,457	£142,668

The Financial Statements were approved by the Management Committee on 2nd May, 1985

DAVID LETHAM, President
JAMES FARRY, Secretary

is designed for 'festivities' in their centenary year 1990, mainly because of the complex taxation implications. The policy of distributing all its revenues to the membership is short-term thinking at its worse and will in the long term serve no useful purpose in that the money is only going to bail out the less financially stable clubs. The laws of economic survival should be allowed to prevail letting the more successful clubs thrive without the drain on resources by the lesser ones. The League, by securing 'reserves', would be able to plan strategically the way ahead.

The extent of the severe decline in public demand for the professional game threatened the complete collapse of the football industry in the late 1970s. Since then a levelling off has provided its administrators with a lifeline in the form of a breathing space to allow a rethink and develop appropriate counter offences before the cessation of the respite, when the game may again be sucked into the vortex of falling revenues and rising costs. That is unless a complete turnaround is achieved. Indeed the chequered history of the SFL makes its plight all the more galling in that large sums of money at one time flowed freely in and out of the game and that this lack of policy combined with the lack of foresight in marketing terms has contributed greatly to its present predicament. Indications are that the honing rather than abandonment of current thinking will hasten the reversal of trends already under way, auguring well for the future.

Case Index

Anglo-Saxon Artist Limited (Marketing Mix Strategies)   255

Auto-Main (Marketing Mix Strategies)   246

AVIS Rent-a-Car (Distribution Management)   207

Bartels Paperbacks (Marketing Mix Strategies)   225

Bovill & Boyd Limited (Strategic Marketing)   53

British Aerospace Warton (New Product Development)   158

Clydesdale Products (Organizational Buying Behaviour)   79

Dawson & Company Limited (Strategic Marketing)   24

Deckgard (Marketing Orientation/Marketing Information Systems)   130

E & R Products (Strategic Marketing)   19

Europack (International Marketing)   295

Flexible Technology Limited (International Marketing)   284

George Hobson Limited (Marketing Policy and Strategy)   58

Independent Bookshop Limited (Segmentation and Targeting)   135

INFORAK (New Product Development)   168

Kilroy Products (Advertising Management)   196

The Langport Building Society (Advertising Management)   201

Massey-Ferguson–Agromet-Motoimport (Poland) (International
  Marketing)   262

MIT Tractors (Pricing Policy)   187

Passcard (Strategic Marketing)   69

POK Electronic Systems (Pricing Policy)   190

Scottish Express International (Physical Distribution/Marketing
  Information Systems)   216

Scottish Foam Limited (Strategic Marketing)   35

The Scottish Football League (Non-Profit Marketing)   320

The Scottish National Orchestra (Non-Profit Marketing)   308

Southern Precision Engineering (Organizational Buying
  Behaviour/Personal Selling)   104

Strathspey Ski Centre (Marketing Mix Strategies)   232

Weighill Hotel, Glasgow (Marketing Information Systems)   118

Sheila Silver Library
Self Issue
Leeds Beckett University

Customer name: Rodrigues, Edgar Da Silva Berna (Mr)

Customer ID: 0771124737

Title: Cases in marketing management
ID: 1700939607
Due: 30/6/2015,23:59

Total items: 1
27/05/2015 12:29
Checked out: 1
Overdue: 0
Hold requests: 0
Ready for pickup: 0

Need help? Why not Chat with Us 24/7?
See the Need Help? page on the library
website: library.leedsbeckett.ac.uk